Ricœur at the Limits of Philosophy

Can finite humans grasp universal truth? Is it possible to think beyond the limits of reason? Are we doomed to failure because of our finitude? In this clear and accessible book, Barnabas Aspray presents Ricœur's response to these perennial philosophical questions through an analysis of human finitude at the intersection of philosophy and theology. Using unpublished and previously untranslated archival sources, he shows how Ricœur's groundbreaking concept of symbols leads to a view of creation, not as a theological doctrine, but as a mystery beyond the limits of thought that gives rise to philosophical insight. If finitude is created, then it can be distinguished from both the Creator and evil, leading to a view of human existence that, instead of the 'anguish of no', proclaims the 'joy of yes'.

Barnabas Aspray is a lecturer in philosophy of religion at King's College, London. He received his PhD from the University of Cambridge in 2020 and is an active member of the International Network of Philosophy of Religion, Porticus Talents for Good, and the Las Casas Institute for Social Justice at Oxford.

Ricœur at the Limits of Philosophy

God, Creation, and Evil

BARNABAS ASPRAY
University of Oxford

Shaftesbury Road, Cambridge CB2 8EA, United Kingdom

One Liberty Plaza, 20th Floor, New York, NY 10006, USA

477 Williamstown Road, Port Melbourne, VIC 3207, Australia

314–321, 3rd Floor, Plot 3, Splendor Forum, Jasola District Centre, New Delhi – 110025, India

103 Penang Road, #05–06/07, Visioncrest Commercial, Singapore 238467

Cambridge University Press is part of Cambridge University Press & Assessment, a department of the University of Cambridge.

We share the University's mission to contribute to society through the pursuit of education, learning and research at the highest international levels of excellence.

www.cambridge.org
Information on this title: www.cambridge.org/9781009186759

DOI: 10.1017/9781009186735

© Cambridge University Press & Assessment 2022

This publication is in copyright. Subject to statutory exception and to the provisions of relevant collective licensing agreements, no reproduction of any part may take place without the written permission of Cambridge University Press & Assessment.

First published 2022
First paperback edition 2025

A catalogue record for this publication is available from the British Library

ISBN 978-1-009-18674-2 Hardback
ISBN 978-1-009-18675-9 Paperback

Cambridge University Press & Assessment has no responsibility for the persistence or accuracy of URLs for external or third-party internet websites referred to in this publication and does not guarantee that any content on such websites is, or will remain, accurate or appropriate.

For Duncan and Sîan,
with gratitude

Contents

Acknowledgements		*page* ix
	Introduction	1
1	Rage against the System: The Unity of Truth	18
2	A Philosophy of Hope? The Universality of Truth	43
3	Absolutely No Absolutes? Ricœur's Encounter with Thévenaz	65
4	Finitude and the Infinite: The God of the Philosophers	86
5	Finitude and Evil: The Crucial Distinction	118
6	Rightly Relating Evil and Finitude	145
7	The Poetic Symbol of Creation	167
8	The Mysterious Unity of Creation	186
9	The Original Goodness of Creation	205
	Conclusion: New Frontiers between Philosophy and Theology	223
Bibliography		229
Index		245

Acknowledgements

The idea for this book grew out of my doctoral thesis which I pursued at the University of Cambridge under the supervision of Professor Janet Soskice. I am grateful above all to her for her patient and careful attention, and for encouraging me to rework my thesis into a book. Many thanks also to Amy Daughton and David Ford, whose enthusiasm for Ricœur during MPhil supervisions encouraged me to go deeper in exploring this great thinker. I have much gratitude for friends who gave of their time to read a chapter and provide helpful feedback: to Simone Kotva, Nadya Pohran, Alison Scott-Baumann, Blake Allen, Nathan Lyons, and Ragnar Misje Bergem: this book is better than it would have been without your input. Thank you! A special thanks to Christina Gschwandtner for her friendship, advice, and encouragement in the later stages of production. She went beyond the call of duty to help me in my academic career and I owe her much for it.

The journey that led me into philosophy of religion began long before Cambridge. I am grateful to my parents for their continual love and support of my somewhat questionable career choices, and for their warm endorsement of the value of thinking theologically. I am also particularly thankful to David Hollow, the first to predict that I would become a professional theologian, four years before I had begun any full-time academic study of theology. He did not suggest it, as most people would. He told me that it would happen. His unflagging belief in me and my calling has been an invaluable encouragement. Thanks more widely to Community Church Harlesden, who supported me financially for the first two years of my theological study, and who showed unfailing enthusiasm and encouragement for my rather preternaturally obsessive theological interests.

Finally, on both a personal and an academic level, I am above all thankful to my wife, Silvianne, who read my entire book with painstaking care, but more importantly provided me with indispensable love, comfort, and companionship throughout. I love the way our journey together has begun, and I look forward to its continued unfolding within divine providence and love.

Introduction

Does philosophy have limits? Yes and no.

No, because nothing is 'out of bounds' for philosophy. There is nothing philosophy is forbidden to question, doubt, and explore. Philosophy seeks to understand and explain all of reality without remainder: as Aristotle said, its scope is nothing less than 'being', that is, everything that is. In that sense, there can be no limits to philosophy.

But also yes, because no philosophy has ever existed without an author. All philosophy proceeds from a human mind, with its own situation and way of reasoning, a mind with limitations to what it can learn, experience, and conceive. Philosophy has limits, therefore, because it is done by beings who have limits, in other words, who are *finite*. The 'limits of philosophy' are drawn by the finitude of the human condition.

This book takes 'finitude', and the limits set by finitude, to be the keystone of Paul Ricœur's philosophy. In all his writings Ricœur shows a rigorous concern not to transgress the boundaries of what is possible for human thought as finite. But at the same time, he pushes philosophy to its outermost limits in order to peek, as through a glass darkly, at what lies beyond. How is this possible? Because, as Hegel famously remarked, to know a limit as a limit is already to have gone beyond it.[1] One cannot

---

[1] 'Something is already transcended by the very fact of being determined as a limitation. For a determinateness, a limit, is determined as limitation only in opposition to its other in general, that is, in opposition to that which is without its limitation; the other of a limitation is precisely the beyond with respect to it' (G. W. F. Hegel, *The Science of Logic*, ed. and trans. George Di Giovanni [Cambridge: Cambridge University Press, 2010], 106); translation modified: 'daß etwas als Schranke bestimmt ist, darüber bereits hinausgegangen ist. Denn eine Bestimmtheit, Grenze ist als Schranke nur bestimmt im Gegensatz

describe a boundary line without referring in some way to both sides of it. For example, the outline of France shows one side of the outline of Spain: thus to remain within the limits of France means knowing something, however little, of the shape of Spain. Similarly, for Ricœur, to know the limits of human reason means to have a shadowy (apophatic) outline of whatever is on the other side of them.

This book situates Ricœur's concept of finitude in the wider context of twentieth-century French philosophy, showing both that Ricœur is asking the same questions others were asking and that his answers are strikingly unique. What it means to be finite and human was arguably the dominant question of twentieth-century thought as a whole. From Bergson's analysis of free will, Merleau-Ponty's descriptions of embodiment, Sartre's 'Existentialism is a Humanism', and de Beauvoir's seminal explorations of gender, to Lacan's investigations of the unconscious, Henry's phenomenology of life, Arendt's politically inflected anthropology, Kristeva's insights concerning the 'other', and Foucault's histories of sexuality, power and discipline – in these and countless other works, the 'human condition' is the focus of enquiry.

To this Ricœur is no exception. He gave the name 'philosophical anthropology' to his work, which he considered an 'urgent task for contemporary philosophy'.[2] As Brian Gregor says, Ricœur 'wrote on many topics and problems, but the concern that unites them all is the question of philosophical anthropology: what does it mean to be a human being?'[3]

But unlike his twentieth-century contemporaries, Ricœur did not think it possible to isolate anthropology from other questions, such as those concerning universal truth, God, evil, and the origin of the world. 'Far from constituting the first question philosophy can raise', Ricœur claims in Kantian fashion, 'the question "what is man?" comes at the end of a series of prior questions'.[4]

---

gegen sein Anderes überhaupt als gegen sein Unbeschränktes; das Andere einer Schranke ist eben das Hinaus über dieselbe' (G. W. F. Hegel, *Die Wissenschaft der Logic*, vol. 1, Werke 5 [Frankfurt: Suhrkamp, 1970], 145). Of course, this is precisely what Heidegger denies, and will be discussed in more detail in Chapter 4.

[2] Paul Ricœur, *Philosophical Anthropology* (Cambridge: Polity Press, 2016), 1. 'L'anthropologie philosophique est devenue une tâche urgent de la pensée contemporaine' (Paul Ricœur, *Anthropologie philosophique*, ed. Johann Michel and Jérôme Porée, Écrits et conférences 3 [Paris: Éditions du Seuil, 2013], 21).

[3] Brian Gregor, *Ricœur's Hermeneutics of Religion: Rebirth of the Capable Self* (Lanham: Lexington Books, 2019), 4.

[4] Ricœur, *Philosophical Anthropology*, 195. 'La question *qu'est-ce que l'homme?*, loin de constituer la première question que la philosophie puisse se poser, vient à la fin d'une série de questions préalables' (Ricœur, *Anthropologie philosophique*, 306).

To be sure, Ricœur often wrote philosophy that aimed to describe the human condition in abstraction from metaphysical concerns,[5] but as we shall see, he never saw his methodological bracketing either as entirely pure or as providing a self-sufficient picture of what it means to be human. As Pamela Sue Anderson notes, Ricœur's 'philosophy of the will reveals that, for him, a comprehensive philosophical anthropology is inevitably tied to theological reflection'.[6] Ricœur argued that there is no metaphysically neutral point of view from which humanity can be studied, and that even though we may temporarily bracket out wider issues to narrow our focus, our philosophy is always coloured by our implied position concerning the big questions about truth, God, evil, and creation, and our understanding of the human condition is not complete without addressing them.

Ricœur's willingness to explore what lies beyond the human places him in stark contrast to Martin Heidegger, whose concept of finitude was and still is the most influential in both philosophy and theology and because of that will be the primary point of comparison to Ricœur. Heidegger denies that it is meaningful to speak of anything beyond the limits of human finitude. For Heidegger, finitude is a standalone category without an opposite. Ricœur, on the other hand, wrestles continually with two 'opposites' or non-finites and how they interact with finitude – the infinite (or God, or transcendence) and non-being (or evil). Where Heideggerian finitude is total immanence and therefore nothing but finitude, Ricœurian finitude is dialectically related to an infinitude that enables an openness to transcendence. Similarly, where Heidegger rejects the idea that 'fallenness' leads to any concept of a primordial unfallen state, Ricœur uses the productive faculty of the imagination to offer a picture of innocent finitude prior to its invasion by the corruption of evil.

In summary, we may say that Ricœur sees human finitude as *created*. This has implications for more than finitude itself. If finitude is created, then there is a creator (the infinite). If the creator is good, then created finitude is good, which means that evil cannot belong to it by nature. Therefore if finitude is created, it is framed between two things that are not itself, one positive and one negative, one conventionally called God and the other evil.

---

[5] See, for example, Paul Ricœur, *Freedom and Nature: The Voluntary and the Involuntary*, trans. Erazim Kohák (1950; repr., Evanston: Northwestern University Press, 1966); Paul Ricœur, *Le volontaire et l'involontaire*, Philosophie de la volonté 1 (Paris: Aubier, 1949).

[6] Pamela Sue Anderson, *Ricœur and Kant: Philosophy of the Will* (Atlanta: Scholars Press, 1993), 3.

Does the category of 'creation' not turn Ricœur's thought into theology? No, because Ricœur never invokes the authority of a revealed tradition as a substitute for argument, nor does he claim that God, creation, or evil can be grasped by philosophy as determinate concepts. In Ricœur's own language, they are *symbols*: ideas drawn from outside philosophy that cannot be exhaustively explained within philosophy, but that shed light on aspects of the human condition that philosophy can meaningfully talk about.

PAUL RICŒUR'S LIFE AND WORK

Why read or write about Paul Ricœur? Simply because he is universally recognised as one of the twentieth century's leading philosophers of religion. His philosophy of finitude is among the most important resources available for contemporary discussions. A chorus of voices have recently named Ricœur one of the 'most influential',[7] 'greatest',[8] 'most important',[9] and 'foremost'[10] philosophers of the twentieth century, not only in philosophy but across the humanities disciplines. In the case of theology and philosophy of religion, David Ford considers Ricœur (with Bonhoeffer) *the* greatest Christian thinker of the last hundred years;[11] Boyd Blundell names Ricœur (with Barth) as a 'major power' behind a North American 'proxy war' between rival theological schools of thought;[12] Jürgen Werbick calls him 'one of the contemporary

---

[7] 'In the realm of the humanities, Paul Ricœur (1913–2005) is widely viewed as one of the most influential philosophers of the twentieth century' (Martijn Boven, Eddo Evink, and Gert-Jan van der Heiden, 'Paul Ricœur and the Future of the Humanities', *International Journal of Philosophy and Theology* 75, no. 2 [15 March 2014]: 112).

[8] 'Paul Ricœur (1913–2005) was one of the greatest Western philosophers of the twentieth century' (Alison Scott-Baumann, *Ricœur and the Hermeneutics of Suspicion* [London: Continuum, 2009], 1).

[9] 'Paul Ricœur is widely regarded as one of the most important philosophers of the 20th century' (David Kaplan, 'Paul Ricœur and the Philosophy of Technology', in Farhang Erfani, ed., *Paul Ricœur: Honoring and Continuing the Work* [Lanham: Lexington Books, 2011], 21).

[10] 'Paul Ricœur ... is widely regarded as the foremost living phenomenologist' ('Preface', in Lewis Edwin Hahn, ed., *The Philosophy of Paul Ricœur*, vol. 22, The Library of Living Philosophers [Chicago: Open Court, 1995], xvii).

[11] Personal conversation with David Ford, former Regius Professor of Divinity at the University of Cambridge.

[12] Boyd Blundell, *Paul Ricœur between Theology and Philosophy: Detour and Return* (Bloomington: Indiana University Press, 2010), 13. Blundell is referring to the classic 1980s Chicago/Yale feud, which attained legendary status in theological circles. For more on this, see Paul DeHart, *The Trial of the Witnesses: The Rise and Decline of Postliberal Theology* (Oxford: Blackwell, 2006).

philosophers who has had the greatest influence on theology;'[13] and Dan Stiver calls Ricœur's philosophy 'one of the best conversation partners for contemporary Christian theology'.[14] Finally, Anthony Thiselton writes that 'Ricœur will have a lasting impact on the future of Christian theology.'[15]

Ricœur's wide-reaching influence and importance lies not only in the quality of each of his works, but in the seventy-year span over which they were written, bringing continuity to an otherwise torn and fragmented century. How many other authors have published material from both before World War II and after 9/11?[16] Paul Ricœur's life was deeply intertwined with the tumultuous history of France in the twentieth century, and the sufferings that come with being finite were imprinted deeply on his experience.[17] Born in 1913, he lost both his parents before his third birthday – his mother from illness and his father in the trenches of World War I. He and his sister were raised by their grandmother and their aunt. A soldier in World War II, he was captured by the German army and sent to a prisoner-of-war camp in 1940 where he spent the next five years until the end of the war. He was deeply enmeshed in the affairs of 1968 and, while attempting the role of mediator between his institution and its revolutionary students, suffered minor physical assault from a student with a waste-paper basket lid.[18] Following this, he resigned from teaching in France for a number of years and took up positions at Louvain and the University of Chicago. In his personal life, he experienced both the stability of a happy marriage which lasted sixty-three years until the death of his wife Simone in 1998, and the tragic rupture caused by the suicide of one of his five children.[19] Ricœur continued writing and publishing into

---

[13] Jürgen Werbick, 'Foreword', in Maureen Junker-Kenny and Peter Kenny, eds., *Memory, Narrativity, Self and the Challenge to Think God: The Reception within Theology of the Recent Work of Paul Ricœur* (Münster: LIT, 2004), ix.

[14] Dan R. Stiver, *Ricœur and Theology* (London: T & T Clark, 2012), 146.

[15] Anthony C. Thiselton, *Hermeneutics: An Introduction* (Grand Rapids: Eerdmans, 2009), 228.

[16] See, for example, Ricœur's first article, 'L'appel de l'action. Réflexions d'un étudiant protestant', *Terre nouvelle* 2 (June 1935); and at the other end, his last book, *Parcours de la reconnaissance* (Paris: Stock, 2004).

[17] As Alison Scott-Baumann writes, Ricœur's 'personal and academic life was marked indelibly by major events of the twentieth century' (Alison Scott-Baumann, *Ricœur and the Negation of Happiness* [London: Bloomsbury, 2013], ix).

[18] Charles E. Reagan, *Paul Ricœur: His Life and His Work* (Chicago: University of Chicago Press, 1996), 35.

[19] François Dosse, *Paul Ricœur: les sens d'une vie*, 2nd ed. (Paris: La Découverte, 2008), 521.

his nineties, and after he died in 2005 the notes found on his desk were published posthumously.[20]

The astounding longevity of Ricœur's career is matched only by the breadth of topics he considered. These develop our understanding of what it means to be finite human beings in numerous directions. Stiver writes that Ricœur 'made significant intersections not only with quite varied areas in philosophy but also with religion, literature, psychoanalysis, and sociology', not to mention history, linguistic, politics, and theology.[21] Within philosophy the number of topics to which he contributed is almost uncountable. Arrien makes a start: 'the will, the symbol, evil, truth, history, imagination, metaphor, narrative, language, time, the self, etc.'[22] We might add: interpretation, the unconscious, memory, justice, ideology, the sacred, the other – and the list is still far from comprehensive. But I also agree with Arrien that 'there is nonetheless a centre ... to this seeming plurality of fields of investigation: namely, "the human" who discovers "themselves"'.[23] As noted above, philosophical anthropology is his focus.

In terms of religion, Ricœur's grandparents were of Huguenot descent and raised him a devout Protestant, a tradition for which he says 'reading the Bible was central'.[24] His wife, a childhood friend, was from the same confessional background.[25] Being Protestant in a Catholic country was not always easy for Ricœur, but with the rising tide of atheism he found he had more in common with his Catholic friends, especially the philosophical ones, than with anyone else, and it is evident that they drew much support from one another.[26] Ricœur never seems to have radically

---

[20] Paul Ricœur, *Living up to Death* (Chicago: University of Chicago Press, 2009); Paul Ricœur, *Vivant jusqu'à la mort. Suivi de fragments* (Paris: Éditions du Seuil, 2014).

[21] Stiver, *Ricœur and Theology*.

[22] My translation: 'la volonté, le symbole, le mal, la vérité, l'histoire, l'imagination, la métaphore, la narration, le langage, le temps, le soi' (Sophie-Jan Arrien, 'Introduction: Paul Ricœur (1913–2013): méthode et finitude', *Philosophiques* 41, no. 2 [2014]: 234).

[23] My translation: 'Il y a pourtant bien un centre, me semble- t-il, à cette pluralité apparente de champs d'investigation, à savoir "l'homme" qui se découvre "soi"' (Arrien, 'Introduction').

[24] Paul Ricœur, *Critique and Conviction: Conversations with François Azouvi and Marc de Launay* (Cambridge: Polity Press, 1998), 6. 'C'était un milieu très imprégné par la lecture de la Bible' (Paul Ricœur, *La critique et la conviction: entretien avec François Azouvi et Marc de Launay* [Paris: Calmann-Lévy, 1995], 16).

[25] Ricœur, *Critique and Conviction*, 10. 'Je me suis marié ... en 1935, avec une amie d'enfance du milieu protestant' (Ricœur, *La critique et la conviction*, 22).

[26] His later friendship with the Jewish philosopher Emmanuel Lévinas was also valuable to him.

doubted his faith. At the end of his life he speaks of his faith as 'a chance transformed into a destiny by continuous choice'.[27] He means by this both: (1) that due to the family he was born into, he did not choose his Protestant Christian upbringing; and (2) that he nonetheless remains responsible for his continual personal choice to remain a Christian, a responsibility which is discharged by providing 'plausible arguments, that is, ones worthy of being pleaded in a discussion with good-faith protagonists, who are in the same situation as me, incapable of rendering fully rational the roots of their convictions'.[28]

RICŒUR'S PHILOSOPHICAL MENTORS

Of course, Ricœur's philosophy did not emerge in a vacuum. He was deeply influenced both by prevailing schools of thought and by individual philosophers. He became the thinker he was through dialogue with certain key mentors, two of whom stand out in significance during the early stages of his career: the French Catholic philosopher Gabriel Marcel and the German existentialist Karl Jaspers, who has already been mentioned. These two philosophers will appear in dialogue with Ricœur throughout this book, and they deserve a brief introduction.

In 1934, shortly after finishing his Master's thesis, the twenty-one-year-old Ricœur was introduced to the famous 'Friday evenings' of philosophical discussion which took place at the home of a high school philosophy teacher, musician, playwright, and recent Catholic convert Gabriel Marcel. Fifteen years his senior, Marcel rapidly became both mentor and close friend to Ricœur, who promptly devoured everything Marcel had published.[29] Although Ricœur claims he 'never submitted to the intellectual constraints of being [Marcel's] disciple',[30] nonetheless during his captivity in a German prisoner-of-war camp, he wrote often

---

[27] Ricœur, *Living up to Death*, 62. 'Un hasard transformé en destin par un choix continu' (Ricœur, *Vivant jusqu'à la mort*, 99).

[28] Ricœur, *Living up to Death*, 62. 'C'est ce choix dont je suis sommé de rendre compte, ma vie durant, par des arguments plausibles, c'est-à-dire dignes d'être plaidés dans une discussion avec des protagonistes de bonne foi, qui sont dans la même situation que moi, incapables de rendre raison des racines de leurs convictions' (Ricœur, *Vivant jusqu'à la mort*, 100).

[29] Dosse, *Paul Ricœur*, 28–37. See also Ricœur, *Critique and Conviction*, 9; Ricœur, *La critique et la conviction*, 21.

[30] Ricœur, *Critique and Conviction*, 25. 'sans que jamais j'aie subi les contraintes intellectuelles d'un disciple'. Ricœur, *La critique et la conviction*, 44–5.

to Marcel using the address 'Cher Maître', implicitly labelling himself Marcel's student. In one of these letters Ricœur also writes that, outside his own family, Marcel is the person he most longs to see, telling him: 'you have been a principal source of spiritual inspiration for me'.[31]

But who was Gabriel Marcel? Born in 1889 in Paris, Marcel's childhood was characterised by much travel due to his father's profession. He was fluent in both English and German and wrote his Master's thesis on a comparison of the philosophies of Coleridge and Schelling.[32] During World War I Marcel worked for the Red Cross and was tasked with informing the families of soldiers who were found dead or missing, a task that he admits deeply affected his philosophy, impressing on him the mortality and fragility of being human.[33] Although Marcel loved to write plays, these were not received with great acclaim by the general public. His philosophical writings, on the other hand, became caught up in a renewal movement that shook the academic world, even though the name of that movement, 'existentialism', was never much to Marcel's taste, nor were many of the tenets that came to be associated with it.

After an upbringing of vague agnosticism, Marcel converted to Catholicism in his forties as a result of his personal philosophical journey and the influence of various devout Christian friends.[34] Because of the faith commitments shared by Marcel and Ricœur, and the personal friendship they enjoyed over and above any mutual philosophical interest, I am convinced that Marcel was the single strongest influence on Ricœur during this early period of his career.[35]

---

[31] My translation: 'Vous avez été pour moi un principe générateur dans l'ordre de l'esprit' (Paul Ricœur, 'Paul Ricœur to Gabriel Marcel', 21 February 1943, Fonds Gabriel Marcel). Letter written by G. Fougeirol with an appendix by Paul Ricœur. The Fonds Gabriel Marcel, where these letters from Paul Ricœur to Gabriel Marcel can be found, is at the Bibliothèque Nationale de France, Paris.

[32] This was published fifty years later as Gabriel Marcel, *Coleridge et Schelling* (Paris: Aubier, 1971).

[33] See Gabriel Marcel, 'An Autobiographical Essay', in *The Philosophy of Gabriel Marcel*, ed. Paul Arthur Schilpp and Lewis Edwin Hahn, Library of Living Philosophers (LaSalle: Open Court, 1984), 20.

[34] Marcel writes about his conversion and other life events in his autobiography, *Awakenings: A Translation of Marcel's Autobiography*, trans. Peter Rogers (Milwaukee: Marquette University Press, 2002); Gabriel Marcel, *En chemin, vers quel éveil?* (Paris: Gallimard, 1971).

[35] *Contra* Jérôme Porée: see his 'Karl Jaspers', in Scott Davidson, ed., *A Companion to Ricœur's 'Fallible Man'* (Lanham: Lexington Books, 2019), 31.

It was Marcel who first introduced Ricœur to the writings of Karl Jaspers.[36] Although Ricœur only met Jaspers personally twice,[37] the writings of this German philosopher became another great influence on Ricœur in this early period.

Born in 1883 in Oldenburg, Germany,[38] Jaspers arrived late to the professional practice of philosophy. He had been fascinated by philosophical ideas since a teenager, but was put off from formally studying philosophy by what he felt was the arid, scientific style of philosophising that was predominant in the universities, a style that ignored the existential situation of being human.[39] Instead, he studied medicine and began work as a psychiatrist, ending up as a professor of psychology. His psychology department was closely connected to philosophy, and Jaspers found there to be a certain freedom of movement between the two disciplines. At the same time, he became aware of the possibility of another way of doing philosophy than the type of philosophy he had been previously deterred by. This may explain why, in 1922, after seven years teaching psychology at the University of Heidelberg, he was appointed to the chair of philosophy.[40] To begin with, he felt ill-prepared for the post. For the next ten years he published little, and instead embarked on a decade-long reading project, seeking to acquire familiarity with the works of great philosophers throughout history. This eventually led to the 1932 publication of his first properly philosophical work. He gave it the straightforward title *Philosophy*, which he meant 'in the sense of a testimony to philosophy, to practical philosophizing'.[41] Although he

---

[36] See Paul Ricœur, 'Intellectual Autobiography', in *The Philosophy of Paul Ricœur*, ed. Lewis Hahn (Chicago: Open Court, 1995), 7; Paul Ricœur, *Réflexion faite* (Paris: Éditions Esprit, 1995), 17.

[37] Ricœur, *Critique and Conviction*, 21; Ricœur, *La critique et la conviction*, 39.

[38] Suzanne Kirkbright, *Karl Jaspers: A Biography: Navigations in Truth* (New Haven: Yale University Press, 2004), 3.

[39] Karl Jaspers, 'On My Philosophy', in *Existentialism from Dostoevsky to Sartre*, ed. Walter Kaufman (New York: Meridian Books, 1956), 132.

[40] Kirkbright, *Karl Jaspers*, 119. Jaspers gives two different dates for this appointment. In the Afterword to the third edition of *Philosophy*, he says it was in 1920. But Kirkbright's biographical investigations confirm the 1922 date that Jaspers gives in his 'Intellectual Autobiography'; compare: Karl Jaspers, 'Nachwort (1955)', in *Philosophie*, 3rd ed. (Berlin: Springer-Verlag, 1956), xviii; Karl Jaspers, 'Philosophical Autobiography', in *The Philosophy of Karl Jaspers*, ed. Paul Arthur Schilpp, 2nd, augmented ed., Library of Living Philosophers (LaSalle: Open Court, 1981), 34.

[41] Karl Jaspers, 'Epilogue 1955', in *Philosophy*, trans. E. B. Ashton, vol. 1 (Chicago: University of Chicago Press, 1969), 10 'in dem Sinne, daß es von der Philosophie zeugen solle, dem praktischen Philosophieren' (Jaspers, 'Nachwort (1955)', xxi).

subsequently wrote many philosophical works, he later confessed that *Philosophy* remained the one 'closest to my heart'.[42]

Jaspers openly opposed the Nazi regime right from the start, a stance which cost him his professorship in 1937 and his publishing rights in 1938.[43] It also strained his friendship with Heidegger to breaking point.[44] After the war he was reinstated as a professor by the Allied forces and continued to have a prolific and successful career, even though ironically his fame and influence only dwindled in comparison to that of Heidegger.[45]

Jaspers's 900-page *Philosophie* was Ricœur's constant literary companion during the five years of his wartime captivity. Together with a fellow prisoner of war, Mikel Dufrenne, he carefully read and reflected on it and other of Jaspers's works. This period of intense study bore fruit after the war with the publication of a joint work expounding, interpreting, and critically evaluating Jaspers's philosophy for a French audience.[46] An indelible mark had been left on this young philosopher, and although in later decades his references to Jaspers diminished somewhat, Alan Olson argues that 'the influence of Jaspers is a rather constant factor and cannot be confined merely to the earlier Ricœur as some of his followers tend to assume'.[47]

METHOD AND SCOPE OF THIS BOOK

This book restricts itself to Ricœur's writings prior to his turn to hermeneutics in the 1960s. I will occasionally reference Ricœur's later writings when he returns to earlier themes or reflects on his earlier work, but overall I have aimed to present Ricœur's philosophical anthropology prior to his engagement with structuralism, psychoanalysis, hermeneutics, and narrative. Such a limitation has the advantage of showing elements in Ricœur's concept of 'symbols' that are omitted when symbols

---

[42] Jaspers, 'Epilogue 1955', 5. 'das liebste meiner Bücher' (Jaspers, 'Nachwort (1955)', xv).
[43] Jaspers, 'Philosophical Autobiography', 62. One contributing reason for Jaspers's trenchant opposition to Nazism could have been that his wife was Jewish.
[44] Jaspers, 'Philosophical Autobiography', 75/8.
[45] Sarah Bakewell, *At the Existentialist Café: Freedom, Being, and Apricot Cocktails* (London: Vintage, 2016), 193.
[46] Mikel Dufrenne and Paul Ricœur, *Karl Jaspers et la philosophie de l'existence* (Paris: Éditions du Seuil, 1947).
[47] Alan Olson, *Transcendence and Hermeneutics: An Interpretation of the Philosophy of Karl Jaspers* (The Hague: Martinus Nijhoff, 1979), 156.

Method and Scope of This Book 11

are seen merely as hermeneutic theory in embryonic form. It also reveals Ricœur's dependence on Kant's *Critique of the Power of Judgment* when developing not only his concept of symbols, but also his poetics, and even his way of using the biblical narrative of creation to stimulate philosophical thought. More broadly, this early focus serves to prove David Pellauer's claim that 'much of what came later was already implicit in, if not already signaled in, the early work'.[48] I shall show moments where Ricœur's interests in language, metaphor, symbol, ethics, and imagination – themes typically sourced in his later writings – are already present in embryonic form.

As well as Jaspers and Marcel, I will situate Ricœur against the backdrop of a third influence: the French reflexive school of philosophy. This school is represented initially by Léon Brunschvicg (1869–1944), Ricœur's Master's supervisor, as well as Jules Lachelier (1832–1918) and Jules Lagneau (1851–1894), the two interlocutors of Ricœur's Master's thesis; and then later in Ricœur's life by Pierre Thévenaz (1913–1955) and Jean Nabert (1881–1960). These latter two will appear throughout this book as dialogue partners in Ricœur's developing thought.

My focus on these three particular influences on the early Ricœur offers a unique angle in scholarship. This is, first, because Ricœur's connection to French reflexive philosophy has received little scholarly attention.[49] Secondly, while some scholars have pointed to the numerous traces of Marcel's thought on Ricœur,[50] and others have drawn out elements of

---

[48] David Pellauer, 'Remembering Paul Ricœur', in *A Passion for the Possible: Thinking with Paul Ricœur*, ed. Brian Treanor and Henry Isaac Venema (New York: Fordham University Press, 2010), 43.

[49] Notable exceptions include: Pierre Colin, 'Herméneutique et philosophie réflexive', in *Paul Ricœur: les métamorphoses de la raison herméneutique*, ed. Jean Greisch and Richard Kearney (Paris: Éditions du Cerf, 1991); Gregor, *Ricœur's Hermeneutics of Religion*; and Eric Grump, 'Between Conviction and Critique: Reflexive Philosophy, Testimony, and Pneumatology', in *Ricœur as Another: The Ethics of Subjectivity*, ed. Richard A. Cohen and James L. Marsh (Albany: SUNY Press, 2002).

[50] See: Blundell, *Paul Ricœur between Theology and Philosophy*; Boyd Blundell, 'Creative Fidelity: Gabriel Marcel's Influence on Paul Ricœur', in *Between Suspicion and Sympathy: Paul Ricœur's Unstable Equilibrium*, ed. Andrzej Wierciński (Toronto: Hermeneutic Press, 2003), 89–102; Patrick L. Bourgeois, 'Marcel and Ricœur: Mystery and Hope at the Boundary of Reason in the Postmodern Situation', *American Catholic Philosophical Quarterly* 80, no. 3 (2006): 421–33; Patrick Bourgeois, 'Ricœur and Marcel: An Alternative to Postmodern Deconstruction', *Journal of French and Francophone Philosophy* 7, no. 1-2 (2010): 164–75; Julien Farges, 'L'héritage de Gabriel Marcel: Paul Ricœur et la question des limites de la phénoménologie', *Philosophie*, no. 132 (15 December 2016): 31–43.

his relationship to Jaspers,[51] what has not previously been done is to compare and contrast the respective influences of both these thinkers on Ricœur, together with that of his prior training in French reflexion, in order to show how all three interact to form Ricœur's early philosophy.

Another important influence on Ricœur is undoubtedly the phenomenology of Edmund Husserl. Focussing too much on Husserl, however, can have the effect of making other aspects of Ricœur's thought seem like little more than phenomenological heterodoxy. Indeed, it has been argued that the Marcellian strands in Ricœur are often thought of as nothing more than aberrations of the phenomenological method. However, 'what, from the point of view of phenomenology, appears as heresy or heterodoxy in Paul Ricœur's thought is in reality the effect or the counterpart of a fidelity on his part to the cardinal intentions and intuitions of Gabriel Marcel's philosophy'.[52] As we shall see, the same could be said about Jaspers and the reflexive method. Our 'phenomenological bracketing', or 'bracketing of phenomenology', therefore has the advantage of bringing into sharper relief the three aforementioned influences on the early Ricœur – reflexive philosophy, Marcel and Jaspers – which are often eclipsed by focussing on Husserl. I trust that the phenomenological dimension of Ricœur's work remains implicit in my analysis, and I refer the reader to other fine studies that make it explicit.[53]

This book is one of many that highlight Ricœur's relation to one or more figures in the history of thought. In Ricœur one finds a rich confluence of philosophical influences, all of which have an arguable claim to major significance and many of which have an entire monograph devoted to them: Plato, Aristotle, Augustine,[54] Spinoza, Descartes,

---

[51] See: Olson, *Transcendence and Hermeneutics*; Mark Gedney, 'Jaspers and Ricœur on the Self and the Other', *Philosophy Today* 48, no. 4 (1 December 2004): 331; Charles Courtney, 'Reading Ciphers with Jaspers and Ricœur', *Existenz* 1, no. 1–2 (2006), https://existenz.us/volumes/Vol.1Courtney.html.

[52] My translation: 'Ce qui, du point de vue de la phénoménologie, apparaît comme hérésie ou hétérodoxie dans la pensée de Paul Ricœur est en réalité l'effet ou la contrepartie d'une fidélité de sa part aux intentions et aux intuitions cardinales de la philosophie de Gabriel Marcel' (Farges, 'L'héritage de Gabriel Marcel', 31).

[53] Dermot Moran, 'Husserl and Ricœur: The Influence of Phenomenology on the Formation of Ricœur's Hermeneutics of the "Capable Human"', *Journal of French and Francophone Philosophy* 25, no. 1 (1 September 2017): 182–99; Don Ihde, *Hermeneutic Phenomenology: The Philosophy of Paul Ricœur* (Evanston: Northwestern University Press, 1971); Ted Klein, 'Ricœur and Husserl', *Iliff Review* 35, no. 3 (1978): 27–36; David Pellauer, *Ricœur: A Guide for the Perplexed* (London: Continuum, 2007), 10–12.

[54] Isabelle Bochet, *Augustin dans la pensée de Paul Ricœur* (Paris: Editions Facultés Jésuites de Paris, 2004).

Kant,[55] Hegel,[56] Kierkegaard, Heidegger,[57] Barth,[58] etc. Many of these sources of Ricœur's thought are explored, directly or indirectly, in what follows. French reflexive philosophy is a channel for much Cartesian thought, as is Jaspers's philosophy for Kierkegaardian thought. Chapter 8 makes an original contribution to our understanding of Kant's influence on Ricœur. Ricœur's Platonic overtones shall make an appearance as part of the argument of Chapter 4. Conversely, this study will show that the influence of Barth on Ricœur is less than is often believed. Other figures are already known to be less significant for Ricœur's earlier period. Heidegger's influence on Ricœur increased over time: it was only 'little by little', Ricœur says in the '90s, 'that I was caught up in the Heideggerian wave', as part of his 'hermeneutic turn'.[59] Likewise Aristotle and Spinoza play a greater role in Ricœur's later thought and their influence is not prominent in this study.

Where I make use of untranslated materials, my policy has been to provide an English translation in-text and to place the original French in a footnote. One translation choice may require explaining: I have rendered the French word *l'homme* (man) as 'the human' for the sake of gender inclusivity, even though the English expression is somewhat clumsy. *L'homme* is a properly philosophical term in French and does not mean 'humanity', but refers to what is true about any individual human being.[60]

OUTLINE OF THE ARGUMENT OF THIS BOOK

The aim of this book is to show the many connections between Ricœur's early philosophical anthropology of finitude and broader 'metaphysical' themes such as universal truth, God, evil, and creation. In circular

---

[55] Anderson, *Ricœur and Kant*.
[56] George Ille, *Between Vision and Obedience – Rethinking Theological Epistemology: Theological Reflections on Rationality and Agency with Special Reference to Paul Ricœur and G. W. F. Hegel* (Cambridge: James Clarke & Co, 2014).
[57] Patrick Bourgeois and Frank Schalow, *Traces of Understanding: A Profile of Heidegger's and Ricœur's Hermeneutics* (Amsterdam: Rodopi, 1990).
[58] Mark Wallace, *The Second Naiveté: Barth, Ricœur, and the New Yale Theology* (Macon: Mercer, 1990).
[59] Ricœur, *Critique and Conviction*, 22. 'Ce n'est que peu à peu que j'ai été pris dans la vague heideggerienne' (Ricœur, *La critique et la conviction*, 39).
[60] As Anderson notes, 'Because *l'homme* when used in French phenomenology, has tended to serve as a generic reference for humankind Ricœur remains unaware of the issue of gender in this context' (Anderson, *Ricœur and Kant*, 3).

fashion typical of Ricœur's 'hermeneutic' thought, these themes both *influence* and *are influenced by* his understanding of what it means to be finite and human.

The question of how finitude relates to the nature of philosophy as the search for truth is essential groundwork for understanding Ricœur's philosophical method. Chapter 1, 'Rage against the System: The Unity of Truth' therefore sets the scene for everything that follows by outlining Ricœur's answer to this question in its historical context. It argues that Ricœur's methodology is a product of the joint influence of the two schools of thought in which he had been trained: French reflexive philosophy and existentialism. From the reflexive method Ricœur learns that philosophy's nature is to seek systematic unity. But the existentialists make him aware of the over-reaching pretention of any human claim to grasp the totality of truth suggesting that we should focus instead on concrete particulars. Mediating between these two extremes, Ricœur construes systematising as the ultimate never-finished goal of philosophy.

Chapter 2, 'A Philosophy of Hope? The Universality of Truth', makes the case that Ricœur mediates between the particularity of the individual philosopher and the universality of philosophical truth-claims. He does this by showing that it is impossible not to make universal claims, but that these must be always provisional. Ricœur's philosophy is thus a philosophy of hope, avoiding the pitfalls of despair (the truth cannot be attained) on the one hand and arrogance (the truth has been attained) on the other: rather the truth is always partially attained and the goal of philosophy is to attain more of it. This search is founded on hope, both that we can attain partial truth now and that the fullness of truth will be given in the eschaton.

Chapter 3, 'Absolutely No Absolutes? Ricœur's Encounter with Thévenaz', introduces the Barthian philosopher Pierre Thévenaz, a close friend and contemporary of Ricœur. Thévenaz dubbed his thought a 'philosophy without absolutes'. Ricœur appreciated much about Thévenaz's approach, yet he also pushed back, showing how one cannot avoid absolutes in philosophy even by the self-contradiction of ruling them out absolutely. Over the course of this debate it becomes clear throughout that 'the Absolute' is being used by all parties as a covert philosophical term for 'God'.

Chapter 4, 'Finitude and the Infinite: The God of the Philosophers', contends that Ricœur's concept of finitude contains an implicit argument for the existence of God. Unlike almost every other French philosopher of his time, Ricœur argues that human finitude cannot be understood in isolation from the question of the meaning of transcendence. Moreover, he departs from the almost ubiquitous identification of 'the human' with pure finitude in twentieth-century continental philosophy. For Ricœur, we would not be aware of our finitude if we were nothing but finitude. The fact that we know ourselves as finite reveals an infinitude equally present in the human constitution. To be human is therefore to be a paradoxical mixture of finitude and infinitude. This infinitude is only grasped apophatically, through a negation of finitude. But although it is only known negatively, the infinite itself is not negative but positive, an original affirmation of being. Philosophy can therefore dimly grasp God in a sort of negative outline of what is not true of him, without being able to give it any positive substance.

Chapter 5, 'Finitude and Evil: The Crucial Distinction', looks in the opposite direction, at the relation of human finitude to evil. Ricœur later explained why he gave the title *Finitude and Guilt* to Part II of *Philosophy of the Will*: it was because 'my problem was to distinguish between finitude and guilt. I had the impression, or even the conviction, that these two terms tended to be identified in classical existentialism at the cost of both experiences'.[61] Surprisingly little scholarship takes note of this explicit aim of Ricœur's, yet it is fertile ground, not only for philosophy but also for theology. As Judith Wolfe suggests, 'Modern theology ... has too often neglected the task of a rigorous engagement [with] the complex relationship between finitude and sinfulness.'[62] Similarly, Ricœur believes that a confusion of finitude with evil/guilt pervades the philosophy of his time. For him, finitude is ontological, part of our unchosen human constitution, whereas it is intrinsic to the experience of guilt that we *could have* chosen otherwise.

Chapter 6, 'Rightly Relating Evil and Finitude', shows how Ricœur reframes the relationship between finitude and evil. Ricœur seeks to uncover the structures of human existence prior to their corruption by evil, in order to show that evil is a historical aberration that corrupts an originally good human nature. But Ricœur does not confuse goodness with perfection; he sees a necessary maturity that takes place in human

---

[61] This quotation is from a presentation Ricœur gave to the Divinity School of the University of Chicago, 5 May 1971, that was later published as an appendix to the English translation of *The Rule of Metaphor*. See Paul Ricœur, *The Rule of Metaphor: Multi-Disciplinary Studies of the Creation of Meaning in Language*, trans. Kathleen McLaughlin, John Costello, SJ, and Robert Czerny (London: Routledge, 1978), 372.
[62] Judith Wolfe, *Heidegger and Theology* (London: Bloomsbury, 2014), 196.

history that is separate from the need to restore corrupted humanity. He draws inspiration from Irenaeus' account of an immature innocence prior to the fall, and from the biblical allusion to the serpent which symbolises an evil anterior to humanity.

In Chapter 7, 'The Poetic Symbol of Creation', we take a 'theological turn'. Even though Ricœur kept the two disciplines of theology and philosophy strictly separate, his thought reveals the mutual enrichments that emerge from the two listening to each other. As theologian Andrew Davison says, 'we can be *more philosophical* in order to be *more theological*',[63] and philosopher Emmanuel Falque concurs from the other side that 'the better one theologizes, the more one philosophizes'.[64] This chapter therefore examines the impact of the Christian doctrine of creation on Ricœur's philosophy. Ricœur intended his projected third part of *Philosophy of the Will* to be what he calls a 'poetics' of the will.[65] Methodologically this meant lifting the brackets he had placed around transcendence and describing human subjectivity in light of religious symbols such as God, creation, and redemption. These function for Ricœur as a 'symbol', meaning an object opaque to philosophy but which can illuminate areas of philosophical thought. What is rarely noticed, however, is that the primary 'poetic symbol' for Ricœur is that of viewing human subjectivity as *created*: 'poetry is the art of *conjuring up the world as created*. It is in effect the *order of creation* which [the first Part] holds in suspension'.[66] Although several studies have explored the religious dimension of Ricœur's early 'poetics', none so far has focussed on the role of creation as the ultimate poetic symbol that underlies Ricœur's thought. To see Ricœurian finitude as fundamentally *created* finitude adds a new perspective to the problematics of the three preceding chapters.

Chapter 8, 'The Mysterious Unity of Creation', argues that Ricœur puts the symbol of creation to work in his philosophy to unify the

---

[63] Andrew Davison, *The Love of Wisdom: An Introduction to Philosophy for Theologians* (London: SCM Press, 2013), ix. Italics original.

[64] Emmanuel Falque, *Crossing the Rubicon: The Borderlands of Philosophy and Theology*, trans. Reuben Shank (New York: Fordham University Press, 2016), 107. Original italicised: '*Plus on théologise, mieux on philosophe*' (Emmanuel Falque, *Passer le Rubicon: philosophie et théologie : essai sur les frontières* [Paris: Éditions Lessius, 2013], 175).

[65] Ricœur, *Freedom and Nature*, 30. Italics original: 'L'achèvement de l'ontologie du sujet exige un nouveau changement de méthode, l'*accès à une sorte de "Poétique"* de la volonté' (Ricœur, *Le volontaire et l'involontaire*, 32).

[66] Ricœur, *Freedom and Nature*, 30. Italics mine: 'Au sens radical du mot, la poésie est l'art de conjurer le monde de la création. C'est en effet l'ordre de la création qui est tenu en suspens par la description' (Ricœur, *Le volontaire et l'involontaire*, 32).

fragmented elements of being: subjectivity and objectivity, freedom and nature. Creation is the source of inspiration for Ricœur's insights concerning the relation of finitude to truth, transcendence, and evil. Creation leads Ricœur to affirm the ultimate unity of reality, even though we can only articulate it in paradoxes of subject and object.

Chapter 9, 'The Original Goodness of Creation', makes the case that Ricœur persistently seeks the originally good essence of all things because he sees them as created by a good Creator and therefore good. In contrast to Sartre's philosophy of refusal which remains angry and disappointed that it is not infinite, that it is not God, Ricœur develops his concept of *consent*, which means humbly submitting to the reality I cannot control in the belief, or more precisely the hope, that it is fundamentally good and created by a good Creator.

The conclusion draws these threads together and offers some suggestions concerning what this study contributes to the much-debated issue of the relationship between philosophy and theology in Ricœur. Each of the preceding themes brings to light its own point of contact between the two discourses, revealing a fecund interaction and harmonious mutual interchange, at the heart of Ricœur's thought, between his philosophy and his faith.

I

Rage against the System
The Unity of Truth

> The driest argument has its hallucinations, too hastily concluding that its net will now at last be large enough to hold the universe. Men may dream in demonstrations, and cut out an illusory world in the shape of axioms, definitions, and propositions, with a final exclusion of fact signed Q.E.D. No formulas for thinking will save us mortals from mistake in our imperfect apprehension of the matter to be thought about.
>
> George Eliot[1]

What does our human finitude mean for our quest for truth? This question cannot be ignored because our finitude puts limits on our capacity for knowledge, preventing us from grasping truth in its totality. Thus the way we understand our own finitude both determines, and is determined by, the way we pursue truth and the kind of truth we will claim to be able to possess. Any beliefs we have about how to do philosophy will be dependent on a prior understanding of what we are as human beings and what kind of philosophy we are capable of.

The question of how human finitude limits the search for truth was one of the major concerns of twentieth-century philosophy and Ricœur has much to say about it. It is essentially the question of philosophical method, or what we might call the 'epistemology of finitude', the quest for knowledge and truth in light of our finite capacities. The first two chapters of this book explore Ricœur's philosophical method and his reasons for it, preparing the ground for the more ontological questions about finitude.

---

[1] George Eliot, *Daniel Deronda* (London: Penguin Books, 1993), 514.

Rage against the System: The Unity of Truth

In this first chapter, we explore Ricœur's conception of what it means for finite beings to search for systematic, synthetic, and unified truth. We shall find that Ricœur conceives systematicity as a never-finished task, which goes awry if it is abandoned either because a philosopher thinks they have finished it, or because they give up hope of finishing it. Ricœur displays a 'combination of the desire for synthesis and the recognition of diversity', as Charles Taylor elegantly put it.[2] Taylor also describes Ricœur as 'fully aware of the temptations, of the distortions, and ultimately of the totalitarian intent of the premature synthesis',[3] while at the same time recognising the necessity for thought to posit the unity of being. Ricœur resolves this tension by an appeal to eschatological unity that is only partly realised in the present: 'the reconciliation between the necessary unity and the seemingly incommunicable diversity in man, in societies or in history, is to be found in an eschatology of which the present offers us only a small part "on deposit"'.[4]

We shall also find that Ricœur mediates between the premature synthesising of French reflexion, and the disillusioned fragmentation of existentialism. Ricœur is well known as a conciliatory figure who finds common ground between opposing positions (Gadamer and Habermas,[5] phenomenology and psychoanalysis,[6] Kant and Hegel,[7] etc.). But the mediation between French reflexive philosophy and existentialism has so far gone unnoticed, probably because Ricœur never draws attention to it or names it as such, and because many scholars neglect the 'crucial and pivotal influence of the French reflexive philosophical tradition', as Eric Grump observes.[8] French reflexion's influence on Ricœur is one pole of a tension in his method; the other pole is existentialism. Let us briefly turn to examine these two types of philosophy.

---

[2] Charles Taylor, 'History and Truth (Book Review)', *The Journal of Philosophy* 65, no. 13 (1968): 402.
[3] Taylor, 'History and Truth'.
[4] Taylor, 'History and Truth', 403.
[5] See Paul Ricœur, 'Hermeneutics and the Critique of Ideology', in *Hermeneutics and the Human Sciences: Essays on Language, Action and Interpretation*, ed. and trans. John Thompson (Cambridge: Cambridge University Press, 1981), 23–60.
[6] See Paul Ricœur, *Freud and Philosophy: An Essay on Interpretation*, trans. Denis Savage (New Haven: Yale University Press, 1970); Paul Ricœur, *De l'interprétation: Essai sur Freud* (Paris: Éditions du Seuil, 1965).
[7] See Paul Ricœur, 'Hope and the Structure of Philosophical Systems', in *Figuring the Sacred: Religion, Narrative, and Imagination*, ed. Mark I. Wallace, trans. David Pellauer (Minneapolis: Fortress Press, 1995), 203–16.
[8] Grump, 'Between Conviction and Critique', 170.

FRENCH REFLEXIVE PHILOSOPHY

Before either existentialism or phenomenology became known in France, the reflexive method was the most common way of doing philosophy.[9] Ricœur remained committed to this method long after it went out of fashion, indeed until the end of his life. In 1986 he gave a brief description of how he understood it:

> By reflexive philosophy, I mean broadly speaking the mode of thought stemming from the Cartesian cogito and handed down by way of Kant and French post-Kantian philosophy, a philosophy that ... was most strikingly represented by Jean Nabert.[10]

In other words, reflexion is a style of philosophising that begins and ends with the thinking subject, a feature common to both Descartes and Kant. As Brian Gregor puts it, 'reflexive philosophy is primarily concerned with the possibility of self-knowledge. Through the act of reflection, the thinking subject attempts to step back and reflect on what consciousness is doing when it knows, when it values, and when it wills'.[11]

By the time Ricœur began his studies, reflexive philosophy had become idealist in nature and had risen to the status of the dominant strand of philosophy in France. Ricœur's director of studies, Léon Brunschvicg, was reflexion's greatest representative, and his Master's thesis was a comparison of two recently deceased reflexive philosophers (also known at the time as spiritualists), Jules Lachelier and Jules Lagneau.[12] After World War II, the reflexive method continued to exert a live influence on Ricœur through

---

[9] This tradition had many overlaps with the nineteenth-century spiritualist movement. See Gilbert Varet, 'Spiritualisme et philosophie réflexive', *Revue des Sciences Philosophiques et Théologiques* 74, no. 1 (1990): 23–34. The label 'spiritualism' was not fashionable by Ricœur's time, which is perhaps why he does not use it.

[10] Paul Ricœur, *From Text to Action*, trans. Kathleen Blamey and John B. Thompson (Evanston: Northwestern University Press, 1991), 12. 'Par philosophie réflexive, j'entends en gros le mode de pensée issu du *Cogito* cartésien, à travers Kant et la philosophie post-kantienne française peu connue à l'étranger et dont Jean Nabert a été pour moi le penseur le plus marquant' (Paul Ricœur, *Du texte à l'action* [Paris: Éditions du Seuil, 1986], 25).

[11] Gregor, *Ricœur's Hermeneutics of Religion*, 12.

[12] Paul Ricœur, *Méthode réflexive appliquée au problème de Dieu chez Lachelier et Lagneau* (Paris: Éditions du Cerf, 2017). Lachelier is often also grouped with the spiritualist movement (see Frederick Copleston, *19th and 20th Century French Philosophy*, A History of Philosophy 9 [London: Continuum, 2003], 155–77). According to Leonard Lawlor, Lachelier was 'among the most influential philosophers in France in the second half of the nineteenth century' (translator's footnote in Jean Wahl, *Transcendence and the Concrete: Selected Writings*, ed. Alan Schrift and Ian Alexander Moore [Bronx: Fordham University Press, 2016], 36).

his interactions with Pierre Thévenaz, and Jean Nabert – the latter being known as reflexion's last great representative, who Ricœur says 'was to have a decisive influence on me in the 1950s and 1960s'.[13] We will see this influence when examining how Thévenaz (Chapter 3) and Nabert (Chapter 4) contributed to Ricœur's philosophical understanding of God.[14]

However, reflexive philosophy was not *quite* the first philosophy Ricœur learned.[15] It was his earliest *University* formation, but his thought had already been shaped by his high school teacher, Roland Dalbiez. As the first Frenchman to write a philosophy thesis on Freud, Dalbiez continually challenged the pretensions of pure consciousness to grasp universality and to be transparent to itself. In addition, Dalbiez prepared Ricœur for a critical relationship to idealism, which, Ricœur recalls, was Dalbiez's 'main adversary'. Dalbiez suspected idealism of 'inducing thought to hold in its grasp only emptiness; deprived of reality in this way, thought was forced to turn narcissistically back upon itself'.[16] In his intellectual autobiography, Ricœur, speaking of Dalbiez, says, 'I owe to my first philosophy teacher the resistance that I have opposed to the claim to immediacy, adequation, and apodicticity made by the Cartesian cogito and the Kantian "I think", when my subsequent university studies brought me under the influence of the French heirs to these two founders of modern thought'.[17] In Ricœur's Master's thesis we can see him making use of these lessons he had learned from Dalbiez, criticising the reflexive tendency to focus exclusively on universal elements of human nature at the expense of all that distinguishes one person from another. 'The followers of the reflexive method', he observes, 'often forget that I am not only an individual, but a person', not only an identical instance of humanity, but a unique personality with his or her own distinctive way of

---

[13] Ricœur, 'Intellectual Autobiography', 6. 'Jean Nabert devait m'influencer de façon plus décisive dans les années cinquante et soixante' (Ricœur, *Réflexion faite*, 15).
[14] See the sections on 'Pierre Thévenaz and the Philosophy without Any Absolute' in Chapter 3 and 'Transcendence as Original Affirmation' in Chapter 4.
[15] Contra Gregor, who writes that reflexive philosophy was Ricœur's 'earliest philosophical formation': Gregor, *Ricœur's Hermeneutics of Religion*, 12.
[16] Ricœur, 'Intellectual Autobiography', 4. 'L'adversaire principal était l'idéalisme, suspecté de laisser la pensée refermer sa prise sur le vide, privée de réel, la pensée était contrainte de se replier narcissiquement sur soi-même' (Ricœur, *Réflexion faite*, 12).
[17] Ricœur, 'Intellectual Autobiography', 4. 'Je suis persuadé aujourd'hui que je dois à mon premier maître de philosophie la résistance que j'opposai à la prétention à l'immédiateté, à l'adéquation et à l'apodicticité du cogito cartésien, et du "je pense" kantien, lorsque la suite de mes études universitaires m'eut conduit dans la mouvance des héritiers français de ces deux fondateurs de la pensée moderne' (Ricœur, *Réflexion faite*, 12).

thinking.[18] The very method that wishes to grasp all of reality has omitted one of its dimensions, Ricœur observes.

Although the reflexive method was neither the first nor the last of the formative influences on Ricœur, it left an indelible mark on him. He never abandoned reflexive philosophy's hallmark commitment to careful, systematic rationality that seeks universal truth. Gregor rightly underlines this element, writing that the reflexive tradition was 'formative for Ricœur and remained influential throughout all of his subsequent work, including his philosophy of religion. If we want to understand Ricœur, then, we need to understand something about reflexive philosophy'.[19] Although Ricœur 'modifies that tradition in significant ways',[20] he nonetheless 'remains committed to a modified, chastened form of the reflexive method as a way to pursue self-understanding'.[21]

For French reflexion, the finitude of human thought is expressed in its idealist insistence that we are unable to grasp reality 'in itself', being able to comprehend things only as they appear to our finite minds. But the reflexive school did not see finitude as something that impedes our ability to determine what is true (for the thinking subject) in a universally valid and systematically unified manner. French reflexion was characterised by a systematic approach to truth. This was rarely made explicit, since it was understood that all philosophy by nature aims to be systematic in order to capture truth in its totality and unity.

For the following generation of philosophers, however, finitude would be understood in a very different way.

EXISTENTIALISM

The upsurge of the philosophies that later came to be known as existentialist was arguably the first major philosophical 'event' of the twentieth century for both France and Germany.[22] In spite of this, to give a precise

---

[18] My translation: 'Les partisans de la méthode réflexive oublient souvent que je ne suis pas seulement un individu, mais une personne' (Ricœur, *Méthode réflexive*, 39).
[19] Gregor, *Ricœur's Hermeneutics of Religion*, 12.
[20] Gregor, *Ricœur's Hermeneutics of Religion*, 11.
[21] Gregor, *Ricœur's Hermeneutics of Religion*, 4.
[22] For example, Frédéric Worms divides twentieth-century French thought into three waves. The first is a prolongation of nineteenth-century debates over spiritualism. These debates are then suddenly swept off the scene by the irruption of existentialism, the second wave. Existentialism eventually gives way, to the 'third wave' of structuralist and post-structuralist concerns in the 1960s. See Frédéric Worms, *La philosophie en France au XXe siècle: moments* (Paris: Gallimard, 2009).

definition of existentialism is notoriously difficult.²³ It is equally hard to determine who counts as an existentialist. As Alan Schrift says, 'the range of thinkers and writers associated with existentialism makes it difficult to isolate any set collection of theses to which all would agree'.²⁴ This is no coincidence, but fits the existentialists' very aversion to abstractions, to lumping things together in a general category at the expense of their concrete individuality. On the other hand, it is hard to study philosophy in the 1930s and 1940s and deny that a new way of philosophising erupted which exerted enormous influence not only on philosophy, but also on literature, history, theology and psychology.²⁵ The difficulties associated with the existentialist label do not prevent it from serving as a heuristic to identify common features of the philosophies of the time. Scholars have characterised existentialism as a philosophy 'about the concrete individual',²⁶ concerned with 'individual, concrete human existence',²⁷ that 'takes as its starting point the individual's existence'.²⁸

Four names are regularly grouped together by Ricœur and other writers as the seminal existentialist philosophers: Martin Heidegger, Karl Jaspers, Gabriel Marcel, and Jean-Paul Sartre.²⁹ According to Marcel, it was Sartre who first made this fourfold canonisation on the occasion of his famous 1945 address, *L'existentialisme est un humanisme*.³⁰ But Sartre was the only one of the four who willingly accepted the label 'existentialist',³¹ and his association with the other three may have only

---

²³ As noted in (*inter alia*) Jon Stewart, ed., *Kierkegaard and Existentialism*, Kierkegaard Research: Sources, Reception and Resources 9 (Farnham: Ashgate, 2011), ix; Bakewell, *At the Existentialist Café*, 33; Kevin Aho, *Existentialism: An Introduction* (Cambridge: Polity Press, 2014); Will Herberg, ed., *Four Existentialist Theologians* (Garden City: Doubleday Anchor Books, 1958), 3

²⁴ Alan D. Schrift, *Twentieth-Century French Philosophy: Key Themes and Thinkers* (Malden: Blackwell, 2009), 32.

²⁵ In theology Diogenes Allen notes that, 'For nearly half of the twentieth century existentialism was the only contemporary philosophical current with which theology had any vital contact'. Diogenes Allen and Eric Springsted, *Philosophy for Understanding Theology*, 2nd ed. (Louisville: Westminster John Knox Press, 2007).

²⁶ Thomas Flynn, *Existentialism: A Very Short Introduction* (Oxford: Oxford University Press, 2006), xii.

²⁷ Bakewell, *At the Existentialist Café*, 34.

²⁸ Steven Earnshaw, *Existentialism: A Guide for the Perplexed* (London: Continuum, 2006), 1.

²⁹ Paul Ricœur, *Gabriel Marcel et Karl Jaspers: philosophie du mystère et philosophie du paradoxe* (Paris: Éditions du Temps présent, 1948), 18, 33, 154.

³⁰ Gabriel Marcel, *Tragic Wisdom and Beyond*, trans. Peter McCormick and Stephen Jolin (1968; repr., Evanston: Northwestern University Press, 1973), 237.

³¹ Flynn, *Existentialism*, xii.

become common currency due to the enormous influence of that very address.

Those called existentialists were most united in their opposition to 'the whole tradition of classical philosophy since Plato' (according to Jean Wahl, who wrote one of the first introductions to the movement).[32] A particular *bête noire*, however, was Hegel, who represented the last of the great Western philosophical systems constituted by 'objectivity, necessity, universality, and totality'.[33] Jaspers described the whole of Western philosophy from Plato to Hegel as characterised by 'objective, confident, absolute rationality'.[34] The existentialists considered Kierkegaard and Nietzsche to be the first break in this totalising pattern of philosophy and the great nineteenth-century 'precursors' to existentialism,[35] 'to whom', Mairet tells us, 'all existential thinkers acknowledge their indebtedness'.[36]

For the existentialists, the great failure of nineteenth-century philosophy was its presumption of a universal perspective which led to totalising systems of thought. The existentialists insisted, by contrast, on our inability to see reality from a 'God's-eye view'. This insistence took the form of a renewed emphasis on *human finitude*. French reflexion, said the existentialists, had transgressed the finite limits of human knowledge by its claims to universal knowledge and closed systems of thought. Instead, philosophy should restrict itself to a humbler focus on particular elements of the human condition without attempting to integrate these into any overarching system.

A crucial difference between reflexive philosophy and existentialism lies in their opposing attitudes towards the urge to build a 'philosophical system'. While reflexive philosophers expended their efforts to produce comprehensive systems that place every truth in the context of a wider

---

[32] Jean Wahl, *Philosophies of Existence: An Introduction to the Basic Thought of Kierkegaard, Heidegger, Jaspers, Marcel, Sartre*, trans. F. M. Lory (New York: Schocken Books, 1969), 12. 'Ces philosophies ... s'opposent en fait à toute la tradition de la philosophie classique depuis Platon' (Jean Wahl, *Les philosophies de l'existence*, 2nd ed. [Paris: Librarie Armand Colin, 1959], 20).

[33] Wahl, *Philosophies of Existence*, 13. '... d'objectivité, de nécessité, d'universalité, de totalité' (Wahl, *Les philosophies de l'existence*, 22).

[34] Karl Jaspers, *Reason and Existenz*, trans. William Earle (London: Routledge, 1956), 128. 'Hegel war das Ende der abendländischen Philosophie der objektiven, selbstgewissen, absoluten Vernünftigkeit' (*Vernunft und Existenz*, 3rd ed. [Bremen: Johs. Storm Verlag, 1949], 102).

[35] Bakewell, *At the Existentialist Café*, 17.

[36] Jean-Paul Sartre, 'Translator's Introduction', in *Existentialism and Humanism*, trans. Philip Mairet (London: Methuen, 1948), 5; see also Stewart, *Kierkegaard and Existentialism*, ix.

totality, most existentialists by contrast saw such systems as a temptation and a betrayal of the heart of philosophy. Kierkegaard and Nietzsche are the primary influences in this rejection of systematic philosophy. As Jaspers put it, for them, 'the system is ... a detour from reality and is, therefore, lies and deception'.[37] Emmanuel Mounier specifies Hegel as Kierkegaard's main opponent, writing that 'Kierkegaard ranges himself against the Hegelian Absolute System, the systematization of system'.[38]

There is no doubt that Ricœur was influenced by Kierkegaard in this area alongside many others, as Huskey has shown.[39] But a stronger and more direct influence comes from his mentor, Marcel, who takes the rejection of systems to the furthest extreme, as we shall see. But the form Marcel's influence takes is not straightforward. Ricœur is a much more systematic thinker than Marcel by disposition – in fact, this is probably the greatest difference between the two thinkers. I suggest, with Blundell, that Marcel's influence is instead found in his *restraining* Ricœur from excessive systematisation: 'It was Marcel who continually strove to temper Ricœur's "systematic spirit", fearing that Ricœur himself would fall victim to what Marcel called the "spirit of abstraction".'[40]

GABRIEL MARCEL: SYSTEMATICALLY AGAINST SYSTEMS

Nobody is more violently opposed to philosophical systems than Marcel. For Marcel, systems are the antithesis of true philosophy: they are closed where philosophy should be open, abstract where philosophy should be concrete, arrogant where philosophy should be humble, and presuming a divine perspective where philosophy should admit its own finitude. Systems have no redeeming feature for Marcel. He sees the temptation to build a system as the original temptation of Adam and Eve: to forget human finitude and aspire to be like God, knowing, naming, and

---

[37] Jaspers, *Reason and Existenz*, 26. 'Das System ist ihnen Ablenkung von der Wirklichkeit, darum Lüge und Täuschung' (Jaspers, *Vernunft und Existenz*, 12).

[38] Emmanuel Mounier, *Existentialist Philosophies: An Introduction*, trans. Eric Blow (London: Rockliff, 1948), 4. 'Kierkegaard se dresse contre le système de Hegel, le Système absolu, systématisation du système' (Emmanuel Mounier, *Introduction aux existentialismes* [Paris: Éditions Denoël, 1947], 9).

[39] See R. K. Huskey, *Paul Ricœur on Hope: Expecting the Good* (New York: Peter Lang, 2009), 27–31. On the broader influence of Kierkegaard on Ricœur, see Timo Helenius, 'Ricœur's Kierkegaard', *International Journal of Philosophy and Theology* 80, no. 4–5 (20 October 2019): 356–73. Helenius's article does not, however, mention the attitude towards philosophical systems among the influences of Kierkegaard on Ricœur.

[40] Blundell, 'Creative Fidelity', 90.

ordering all things. It is, in short, the temptation of pride, and for Marcel, 'humility cannot bring forth a system'.[41]

Marcel sees system-building as an arrogant pretention to Godhood because it is inseparable from the totalising impulse, the desire to comprehend everything. 'No systematisation is possible', he tells us, 'without constant recourse to the notion of totality'.[42] Because philosophy is fundamentally an attempt to grasp reality, to totalise means to claim a complete and final grasp on reality that explains everything fully and without remainder. But this implies an absolute or universal point of view, a 'central observatory from which the universe may be contemplated in its totality'.[43] Marcel speaks of the system-builder as someone who 'claims to install himself at the center of being'.[44] Additionally the system is closed by its very nature: 'System means closed totality and complete immanence.'[45] Closure implies that nothing new can ever be learned, discovered, or even occur in history. More pointedly from a religious perspective, closure prevents the possibility of any transcendent revelation coming from outside the universe. Marcel demonstrates this by a thought experiment: 'Suppose that an absolute addition, an entirely unsought gift has been made to man – whether to some men or to all in the course of history', he imagines. The systematic philosopher is compelled to ignore it for fear that it will break apart her system, and must 'refuse to allow an intrusion to take place in a system regarded as closed'.[46]

This temptation to aspire to Godhood by system-building occurs because of the negative impulses of *domination*, *possession*, and *control*,

---

[41] Kenneth T. Gallagher, *The Philosophy of Gabriel Marcel* (New York: Fordham University Press, 1962), 6.
[42] Gabriel Marcel, 'Author's Preface to the English Edition', in *Metaphysical Journal*, trans. Bernard Wall (London: Rockliff, 1952), XII.
[43] Gabriel Marcel, *Creative Fidelity*, trans. Robert Rosthal (1940; repr., New York: Crossroad, 1982), 4. 'Je ne puis sans contradiction penser l'absolu comme un observatoire central d'où l'univers serait contemplé dans sa totalité' (Gabriel Marcel, *Du refus à l'invocation* [Paris: Gallimard, 1940], 8).
[44] Marcel, *Creative Fidelity*, 4. 'Le métaphysicien "prétend se transporter au cœur de l'être ou retrouver l'acte primitif dont dépendant à la fois mon être propre et l'être du monde (Lavelle, *De l'acte*, art. I)"?' (Marcel, *Du refus à l'invocation*, 8).
[45] Gabriel Marcel, 'Some Reflections on Existentialism', *Philosophy Today* 8, no. 4 (1964): 250.
[46] Gabriel Marcel, *Being and Having*, trans. Katharine Farrer (1935; repr., London: Dacre Press, 1949), 133. 'À supposer qu'un apport absolu, un don entièrement gratuit ait été fait à l'homme – que ce soit à quelques-uns ou à tous – au cours de l'histoire.... On refuse en somme ici de laisser se produire une certaine intrusion dans un système regardé comme clos' (Gabriel Marcel, *Être et avoir* [Paris: Aubier, 1935], 193).

Marcel tells us. The desire for *domination* is competitive, seeking a superior viewpoint to others, and the more tightly linked one's system of ideas, the more they form a unified whole which gives the impression of inhabiting an impenetrable fortress: 'Systematization satisfies the need to confront the adversary with a compact unity which one believes can intimidate him.'[47] In the early twentieth century many philosophers felt threatened by the positivism of modern science. In response, they felt the need for their own alternative complete account of reality which would have a similar level of rigour and finality. He says sardonically that owning a system 'diminishes the inferiority complex philosophers have had for the last fifty years with the development of the empirical sciences'.[48] Secondly, systems also satisfy the impulse to *possess* ideas like objects that can be arranged in a certain order. The more one objectifies knowledge, the more one can think of knowledge as something one owns, like property, and one can put one's name to and exploit to one's own advantage. Systems require objects to manipulate and arrange: 'objectivity is bound up with the existence of a system of questions and answers, but conversely such a system supposes objectivity'.[49]

But for Marcel, some things can never be conceived as objects without destroying their very nature, the best example being God. 'God is not an object', he tells us, but neither is he a subjective feeling. He is not 'simply the conceptualised expression of a particular manner of being or of feeling'.[50] God transcends the subject/object divide, breaking open any system in which we might want to place him.

Marcel points to our finitude, our non-Godlike status, as sufficient reason why we cannot grasp reality by means of a system. 'In succumbing to the temptation of system-building', he writes, 'isn't there a tendency

---

[47] Marcel, *Creative Fidelity*, 188. 'Systémisation répond au souci d'opposer à l'adversaire un bloc compact que l'on croit susceptible de l'intimider' (Marcel, *Du refus à l'invocation*, 242).

[48] Marcel, *Creative Fidelity*, 4. 'En procédant par définitions et par théorèmes, on espère réduire définitivement le complexe d'infériorité qui ronge tant de philosophes depuis un demi-siècle en présence du progrès des sciences particulières' (Marcel, *Du refus à l'invocation*, 8).

[49] Gabriel Marcel, *Metaphysical Journal*, trans. Bernard Wall (1927; repr., London: Rockliff, 1952), 140. 'L'objectivité est liée à l'existence d'un système de questions et de réponses, mais inversement ce système suppose une objectivité' (Gabriel Marcel, *Journal métaphysique* [Paris: Gallimard, 1927], 139).

[50] Marcel, *Metaphysical Journal*, 261. 'Dieu n'est pas objet ... [ou] simplement l'expression conceptualisée d'une certaine manière d'être ou de sentir' (Marcel, *Journal métaphysique*, 254).

to forget that any philosophy worthy of is name is impossible without an investigation of our condition as existing and thinking beings …?'[51] Our finite condition means, for him, that we can never have an external standpoint on the universe, on Being itself, from which we could survey it and produce an abstract system of ideas. I am unavoidably part of the universe I try to conceptualise. I am always involved, engaged, viewing the world from a particular finite perspective: 'I cannot really stand aside from the universe, even in thought. Only by a meaningless pretence can I place myself at some vague point outside it.'[52]

As a Christian, Marcel equates finitude with the state of being a creature rather than the Creator. Our created condition is the basis for humility, as he says in an interview with Ricœur:

> From the moment someone has a system, it seems to me he is concerned with exploiting it and managing it…. I have found it less and less possible to situate myself at some central point of view which would be like that of God. This would be a pretension completely incompatible with our status as creatures, it seems to me. That is why I have always emphasized the importance of humility on the philosophical level, the humility directly opposed to pride, to *hubris*.[53]

It is noteworthy how in this passage and others Marcel connects epistemological concerns with dispositions like pride and humility. This connection will be important when we consider the status Ricœur gives to hope. Pride, humility, and hope are, for Marcel and Ricœur, not merely emotions or affective consequences, but causal origins of our philosophical stance, orientations of our very being that have a decisive effect on how we understand ourselves and the world.

Marcel was performatively faithful to his rejection of systems. His first two books were simply notes from his journals, his thoughts ordered

---

[51] Marcel, *Creative Fidelity*, 4. 'Lorsqu'on s'abandonne à la tentation du systématique, ne s'expose-t-on pas le plus souvent à oublier qu'une philosophie digne de ce nom n'est pas possible sans un approfondissement de notre condition d'êtres existants et pensants …?' (Marcel, *Du refus à l'invocation*, 8).

[52] Marcel, *Being and Having*, 19. 'Je ne peux pas, même en pensée, me mettre réellement à part de l'univers, ce n'est que par une fiction inintelligible que je peux me situer en je ne sais quel point extérieur de lui' (Marcel, *Être et avoir*, 23).

[53] Marcel, *Tragic Wisdom*, 252. 'A partir du moment où on a un système, on se préoccupe de l'exploiter, de le gérer … il m'est apparu toujours plus clairement qu'il était impossible pour moi de me placer à un point de vue central qui serait en quelque sorte le point de vue de Dieu, qu'il y avait là une prétention qui me semblait tout à fait incompatible avec notre statut de créature: d'où la place que j'ai été amené à accorder à l'humilité sur le plan philosophique, l'humilité par opposition à l'orgueil ou à *l'hybrisme*' (Paul Ricœur and Gabriel Marcel, *Entretiens* [Paris: Aubier-Montaigne, 1968], 117–18).

by the date in which they occurred to him, which he did not re-arrange before publishing. His subsequent books are less radically disordered, comprising essay collections, but to compensate for this he feels the need to disclaim any pretence at system-building in the preface of each. 'The reader will find nothing in the present volume remotely resembling a system of metaphysics', he asserts in one.[54] In another he warns that 'it would be a mistake to look [in this book] for the outline of a system'.[55]

Marcel's alternative approach is to champion a perpetual openness to the new, which he calls *disponibilité*, a French word often translated as 'disposability' or 'availability'. According to Gallagher, *disponibilité* evokes connotations of 'openness, release, abandonment, welcoming, surrender, readiness to respond'.[56] For Marcel, it means the willingness to 'maintain thought in the state of "openness", in contradistinction to a systematised dogmatics closed in on itself'.[57] This openness must be constantly renewed because we are always in danger of closing ourselves off in habitual patterns of thought. Marcel observes the ease with which certain habits of thought and attention can fossilise our worldview:

> As my life becomes more and more an established thing, a certain division tends to be made between what concerns me and what does not concern me ... Each one of us thus becomes the centre of a sort of mental space, arranged in concentric zones of decreasing interest and decreasing adherence, and to this decreasing adherence there corresponds an increasing non-disposability.[58]

This passage shows how Marcelian *disponibilité* is directly opposed to the frame of mind that leads to the formation of closed systems. When we are not open to the new, we begin to feel that we already understand everything, but that is only because we are simply not looking beyond what we are familiar and comfortable with. Marcel insists that

---

[54] Marcel, *Creative Fidelity*, 3. 'On chercherait vainement dans le présent volume quoi que ce soit qui ressemble à l'exposition systématique d'une métaphysique (Marcel, *Du refus à l'invocation*, 7).
[55] Marcel, *Tragic Wisdom*, xxxi. 'L'on commettrait sans doute une erreur en jugeant ... d'en dégager les linéaments d'un système' (Gabriel Marcel, *Pour une sagesse tragique et son au-delà* [Paris: Plon, 1968], 9).
[56] Gallagher, *The Philosophy of Gabriel Marcel*, 26.
[57] Marcel, 'Author's Preface to the English Edition', XIII.
[58] Marcel, *Being and Having*, 70-1. 'À mesure que je m'établis davantage dans la vie, une certaine répartition qui s'apparait à elle-même comme rationnelle tend à se faire entre ce qui me regarde et ce que ne me regarde pas. Chacun de nous devient ainsi le centre d'une sorte d'espace mental qui se dispose suivant des zones concentriques d'adhérence décroissante, d'intérêt décroissant, et à cette adhérence décroissante correspond une indisponibilité croissante' (Marcel, *Être et avoir*, 102).

this fossilisation and closure of our minds is not an inevitable process. *Disponibilité* means being prepared for something new to enter our lives and disrupt the order we have made of our world. It is a continual choice that 'can only occur in a being who is not a closed or hermetic system into which nothing new can penetrate'.[59]

An essential weapon against the fossilisation of our worldview, a weapon that keeps us *disponible*, in Marcel's view, is *communication*. Communication keeps us receptive to the insights and perspectives of others, the corner of the truth they hold that is otherwise invisible to us. 'There is a region of fructifying obscurity', Marcel writes, 'transcending the closed systems in which thought imprisons us, where beings may communicate, where they *are* in and by the very act of communication'.[60]

There is no doubt that Ricœur's work is marked by an awareness of the many problems that come from closed or totalising systems. Still, Ricœur formulates these problems in his own way which is different from Marcel while at the same time bearing the trace of Marcel's way of thinking.

Ricœur begins the critique of closed systems by pointing us to the endless complexity of history, something of which historians will be much more conscious than philosophers. A closed philosophical system, Ricœur says, does 'violence to the facts' by forcing the immense richness and detail of history into a procrustean bed. He describes the professional historian's nagging fear that philosophy 'will crush history with its system-building mentality'.[61] To combat this tendency the philosopher must remember that 'history is extraordinarily rich; it allows for many other interpretations'.[62]

As well as doing violence to the *past*, Ricœur points out that closed systems ignore the possibility of new insight in the *future*. This means that any closed system is always *prematurely* closed, seeing itself as already in the eschatological fullness of knowledge. Like the existentialists, Ricœur

---

[59] Marcel, *Creative Fidelity*, 48. 'L'admiration ... ne peut se produire qu'au sein d'un être qui ne ferme pas avec lui-même un système clos, hermétique, dans lequel rien de neuf ne peut plus pénétrer' (Marcel, *Du refus à l'invocation*, 68).

[60] Marcel, *Creative Fidelity*, 35. italics original: '... par delà les systèmes clos où le jugement nous enferme, une sorte d'indistinction féconde où les êtres communiquent, où ils *sont* dans et par l'acte même de communication' (Marcel, *Du refus à l'invocation*, 52).

[61] Paul Ricœur, *History and Truth*, trans. Charles Kelbley (Evanston: Northwestern University Press, 1965), 34. 'n'écrase l'histoire sous l'esprit du système' (Paul Ricœur, *Histoire et vérité* [Paris: Éditions du Seuil, 2001], 43).

[62] Ricœur, *History and Truth*, 185. 'L'histoire est bien riche; elle permet bien d'autres systèmes de lecture' (Ricœur, *Histoire et vérité*, 211).

sees nineteenth-century philosophies as a parade example of this. 'The heritage of the nineteenth century', he says, is 'the abuse of premature syntheses'.[63] He also shows how such premature syntheses (we might also call these 'overly realised eschatologies') easily transition from theory to practice, as the system imposes its categories on the present day: 'As soon as the exigency for a single truth enters into history as a goal of civilization, it is immediately affected with a mark of violence. For one always wishes to tie the knot too early. The *realized* unity of the truth is precisely the initial lie.'[64]

What is more, Ricœur observes that closed systems cannot account for the reality of *evil*. This is because evil, by its very nature, brings chaos to order, nonsense to sense, and division to unity. Prior to his exposure to existentialism, Ricœur can already see that the reflexive philosophies in which he had been trained fail to deal appropriately with the problem of evil. In his 1934 Master's thesis, he claims that the problem of evil is 'where every philosophy breaks apart'.[65] 'I do not believe', he adds, 'that any philosophy escapes it'.[66] But fifty years later, after passing through existentialism, he will no longer think that all philosophy is totalising by nature, seeing evil instead as a helpful stimulus to hold us back in 'our penchant for totalising systems'.[67] Evil, he says, 'calls into question ... a way of thinking ... submitted to both the rule of noncontradiction and that of systematic totalisation', which means that dealing with the problem of evil enables philosophy to avoid such totalising ways of thinking.[68]

---

[63] My translation: 'L'héritage du XIXe siècle n'est-il pas l'abus des synthèses prématurées[?]' (Paul Ricœur, *Lectures 2: la contrée des philosophes* [Paris: Éditions du Seuil, 1999], 155–6).

[64] Ricœur, *History and Truth*, 176. 'Dès que l'exigence d'une vérité-une entre dans l'histoire, comme une tâche de civilisation, elle est aussitôt affectée d'un indice de violence; car c'est toujours trop tôt qu'on veut boucler la boucle. L'unité *réalisée* du vrai est précisément le mensonge initial' (Ricœur, *Histoire et vérité*, 200).

[65] My translation: '... où viennent se briser toutes les philosophies' (Ricœur, *Méthode réflexive*, 215).

[66] My translation: '... je ne crois pas qu'aucune philosophie y échappe' (Ricœur, *Méthode réflexive*, 217).

[67] My translation (paragraph not in English translation): '... notre penchant pour la totalisation systématique' (Paul Ricœur, 'Le mal: un défi à la philosophie et à la théologie', in *Lectures 3: aux frontières de la philosophie* [Paris: Éditions du Seuil, 1994], 212).

[68] Paul Ricœur, 'Evil: A Challenge to Philosophy and Theology', in *Figuring the Sacred: Religion, Narrative, and Imagination*, ed. Mark I. Wallace (Minneapolis: Fortress Press, 1995), 249. 'Ce que le problème met en question, c'est un mode de penser soumis à l'exigence ... à la fois de non-contradiction et de totalité systématique' (Ricœur, 'Le mal', 211).

But Ricœur goes on to warn that if we ignore evil in our desire for a complete system of thought, we will *cause* evil by our imposition of false categories on reality. From the *theoretical* failures of systems Ricœur transitions to their disastrous *practical* results in the ethical sphere. 'The true evil, the evil of evil, shows itself in false syntheses, that is to say, in the contemporary falsifications of the great undertakings of totalization of cultural experience, that is, in political and ecclesiastical institutions. In this way, evil shows its true face – the evil of evil is the lie of premature syntheses, of violent totalizations.'[69] Ricœur then describes how the transition happens: It 'takes place historically when a sociological *power* inclines toward, and more or less completely succeeds in regrouping all orders of truth and in forcing men to the violence of unity'.[70] The system only has room for certain types of people and behaviour. People who do not conform are either excluded or forced into a procrustean bed which inhibits their true nature: 'the more the system flourishes, the more its victims are marginalized. The success of the system is its failure. Suffering ... is what is excluded from the system'.[71] The ethical lesson to be learned from the violence of closed systems, from premature attempts to realise the unity of truth in history through a particular society, for Ricœur, is to remember that 'the spirit of truth is to respect the complexity of the various orders of truth; it is the recognition of plurality'.[72]

However, despite the many negative traits and abuses of philosophical systems, Ricœur discerns a positive core to systematic thought. In the case of philosophical systems, this means that Ricœur does not condemn

---

[69] Paul Ricœur, *The Conflict of Interpretations* (Evanston: Northwestern University Press, 1974), 439. 'Le mal véritable, le mal du mal, se montre avec les fausses synthèses, c'est-à-dire avec les falsifications contemporaines des grandes entreprises de totalisation de l'expérience culturelle, dans les institutions politiques et ecclésiastiques. Alors le mal montre son vrai visage; le mal du mal est le mensonge des synthèses prématurées, des totalisations violentes' (Paul Ricœur, *Le conflit des interprétations. Essais d'herméneutique* [Paris: Éditions du Seuil, 1969], 429).

[70] Ricœur, *History and Truth*, 189. Italics original: 'Ce glissement se produit historiquement quand un *pouvoir* sociologique incline et réussit plus ou moins complètement à regrouper tous les ordres de vérité et à ployer les hommes à la violence de l'unité' (Ricœur, *Histoire et vérité*, 216).

[71] Ricœur, 'Evil', 257. Translation modified: 'Plus le système prospère, plus les victimes sont marginalisées. La réussite du système fait son échec. La souffrance ... est ce qui s'exclut du système' (Ricœur, 'Le mal', 225–6). Here as elsewhere, 'translation modified' means I have altered the published English text to match the original French more closely.

[72] Ricœur, *History and Truth*, 189. 'L'esprit de vérité est de respecter la complexité *des* ordres de vérité, c'est l'aveu du pluriel' (Ricœur, *Histoire et vérité*, 216).

systematic thinking in itself, but only its excesses in various forms of nineteenth-century thinking, including the reflexive philosophy that was his own initial training. He does not let go of reflexive philosophy's systematic impulse, however, but rather modifies it to take a more humble and provisional stance more suited to the finitude of the human condition.

KARL JASPERS: DISTINGUISHING 'SYSTEM' AND 'SYSTEMATIC'

But what Ricœur does is not without precedent. His other mentor, Karl Jaspers, helps him find a mediating attitude to systems in several significant ways. Ricœur calls Jaspers 'more systematic than Marcel. Even his critique of the system is more systematic'.[73] He credits Jaspers with 'opening the way ... to an ontology which excludes the system and [at the same time] permits a coherent and ordered systematic'.[74]

Jaspers is an exception among the existentialists for his more nuanced approach to systematic thought. He introduces a distinction between 'system' (closed, brittle, fixed synthesis) and 'systematic' (unified, integrated, open, and in process) which becomes crucial for Ricœur. Wahl describes Jaspers's philosophy as 'both the negation of every system and the affirmation that a system is necessary for the intensity of the life of the mind'.[75] Jaspers recognises that there is something unavoidably systematic about thought because we want our ideas to make sense in light of one another: 'Thinking is by nature systematic. When I think I do not stick to one rudiment of a thought, nor do I merely put thoughts side by side; I relate them to each other.'[76] There is something natural about the

---

[73] My translation: '... plus systématique que G. Marcel. Sa critique du système est elle-même plus systématique' (Ricœur, *Marcel et Jaspers*, 62).

[74] My translation: '... frayer la voie à une ontologie ... qui exclut le système et permet une systématique ordonnée et cohérente' (Mikel Dufrenne and Paul Ricœur, *Karl Jaspers et la philosophie de l'existence* [Paris: Éditions du Seuil, 1947], 374).

[75] Jean Wahl, 'The Problem of Choice: Existence and Transcendence in the Philosophy of Jaspers', *Journal of French and Francophone Philosophy* 24, no. 1 (12 October 2016): 224. '... à la fois négation de tout système et affirmation qu'un système est nécessaire à l'intensité de la vie de l'esprit' (Jean Wahl, 'Le problème du choix, l'existence et la transcendance dans la philosophie de Jaspers', *Revue de Métaphysique et de Morale* 41, no. 3 [1934]: 405).

[76] Karl Jaspers, *Philosophy*, trans. E. B. Ashton, vol. 1 (1932; repr., Chicago: University of Chicago Press, 1969), 276. 'Denken ist schon von Natur systematisch: [E]s bleibt nicht bei einem Gedanken im Ansatz stecken, stellt Gedanken nicht bloß nebeneinander, sondern geht auf ihre Beziehung' (Karl Jaspers, *Philosophie*, 2nd ed. [Berlin: Springer-Verlag, 1948], 232).

desire to connect one thing to another, to 'go beyond all single objectivities to a systematic unity that would be complete in the totality of these unities'.[77]

For Jaspers, the system is a never-attainable goal that gives direction to philosophical thought, but that would end all philosophical thought if it believed itself to have arrived. We can never have a finished and complete system of thought, for two reasons. First, being does not present itself to us as a unity. Being is fragmented into three types, which he first calls 'Objective Being, Subjective Being, Being-in-Itself',[78] and later recasts as 'the world, freedom, and transcendence',[79] the unity of which can never be found or demonstrated. 'The fragmentation in which being appears', Jaspers says, 'will not permit me to find an overall being, a being which, for generally valid insight, would include the fragmentation in a way that we might understand'.[80] Secondly, a complete system would deny the incompletion of our human existence, which is 'always en route: I have lost it when I imagine myself at the goal'.[81] Therefore a complete system is only possible at the eschatological horizon: 'If eternal being itself could be the object and point of departure of our philosophizing, its systematics would be the only true one. Philosophy would be complete.' That is why 'to philosophize in such a system, in temporal existence, is to anticipate what we might grasp at the end of days but can now only try to read for fleeting moments'.[82] The impossibility of knowing the future means that 'no systematics of philosophizing can be

---

[77] Jaspers, *Philosophy*, 1969, 1:90. 'über alle einzelne Gegenständlichkeit ... zu einer systematischen Einheit, welche ihre Vollendung in der Totalität dieser Einheiten, der einen Welt, hätte' (Jaspers, *Philosophie*, 46).

[78] Jaspers, *Philosophy*, 1969, 1:47. 'Objektsein, Ichsein, Ansichsein' (Jaspers, *Philosophie*, 4).

[79] Jaspers, *Philosophy*, 1969, 1:282. 'Welt, Freiheit, Transzendenz' (Jaspers, *Philosophie*, 238).

[80] Jaspers, *Philosophy*, 1969, 1:281. Translation modified: 'Die Zerrissenheit des Seins, in der es ... erscheint, läßt kein übergreifendes Sein finden, das für allgemeingültige Einsicht die Zerrissenheit in sich schlösse, so daß diese aus ihm begreiflich würde' (Jaspers, *Philosophie*, 237).

[81] Jaspers, *Philosophy*, 1969, 1:279. 'Existenz ist immer nur auf dem Wege; sie hat sich verloren, wenn sie sich am Ziel wähnt' (Jaspers, *Philosophie*, 235).

[82] Jaspers, *Philosophy*, 1969, 1:279. 'Würde das Sein in seiner Ewigkeit Gegenstand und Ausgang unseres Philosophierens sein können, so wäre dessen Systematik die allein wahre. Diese würde die Philosophie zur Vollendung bringen, welche damit aufhören würde, Philosophieren zu sein.... In einem solchen System nimmt das Philosophieren im Zeitdasein vorweg, was es ergreifen könnte am Ende der Tage, jetzt aber nur ... jeweils einen Augenblick zu lesen versucht' (Jaspers, *Philosophie*, 235).

conclusive, not even if it had a place in its schema for whatever is historically yet to come'.[83]

Jaspers puts philosophy in a tension between the unavoidably systematic nature of our thinking, and the unavoidably temporal, provisional, incomplete nature of any system we produce. Philosophy would cease to be philosophy if it abandoned this tension, either by ceasing to strive for systematicity or by claiming to have achieved it: 'Philosophizing must, as thinking, always strive for a system, but in any complete system it would be mired.'[84] He concludes that 'unity is a true guidepost, never a truly existing object'.[85] In Jaspers's own work we see him striving to enact this balance between systematicity and openness. The first impression one has when reading *Philosophy* is that it is enormously systematic. As Ricœur observes, Jaspers's 'critique of system ... does not seem at first glance to be reflected in the form of his work'.[86] The three volumes of *Philosophy* correspond with the three types of being, and each chapter is neatly divided into sections, subsections, and headings which deal exhaustively with all angles of the topic. But in spite of this impression, Jaspers insists that 'as a whole [*Philosophy*] is not a system. The individual chapters need not be read in the order in which they occur'.[87] Ricœur calls the chapter division in *Philosophy* 'more organic than logical', because the whole work is reflected in each of the parts.[88]

PAUL RICŒUR: THE UNITY OF THE SYSTEM AS ESCHATOLOGICAL HOPE

Karl Jaspers provides Ricœur with a model, helping him to retain the positive impulse in French reflexion while also attenuating it in view of a humbler recognition of the limits of human finitude. In particular,

---

[83] Jaspers, *Philosophy*, 1969, 1:283. '[Keine] Systematik des Philosophierens ... kann eine Geschlossenheit auch nicht in der Form eintreten, daß etwa alles noch geschichtlich Werdende im Schema des Systems den ihm bereiten Ort fände' (Jaspers, *Philosophie*, 238–9).

[84] Jaspers, *Philosophy*, 1969, 1:277. 'Philosophieren würde im System, das es als Denken doch stets erstreben muß, versanden, wenn es sich vollenden würde' (Jaspers, *Philosophie*, 233).

[85] Jaspers, *Philosophy*, 1969, 1:136. 'Einheit ... hat ... jeweils Wahrheit nur als wegweisend, nicht als der daseiende Gegenstand dieser Einheit' (Jaspers, *Philosophie*, 89).

[86] My translation: 'la critique du système ... ne semble pas à première vue se refléter dans la forme de ses ouvrages' (Ricœur, *Marcel et Jaspers*, 61).

[87] Jaspers, 'Philosophical Autobiography', 39.

[88] My translation: '... plus organique que logique' (Ricœur, *Marcel et Jaspers*, 61).

Ricœur takes up Jaspers's distinction between 'system' and 'systematic' and makes it a part of his own method.[89] While a *closed system* means the end of philosophy, to be *systematic* is demanded by philosophical rigour, an unavoidable goal of rationality. 'The system', Ricœur summarises, 'is both philosophy's ultimate requirement and its unattainable goal'.[90] Following through this insight has the effect that Ricœur gradually distances himself from Marcel. This becomes manifest early on. For example, when in 1945 a publisher commissioned Ricœur to write a book on Marcel's thought, he wrote to Marcel expressing 'a real anxiety' about the project:

> I ask myself if a book on your work is possible that doesn't betray it and above all betray the essential quality, which is to be always a work in progress that defies any 'summary' or systematic connection. I find in myself a certain taste for systems, at least of systematic exposition, which would run the real risk of adulterating your work.[91]

Ricœur's admission of his 'taste for systems' sounds almost like a guilty confession here, as if he agreed with Marcel that systematicity was nothing more than an evil temptation. Nevertheless, when the book was published in 1948 it was found to be both systematic in nature and containing a number of constructive criticisms of Marcel. While these criticisms do not refer to Marcel's rejection of system, they do identify missing pieces in his philosophy,[92] which Marcel himself recognised as being due to his non-systematic approach. 'It is completely true', Marcel writes to Ricœur, 'that there are certain problems I have never directly addressed, primarily because I never dreamed of providing a system of

---

[89] For example, he speaks of thinking as the attempt to understand 'concepts woven together, if not in a closed system, at least in a *systematic* order' (Ricœur, *Conflict of Interpretations*, 296). Italics original: '... concepts enchaînés selon un ordre *systématique*, sinon dans un système clos' (Ricœur, *Conflit des interprétations*, 292).

[90] Paul Ricœur, 'Doing Philosophy after Kierkegaard', in *Kierkegaard's Truth: The Disclosure of the Self*, ed. Joseph H. Smith (New Haven: Yale University Press, 1981), 340. 'Le système est à la fois la requête ultime de la philosophie et son but inaccessible' (Ricœur, 'Philosopher après Kierkegaard', in *Lectures* 2, 44).

[91] My translation: 'une réelle anxiété: j'en suis à me demander si un livre est possible sur votre œuvre qui ne la trahisse pas et surtout qui n'en trahisse pas la qualité essentielle qui est d'être une recherche constamment en travail qui défie le "résumé," l'enchaînement systématique. Or je découvre en moi un certain goût du système, au moins de l'exposé systématique, qui ferait courir à votre œuvre un réel danger d'adultération' (Paul Ricœur, 'Paul Ricœur to Gabriel Marcel, Le Chambon s/Lignon', 25 November 1945, Fonds Gabriel Marcel, Bibliothèque Nationale de France, Paris).

[92] Ricœur, *Marcel et Jaspers*, 107–8, 175–7.

philosophy. These are nonetheless points on which I should express myself'.[93]

In the end Ricœur came to see nothing wrong with his 'desire for a certain systematism'.[94] Much later, when reflecting on his relationship with Marcel, Ricœur will more confidently own up to this major difference between them: 'As for the systematic spirit Gabriel Marcel cautioned me about, I continue to claim it.'[95] Invoking instead Jaspers's distinction between 'system' and 'systematic', he continues: 'I confess I have always needed order and, if I reject any form of totalizing system, I am not opposed to a certain systematicity.'[96]

But Ricœur does not see Marcel's non-systematicity as going all the way down. Marcel is too great a thinker for his philosophy to be entirely disordered and inconsistent. Here we meet one of the signature marks of Ricœur's genius, in that he finds elements in Marcel's own thinking that point to the positive side of systematicity. He does this by using a different word that Marcel does not object to, even though it means the same thing. In a 1968 interview with Marcel, Ricœur acknowledges that 'there is no Marcellian system', but then points to the 'living *unity* governing all the themes of your philosophy', a characterisation Marcel is willing to accept.[97] This discernment of a 'unity' to Marcel's thought gently points to the connection between unity and systematicity that Marcel was never able to acknowledge. The closed system is merely the corruption of a deeper thing that is positive.[98]

For Ricœur, the positive presupposition of systematic thought is *a belief in the unity of reality*, a presupposition that is not lacking in Marcel's work. Marcel admits that 'the desire to unify [is] the very foundation of

---

[53] My translation: 'Il est tout à fait vrai qu'il y a certains problèmes que je n'ai pas directement abordés, d'abord parce que je n'ai jamais songé à donner un système de philosophie. Ce sont cependant des points sur lesquels je devrai d'exprimer' (Gabriel Marcel, 'Gabriel Marcel to Paul Ricœur', 19 January 1948, 4, Fonds Ricœur). Fonds Gabriel Marcel, Bibliothèque Nationale de France, Paris.

[54] Paul Ricœur, 'My Relation to the History of Philosophy', *Iliff Review* 35, no. 3 (1978): 5.

[55] Ricœur, *Critique and Conviction*, 25. 'Quant à l'esprit systématique contre lequel Gabriel Marcel me mettait en garde, je continue à le revendiquer' (Ricœur, *La critique et la conviction*, 44).

[56] Ricœur, *Critique and Conviction*, 25. 'J'avoue que j'ai toujours eu besoin d'ordre et, si je récuse toute forme de système totalisant, je ne suis pas opposé à une certaine systématicité' (Ricœur, *La critique et la conviction*, 44).

[57] Marcel, *Tragic Wisdom*, 251. Italics mine: 'Il n'y a pas de système marcellien ... l'unité vivante qui règne entre tous les thèmes' (Ricœur and Marcel, *Entretiens*, 115).

[58] Chapter 5 expounds this signature Ricœurian move, that of finding the hidden positive behind the explicit negative.

intellectual life',[99] but he does not seem to have used this insight to salvage a positive meaning to systematicity. As Gallagher puts it, for Marcel to reject all systematisation is 'to slight one of the profound exigences of the subject, the exigence for unity'. This exigence, Gallagher says, is 'a participation in the unity which binds being together. To see conceptually is to see partially, but to think is to orientate oneself towards the no-longer-partial'.[100]

In other words, Ricœur agrees with Jaspers, that 'thinking is by nature systematic' because of the mind's deeply rooted desire for unity.[101] 'One cannot profess multiplicity', Ricœur insists, 'without denying oneself. There is some reason why the spirit inevitably searches within objects for the unity which it sees, knows, wishes, and believes in. In any case, plurality cannot be the absence of relations'.[102] It is impossible, Ricœur highlights, not to have a certain level of unity to one's thought, whether implicit or explicit, conscious or unconscious. The more we try to avoid being systematic, the more we shall have to do so systematically and thus in a way that negates itself. 'Truth cannot be multiple', Ricœur says, 'without repudiating itself. The True and the One are two interchangeable notions'.[103] The search for unity is an unavoidable part of the search for truth, because 'the question of truth culminates in the problem of the total unity of truths'.[104]

Unlike Jaspers, however, Ricœur sees this unity not only as a demand of the mind but as a presupposition about reality itself, in spite of how fragmented reality may appear to us. There is something tragic in Jaspers's position that the mind longs for a unity that doesn't really exist. That is why Ricœur labels Jaspers's philosophy one of 'paradox', and we shall see in Chapter 8 how he exposes a latent idealism in Jaspers for

---

[99] Marcel, *Being and Having*, 188. 'Le besoin d'unité … fait peut-être le fond même de l'intelligence' (Marcel, *Être et avoir*, 273).
[100] Gallagher, *The Philosophy of Gabriel Marcel*, 148–9.
[101] Jaspers, *Philosophy*, 1969, 1:276. 'Denken ist schon von Natur systematisch' (Jaspers, *Philosophie*, 232).
[102] Ricœur, *History and Truth*, 192. 'On ne peut professer le multiple sans se nier soi-même. Ce n'est pas pour rien que l'esprit cherche invinciblement du côté de l'objet l'unité de ce qu'il voit, de ce qu'il sait, de ce qu'il veut et de ce qu'il croit. Aussi bien la pluralité ne peut être l'absence de relations' (Ricœur, *Histoire et vérité*, 219).
[103] Ricœur, *History and Truth*, 192. 'La vérité ne peut être finalement multiple sous peine de se renier elle-même. Le Vrai et l'Un sont deux notions permutables' (Ricœur, *Histoire et vérité*, 219).
[104] Ricœur, *History and Truth*, 189. 'La question de la vérité culmine dans le problème de l'unité totale des vérités' (Ricœur, *Histoire et vérité*, 216).

Paul Ricœur: The Unity of the System as Eschatological Hope 39

this reason.[105] It is also why, compared to Ricœur, Jaspers's position still retains an element of despair. It has given up, not only on the unity of thought, but also on the unity of being.

However, if Ricœur wants to hold onto the unity of being, he is faced with a problem. Can we affirm unity without falling back into the arrogance of claiming to *possess* that unity? On the other hand, if we cannot possess unity in a closed system, what guarantee is there that it is real? And if we have no guarantee, how do we avoid sliding into despair?

It is at this point that the methodological and even ontological function of *hope* manifests itself in Ricœur's philosophy. In Chapter 2 we will explore the foundational role of hope in Ricœur's philosophy in greater depth, but here we may already note the striking way he connects unity, hope, and ontology. 'The *Unity* of Truth', he writes, 'is the relation between the duty of thought and a kind of ontological hope'.[106] His remarkable use of the adjective 'ontological' shows the influence of Marcel.[107] As we have seen, for Marcel, hope is more than an emotion, more even than an ethical virtue downstream from epistemological concerns, but rather it is constitutive of how we search for truth. Similarly for Ricœur, 'the philosophical impact of hope has an important bearing on reflection'.[108] Hope can be called ontological because it establishes a positive relationship between our being and the being of ultimate reality. In a later article, Ricœur will instead call hope 'structural' to philosophy, drawing on its place in Kant. There he sets up a direct conflict between hope and closed systems, writing that hope brings about a 'structural change within philosophical discourse … [which] concern[s] what we might call the act of closing this discourse'.[109]

Hope is not a theme that comes after other themes, an idea that closes the system, but an impulse that opens the system, that breaks the closure of the system; it is a way of reopening what was unduly closed. In that sense it belongs to the structure of the system as such.[110]

---

[105] See Section 4.2.2, 'Paul Ricœur: The Superiority of Mystery to Paradox'. That chapter shows in addition that Ricœur's belief in the unity of being originates from his commitment to the Christian doctrine of creation.
[106] Ricœur, *History and Truth*, 54. Italics original: '*L'Unité* de la Vérité … c'est celui du rapport entre le devoir de penser et une sorte d'espérance ontologique' (Ricœur, *Histoire et vérité*, 65–6).
[107] This is also another way he develops an idea from Marcel beyond anything Marcel himself did.
[108] Ricœur, *History and Truth*, 12. 'L'impact philosophique de l'espérance c'est l'allure même de la réflexion' (Ricœur, *Histoire et vérité*, 19).
[109] Ricœur, *Figuring the Sacred*, 203.
[110] Ricœur, *Figuring the Sacred*, 211.

This quote shows that it is a mistake to think that Ricœur is aiming for an objective guarantee, and that Ricœurian hope is hope *for* total transparency and certainty, the closure of the system (this is the view of Stuart Hackett, for example, whom I engage in Chapter 2). That is not the object of hope for Ricœur. Hope is not a guarantee in any apodictic sense; it does not prove the unity of being. On the contrary, if the unity of being could be 'objectively guaranteed', there would be no need for hope.

Hope is the narrow path between the twin errors of closed systems and inconsistency, chaos and incoherence. Against arrogance, hope teaches us that total unity is not accessible to us: 'Hope tells me that there is a meaning and that I should seek it. But it also tells me that this meaning is hidden.'[111] It is hidden because we do not have the fullness of knowledge. Against despair, Ricœurian hope maintains the *'eschatological* character of unity', an inherently Christian idea that both preserves the final unity of all things and at the same time prevents that unity from being imposed in history through violence.[112]

What, then, is the unity of truth for the Christian? It is an eschatological representation, the representation of the 'last day'. The 'recapitulation of all things in Christ', in the words of the Epistle to the Colossians, signifies both that unity will be 'manifested at the last day' and that unity is not to be found in history.[113]

But eschatological unity would not be sufficient armament against despair if it left us with a total disconnect, in the present, between our mind's demand for unity and our inability to achieve it before the end of history. That is why Ricœurian hope also gives us the ability to achieve a *partial, provisional* unity in the present, an imperfect correspondence between our minds and reality which we sustain as a *'working hypothesis'*,[114] a never-ending task or quest. For Ricœur, our hope is that 'the unity of the charity of Christ is *already* the hidden meaning of the multiple.... It is therefore in hope that all things are one, that all truths are in the unique

---

[111] Ricœur, *History and Truth*, 95. 'L'espérance me dit: il y a un sens, cherche un sens. Mais elle me dit: ce sens est caché' (Ricœur, *Histoire et vérité*, 110).

[112] Ricœur, *History and Truth*, 185. Italics original: 'le caractère *eschatologique* de l'unité' (Ricœur, *Histoire et vérité*, 211).

[113] Ricœur, *History and Truth*, 181. 'Qu'est-ce alors, pour le chrétien, que l'unité du vrai? Une figure eschatologique, la figure du "dernier jour". La "récapitulation de toutes choses en Christ", selon l'épître aux Colossiens, signifie à la fois que l'unité sera "manifestée au dernier jour" et que l'unité n'est pas une puissance de l'histoire' (Ricœur, *Histoire et vérité*, 207).

[114] Ricœur, *History and Truth*, 185. Italics original: 'hypothèse *de travail*' (Ricœur, *Histoire et vérité*, 211).

Truth'.[115] The unity of our thought (both with itself and with reality) is always provisional and open. Unification thus becomes the never-ending 'task of conquering the diversity of our field of knowledge'.[116]

Hope belongs to the human condition ontologically, because it is the positive stimulus behind the philosophical drive for order, unity, and systematicity. Philosophy ceases to be philosophy if it ceases *searching for unity*, either because it claims to have found it (arrogance, closed system) or because it claims it cannot be found (despair, fragmentation, incoherence). A philosophy of hope looks to unity as a guiding star. Our finitude makes any attainment of unity always incomplete, imperfect, and needing constant correction. Hope respects the mind's demand for unity and coherence as a goal, working towards a partial and provisional unity, but relegates its final achievement to an eschatological horizon.

From this we can already see what we will further explore in Chapter 8, namely, that the particular kind of finitude Ricœur has in mind is the finitude of a created being. This is because finitude by itself would have no reason to hope for final unity. If finitude were not *created* finitude, then any hope for the ultimate unity of reality, in spite of our own inability to achieve it, might be vain and empty.

CONCLUSION

Systematic thought – exemplified by reflexive philosophy and German idealism – has both a positive and a negative impulse in Ricœur's view. It is driven by the human 'will to unity', but this will has an 'ambiguous nature' because it is 'at once the goal of reason and violence'.[117] The goal of reason is the positive impulse: The quest for unity, coherence, consistency, and order. The negative impulse is the lust for control, domination, and totalisation that leads to pride, exclusion of the other, and detachment from the real world.[118] Therefore, despite the many abuses

---

[115] Ricœur, *History and Truth*, 196. 'L'unité de la charité du Christ est déjà le sens caché du multiple.... C'est donc en espérance que toutes choses sont unes, que toutes les vérités sont dans l'unique Vérité' (Ricœur, *Histoire et vérité*, 224).
[116] Ricœur, *History and Truth*, 42. Translation modified: 'La vérité se présente à nous comme une idée régulatrice, comme la tâche ... de vaincre la diversité de notre champ de connaissance' (Ricœur, *Histoire et vérité*, 52).
[117] Ricœur, *History and Truth*, 166. 'Le caractère ambigu de notre volonté d'unité, à la fois comme tâche de la raison et comme violence' (Ricœur, *Histoire et vérité*, 188).
[118] One Ricœur's use of positive and negative, see Alison Scott-Baumann, *Ricœur and the Negation of Happiness* (London: Bloomsbury, 2013).

that Ricœur is aware of in systematic philosophy, he also sees its necessity if one is to avoid inconsistencies, contradictions, and lacunae in one's worldview. Where Marcel condemns systematic thought as a violation of the openness necessary to finite human beings, Ricœur responds that 'truth is characterized principally by the passion for unity'.[119] We systematise in order to attain a level of coherence in our thought, our world, and finally our action. That coherence is not guaranteed *epistemologically*, but it is aimed at *ontologically* by means of the hope at the heart of our finite human condition.

---

[119] Ricœur, *History and Truth*, 6. 'La vérité ... est caractérisée principalement par la passion de l'unité' (Ricœur, *Histoire et vérité*, 12).

2

A Philosophy of Hope?

The Universality of Truth

> Philosophy means to be on the way
> Karl Jaspers[1]

Hope is the methodological keystone of Ricœur's philosophy. As a method, hope means the commitment to searching for truth based on the belief that we can grow in understanding, but that we can never attain the fullness of truth. In the last chapter we saw how hope provided a third way between the closed system (which has no need for hope because it knows everything already) and the chaos and fragmentation of unsystematicity (which has no hope that reality is ultimately unified). This chapter is about how hope mediates between the universal and the particular, that is to say, the universal aspirations of philosophy and the particular situation in history and culture of an individual philosopher. We shall find Ricœur mediating, again, between the universalising tendencies of French reflexion and the particularising tendencies of existentialism, producing a 'philosophy of similitude' which reaches in hope towards the universal without ever forgetting the finite particularity of the philosopher.

PREVIOUS SCHOLARSHIP ON RICŒURIAN HOPE

The centrality of hope in Ricœur's philosophical method has gone largely unnoticed, with a couple of notable exceptions. One scholar, Stuart Hackett, has written on how Ricœur navigates universals and particulars, but his

---

[1] Karl Jaspers, *Way to Wisdom* (New Haven: Yale University Press, 1954), 12. 'Philosophie heißt: auf dem Wege sein' (Karl Jaspers, *Einführung in die Philosophie*, 2nd ed. [Munich: Piper, 1971], 13).

analysis is reactionary and unsatisfying precisely because he does not see the function of hope for Ricœur. He begins well, observing that for Ricœur, 'the basic problem of philosophical methodology is that of reconciling philosophy's traditional goal of rational universality and objectivity with the complex limitation placed on this goal by man's total existential involvement as entailing both a basic human and singularly individual finitude'.[2] This means that truth itself is 'interpreted as the dialectical tension between such rational universality and such individual singularity'.[3] Therefore the task of philosophy, for Ricœur, is to search 'for the unity of truth in a context of ultimately unresolvable philosophic difference – a contrast which is synthesized, not in actuality, but only in a kind of eschatological hope'.[4]

This is a very good description of Ricœur's methodology, making it all the more surprising that Hackett's next move shows he has failed to understand a fundamental element of Ricœur's position. Hackett accuses Ricœur of being unable to provide a rationale for the status of his own discourse, because Ricœur's assertion of the non-universality of philosophy makes his own position equally non-universal. 'What prevents the whole of Ricœur's own analysis,' Hackett asks, 'from being as contingently relative in all its aspects as he insists, in his theory, is the case with any philosopher's viewpoint?'[5] This is unacceptable, he tells us, because

the very theory that philosophy must be content with a fusion between universality and contingency would then itself either be contingently relative and therefore not a genuinely objective eidetic analysis of man's epistemological situation; or else the theory would indeed be the very sort of rationally objective thesis which, as a theory, it maintains to be impossible for a human knower.[6]

Oddly enough, Hackett does not seem to notice that he has provided the answer to his own objection. Ricœur's theory that philosophy is a universal/contingent fusion is itself neither 'contingently relative' nor 'rationally objective', but is what Hackett himself says: a universal/contingent fusion. Even though Hackett acknowledges that Ricœur is aiming at a middle road, Hackett himself seems unable to escape from a radical either/or dichotomy for which discourse is either completely universal or completely relative; for example, he objects that Ricœur's 'theory of truth is

---

[2] Stuart Hackett, 'Philosophical Objectivity and Existential Involvement in the Methodology of Paul Ricœur', *International Philosophical Quarterly* 9, no. 1 (1969): 12.
[3] Hackett, 'Philosophical Objectivity and Existential Involvement'.
[4] Hackett, 'Philosophical Objectivity and Existential Involvement'.
[5] Hackett, 'Philosophical Objectivity and Existential Involvement', 34.
[6] Hackett, 'Philosophical Objectivity and Existential Involvement'.

again either objectively adequate analysis (at least in principle) or else it is itself culturally contingent'.[7] Is not Ricœur's philosophy precisely the rejection of this alternative? Does not Ricœur speak of the 'apparent dilemma of scepticism and dogmatism'[8] (where scepticism is another word for relativism or subjectivism, and dogmatism for objective certainty)? Does he not put forward hope as precisely the way to *avoid* this false dichotomy? 'We do not have to choose,' he claims, 'between the dogmatism which permits only disciples or enemies and no friends, and the subjectivism which gives each their own truth. Between possessing the truth and choosing one's own truth, there is *hope* of having accessed *something* of the truth'.[9] Throughout Hackett's critique he accuses Ricœur of lacking any 'objective basis'[10] or 'guarantee of objectivity',[11] but he does not seem to notice that Ricœurian hope undermines the need for an 'objective guarantee' of anything. The words 'objective' (as an epistemological term) and 'guarantee' are foreign to Ricœur's writings.[12] As David Stewart points out, by its very nature 'hope guarantees nothing'.[13] If there were an objective guarantee of truth, there would be no need for hope. Hackett is unable to see how hope is a substitute for objective certainty. As I will demonstrate, hope leads the philosopher not to aim for a supposedly objective adequation to reality, but rather to seek the *similitude* of our thoughts to reality. Ricœur never asks us to hope that our understanding of the world is complete or even accurate-though-partial. Instead, philosophy is undergirded by hope that we are '*within* the bounds of truth'.[14] What can justifiably be hoped for is that we have an *approximation* to reality.

[7] Hackett, 'Philosophical Objectivity and Existential Involvement'.
[8] My translation: 'Dilemme apparent du scepticisme et du dogmatisme' (Paul Ricœur, 'Le renouvellement du problème de la philosophie chrétienne par les philosophies de l'existence', in *Le problème de la philosophie chrétienne*, ed. Jean Boisset [Paris: Presses universitaires de France, 1949], 44).
[9] My translation (italics original): 'Nous n'avons peut-être pas à choisir entre le dogmatisme qui ne permet que des disciples et des ennemis et point d'amis, et le subjectivisme qui accorde à chacun sa vérité. Entre posséder la vérité et choisir sa vérité, il y a l'*espérance* d'avoir accédé à *de la* vérité' (Dufrenne and Ricœur, *Karl Jaspers et la philosophie de l'existence*, 278).
[10] Hackett, 'Philosophical Objectivity and Existential Involvement', 35.
[11] Hackett, 'Philosophical Objectivity and Existential Involvement', 34.
[12] We shall see later in this chapter (in the section titled 'Paul Ricœur: A Mediating Philosophy of Similitude') that the word 'objective' is equivocal in English and French, whereas German distinguishes between epistemological and ontological objectivity.
[13] David Stewart, 'In Quest of Hope: Paul Ricœur and Jürgen Moltmann', *Restoration Quarterly* 13, no. 1 (1970): 42.
[14] Ricœur, *History and Truth*, 54. Italics original: '*dans* la vérité' (Ricœur, *Histoire et vérité*, 66).

Other scholars have noticed that hope is important for Ricœur, but they have not shown how it is central to his very method. For example, Rebecca Huskey defines Ricœurian hope as 'an expectation of some future good for oneself and for others, an expectation which must be acted upon to be realized'.[15] This definition rightly highlights the active and practical element in hope which is certainly present. But to call hope an 'expectation' at the theoretical level is weak, when it has a much more fundamental task in Ricœur, orienting the human quest for truth and undergirding the possibility of doing any philosophy at all. Huskey does not mention Ricœur's use of the adjective 'ontological' for hope, nor does she point to its *methodological* function in Ricœur's work, although in fairness she admits that her definition is 'by no means ... the last word on hope',[16] and looks forward to further explorations that build on her own work.

David Stewart does better, in that he notices Ricœur's 'ontological hope'.[17] But while Stewart wonderfully demonstrates how Ricœur *applies* hope to ontological concerns downstream, he does not go upstream to see how hope animates Ricœur's very *methodology* in a fundamental way.

Only two scholars connect hope to Ricœur's method. First, Peter Albano identifies hope as the way Ricœur mediates between Kant and Hegel, in seeing truth as 'the attainment of provisional syntheses within an eschatological horizon'.[18] While this depiction has some validity, both Kant and Hegel were overly confident in their philosophical syntheses from the twentieth-century perspective, however much Kant was also careful to think within strict limits. Secondly, Erin White situates hope not in the centre but at one pole, the other of which is suspicion, thereby characterising Ricœur's method as a mediation 'between suspicion and hope'.[19] For Ricœur, states White, 'hope is tempered by an acknowledgement that symbols can never bestow absolute knowledge or the fulness of being'.[20] This is misleading, however. In Ricœur's philosophy, hope is not *tempered* by the impossibility of absolute knowledge; it is already the substitute *for* absolute knowledge. If absolute

---

[15] Huskey, *Ricœur on Hope*, 193.
[16] Huskey, *Ricœur on Hope*.
[17] Stewart, 'In Quest of Hope', 40.
[18] Peter Albano, *Freedom, Truth, and Hope: The Relationship of Philosophy and Religion in the Thought of Paul Ricœur* (Lanham: University Press of America, 1987), 117.
[19] Erin White, 'Between Suspicion and Hope: Paul Ricœur's Vital Hermeneutic', *Literature and Theology* 5, no. 3 (1991): 311–21.
[20] White, 'Between Suspicion and Hope', 320.

knowledge were a reality, no hope would be necessary. Ricœur makes this clear when he writes: 'between hope and absolute knowledge we have to choose'.²¹ Ricœur's method, therefore, is not 'between' suspicion and hope; hope is itself the road 'between' arrogance and despair, totality and nihilism.

GABRIEL MARCEL: UNIVERSAL TRUTH IS NOT UNIVERSAL PROOF

We now turn to the context in which Ricœur was writing, a context polarised by opposing views on how to relate the universal and the particular in philosophy. These went to such extremes in some cases that Maurice Blondel accused the existentialist movement, especially Sartre, of having 'revived the divorce between the individual and the universal'.²²

Reflexive philosophy stands at one extreme, being concerned only with universal truth. In fact, the quest to establish universal truth is the core aim of French reflexion.²³ Here the particularities of individual thinking subjects are seen not as a source of richness, but as an obstacle to be overcome. Ricœur puts it this way: for French reflexion,

the truth is not an aspect of my individual thinking; doubtless it must appear in individual minds, but the function of reflection is not to describe individual modes of appearance of thought, but their validity, their truth, their universal form.²⁴

In other words, universal truth is the only kind of truth that matters. Truth, by its very definition, transcends any individual or particular perspective.

On the other end of the spectrum we have existentialism's rejection of generalisations, abstractions, and thought that claims universal validity.

---

²¹ Ricœur, *Figuring the Sacred*, 212.
²² Maurice Blondel, 'The Inconsistency of Jean Paul Sartre's Logic', *The Thomist* 10. no. 4 (1947): 395.
²³ As Jean Greisch writes, reflexive philosophy 'looks in two distinct directions: at times it is reflection on the conditions of possibility of true knowledge, and consequently of the *universality* which grants it; at other times it is the intimacy of the life of consciousness which supports this' (my translation [italics mine]: 'La philosophie réflexive regarde en deux directions distinctes: tantôt, c'est la réflexion sur les conditions de possibilité du savoir vrai et, partant, l'universalité de la raison qui prime; tantôt, c'est l'intimité de la vie de la conscience qui l'emporte' [Jean Greisch, 'Préface', to Ricœur, *Méthode réflexive appliquée au problème de Dieu chez Lachelier et Lagneau*, 12–13]).
²⁴ My translation: 'La vérité n'est point un trait de ma pensée individuelle: sans doute faut-il que la pensée apparaisse dans ses esprits individuels, mais la réflexion n'a pas pour fonction de décrire les modes individuels d'apparition de la pensée, mais leur validité, leur vérité, leur forme universelle' (Ricœur, *Méthode réflexive*, 37).

A popular book that signalled this new wave was Jean Wahl's *Towards the Concrete*, published in 1932.[25] The book is an attack on German idealism for having retreated into the structures of human thought and thus abandoned the concreteness of reality itself. But, announces Wahl, the project of German idealism has failed: 'We see thought run aground on the real in its attempt at idealization and run aground on the particular when it attempts to generalize. Reality and particularity are united'.[26] The clarion call 'towards the concrete' became a kind of early *motif* of the existentialist movement.

Jean Wahl's landmark book comprised three studies of seminal figures in the existentialist move away from abstractions and towards the concrete, one of whom was Gabriel Marcel himself. Moreover, Marcel seemed happy with the way Wahl characterises his thought, defining his own philosophy as marked from beginning to end by a 'suspicion of generalities',[27] as well as 'an obstinate and untiring battle against the spirit of abstraction'.[28]

What does Marcel mean by the 'spirit of abstraction'? He is not against abstraction per se and distinguishes between 'abstraction as such, and … the spirit of abstraction',[29] the former being a necessary and natural process of thinking, and the latter being the deception that reduces everything to those elements in it which correspond to some universal theory, producing 'general formulations of the type, "This is only that …, This is nothing other than that …"'.[30] For example, he considers how Marxist theory treats art merely in terms of what it reveals about the economic situation in which it was produced: 'there cannot be a rational justification of any sort for the act by which one claims to subordinate the

---

[25] Jean Wahl, *Vers le concret: études d'histoire de la philosophie contemporaine: William James, Whitehead, Gabriel Marcel* (Paris: Vrin, 2004).

[26] Jean Wahl, *Transcendence and the Concrete: Selected Writings*, ed. Alan Schiff and Ian Alexander Moore (Bronx: Fordham University Press, 2016), 51. Translation modified: 'On voit la pensée se heurter au réel dans son effort d'idéalisation, et se heurter au particulier dans son effort de généralisation. Réalité et particularité [sont] unies' (Wahl, *Vers le concret*, 44).

[27] Marcel, *Tragic Wisdom*, xxxiv. 'la méfiance à l'endroit du global, qui a marqué tant de mes démarches' (Marcel, *Pour une sagesse tragique*, 13).

[28] Gabriel Marcel, *Man against Mass Society* (South Bend, Indiana: Gateway Editions, 1978), 1. 'une lutte opiniâtre menée sans relâche contre l'esprit d'abstraction' (Gabriel Marcel, *Les hommes contre l'humain* [Belgium: Éditions Universitaires, 1991], 13).

[29] Marcel, *Man against Mass Society*, 155. 'abstraction et esprit d'abstraction' (Marcel, *Les hommes contre l'humain*, 98).

[30] Marcel, *Man against Mass Society*, 156. 'des formules générales du type "ceci n'est que cela …, ceci n'est pas autre chose que cela …"' (Marcel, *Les hommes contre l'humain*, 99).

characteristics of artistic creation, at a given epoch, to the prevailing economic conditions of that epoch'.[31]

Marcel's attacks on the spirit of abstraction are bound up with his broader critiques of German idealism's objectivization, universalisation and systematisation of knowledge. For Marcel, abstraction is the process which generalises things, which distances oneself from them in an attempt to describe them objectively, and which claims universal validity for what it says. Marcel's critiques of abstraction and generalisation fall into three categories.

Marcel critiques abstractions because they tend to make things more and more into objects we can control. By contrast, he holds that the most important themes in metaphysics can never be treated as objects with universal validity. 'The central theme of the *Metaphysical Journal*,' says Gabriel Marcel, 'and, of course, of subsequent works, is precisely the impossibility of thinking of being as object'.[32] This is because to think of being as object

> presupposes the initial action by which I separate myself from the world, as I separate myself from the object which I consider in its different aspects.... [But] I cannot really stand aside from the universe, even in thought. Only by a meaningless pretence can I place myself at some vague point outside it.[33]

I cannot, continues Marcel, 'place myself in front of [the universe] so as to judge it', because 'I am *part of it*'.[34] I cannot look at my own eyes, turn around and examine the zero-point from which my perception radiates outward. I am always already involved in what I am thinking about.

Metaphysics and ontology, then, cannot be objectified; they belong to the realm Marcel calls 'mystery' rather than 'problem'. The essential

---

[31] Marcel, *Man against Mass Society*, 156. 'Il ne peut pas y avoir de justification rationnelle, quelle qu'elle soit, de l'acte par lequel on prétend subordonner les caractères de la création artistique à une époque donnée aux conditions économiques qui prévalent à cette même époque' (Marcel, *Les hommes contre l'humain*, 98).

[32] Marcel, 'Author's Preface to the English Edition', VIII. Marcel uses the word 'being' to refer to reality as it is, without any automatic connection to God, and the word 'object' in the sense common to positivism and idealism as something whose properties depend in no way on subjective disposition or point of view, that remains what it is regardless of who is looking at or talking about it.

[33] Marcel, *Being and Having*, 19. 'suppose ... l'acte initial par lequel je me sépare du monde, comme je me sépare de l'objet que je considère sous ses différents aspects.... [Mais] je ne peux pas, même en pensée, me mettre réellement à part de l'univers, ce n'est que par une fiction inintelligible que je peux me situer en je ne sais quel point extérieur à lui' (Marcel, *Être et avoir*, 23).

[34] Marcel, *Metaphysical Journal*, 236. Italics mine: 'Comment me placer devant cette œuvre [l'univers] pour la juger; d'elle je fais partie' (Marcel, *Journal métaphysique*, 230).

difference between a problem and a mystery is that an enquiry about mystery redounds on the enquirer:

> Wherever a problem is found, I am working upon data placed before me.... [But] when the inquiry is about Being, the ontological status of the questioner becomes of the highest importance.... The whole reflexive process remains within a certain assertion which I *am* – rather than which I *pronounce*.... Thereby we advance into the realm of the metaproblematic, that is, of mystery. A mystery is a problem which encroaches upon its own data and invades them, and so is transcended *qua* problem.³⁵

Because we cannot separate ourselves from metaphysical enquiry, the enquiry is not something we can control or use to our own pre-decided ends; rather, it transforms us in an essential way. 'As we raise ourselves towards Reality,' Marcel says, 'we find that it cannot be compared with an object placed before us on which we can take bearings: and we find, too, that we are ourselves actually changed in the process'.³⁶

Rather than abstractions, generalisations, and forms of knowledge and truth that are objectively verifiable, Marcel's philosophy is focussed on the concrete individual. His writing style is profoundly affected by this unwillingness to engage in truth at the objective or abstract level. His philosophical works are full of phrases like 'it seems to me', 'I believe', 'I notice', 'my impression is', as well as personal anecdotes which illustrate the points he is trying to make.

However, Marcel is not a complete particularist who imagines that nothing he is saying has universal value. His metaphysics makes no pretence at having any objective validity, but he nonetheless thinks it is true. Before Marcel could grasp the place of universals in thought, he had to dissociate the concept of universal *truth* from universal *validity*, meaning that a thing can be true for everyone without being *provable* by means of universal reason. Marcel notices that faith, religion, and God do not

---

³⁵ Marcel, *Being and Having*, 171. Translation modified: 'Là où il y a problème je travaille sur des données placées devant moi, mais ... là où l'interrogation porte sur l'être ... le statut ontologique du questionnant vient au premier plan.... Tout le processus réflexif demeure intérieur à une certaine affirmation que *je suis* plutôt que je ne *la profère*.... Par là nous pénétrons dans le méta-problématique, c'est-à-dire dans le mystère. Un mystère, c'est un problème qui empiète sur ses propres données, qui les envahit et se dépasse par là-même comme problème' (Marcel, *Être et avoir*, 249–50).

³⁶ Marcel, *Being and Having*, 169. 'Plus nous nous élevons vers la réalité ... plus elle cesse d'être assimilable à un objet posé devant nous sur lequel nous prenons des repères, et en même temps plus nous nous transformons effectivement nous-mêmes' (Marcel, *Être et avoir*, 247).

seem to fit the either/or of subjective-particular or objective-verifiable. He rejects the idea that faith is purely subjective, like musical taste, because

> the man of faith is in fact making affirmations about reality, which the music-lover, of course, is not. Are these affirmations valid? The unbeliever ... would no doubt say 'Yes, they are valid for the man who makes them.' But this is equivalent to saying that they are false, for the man who makes these assertions claims that they are for everybody and not only for himself.[37]

Marcel recognises that it is of the very nature of faith not to be rationally provable: 'Were faith converted into certitude it would be denied as faith.'[38] But he also realises that faith in God transcends, not only the subject/object dichotomy, but also the dichotomy between universally provable truth and personal feelings. 'We commonly suppose,' he observes, 'that if God is not an object, he is simply the conceptualised expression of a particular manner of being or of feeling which is properly mine. ... This either-or ought to be rejected[:] faith, though not an objective mode of apprehension, cannot therefore be reduced to a more personal disposition'.[39] In this way Marcel arrives at a notion of universal truth which does not equate to universal provability or to objective certainty. Marcel has the insight to see that something can be universally true without, due to our finitude, being universally provable. We must dissociate '*the true* and the *universally valid*', ('valid' meaning provable on universally agreed grounds').[40]

Human finitude for Marcel, then, does not mean that we can have no universal beliefs – on the contrary, we cannot avoid doing so. Rather, our finitude prevents us from *proving* those claims universally or objectively.

---

[37] Marcel, *Being and Having*, 205. Translation modified: 'Celui qui a la foi, en effet, émet certaines affirmations portant sur la réalité; ce n'est point là le cas de l'amateur de musique. Ces affirmations sont-elles valables ou non? Dans le cas qui nous occupe, on répondra sans doute: "Oui, pour celui qui les énonce." Mais ceci revient tout de même à dire qu'elles sont fausses, car précisément celui qui les énonce prétend ne pas les énoncer seulement pour lui-même, mais pour tous' (Marcel, *Être et avoir*, 200).
[38] Marcel, *Metaphysical Journal*, 41. 'La foi se nierait en se convertissant en certitude' (Marcel, *Journal métaphysique*, 42).
[39] Marcel, *Metaphysical Journal*, 261. 'On admet communément que si Dieu n'est pas objet, il est simplement l'expression conceptualisée d'une certaine manière d'être ou de sentir qui est proprement *mienne*. ... L'alternative devait être rejetée: la foi, tout en n'étant pas un mode d'appréhension objective, ne se réduisait pas pour cela à une simple disposition personnelle' (Marcel, *Journal métaphysique*, 254).
[40] Gabriel Marcel, *The Mystery of Being*, trans. G. S. Fraser, vol. 1 (Chicago: Regnery Publishing, 1950), 18. 'dissocier ... vérité et universelle validité' (Gabriel Marcel, *Le mystère de l'être*, vol. 1 [Paris: Aubier, 1951], 25).

Since we can neither prove our universal claims, nor avoid making them, there is no option but to have faith. Faith in this context means holding something as true when it can never be certain. Our finitude, for Marcel, is the reason why we cannot do without faith.

KARL JASPERS: RADICAL FLIGHT TO THE INDIVIDUAL

Marcel's focus on concrete particulars and on truth that cannot be universally proven has much in common with Jaspers. For Jaspers, philosophy therefore 'starts with our situation'.[41] We cannot begin philosophy from abstractions. We are always in a situation from which our reflection takes its starting point. It is part of our very nature as individuals to be unable to know things from an absolute or universal standpoint: 'If the universal were the truth pure and simple, if I could know the truth, I as myself would only be an accidental, interchangeable addition. ... I cannot live in an *absolute* universality without evaporating as myself'.[42]

Unlike Marcel, however, Jaspers understands finitude primarily by means of *historicity*, a feature which will become important for Ricœur. In Jaspers's philosophy, our historicity is the origin of our unique, finite perspective on the world, without which we would not be who we are. Our desire for objective truth makes us suffer our historical finitude as a destabilising force: 'We want to be delivered from historicity.... We want something solid to give us a guarantee.'[43] But this is impossible; our historical rootedness is the zero-point from which we see anything at all, which by definition we cannot see but is the condition from which we see anything else: '*There is no getting beyond the source* [because] I cannot stand at my own back.'[44]

---

[41] *Philosophy*, 1969, 1:43. 'Ausgang des Philosophierens von unserer Situation' (*Philosophie*, 1).

[42] Karl Jaspers, *Philosophy*, trans. E. B. Ashton, vol. 2 (Chicago: University of Chicago Press, 1969), 114. 'Wäre das Allgemeine das Wahre schlechthin, könnte man das Wahre wissen, so käme man als Selbst nur hinzu, zufällig und auswechselbar; ... Es ist unmöglich, im Allgemeinen als dem Absoluten zu leben, ohne als Selbst Verblasen zu werden' (Jaspers, *Philosophie*, 407–8).

[43] Jaspers, *Philosophy*, 1969, 2:124. 'Man möchte befreit sein von der Geschichtlichkeit.... Ein Festes soll uns Garantie ... schaffen' (Jaspers, *Philosophie*, 418).

[44] Jaspers, *Philosophy*, 1969, 2:117. Italics original: 'Geschichtliches Bewußtsein als ein sich verwirklichendes Sein ist kein möglicher *Standpunkt*, den man neben anderen Standpunkten klassifizieren könnte.... *Es ist unmöglich, noch hinter den Ursprung zu kommen*; denn existierend kann ich nicht hinter mich selbst treten' (Jaspers, *Philosophie*, 410–11).

Jaspers's stress on the historicity of our finitude means that he understands philosophy primarily as an activity. In fact, 'Jaspers hardly ever speaks of "philosophy"', Richard Grabau notes; 'Instead, he prefers to use the present infinitive of the verb "philosophieren" which I have translated as "philosophizing". By using this term Jaspers stresses the fact that philosophy is an activity, a movement of thought that knows no end and produces no set of doctrines, theories, or even concepts'.[45] 'The essence of philosophy,' he continues, 'is not the possession of truth but the search for truth.... Philosophy means to be on the way. Its questions are more essential than its answers, and every answer becomes a new question'.[46] This understanding of philosophy as a continual search is something we see lived out in the whole of Ricoeur's philosophical career.

From our historicity, Jaspers draws the consequence that each individual human is radically unique and non-comparable: Human selfhood is *'never universal*, and thus not a case that might be subsumed as particular under a universal'.[47] We speak of human selves as if they belonged into some overarching category, but this is an illusion of language: 'I speak of the self as if it were a universal whose structures I demonstrate, but I can mean only my own self for which nothing can substitute.'[48] The word 'self', Jaspers says: 'becomes my sign for referring to my unified conception of myself and the self.... I speak also of the many selves and of their Existenz; but I cannot mean it that way, because the many do not exist as cases of a universal'.[49]

---

[45] Richard Grabau, 'Preface', in *Philosophy of Existence*, by Karl Jaspers (Philadelphia: University of Pennsylvania Press, 2010), xii.

[46] Jaspers, *Way to Wisdom*, 12. 'Das Suchen der Wahrheit, nicht der Besitz der Wahrheit ist das Wesen der Philosophie, mag sie es noch so oft verraten im Dogmatismus, daß heißt in einem in Sätzen ausgesprochenen, endgültigen, vollständigen und lehrhaften Wissen. Philosophie heißt: auf dem Wege sein. Ihre Fragen sind wesentlicher als ihre Antworten, und jede Antwort wird zur neuer Frage' (Jaspers, *Einführung in die Philosophie*, 13).

[47] Jaspers, *Philosophy*, 1969, 2:5–6. Translation modified (italics original): '*Existenz* als sie selbst ist *nie allgemein*, darum nicht der Fall, der als ein besonderer unter ein Allgemeines subsumierbar ist' (Jaspers, *Philosophie*, 297).

[48] Jaspers, *Philosophy*, 1969, 2:16. 'So spricht Existenzerhellung vom Selbst zwar wie von einem Allgemeinen, dessen Strukturen sie aufweist, aber sie kann nur mich selbst treffen wollen, der ich unvertretbar bin: ich bin nicht das Ich, sondern ich selbst' (Jaspers, *Philosophie*, 307).

[49] Jaspers, *Philosophy*, 1969, 2:16. 'Selbst wird das signum, durch das ich treffe, was ich als mich selbst und das Selbst ineinsfassend denke. — Existenzerhellung spricht weiter von den vielen Selbst als den Existenzen: sie kann es aber so nicht meinen, da es die Vielen als Exemplare eines Allgemeinen nicht gibt' (Jaspers, *Philosophie*, 307–8). The German word 'Existenz' was left untranslated by Jaspers's English translator because it is a technical term used by Jaspers in a unique way. In common German speech, it means simply existence', but Jaspers uses it to mean *human* existence as distinguished from other kinds of existence.

Jaspers is not saying that *all* knowledge and truth are purely individual. He reserves a realm for universally verifiable truth in the domain of the sciences and all areas of knowledge that deal with the objective, external world. But for the *internal* world of the human subject, there is no universality, only individuality. As Emmanuel Mounier puts it, for Jaspers, 'Philosophy can never lead me to discover *the* truth; it can only lead me to discover *my own* truth which applies to me.'[50]

Jaspers returns from the brink of what would otherwise be complete isolation by developing a philosophy of *communication*, probably the best and most enduring element of his entire corpus and the theme from which Ricœur will benefit most. Communication, for Jaspers, is the beating heart of authentic philosophising. Communication presupposes both that no individual has all the answers and that we can learn from one another and grow in knowledge; it is the 'third way' between totalising universalism and isolating individualism: '*I am* only by interacting with other[s].... An isolated human being exists only as a boundary concept, not in fact.'[51]

PAUL RICŒUR: A MEDIATING PHILOSOPHY OF SIMILITUDE

Both Marcel and Jaspers have emphasised the necessity of communication in a way that has an indelible mark on Ricœur. 'It is impossible to overestimate,' Ricœur says, 'the place of the reflections by G. Marcel and K. Jaspers ... on the lines of "communication" which are built with the other at the very heart of our existence'.[52] Indeed, Ricœur's mediating impulse arises from the conviction that both parties in a conflict deserve our attention, and that neither should be ignored: 'On the road that ascends from my situation toward the truth, there is only one way of moving beyond myself, and this is *communication*. I have only one means of emerging from myself: I must be able to live within another.

---

[50] Mounier, *Existentialist Philosophies*, 111. 'La philosophie doit renoncer à l'extension, tentation de l'idée traditionnelle de vérité, pour l'étroitesse profonde.... Elle ne me conduit ainsi jamais à la vérité, mais à ma vérité' (Mounier, *Introduction aux existentialismes*, 116).

[51] Jaspers, *Philosophy*, 1969, 2:52. 'Schon als *empirisches Dasein* bin ich *nur* durch das andere Dasein in Wechselwirkung.... Ein isoliertes Menschenwesen ist nur als Grenzvorstellung, nicht faktisch' (Jaspers, *Philosophie*, 343).

[52] My translation: 'Il est impossible de surestimer la place que tiennent chez G. Marcel et chez K. Jaspers les réflexions sur ... les liens de "communication" qui se nouent avec autrui, au cœur même de l'existence de chacun' (Ricœur, *Marcel et Jaspers*, 157).

Communication is a structure of true knowledge.'[53] Ricœur sees communication as the only way to prevent building a closed 'totalising system' of philosophy, reminding us that we only ever have part of the truth and that to grow in the truth we must listen to those around us: 'Communication rules out any pretension to encompass or reduce the other to a part of my total discourse.... Truth, as Jaspers says, is nothing else than "philosophizing-in-common".'[54]

Nonetheless, Ricœur also has some reservations about the extent to which Marcel and Jaspers have taken their rejection of objective and universal truth. Unlike them, 'Ricœur does not want to give up all notions of universality,' as Gregor notes.[55]

Ricœur's criticism of Marcel concerns his failure to find a positive role for objectivity and abstraction. While agreeing with Marcel's critique of the arrogant pretentions to grasp objective knowledge, he notices that Marcel's treatment of objectivity remains only negative. Part of the problem is that the term 'objective' is ambiguous in French (and English). In French, 'objectivity designates both the being of the object immanent to the subject and the objective character of the knowledge of that object'.[56] German has two different words for these things. *Gegenstand* refers to an object in the world, rarely a cause of dispute. *Objekt*, on the other hand, is an epistemologically stronger term, meaning 'the object for objective knowledge, that is, which claims rigour and universality'.[57] The objectivity against which Marcel so persistently battles is objective knowledge, not the existence of objects. If Marcel had more closely examined the different meanings of 'object', Ricœur suggests, he might have been able to find more positive forms of objectivity than the ones he attacks: 'A positive evaluation of objectivity in general ... would supply a fecund

---

[53] Ricœur, *History and Truth*, 51. 'Sur le chemin qui monte de ma situation en direction de la vérité, il n'est qu'une voie de dépassement, la *communication*. Je n'ai qu'un moyen de sortir de moi-même: c'est de me dépayser en autrui. La communication est une structure de la connaissance vraie' (Ricœur, *Histoire et vérité*, 62).

[54] Ricœur, *History and Truth*, 67. 'La communication exclut toute prétention d'englober, de réduire l'autre à une partie de mon discours total.... La vérite, comme dit Jaspers, n'est pas autre chose que le "philosopher en commun"' (Ricœur, *Histoire et vérité*, 80).

[55] Gregor, *Ricœur's Hermeneutics of Religion*, 19.

[56] My translation: 'L'objectivité désigne aussi bien l'être de l'objet immanent au sujet et le caractère objectif de la connaissance de cet objet' (Dufrenne and Ricœur, *Karl Jaspers et la philosophie de l'existence*, 32).

[57] My translation: 'l'objet pour une connaissance objective, c'est-à-dire qui prétend à la rigueur et à l'universalité' (Dufrenne and Ricœur, *Karl Jaspers et la philosophie de l'existence*).

development to the work of G. Marcel.'[58] Similarly, Ricœur says that Marcel could have reflected on the nature of laws and institutions to find a positive side to abstractions: 'There is a spirit of abstraction which is at the base of the *Habeas corpus*.... A state of law ... is a permanent conquest of abstraction over the arbitrariness of the prince ... and the anarchy of the crowd.'[59]

These criticisms are minor, however. Overall Ricœur has a positive appraisal of Marcel's treatment of the universal/particular problem: 'Marcellian thinking attempts to escape from the choice between the universal and the particular',[60] because of his discovery that *faith* enables us to believe in universal truth without needing to prove it objectively.

Perhaps the absence of a role for faith is the cause of the more serious weaknesses that Ricœur discerns in the work of Karl Jaspers, in which he discerns an odd mixture of humility and dogmatism. Jaspers insists that he has no desire to recruit disciples, that every philosophy will be different, and philosophy by its nature cannot command dogmatic authority. But Jaspers also thinks, Ricœur points out, that what he is saying is true, not just for him but for everyone else: 'On the one hand, his work is inimitable and invites me to follow myself and not him.' But on the other hand, it still demands that 'every human being worthy of the name must recognise it'.[61] He characterises Jaspers's philosophy as driven by two opposing impulses: 'the first, developed systematically, underlines the singularity of the individual, of the unique'. But 'the second ... which remains implicit, tends towards a universal doctrine of man'. Ricœur then makes this crucially important observation: that the second impulse 'rescues the philosophical character of the first', without

---

[58] My translation: 'Une évaluation positive de l'objectivité en général, une description plus nuancée de ses divers niveaux et surtout la recherche d'une forme de l'objectification moins dégradée que celle de l'empirisme positiviste, fournirait sans doute à l'œuvre de G. Marcel un rebondissement fécond' (Ricœur, *Marcel et Jaspers*, 108).

[59] My translation: 'Il y a un esprit d'abstraction qui est la base de l'*Habeas corpus*, des libertés municipales et bourgeoises, du droit civil et pénal, du droit social moderne.... L'on envisage difficilement la réflexion du philosophe existentiel qui ne serait point protégée par la loi et par un état de droit qui est une conquête permanent de l'abstraction sur l'arbitraire du prince, le privilège des grands et l'anarchie de la foule' (Ricœur, *Marcel et Jaspers*, 176).

[60] Paul Ricœur, 'Gabriel Marcel and Phenomenology', in *The Philosophy of Gabriel Marcel*, ed. Schilpp and Hahn, 481.

[61] My translation: 'Pour une part son œuvre est inimitable et m'invite à *me* suivre et non lui, ... pour une autre part elle est exemplaire en ce sens que tout homme digne de ce nom doit s'y reconnaître' (Dufrenne and Ricœur, *Karl Jaspers et la philosophie de l'existence*, 331).

which it would no longer be philosophy.[62] Philosophy loses its essence if it gives up any claim to universal truth although knowing this to be unattainable.

This oscillation between singularity and universality, Ricœur observes, leads to a sort of contradiction running throughout Jaspers's work that he does not seem aware of. Jaspers emphasises again and again that each individual is unique, incomparable, that they cannot be collected into a general category. But he betrays this individuality by the very nature of his writing. He tells us nothing about his own individual life, rather he tells us about human life in general. Ricœur makes this point in an amusing way:

> [Jaspers] does not recount *his own* singularity; he illuminates *the* singularity which has to do with the human condition. That is why he is a philosopher and not a novelist, why his book is called 'Philosophy' and not 'intimate journal'.[63]

What is the difference between a work of philosophy and an intimate journal? The former makes universal claims by its very nature, even if these claims are negative. Jaspers writes that philosophy betrays human individuality when it 'claims to know it ... with the language of universality'.[64] And yet, Ricœur observes, Jaspers himself makes an implicit 'claim to universality which surpasses his doctrine of the individual';[65] he affirms the uniqueness of each human individual, but 'despite himself describes it in universal terms'.[66]

Ricœur suggests a possible solution to the difficulty Jaspers has created for himself. This would be to show that the human individuality, 'even though it is always the unique act of a unique subject, nonetheless participates in the universal'. Unfortunately, Ricœur laments, Jaspers has not developed this 'idea of an affinity (which we would call ontological)

---

[62] My translation: 'La première, systématiquement développée, souligne la singularité de l'individu, de l'unique.... La seconde ... qui reste implicite, tend à une doctrine universelle de l'homme.... sauve le caractère philosophique de la première' (Dufrenne and Ricœur, *Karl Jaspers et la philosophie de l'existence*, 330).

[63] My translation (italics original): 'Il ne raconte pas *sa* singularité; il éclaire *la* singularité qui tient à la condition humaine. C'est par là qu'il e8st philosophe et non romancier, que son œuvre s'appelle "Philosophie" et non "Journal intime"' (Dufrenne and Ricœur, *Karl Jaspers et la philosophie de l'existence*).

[64] My translation: 'prétendrait la connaître ... avec le langage de l'universalité' (Dufrenne and Ricœur, *Karl Jaspers et la philosophie de l'existence*, 112).

[65] My translation: 'prétention à l'universalité qui dépasse sa doctrine de l'individu' (Dufrenne and Ricœur, *Karl Jaspers et la philosophie de l'existence*, 331).

[66] My translation: 'l'énonce malgré lui en termes universels' (Dufrenne and Ricœur, *Karl Jaspers et la philosophie de l'existence*, 328).

between [individual] Existenz and the universal; he does not pose the problem of the reality of 'human nature'.[67]

Ricœur then turns to his own (and Mikel Dufrenne's) fuller solution to the problem of how to relate individuality and universality, a solution that avoids the extremes of both nineteenth-century universalism and twentieth-century individualism. This 'third way' between these two pitfalls Ricœur names a 'philosophy of similitude'. A philosophy of similitude, Ricœur argues, is the '*a priori* condition of a philosophy of Existenz' and the only way that existentialism 'can save itself as philosophy'.[68]

What constitutes such a philosophy of similitude? On the one hand, a philosophy of similitude acknowledges that pure particularity is just as impossible as pure universality: 'Whoever wishes to be nothing but singular never succeeds; neither does whoever wishes to be nothing but universal.'[69] Instead, philosophy remains in tension between these two poles: 'Philosophy is always midway between the most vast and communal existential possibilities and the most personal existential reality.'[70] On the other hand, a philosophy of similitude is a *corrective* to the universalist excesses of the nineteenth century, rather than a *reaction* that swings to the opposite extreme. On the one hand, it does not restore to thought the universal verifiability that was the obsession of German idealism. It is not 'a new knowledge', says Ricœur (using the term 'knowledge' in the rationalist sense of objective, conclusive certainty). Rather, for this philosophy 'everything remains contestable'.[71] On the other hand, it does not retreat from the task of philosophy which is to reach for the universal. Its vocation is 'not to destroy the similitude of man, but on the contrary to push the limits of similitude beyond

---

[67] My translation: 'Bien qu'elle soit toujours l'acte unique d'un sujet unique, participe pourtant à l'universel ... idée d'une affinité que nous dirions volontiers ontologique entre l'existence et l'universel' (Dufrenne and Ricœur, *Karl Jaspers et la philosophie de l'existence*, 112).

[68] My translation: 'condition *a priori* d'une philosophie de l'existence ... peut se sauver comme philosophie' (Dufrenne and Ricœur, *Karl Jaspers et la philosophie de l'existence*, 342).

[69] My translation: 'Qui veut n'être que singulier n'y arrive point; qui veut n'être qu'universel n'y arrive pas non plus' (Dufrenne and Ricœur, *Karl Jaspers et la philosophie de l'existence*, 329).

[70] My translation: 'La philosophie est toujours à mi-chemin des possibilités existentielles les plus vastes et les plus communes et de la réalité existentielle la plus personnelle' (Dufrenne and Ricœur, *Karl Jaspers et la philosophie de l'existence*, 340).

[71] My translation: 'un nouveau savoir ... tout reste contestable' (Dufrenne and Ricœur, *Karl Jaspers et la philosophie de l'existence*, 334).

the intellectual equipment of man to which classical philosophy had reduced it'.[72]

Ricœur argues furthermore that a philosophy of similitude is the basis for both the possibility and the necessity of *communication*. In a signature Ricœurian move, Ricœur uses Jaspers's own central emphasis to rescue a defect in Jaspers's philosophy, protecting (in his view) the very possibility of existential philosophy itself: 'It is because reason ... connects individuals in communication that existential philosophy is possible.'[73]

Finally, and most importantly, a philosophy of similitude is founded on the unverifiable *hope* that there is a universal dimension to what it says. It is not a vain, foolish hope for pure universality; it is 'the hope of a philosopher who has lost her naïveté and who knows that no philosophy is the universal philosophy, immutable, exhaustive, but is always marked by the unique choice of each, by the history which situates it, by the dialogue which puts it again in question.'[74] This hope of universality is what makes anything worth saying to anyone else. This means that the universal dimension is inherent in the nature of language. Jaspers has been forced to assign a corrupting role to language in order to protect the radical singularity of each human individual. But, Ricœur says, language is also part of human existence and therefore must have a positive side to it. Language is by its nature universal, because to name something is to place it in a general category:

We speak of *freedom, the origin, historicity*, even though there are only freedoms, origins, historicities which are not different examples of the same model, but original. Thus the moment we return to grasp existence in the unique and incommunicable experience of the subject, we conceive it again. And we cannot do otherwise, because to renounce thought is to renounce existence.[75]

---

[72] My translation: 'non de détruire la similitude de l'homme, mais au contraire de repousser les limites de la similitude au-delà de l'équipement intellectuel de l'homme où la philosophie classique l'avait réduite' (Dufrenne and Ricœur, *Karl Jaspers et la philosophie de l'existence*, 331).

[73] My translation: 'C'est parce que la raison ... lie les individus dans la communication, qu'une philosophie existentielle est possible' (Dufrenne and Ricœur, *Karl Jaspers et la philosophie de l'existence*, 337).

[74] My translation: 'l'espoir d'un philosophe qui a perdu la naïveté et qui sait que nulle philosophie n'est la philosophie universelle, immuable, exhaustive, mais qu'elle est toujours marquée par le choix unique de chacun, par l'histoire qui le situe, par le dialogue qui le remet en question' (Dufrenne and Ricœur, *Karl Jaspers et la philosophie de l'existence*, 339). Do we detect here the beginning traces of Ricœur's celebrated 'second naïveté'?

[75] My translation (italics original) 'Nous parlerons de *la* liberté, de *l'*origine, de *l'*historicité, alors qu'il n'y a que *des* libertés, *des* origines, *des* historicités qui ne sont point des exemplaires différents d'un même modèle, mais des styles originaux. Ainsi, au moment que

Ricœur's point is that *to speak at all is to presuppose hope in the universal dimension of language*. 'How can an Existenz', he asks, 'open itself to another Existenz and awaken an echo in the other, how would language and a mediation be possible, as inadequate as they may be, ... if a certain similitude of man is not recognised? Similitude is the *a priori* condition of all mediation'.[76] Even the most personal statements have a universal element to them in view of their being statements, attempts to communicate something to someone else: 'Without any hope of universality, a personal confession would be pointless.'[77] Even to assert that something is unique is to claim universality to the assertion: 'It is this hope to speak of all and for all which accompanies this philosophy of the unique.'[78]

In sum, Ricœur's method is based on an understanding of human beings as finite creatures who participate in the truth without possessing the whole of it. Its key characteristic is hope. His philosophy is profoundly shaped by the way Jaspers and Marcel, in their different ways, see finitude as constituted by the fact that we are *inside* reality, historically, corporeally, perspectivally, and therefore reality itself cannot be objectively grasped. Marcel in particular is the driving influence[79] behind Ricœur's 'elevation of hope to the level of a philosophical category'.[80] As we saw in the last chapter, it is due to Marcel that Ricœur goes so far as to call hope 'ontological'.[81] But Ricœur goes further than Marcel in making hope integral to his philosophical method. Marcel's rich reflections

---

nous renvoyons pour saisir l'existence à l'expérience unique et intransmissible du sujet, nous nous proposons encore de la penser. Et nous ne pouvons faire autrement. Car renoncer à la pensée, c'est renoncer à l'existence' (Dufrenne and Ricœur, *Karl Jaspers et la philosophie de l'existence*, 112).

[76] My translation: 'Comment une existence s'ouvrirait-elle à une autre existence et éveillerait-elle un écho chez l'autre, comment un langage et une médiation même inadéquate seraient-ils possibles, ... si une certaine similitude de l'homme ne s'y faisait reconnaître? La similitude est la condition *a priori* de toute médiation' (Dufrenne and Ricœur, *Karl Jaspers et la philosophie de l'existence*, 334).

[77] My translation: 'Sans espoir d'universalité, une confession personnelle serait oiseuse' (Dufrenne and Ricœur, *Karl Jaspers et la philosophie de l'existence*, 339).

[78] My translation: 'C'est cet espoir de parler de tous et pour tous qui accompagne cette philosophie de l'Unique' (Dufrenne and Ricœur, *Karl Jaspers et la philosophie de l'existence*.).

[79] As Patrick Bourgeois observes. See Patrick L. Bourgeois, 'Marcel and Ricœur: Mystery and Hope at the Boundary of Reason in the Postmodern Situation'. *American Catholic Philosophical Quarterly* 80, no. 1 (2006): 421–33.

[80] Stewart, 'In Quest of Hope', 44.

[81] Ricœur, *History and Truth*, 54; Ricœur, *Histoire et vérité*, 66.

on hope are many and varied,[82] but in true Marcellian form they are unsystematic and disconnected. For Ricœur, on the other hand, hope becomes the methodological keystone that sustains the tension between the limitations of human finitude and the unavoidably universal aspirations of philosophy.

Yet Ricœur also retains more of the nineteenth-century spirit than his two mentors. His commitment to the reflexive method places him in stark contrast to them in multiple ways. Where Jaspers sees in language only the deceptive temptation to false universals, an unfortunate defect, Ricœur points out that hope in the universal thrust of language is essential to communication, thus essential to philosophy. Likewise, where Marcel sees in abstractions only an escape from concrete reality, Ricœur sees abstractions as essential to thought and thus to philosophy. Where Jaspers radicalises human individuality to the point where 'humanity' is a meaningless word, Ricœur shows that communication presupposes a common humanity in which individual humans participate.

CONCLUSION

Ricœur construes philosophy as a journey on which truth is found only in part, like breadcrumbs along the way. He thereby invites us to see the essence of philosophy, not in its answers, but in its task and goals. He defines philosophy as a *search motivated by hope* that holds finite human contingency in tension with universal truth, eluding the false alternatives of certainty and relativity, arrogance and despair, or in his words 'skepticism which refuses to look for meaning and fanaticism which declares it prematurely'.[83] This middle road he calls a *philosophy of similitude*, the idea that our thought always *both* participates in universal truth *and* contains elements of our own individual point of view. This philosophy of similitude is founded on the hope that our ongoing quest for truth is not in vain, that we are getting closer to the

---

[82] For Marcel's writings on hope, see, *inter alia*: Marcel, *Being and Having*, 74–9; Marcel, *Être et avoir*, 104–11; Gabriel Marcel, *Homo viator: Introduction to the Metaphysic of Hope*, trans. Emma Craufurd (New York: Harper Torchbook, 1962); Gabriel Marcel, *Homo viator: prolégomènes à une métaphysique de l'espérance* (Paris: Aubier, 1944). Doubtless Ricœur's use of hope is also a sign of his participation in the Kantian tradition (in view of Kant's famous third question, 'What can I hope for?' in which he places religious belief), but this influence is more in the background for Ricœur.

[83] Ricœur, *History and Truth*, 12. 'scepticisme qui renonce à chercher le sens, [et] fanatisme qui le donne prématurément' (Ricœur, *Histoire et vérité*, 19).

truth, but that we will never arrive at its fullness until the end of time: 'The unity of truth is a timeless task only because it is at first an eschatological hope.'[84]

Ricœur is not only personally convinced of the unity of truth.[85] He posits hope not merely as a private preference or an arbitrary choice. For him hope is not voluntaristic. It is the centrepiece of his method, not by fiat, but because he sees it as an essential requirement of all philosophising. But Ricœur is also aware that his hope comes from his Christian convictions, and this awareness causes him to articulate an unusual relationship between philosophy and theology where they depend on each other to exist at all: 'to live Christian hope philosophically [is] the directive principle of reflection – for the conviction of the ultimate unity of truth is the very Spirit of Reason'.[86] Even if the unity of truth will only be revealed at the end of history, the hope that even now we participate in the truth is sustained only by the conviction that truth *really is* one and universal, a conviction that cannot be proven.[87]

Ricœur's philosophy of similitude thus underpins the validity of any philosophising at all and of any communication. It shows that we are always torn between our own particularity and the universality inherent in language. As philosophers, we are continually tempted to forget our finite origins and make universal claims without foundation. To avoid this temptation, 'consciousness … must confess its own finitude, its particularity hidden in the claim to universality'.[88] But it ceases to be philosophy if it lets go of its fundamental task: the 'search for universality'.[89]

---

[84] Ricœur, *History and Truth*, 55. 'L'unité du vrai n'est une tache intemporelle que parce que d'abord elle est une espérance eschatologique' (Ricœur, *Histoire et vérité*, 68).

[85] That is why to point to hope as Ricœur's signature characteristic is much more than 'vacuous, oracular piety,' in Stephen Tyman's words (see Stephen Tyman, 'Ricœur and the Problem of Evil' in Hahn, *The Philosophy of Paul Ricœur*, 22:452).

[86] Ricœur, *History and Truth*, 7. 'J'entrevois … qu'il est possible … de vivre philosophiquement l'espérance chrétienne comme raison régulatrice de la réflexion, car la conviction de l'unité finale du vrai, c'est l'Esprit même de la Raison' (Ricœur, *Histoire et vérité*, 13).

[87] In a later article Ricœur draws a sharper distinction between philosophy and theology, placing hope at the centre of each but in different ways. Philosophy learns something from the Christian message of hope, something about its own stimulus towards truth, yet philosophy must still 'remain within the limits of reason alone' ('Hope and the Structure of Philosophical Systems', in Ricœur, *Figuring the Sacred*, 216).

[88] My translation (paragraph not in English translation): 'La conscience … doit confesser sa propre finitude, sa particularité dissimulée dans sa prétention à l'universalité' (Ricœur, 'Le mal', 224).

[89] My translation: 'recherche d'universalité' (Ricœur, 'Renouvellement de la philosophie chrétienne', 56).

Conclusion

Therefore philosophy is by its nature the *search for universal truth by finite, individual beings*:

> The search for truth, it seems, is characterized by being stretched, so to speak, between two poles: a personal situation and a certain intention with respect to being. On the one hand, I have something to discover personally.... And yet, on the other hand, to search for truth means that I aspire to express something that is valid for all, that stands out on the background of my situation as something universal. I do not want to invent or to say whatever I like, but what is. From the very roots of my situation, I aspire to be bound by being. Let being be thought in me – such is my wish for truth. And so the search for truth is itself torn between the 'finitude' of my questioning and the 'openness' of being.[90]

For Ricœur, unity and universality are unavoidable demands of the human mind, but due to our historical finitude our grasp of them is always provisional. Therefore, only a philosophy of hope can sustain its impulse towards unity without either giving up the possibility of attaining it or imagining falsely to have reached universality.

In sum, Ricœur's philosophical method is a careful alloy of French reflexive philosophy and existentialism. Grounded in hope, it avoids the pitfalls of arrogance and despair on either side. Against the overreaching arrogance of French reflexion, he reminds us that philosophy is a *search*, but not *final comprehension* for all time: 'hope does not give us the power to master history or to order it rationally.... No one may write the *philosophia perennis*.'[91] Against existentialist despair, Ricœur insists that our finitude is not an excuse not to claim things as true, to do no active philosophising of our own. Construing philosophy as a search does not exonerate us from making any universal claims. We cannot live or speak without an implicit set of answers to universal questions, but these answers will always be only provisional.

---

[90] Ricœur, *History and Truth*, 50–1 'La recherche de la vérité – pour parler très simplement – est elle-même tendue entre deux pôles: d'une part une situation personnelle, d'autre part une visée sur l'être. D'une part j'ai quelque chose à découvrir en propre.... Et pourtant, d'autre part, chercher la vérité veut dire que j'aspire à dire une parole valable pour tous, qui s'enlève sur le fond de ma situation comme un universel; je ne veux pas inventer, dire ce qui me plaît, mais ce qui est. Du fond de ma situation, j'aspire à être lié par l'être. Que l'être se pense en moi, tel est mon vœu de vérité. Ainsi la recherche de la vérité est-elle tendue entre la "finitude" de mon questionner et "l'ouverture" de l'être"' (Ricœur, *Histoire et vérité*, 61–2).

[91] Ricœur, *History and Truth*, 55–6. 'Cette espérance ne confère pas le pouvoir de dominer l'histoire, de l'ordonner rationnellement.... nul ne peut écrire la *philosophia perennis*' (Ricœur, *Histoire et vérité*, 67–8).

To live on the basis of hope is not easy. It demands that we keep searching, keep pursuing, without any guarantee of certainty. It demands that all of our current opinions remain forever open to revision, and at the same time that we operate on the basis of them in the meantime. It takes courage to hope, without ever knowing, that we are *'within* the bounds of truth'.[92] But for Ricœur the possibility of doing philosophy depends on this hope.

---

[92] Ricœur, *History and Truth*, 54. Italics original: '*dans* la vérité' (Ricœur, *Histoire et vérité*, 66).

3

Absolutely No Absolutes?

Ricœur's Encounter with Thévenaz

> in the image of God he created them
> Genesis 1:27 ESV

Chapters 1 and 2 were concerned with the 'epistemology of finitude', the question of how finite beings can attain truth in spite of their limits. Epistemology cannot be separated from the ontology of finitude, because what we are capable of knowing is dependent on what kind of beings we are. To place the focus on ontology will bring us to the heart of the twentieth-century debates on finitude, which concern the possibility of conceiving the 'infinite', the 'absolute', and the 'transcendent' (all proxy terms for God) in light of the structural limits of finite human reason. In these debates we do not find Ricœur operating in his renowned role of mediator. Rather, we find him fighting on several fronts at once: against Barthians who claim that philosophy can tell us nothing about the divine (because that is the role for revelation); and against Heideggerians who, as it happens, claim the same thing but for different reasons. In the end it is a mediation of sorts: Ricœur is fighting for a productive relationship between philosophy and theology, in a context in which both Barthians and Heideggerians are tearing the two apart such that they no longer speak to each other.

This chapter concerns Ricœur's encounter with Barthianism in the form of its most philosophical representative and close friend of Ricœur, the Swiss Protestant Pierre Thévenaz. I shall then briefly consider the resources Ricœur finds in his mentors, Jaspers and Marcel, before looking at Ricœur's response to Thévenaz.

PIERRE THÉVENAZ AND THE PHILOSOPHY WITHOUT ANY ABSOLUTE

In his 1994 'Intellectual Autobiography', Ricœur wrote:

> My primary concern, which has never wavered, not to mix *genres* together, has ... drawn me closer to the notion of a philosophy without any absolute, a philosophy I saw defended by my deeply regretted friend, Pierre Thevanez [*sic*], who held it to be the typical expression of a Protestant philosophy.[1]

Who was Pierre Thévenaz and what is this 'philosophy without any absolute' that Ricœur has moved towards? And what does this 'philosophy without any absolute' have to do with not mixing genres and being a Protestant? Answering these questions will provide a helpful starting point to an investigation of the true place – and significance – of absolutes in Ricœur's philosophy. The above statement by Ricœur makes clear from the outset that the question of 'absolutes' is really a question concerning the possibility of any point of contact between philosophy and theology. We shall see that Thévenaz's philosophy is marked by a deep ambiguity of meaning, and that when Ricœur confesses a 'closeness' to Thévenaz it is only in relation to one interpretation of his thought.

Thévenaz is the obvious choice of philosopher to compare with Ricœur on the question of absolutes, not only because Ricœur names him explicitly, but because he is contextually closest to Ricœur. Both were born in 1913, and both were francophone Protestant philosophers – a rare set of attributes for any two people to share. Thévenaz was a 'Romand' – a French Swiss – who first met Ricœur in 1948 at a conference in Germany, a meeting Thévenaz described to his wife as a 'sensational encounter'.[2] It was the first of numerous events at which they were both present. But Thévenaz sadly died of illness in 1955 before completing his *magnum opus*, which according to the obituary in *Esprit* would have been called *The Philosophy of Protestantism*.[3] The manuscript of this work was published in 1960 as *La condition de la raison philosophique*; but prior to that, in 1956, a committee published a collection of his essays in the

---

[1] Ricœur, 'Intellectual Autobiography', 13. Italics original: 'Mon souci, jamais atténué, de ne pas mêler les genres m'a plutôt rapproché de la conception d'une philosophie sans absolu, que je voyais défendue par mon regretté ami Pierre Thévenaz, lequel la tenait pour l'expression typique d'une philosophie protestante' (Ricœur, *Réflexion faite*, 26).

[2] My translation: '[Meeting Ricœur was one of] deux rencontres "sensationnelles"' (cited in Sylvie Bonzon, 'Paul Ricœur en Suisse romande: rencontres, liens et héritage', *Revue de Théologie et de Philosophie* 138 [2006]: 294).

[3] 'Pierre Thévenaz', *Esprit*, no. 230/231 (9) (1955): 1640.

two volumes titled *L'homme et sa raison*, to which Ricœur provided a generous preface.[4] Although in his own philosophy Ricœur rarely cites Thévenaz, this Swiss Protestant was a crucial background influence on him, especially in the example he set for how to keep theology and philosophy 'unmixed'.

Thévenaz belongs to the French reflexive tradition of philosophy. His greatest influence is indisputably Karl Barth. André de Muralt has observed the 'striking manner' in which the work of Thévenaz exhibits the 'coming together of the Barthian theology and autonomous reflection'.[5] In the mid-twentieth century Barth was widely assumed to be anti-philosophical,[6] so the figure of a 'Barthian philosopher' is rather striking. Indeed, after the 1942 publication in *In Extremis* of his article 'Théologie barthienne et philosophie', Thévenaz took over from Henry Corbin the role of being what Bernard Reymond calls the primary philosopher 'of the whole French expression of the Barthian movement'.[7] After Barth, Descartes and Kant are Thévenaz's two strongest influences. These influences situate Thévenaz in the French reflexive tradition, along with the fact that his philosophical formation was under Jean de la Harpe, a disciple of the French idealist and immanentist Léon Brunschvicg, who as we saw in Chapter 1 was the leading reflexive philosopher of his day.[8]

Thévenaz's key text for our purposes is 'La philosophie sans absolu' ('Philosophy without Absolutes'), in which he characterises the entire history of philosophy as a war against the absolute.[9] This war begins when the individual awakens to the subjectivity of their perception of the world

---

[4] According to Peter Carpenter in 'Thévenaz and His Philosophy', *Studies in Religion/ Sciences Religieuses* 5, no. 4 (1 March 1976): 331. See Pierre Thévenaz, *La condition de la raison philosophique* (Neuchâtel: Éditions de la Baconnière, 1960); *L'homme et sa raison: raison et conscience de soi*, vol. 1, 2 vols (Neuchâtel: Éditions de la Baconnière, 1956); *L'homme et sa raison: raison et histoire*, vol. 2, 2 vols (Neuchâtel: Éditions de la Baconnière, 1956).

[5] Cited in Carpenter, 'Thévenaz and His Philosophy', 331.

[6] See, for example: Ricœur, *Critique and Conviction*, 6; Ricœur, *La critique et la conviction*, 17; Marcel, *Awakenings*, 124; and Marcel, *En chemin, vers quel éveil?*, 139. This perception has been marginally rectified in Kenneth Oakes, *Karl Barth on Theology and Philosophy* (Oxford: Oxford University Press, 2012).

[7] My translation: 'Le seul vrai philosophe de tout le mouvement barthien d'expression française' (Bernard Reymond, *Théologien ou Prophète? Les francophones et Karl Barth avant 1945* [Lausanne: L'âge d'homme, 1985], 67).

[8] See Bernard Hort, 'Une philosophie sans absolu', *Revue de Théologie et de Philosophie* 120, no. 3 (1988): 356. For a sketch of French reflexive philosophy, see Chapter 1 above, the section titled 'French Reflexive Philosophy'.

[9] Pierre Thévenaz, 'La philosophie sans absolu', in *L'homme et sa raison: raison et conscience de soi*, vol. 1, 187–206.

by discovering that other people see things differently to oneself. They discover, in other words, that their perspective is not 'absolute'. Greek philosophy, the first in the West, sought to overcome this relativity of perspective by eliminating the bias of human subjectivity, like cleaning our spectacles of dirt, purifying our vision in order to attain objective truth. The task of philosophy, for them, was that of purging ourselves of what is contingent in us so that only the absolute remains. Thus the Greeks spoke, says Thévenaz, of conquering our frail humanity in order to access the divine spark deep within us (notice the immediate equation Thévenaz makes between the 'absolute' and the 'divine').[10] But, Thévenaz avers, this Greek project was destined to fail. A human being is by his or her nature defined by finitude and subjectivity. We cannot reach the absolute without estranging ourselves from ourselves, 'absolutizing ourselves', which amounts to destroying ourselves, because our essence is purely and intrinsically subjective, contingent, finite.[11]

The second failed solution, Thévenaz continues, was to see the absolute as the opposite pole to ourselves, to discover our contingent finitude in the '*human relation to the absolute* and no longer that of assimilation to the absolute'.[12] 'The presence of the absolute in immanence or finitude', he explains, 'is no longer conceived ... as a call to self-divinisation, but as a call to discover the true proportions of the human'.[13] For this second model, the absolute can still be known, but precisely as what we are not and can never become. However, Thévenaz points out, this solution still contains at bottom the assumption that our mind has the capacity to grasp something of absolute reality, that 'reason and reality have a common destiny or are united by an eternal ontological decree'.[14] The problem with this second solution, in Thévenaz's evaluation, was that the absolute is precisely what exists independently of all relation to anything, a 'reality totally independent of the mind'.[15] But anything that is totally independent of our conceiving it cannot be conceived *by definition*.

---

[10] Thévenaz, 'La philosophie sans absolu', 190.
[11] Thévenaz, 'La philosophie sans absolu', 199.
[12] My translation (italics original): '*relation de l'homme à l'absolu* et non plus celui de l'assimilation à l'absolu' (Thévenaz, 'La philosophie sans absolu', 192).
[13] My translation: 'La présence de l'absolu dans l'immanence ou dans la finitude n'est plus conçue ... comme un appel à se diviniser, mais comme un appel à découvrir sa mesure d'homme' (Thévenaz, 'La philosophie sans absolu', 193).
[14] My translation: 'La raison droite et la réalité ont un destin commun ou sont solidaires par un décret ontologique éternel' (Thévenaz, 'La philosophie sans absolu', 195).
[15] My translation: 'réalité totalement indépendante de l'esprit' (Thévenaz, 'La philosophie sans absolu', 196).

The third solution, therefore, arrives with Kant and his 'Copernican revolution' which drags human thought out of the heavens and down to earth where it belongs. Human knowledge is always contingent, so the absolute is beyond its grasp. The absolute becomes a 'limit-concept' which we can 'conceive' but not 'know'.[16] Kant thereby retained the absolute or thing-in-itself as a limit-idea, while banishing it from the domain of human knowledge. Problems arose immediately from this third solution, recounts Thévenaz, as the ambiguity and inconsistency of Kant's concept of the 'thing-in-itself' was uncovered by those who attempted to make use of it: 'how, it was effectively asked, can we simultaneously affirm the existence of the thing-in-itself and its unknowable character'?[17] The absolute had to be interpreted *either* as an indication of a mysterious unknowable transcendence, *or* as an indication of the limits of our thought.

Here we arrive at Thévenaz's own (fourth) solution, which belongs to a strand of idealism that radicalised Kant by taking the second of the above options. Thévenaz banishes the thing-in-itself (which he identifies as the absolute) even as a limit-concept, by distinguishing between the concepts of 'limit' (German: *Grenze*) and 'delimitation' (German: *Schranke*). The former indicates something beyond it, but the latter is an ultimate barrier without any conceivable 'other side'; it only indicates the confines of our own finitude. Thévenaz's reason for choosing the latter is that to choose the former always leads to having a concept of the absolute, thereby doing violence to our finite contingent conceptuality. He concludes:

There are two absolutes: the Other which indicates the beyond and which estranges us by divinising us, because in order to reach it we must escape from ourselves and dissolve ourselves in it, absolutizing ourselves. And the Other which indicates the here-below, the irremediably relative absolute, which brings the subject back to itself and permits it to recognise itself in its human condition.[18]

But while the former 'real absolute' does violence to our nature, the latter 'relative absolute' does violence to language. Both absolutes are thus meaningless, and it becomes necessary to 'say goodbye to the absolute'

---

[16] Thévenaz, 'La philosophie sans absolu', 196–7.
[17] My translation: 'comment, en effet, pensait-on affirmer simultanément l'existence de la chose en soi et son caractère inconnaissable?' (Thévenaz, 'La philosophie sans absolu', 198).
[18] My translation: 'Il y a deux absolus: l'Autre qui indique l'au-delà et qui nous aliène en nous divinisant, car pour le rejoindre nous devrions sortir de nous et nous fondre en lui, nous absolutiser nous-mêmes. Et l'Autre qui indique l'en-deçà, l'absolu irrémédiablement relative, qui ramène le sujet à lui-même et lui permet de se reconnaître dans sa condition d'homme' (Thévenaz, La philosophie sans absolu', 199).

as a tool which has fulfilled its use in revealing our contingency to us, but is no longer useful.[19]

But the fight against absolutes, Thévenaz tells us, is never fully over. New absolutes, both conscious and unconscious, continue to arise in philosophy. For example: Kant himself could not resist absolutising his concepts of God, morality, and freedom, slipping them in through the back door of 'practical reason'; the post-Kantians produced the concept of 'Absolute Spirit' which for them was fundamental reality; the positivists absolutized matter; and even Husserlian phenomenology wavers between a disabsolutized methodological reduction and a new absolutisation of itself as an apodictic foundation.[20] These absolutisations continue to reappear due to the mind's deeply rooted temptation to deny its own contingent nature. 'There will only be a true disabsolutization', Thévenaz says, 'when we become conscious of our humanity as limited and put into question, without once again estranging ourselves in a new absolute … into which we might re-absorb or dissolve ourselves, so to speak.'[21]

This kind of 'true disabsolutization' can only take place, Thévenaz contends, by means of a true *conversion* of the human subject. Unlike the ancient forms of 'conversion to the beyond', which led to questionable and spurious metaphysics, this will be a 'conversion of the here-below', which will focus on the true task and scope of philosophy: an analysis of the human condition. This new humble and unpretentious philosophy, which is anthropology, instead of conceiving finitude only negatively by its opposition to the infinite will have a positive account of finitude as sufficient to itself.[22]

If the philosopher could remain at human height, with human proportions in both knowledge and conduct, the reign of absolute philosophy would have definitively come to an end, and what was always the legitimate ambition of all philosophy (to discover the exact measure of subjectivity and its role in knowledge) would perhaps be more satisfied.[23]

---

[19] My translation: 'dire adieu à l'absolu' (Thévenaz, 'La philosophie sans absolu', 200).
[20] Thévenaz, 'La philosophie sans absolu', 200–2.
[21] My translation: 'il n'y a désabsolutisation véritable que si l'homme prend conscience de son humanité comme limitée et mise en question, sans s'aliéner à nouveau dans un nouvel absolu … dans lequel il pourrait pour ainsi dire se résorber ou du moins se fonder' (Thévenaz, 'La philosophie sans absolu', 204).
[22] Thévenaz, 'La philosophie sans absolu', 205.
[23] My translation: 'Si le philosophe pouvait rester à hauteur d'homme, dans sa connaissance comme dans sa conduite, à la mesure humaine, le règne de la philosophie de l'absolu aurait définitivement pris fin et l'ambition légitime de la philosophie de tous les temps (découvrir la mesure exacte de sa subjectivité et sa part dans la connaissance) s'en trouverait peut-être un peu mieux satisfaite' (Thévenaz, 'La philosophie sans absolu', 206).

We could summarise Thévenaz's denial of absolutes in this way: that which is 'real' for finite humans is only ever *our concept of* the real; it is never reality in itself. We cannot conceive anything real outside our minds because by conceiving it, we are putting it in our minds. Our thought cannot escape itself and cease to be thought. In a parallel way, the absolute is only ever our idea of it, but our idea of it can never be absolute because our ideas are contingent by nature. To have an idea of the absolute would mean that there was something inside our minds which corresponded to it, a concept which was adequate to the absolute. Thus there is never, nor could there ever be, any adequation between the absolute and our concepts, and without any adequation, we cannot properly be said to *have a concept* of the absolute.

Like Ricœur, Thévenaz believes in philosophy's autonomy in relation to theology, and he is careful to ensure that his article 'The Philosophy without Absolutes' is a standalone philosophical argument. But this argument is nonetheless deeply interwoven with, and relevant for, his Barthian Protestantism. It is part of Thévenaz's overall project of destroying the 'God of the philosophers' in order to make way for the 'God of Abraham, Isaac, and Jacob'. This famous Pascalian duality is a radical either/or exclusion in Thévenaz's interpretation, without any possible identification or even any overlap between the two.

The Christian God, in Thévenaz's view, is not a philosophical alternative to other conceptions of God. God is not the 'true absolute' as opposed to all the false absolutes – he could not be, because Thévenaz has denied all absolutes: 'the Christian God is not a truer God, philosophically speaking, a God whose attributes would prevail in competition over those of the God of the philosophers'.[24] Rather, God is known only through his action in history.

> The God of Jesus Christ ... can be understood only from the point of view of God's actions on our behalf or from that of the Word made flesh: in this sense the reality of Jesus Christ, recognized in faith, destroys all theoretical speculation about God.[25]

[24] Pierre Thévenaz, 'God of the Philosophers and God of the Christians', trans. Peter Carpenter, *Studies in Religion/Sciences Religieuses* 5, no. 4 (1976): 342. 'Le Dieu chrétien n'est pas un Dieu philosophique plus vrai, un Dieu dont les attributs, dans une compétition avec ceux du Dieu des philosophes' (Pierre Thévenaz, 'Dieu des philosophes et dieu des chrétiens', in *L'homme et sa raison: raison et conscience de soi*, vol. 1, 314).

[25] Thévenaz, 'God of the Philosophers and God of the Christians', 342. 'Le Dieu de Jésus-Christ est un Dieu dont les qualités ... ne se comprennent qu'à partir de l'action de ce Dieu pour nous, à partir du Verbe fait chair: en ce sens, la réalité de Jésus-Christ, reconnue dans la foi, ruine toute spéculation théorique sur Dieu' (Thévenaz, 'Dieu des philosophes et dieu des chrétiens' 314).

Nevertheless, and unlike some forms of Barthianism that see no role for philosophy at all, Thévenaz gives it a crucial role. The essence of philosophy, as he sees it, is *critique*, radical doubt, calling everything into question. It is a wrecking ball that destroys any tower of Babel, any human edifice attempting to reach upwards to the divine. Therefore philosophy's function in faith is to hunt down and destroy all false gods, 'to call into question every idol, every Baal, in other words, the totality of gods conceived and fashioned by man, whether by hand or by reason'.[26] This is not only an apologetic endeavour to create room for the God of revelation to enter. Philosophy remains useful also after conversion to Christianity, because our faith is never free of idolatrous conceptions of God. The 'God of the philosophers' continually creeps into our theology through the back door of unconscious or implicit ideas, and 'philosophy is the only means of exorcising or excising these philosophical or pseudo-philosophical excrescences which exist in the notion of God'.[27] That is why philosophy is 'an essential element in the fight of faith. One must engage in philosophy to guard oneself practically and effectively against the God of the philosophers.'[28]

Philosophy, for Thévenaz, both remains the same and undergoes a dramatic transformation in contact with the God of Revelation. With the conversion to Christianity, it experiences a 'conversion to the here-below', in which 'there is no longer a philosophical God or a philosophical theology, instead there is a philosophy in the presence of God (*devant Dieu*) which, because it is self-questioning, discovers little by little that it is merely human'.[29] Thus the ongoing task of philosophy is to investigate the human condition, about which alone it may truly speak.

---

[26] Thévenaz, 'God of the Philosophers and God of the Christians', 338. 'mettre en question toutes les idoles, tous les baals, c'est-à-dire l'ensemble des dieux conçus ou façonnés par l'homme, que ce soit par sa main ou par sa raison' (Thévenaz, 'Dieu des philosophes et dieu des chrétiens', 309).

[27] Thévenaz, 'God of the Philosophers and God of the Christians', 347. 'Seule, en effet, la philosophie peut exorciser ou exciser ces excroissances philosophiques ou pseudo-philosophiques de la notion de Dieu' (Thévenaz, 'Dieu des philosophes et dieu des chrétiens', 321).

[28] Thévenaz, 'God of the Philosophers and God of the Christians', 349. 'un élément essentiel du combat de la foi. Il faut faire de la philosophie pour se garder du Dieu des philosophes, pour s'en garder en fait, pratiquement, efficacement' (Thévenaz, 'Dieu des philosophes et dieu des chrétiens', 324).

[29] Thévenaz, 'God of the Philosophers and God of the Christians', 345. 'Il n'y a plus de Dieu philosophique ni de théologie philosophique, mais il y a une philosophie devant Dieu qui, peu à peu, parce qu'elle est question pour elle-même, découvre mieux qu'elle n'est qu'humaine' (Thévenaz, 'Dieu des philosophes et dieu des chrétiens', 319).

We might be tempted to see an inconsistency in the two conflicting roles Thévenaz gives to philosophy: first, nothing more than critique, but then also investigation into the human condition. A charitable reading, however, can see these as fundamentally the same thing: when philosophy reflects on the human condition, what it discovers are the true limits of human knowledge, and it discovers this by continually calling everything into question, applying radical doubt to any creeping idol of metaphysical assertions wherever and whenever they appear.

KARL JASPERS: CONCEIVING THE INCONCEIVABLE

Before turning to Ricœur's response to Thévenaz, we shall briefly examine what Jaspers and Marcel have to offer to the question of absolutes, as we have done in the preceding chapters. This will prevent the misconception that Ricœur's position is without precedent, in spite of its uniqueness. We shall see that Ricœur's philosophical anthropology is a development of embryonic suggestions given by his two mentors.

Ricœur finds two clues in Jaspers that become vital for his own conception of transcendence. The first is that a need for absolutes can be discerned, not by turning attention away from 'the human condition', but by finding that part of what it means to be human includes holding something as absolute. The second is that philosophy need not restrict itself only to what can be grasped as a determinate concept: there is room for conceiving transcendence negatively, precisely as 'that which cannot be conceived'.

Like Thévenaz, Jaspers also gives a historical survey of attempts to deny absolutes, culminating in the scepticism of the Greeks that 'there is no truth; or there is truth, but we cannot know it; or we can know it but cannot communicate it'. Even this, he notes, was a 'dogmatics, which still clung to definite statements'. He then gives a final example of the Greek sceptics who achieved the 'consummate skepsis of shunning any statement, even the statement that there is no truth'. But even these could not help making an absolute out of a 'fixed point of independence in refraining from all statements'.[30]

---

[30] Jaspers, *Philosophy*, 1969, 1:257–8. 'Es gibt keine Wahrheit; oder: es gibt wohl eine Wahrheit, aber wir können sie nicht erkennen; oder wir können sie erkennen, aber nicht mitteilen'; 'Dieser Dogmatik, die noch in bestimmten Behauptungen verharrt, hat das antike Denken eine vollendete Skepsis entgegengestellt, die jede Behauptung und auch die Behauptung: es gibt keine Wahrheit, vermeidet'; 'Diese Skepsis ist von großartiger

From this history Jaspers draws the opposite conclusion to Thévenaz. For Jaspers, the absolute is not a perennial temptation into which we continually fall, but an unavoidable necessity of the human mind and of thought:

> Human consciousness cannot help making something absolute even if it does not want to. There is, so to speak, an unavoidable point of the absolute in my mind: if I eliminate something as absolute for me, it will be automatically replaced by something else. The consequence of formulated unbelief is that the points it makes with such lucidity are not chaotically changing tenets of an unconscious, shiftless unbelief but definite absolutes reduced to a bare minimum.[31]

In other words, it is part of 'the human condition' to stand mentally on something held to be absolute, even if this absolute is only provisionally held, even if it cannot be proven rationally or grasped as a determinate object.

Jaspers's philosophy is capable of absolutes because he avoids the total idealism of the kind Thévenaz inhabits. A single sentence by Jaspers designates the weak point in this kind of idealism: 'It is conceivable', Jaspers says, 'that there are things which are not conceivable'.[32] Ricœur quotes this Jaspersian maxim more often than anything else Jaspers says, seeming to see in it a sort of key that unlocks the solipsistic prison of post-Kantian absolute idealism.[33] This statement, combined with Jaspers's point about the need for absolutes, jointly reveal something crucial: the human mind cannot help but believe in the reality of things independently of the mind's grasp of them. This is no proof that they are real: on

---

Konsequenz und durchdringendem Selbstverständnis. Nur der feste Punkt der Unabhängigkeit im Sichenthalten allen Behauptens und die Seelenruhe der völligen Gleichgültigkeit bleibt übrig, alles Gehaltvolle wird ohne Teilnahme übernommen' (Jaspers, *Philosophie*, 213–14).

[31] Jaspers, *Philosophy*, 1969, 1:257–8. 'Das menschliche Bewußtsein kann nicht umhin, etwas absolut zu setzen, auch wenn es nicht will. Es gibt sozusagen einen unausweichlichen Ort des Absoluten für mich. Streiche ich etwas als absolut für mich, so tritt automatisch ein anderes an seine Stelle. Die Konsequenz des formulierten Unglaubens ist es, mit voller Klarheit nicht chaotisch wechselnde Inhalte unbewußten haltlosen Unglaubens, sondern bestimmte bis zur äußersten Dürftigkeit reduzierte Absolutheiten' (Jaspers, *Philosophie*, 213–14).

[32] Karl Jaspers, *Philosophy*, trans. E. B. Ashton, vol. 3 (Chicago: University of Chicago Press, 1969), 35. 'Es ist denkbar, daß es gibt, was nicht denkbar ist' (Jaspers, *Philosophie*, 707).

[33] 'Il est pensable qu'il y ait de l'impensable' – see, *inter alia*: Dufrenne and Ricœur, *Karl Jaspers et la philosophie de l'existence*, 262, 376; Ricœur, *Marcel et Jaspers*, 39, 92, 375. On the precise way idealism fails in this regard, see Graham Priest, 'The Limits of Thought – and Beyond', *Mind* 100, no. 3 (1991): 361–70.

the contrary, it reveals only that the human mind cannot help but have faith in things not rationally proven. It is no coincidence that Jaspers's discussion of absolutes occurs as part of a section titled 'faith and unbelief'. For Jaspers, 'the core of a world view is faith' – faith, indeed, in an absolute that cannot be proven even though it can be doubted.[34]

Jaspers also influenced Ricœur in a second way, by connecting discourse on transcendence to the classical *via negativa* which posits the reality of transcendence at the same time as denying its graspability.

The word 'transcendence' was in dispute at the time. Originating from the Latin *transcendere* meaning 'to climb above or pass over',[35] the term (in French, English, and German) indicates something which is 'beyond' in the most general sense. Usually, this is taken to mean beyond the visible or physical world, which is referred to as 'immanence'. This has led to the traditional association of transcendence with the supernatural, spiritual, or metaphysical, that is, anything 'beyond' the natural or physical, most frequently God. Heidegger and Sartre, however, were both fundamentally opposed to the traditional Platonic and Christian conception of transcendence. They redefined the word 'transcendence' in their philosophies to mean not what is beyond the natural world but what is beyond the human subject. This means that for them transcendence precisely *is* the natural world, bringing about a reversal in meaning.[36]

Jaspers, by contrast, sought to revivify the traditional meaning of transcendence.[37] He remains ambiguous and non-committal about whether

---

[34] Jaspers, *Philosophy*, 1969, 1:255. 'Der Kern der Weltanschauung ist Glaube' (Jaspers, *Philosophie*, 211).
[35] Speer Morgan, 'Transcendence', *The Missouri Review* 36, no. 3 (2013): 5.
[36] In a letter to Marcel, Sartre writes that transcendence for him means 'the existential necessity of being thrown outside oneself towards another really given being (in "flesh and bone")' (my translation: 'Quant à la transcendance, cela signifie pour moi la nécessité existentielle d'être jeté hors de soi vers un autre être donné réellement [en « chair et en os »]' ['Lettre de Jean-Paul Sartre à Gabriel Marcel', *Revue de la BNF* 48, no. 3 (2014): 63]). Similarly for Heidegger, writes Dermot Moran, 'transcendence cannot be understood in any religious-Christian-Platonic sense as towards another non-sensory realm or involving any denial of or renunciation of the world. All transcendence is what he calls "finite transcendence".' Instead, '*Dasein* transcends towards the "world". Transcendence essentially characterises *Dasein* as being-in-the-world.... For Heidegger, transcendence is always *towards the world*.' However, Moran notes that Heidegger abandons the word 'transcendence' in his later writings, because it is still too caught up in the Platonic/religious discourse to which he is most opposed (Dermot Moran, 'What Does Heidegger Mean by the Transcendence of *Dasein*?', *International Journal of Philosophical Studies* 22, no. 4 [2014]: 508–9).
[37] For Jaspers's conception of transcendence, see Chapter 3, 'Karl Jaspers: Conceiving the Inconceivable'.

his transcendence is identical to 'God', probably because many prevalent conceptions of God are too objectified and not transcendent enough. But although Ricœur is fully aware of this, he still explains that when he used the word 'transcendence' in his early writings, it was both 'a Jaspersian term' and 'modestly designated the god of [the] philosophers'.[38] In other words, Ricœur wanted to remain faithful to the traditional conception of transcendence that Jaspers sought to preserve, but to be even more faithful than Jaspers himself by keeping it closely related to God. As Alan Olson puts it, 'the fundamental task of Ricœur is that of making an even stronger case for the reality of Transcendence than we find in Jaspers'.[39]

Jaspers often mentions the influence of Plotinus in his work and his conception of transcendence shows this influence.[40] For Jaspers, as for Plotinus, the only types of propositions appropriate to transcendence are negations, precisely because transcendence is the conception of what cannot be conceived:

I reject, as inapplicable to transcendence, whatever I can conceive. I must not define transcendence by any predicate, must not objectify it in any idea, must not conceive it by any inference. Yet all categories may be used to say that transcendent being is neither a quality nor a quantity, neither a relation nor a cause, that it is not singular, not manifold, not being, not nothingness, and so forth.[41]

This is, of course, the classical formulation of negative theology. Thévenaz dismisses negative theology in a footnote, saying that it is no different from any other pre-Kantian account of the absolute because it is still based on 'the accord between knowledge and being': 'The *via negationis*', he says, 'is a means of re-establishing the superabundant and super-transcendent richness of an inviolate and inexhaustible positive absolute,

---

[38] Ricœur, 'Intellectual Autobiography', 13. 'terme évidemment jaspersien, qui désignait pudiquement le dieu des philosophes' (Ricœur, *Réflexion faite*, 25).

[39] Olson, *Transcendence and Hermeneutics*, 159.

[40] Jaspers hardly ever cites sources in his philosophy. But whenever in autobiographical notes he lists his major influences, Plotinus occupies a prominent place of honour – usually second or third in the list. See, *inter alia*: *Philosophy*, 1969, 1:2; *Philosophie*, vi; 'On My Philosophy', 137.

[41] *Philosophy*, 1969, 3:35. 'Das Resultat solchen Transzendierens als aussprechbarer Satz besteht in Negation. Alles Denkbare wird zurückgewiesen als nicht gültig von der Transzendenz. Transzendenz darf durch kein Prädikat bestimmt, in keiner Vorstellung zum Gegenstand, in keinem Schluß erdacht werden, doch sind alle Kategorien verwendbar, um zu sagen, das Transzendente sei nicht Quantität noch Qualität, nicht Beziehung noch Grund, nicht Eines, nicht Vieles, nicht Sein, nicht Nichts usw.' (*Philosophie*, 707).

Karl Jaspers: Conceiving the Inconceivable

from which all real being proceeds.'[42] Thévenaz's captivity to idealism has prevented him from seeing the merits of an apophatic account of God as the Absolute, in which is found the traditional Christian way of preserving human finitude in the presence of the infinite.

In contrast, Jaspers offers a type of 'accord between knowledge and being' (borrowing Thévenaz's language) that is *inverted* in the manner of Neoplatonic apophaticism. It proceeds from the conception that that which cannot be conceived may still have some reality to it. But because, as we saw in Chapter 2, Jaspers lacks any 'similitude' in his thought which could bind together paradoxes,[43] all he can do is to note this paradox. He cannot go further by recognising that if one can conceive that there is something inconceivable, one can also conceive that there is something partially conceivable, thus opening the way to an *analogia entis* which preserves both the radical otherness of God at the same time as our ability to apprehend (not comprehend) him.

Nonetheless, from an Anselmian point of view, which is greater? The God of Thévenaz who is not absolute because no absolute can be conceived and indeed the very idea of the absolute is incoherent, or the God of negative theology (represented here by the Neoplatonic influence on Jaspers) whose absoluteness is the sign of his greatness equal to and beyond conception? In truth Thévenaz's very conception of 'conception' ends up by being radically solipsistic. His argument against conceiving the absolute is simply that we are not absolute. But to follow this argument to its logical conclusion, we cannot conceive a rock or a tree because we are not a rock or a tree. In the end, the human can only know itself, or even more radically, thought can only think itself. And by extension, if anything else existed in the universe that could think, it could likewise only ever know itself and nothing else. God himself could not 'know' humanity without *being* human. And although this may be an attractive proposition for securing the necessity of the Incarnation, it renders meaningless any reference to the divinity of Christ. Jesus may come to earth as 'God among us', but since the word 'God' has no prior content, Jesus' claim to divinity is meaningless, an empty and unnecessary accruing of labels that add nothing to our understanding of him. Thévenaz's solipsism, like

---

[42] My translation: the words 'l'accord entre le connaître et l'être est assuré' are followed by this footnote: 'Même pour la théologie négative, car la *via negationis* est un moyen de restituer la richesse surabondante et super-transcendante d'un absolu inviolé et inépuisablement positif, d'où procède tout être réel' (Thévenaz, 'La philosophie sans absolu', 191).

[43] See Chapter 2 above for Ricœur's 'philosophy of Similitude'.

Jaspers's paradox, is another example of a philosophy without any *analogy* which could bridge the gap between dissimilar things – humans and rocks, or humans and God – without assimilating them into the totalising grasp of a closed philosophical system.

However, Thévenaz has noticed one thing that Jaspers has not, which accounts for Thévenaz's nervousness about negative conceptions of the absolute. Thévenaz sees clearly that *even the most negative theology must have a positive moment at its very heart*. In Chapter 4 we shall see how this idea of a positivity deeper than any negativity (the 'Original Affirmation') plays a crucial role in Ricœur's thought. Ricœur and Thévenaz agree that we cannot affirm the absolute without some semblance or image of the absolute inside ourselves. For Thévenaz, such a divine image in the human amounts to self-divinisation, making ourselves 'like God' in the way of the serpent's temptation in the garden of Eden. What Thévenaz does not see is that being 'like God' is equivocal: not only a postlapsarian temptation but a prelapsarian gift: the gift given only to humans, of being made in *imago Dei*.

GABRIEL MARCEL: AN UNSOLVED PARADOX

The idea that we cannot even deny our absoluteness without by that very denial participating negatively in some form of absolute – this idea is hinted at by Marcel but without resolution. Although Ricœur does not directly cite Marcel in his philosophical writings on finitude and transcendence, a number of distinctively Ricœurian ideas can be found *in nuce* in Marcel's work.

Marcel had a distant perception of the way in which the human, although contingent, must participate in the absolute in order to conceive it. But for him it always remained an unsolved problem, a paradox which he noticed but did not see how to clarify. This is seen most clearly in his introduction to *Creative Fidelity*, where he attacks the arrogance of nineteenth-century philosophical systems for having forgotten the finitude of the human condition. The problem, Marcel says, is that in building a closed philosophical system, we imagine ourselves in some 'absolute' or 'central' position, some God's-eye perspective from which the world may be seen objectively. But, he objects:

I cannot without self-contradiction conceive the absolute as a central observatory from which the universe may be contemplated in its totality, instead of being apprehended in the partial and oblique way it indeed is by all of us. For I cannot conceive of the existence of such an observatory unless I somehow place myself in it mentally; and it is this very notion which must be declared self-contradictory.[44]

At this point, however, Marcel notices a problem with his own account. He has the insight to see that our recognition of our own finitude implies that we have a conception of the absolute as what we are not. 'It would seem', he says, 'that we here encounter an aporia':

> How indeed can I even refer to 'my point of view' without presupposing that 'absolute point of view' I have declared inconceivable? Perhaps the only reply that can be given to this question is that the notion of a true order of the world as it would be discovered to an observer who occupied a privileged position or who observed it under optimal conditions of perception, is implied in the awareness of this world as it is originally given to me according to a perspective which is mine and no other's.[45]

'This, however', he adds with haste, 'does not entail that such a notion expresses or embodies the advance to a higher level of being urged by all the great philosophical rationalisms.'[46] We participate in an absolute point of view but only negatively, as the ability to imagine what we do not have. Although Ricœur never quotes this passage, the argument he makes in *Fallible Man* will push this same insight to its logical conclusion.

After this Marcel rarely talks about the absolute. But in 1958, he gave a lecture to the Société Française de Philosophie titled 'The Questioning of Being'.[47] In the discussion following that lecture, a certain 'Mr. Bénézé'

---

[44] Marcel, *Creative Fidelity*, 4. 'Je ne puis concevoir l'existence d'un semblable observatoire sans m'y installer en quelque sorte idéalement; c'est donc de cette notion elle-même que je suis tenu de dénoncer le caractère contradictoire' (Marcel, *Du refus à l'invocation*, 8–9).

[45] Marcel, *Creative Fidelity*, 4. Translation modified: 'Il semble pourtant qu'on se trouve ici en présence d'une véritable aporie: comment en effet pourrai-je parler de "mon point de vue" sans l'opposer à ce "point de vue absolu" que je viens de déclarer inconcevable? Peut-être faut-il simplement répondre que l'idée d'une ordonnance véritable du monde, telle qu'elle se découvrirait à un observateur occupant une situation privilégiée ou bénéficiant d'un ensemble optimum de conditions optiques, est impliquée dans le fait de reconnaître que ce monde m'est donné initialement selon une perspective qui est la mienne et rien que la mienne' (Marcel, *Du refus à l'invocation*, 9).

[46] Marcel, *Creative Fidelity*, 4–5. 'sans qu'il faille conclure de là en aucune manière que cette idée exprime ou incarne l'espèce de promotion dans l'être que semblent poser par voie de décret les grandes doctrines intellectualistes' (Marcel, *Du refus à l'invocation*, 9).

[47] This paper, together with the subsequent discussion, was published in Marcel's *Tragic Wisdom*; Marcel, *Pour une sagesse tragique*.

attempts to characterise Marcel's thought in terms of the absolute/relative opposition. Conceived this way, says Bénézé, Marcel is saying that:

> There is no symmetry between the absolute and the relative.... In any relative thing, I always discover the absolute. There is nothing surprising about this, for an absolute that is not everywhere ... would not be absolute.... The relative implies the absolute, but the absolute has no need of the relative; or rather, as the two always go together, in any reflection comparing them I can pass from the relative to the absolute very logically and without contradiction, but this is not true if I try to go the other way.[48]

In reply, Marcel expresses discomfort with this unusual way of representing his own thought, while at the same time admitting that he is 'basically in agreement'.[49]

These cameo appearances at the fringes of Marcel's thought raise two significant points. First, they underline the asymmetry of absolute and relative, which are not equal and opposite like the poles of a magnet. In itself, the relative cannot be conceived without the absolute; but it is only for us, because we are relative, that the absolute also cannot be conceived apart from the relative. Secondly, we cannot affirm our own relativity and deny our possibility to conceive the absolute, without thereby conceiving the absolute negatively in that very denial and thereby claiming absolute knowledge. This paradox will be taken up and clarified by Ricœur in his own philosophical anthropology, to which we now turn.

RICŒUR'S RESPONSE: NO GOD IN PHILOSOPHY MEANS NONE IN THEOLOGY

Most of what Ricœur has to say about Thévenaz is contained in his preface to Thévenaz's posthumously published *L'homme et sa raison*. And since the role of a preface is to recommend a book's contents, his

---

[48] Marcel, *Tragic Wisdom*, 56–7. 'Entre Absolu et Relatif, il n'y a pas symétrie.... Dans n'importe quel relatif, je découvre toujours l'Absolu; ce qui n'a rien d'étonnant, car un absolu qui ne serait point partout ... ne serait pas absolu.... Le relatif suppose l'Absolu, mais l'Absolu n'a pas besoin du Relatif ou plutôt, comme l'un ne va pas sans l'autre, le passage, dans la méditation où je les compare, se fait très logiquement, du relatif à l'absolu et sans contradiction, mais pas du tout le passage inverse' (Marcel, *Pour une sagesse tragique*, 92–3).

[49] Marcel, *Tragic Wisdom*, 59. 'quant au fond d'accord avec vous' (Marcel, *Pour une sagesse tragique*, 95). Later in the discussion, Jean Wahl intervenes to offer an explanation for Marcel's discomfort, which is that Marcel's philosophy always seeks to move beyond traditional categories and terminology and he does not like having his work reinterpreted in traditional language. See *Tragic Wisdom*, 60; *Pour une sagesse tragique*, 96.

appraisal is largely enthusiastic. Ricœur expresses great appreciation for the unflinching radicality of Thévenaz's thought and the challenge it puts to us. But in the final four pages he leaves a few pushbacks in the form of gentle 'questions': about the coherence of Thévenaz's conception of philosophy, about whether finitude can be understood without transcendence, and about whether there can really be no overlap between the God of philosophy and the God of revelation.

First of all, Ricœur asks: how can a philosophy whose only purpose is destructive not end by destroying itself?

> Does not the conversion to the here-below ... lead to a quasi-total obliteration of the initial *motif* of this philosophy, which is to be in the presence of God as a simple human, having recuperated the humanity of reason?[50]

This gentle prod of Ricœur's points in the direction of a significant problem with Thévenaz's account, which Ricœur, in his capacity as preface writer, is generous enough not to press home. Ricœur can see, I suggest, that Thévenaz has unwittingly made an Archimedean point out of the rejection of all Archimedean points. He calls philosophy a 'radical critique' but he does not critique the tools by which philosophy performs this critique. The critique claims to be all encompassing but omits to include itself. Thévenaz has committed the classic mistake of letting an 'absolute' creep into the heart of his philosophy: the rejection of all absolutes. He has absolutised human relativity, by laying down as unshakeably certain the truth that there will never and can never be anything absolute. How else could Thévenaz have such radical certainty that philosophy cannot have any absolute? If a philosophy wishes to deny absolutes but not absolutely (that is to say, without contradicting itself), an absolute must always remain theoretically possible. But if an absolute is theoretically possible, what is the basis for the denial of all absolutes? If Thévenaz, having recognised that he has absolutised de-absolutisation, then proceeds to de-absolutise it, then he has made absolutes possible once again. On the other hand, if an absolute is theoretically *im*possible, that is, absolutely impossible, it has destroyed itself by becoming the very thing it rejects. All this is contained *in nuce* in Ricœur's gentle question about the destruction of philosophy.

---

[50] My translation: 'La conversion à l'en-deçà ... n'aboutissent-ils pas à une oblitération quasi-totale du motif initial de cette philosophie: se tenir devant Dieu comme un simple homme ayant récupéré l'humanité de sa raison?' (Paul Ricœur, *Lectures 3: Aux frontières de la philosophie* [Paris: Éditions du Seuil, 2006], 257).

This critique leads to Ricœur's second question: how can a philosophy of human finitude discover itself except in contrast to what it is not? Here Ricœur notes that Thévenaz implicitly acknowledges that this is what has happened in the history of philosophy:

> In the texts of Thévenaz ... we see that the finitude of Cartesian humanity is only found by contrast with the *being* that it does not have, that it cannot give itself, that it is not.... Every philosophy of immanence is charged with giving an account of the possibility of its reflexion. Thévenaz's philosophy ... cannot complete its movement to the here-below; the return to the human can only be one pole of a tension between the worldliness of consciousness, lost in the world, and the emergence of reflexion.[51]

This is another way of expressing the self-contradiction in Thévenaz's absolute denial of absolutes. How can the critique, the calling into question, be trusted if it is not grounded in its own unquestioned reliability? How can a philosophy even reflect on the human condition without any transcendental guarantee of the validity of reflection?

Thirdly and finally, Ricœur asks how philosophy can recognise God as God, if it can have no concept of God.

> Pierre Thévenaz proposes and practices a philosophical conversion from an 'absolute reason in God' to a 'human reason in the presence of God.' ... The question that imposes itself is how the 'in the presence of God' is still part of philosophical reflection insofar as philosophical. As believers, we confess our philosophical responsibility in the presence of God; but as philosophers, do we know we are in the presence of God?[52]

Ricœur asks how we can know we are in God's presence, as philosophers. This question opens up an avenue of thinking that leads to some quite serious difficulties with Thévenaz's conception of the relationship between philosophy and theology. If between the 'God of the

---

[51] My translation: 'Dans les textes de Thévenaz ... on y verra que la finitude de l'homme cartésien n'est conquise que par le contraste avec l'être qu'il n'a pas, qu'il ne peut se donner, qu'il n'est pas.... Toute philosophie de l'immanence a la charge de rendre compte de la possibilité de la réflexion. Or la philosophie de Pierre Thévenaz ... ne peut achever son mouvement vers l'en-deçà, le retour à l'humain ne peut y être qu'un des pôles d'une tension entre la mondanéité de la conscience, perdue au monde, et l'émergence de la réflexion' (Ricœur, *Lectures 3*, 257–8).

[52] My translation: 'La conversion philosophique proposée et pratiquée par Pierre Thévenaz est celle d'une "raison absolue en Dieu" en une "raison humaine *devant* Dieu" ... La question se pose de savoir si et comment le "devant Dieu" fait encore partie de cette réflexion philosophique en tant que philosophique. Le croyant confesse sa responsabilité de philosophe devant Dieu; mais le philosophe sait-il qu'il est devant Dieu?' (Ricœur, *Lectures 3*, 257).

philosophers' and the 'God of Abraham, Isaac and Jacob', there is total equivocity and no possible comparison, we must ask whether there is any need for the two conceptions to exclude one another? If the Christian God can only be known through his actions in history, why label the agent of all these actions 'God', thereby confusing him unnecessarily with the philosophical God who is unrelated to him? What is to prevent the God of revelation from referring to nothing more than a powerful invisible life form that used to roam around the Middle East in the Iron Age, and was either deceived or deceptive in its claims to uniqueness, omnipotence, and omnipresence? Maybe the Christian God was created too, and either doesn't know it, or doesn't wish us to know it, in a manner similar to the myth of Prometheus. If the Christian God is not absolute, then there is no reason to trust 'absolutely' anything he says about himself or about the world.

Ricœur's own answer to this question is to put it down to a certain ambiguity in Thévenaz's work, which hovers between a purely iconoclastic philosophy and one with the ability coherently to see itself as 'in the presence of God'. Another interpreter of Thévenaz, Gabriel Widmer, reformulates the same ambiguity as one that 'hesitates between an atheist conclusion (philosophy without absolutes) and a Christian conclusion'.[53] Conversely, Domenico Jervolino sees this ambiguity not as a flaw but as a necessary expression, by a Christian philosopher, of the real gap between faith and philosophy in a secular age.[54] Nonetheless, even Jervolino acknowledges that Ricœur is 'less radical' than Thévenaz, and 'does not completely share his friend's philosophical position'.[55] Rather than Tertullian's radical opposition between Athens and Jerusalem, Ricœur is more inclined, in the tradition of Justin Martyr, to find 'seeds of truth in the Greek philosophers, the *logoi spermatikoi*, forerunners of the one and only Logos'.[56] In other words, Ricœur sees more fruitful contact between philosophy and theology than the radical rupture that Thévenaz, following Barth, considers crucial to the purity of the Protestant gospel.

---

[53] My translation: 'hésite entre une conclusion athée (philosophie sans absolu) et une conclusion chrétienne (philosophie de la vocation et de la responsabilité)' (Gabriel Widmer, 'Un essai de philosophie protestante: *L'homme et sa raison*, de Pierre Thévenaz', *Revue de Théologie et de Philosophie* 12, no. 2 [1962]: 105).
[54] Domenico Jervolino, 'Pierre Thévenaz et la condition humaine de la raison', 1975, 184.
[55] Domenico Jervolino, *The Cogito and Hermeneutics: The Question of the Subject in Ricœur*, trans. Gordon Poole (Dordrecht; London: Kluwer Academic, 1990), 57, 55.
[56] Jervolino, *The Cogito and Hermeneutics*, 57.

Ricœur rarely ever mentions Thévenaz again, apart from two brief appearances in 1990 and 1994, both of which simply state Ricœur's growing *rapprochement* to Thévenaz's concept of a philosophy without absolutes.[57] This leaves us with an unsolved problem. Given Ricœur's criticisms of Thévenaz's 'philosophy without any absolute', why does Ricœur claim, in 1994, that his own philosophy follows Thévenaz in being 'without absolutes'? As Greisch asks perceptively, 'how much weight should we give this confession'?[58] I suggest two answers to this question. First, the context in which Ricœur invokes Thévenaz's phrase is one in which he has expressed his commitment never to 'mix the genres' of philosophy and theology. This sharp separation was motivated more by pragmatic career considerations than by any pretentions to disciplinary purity. 'When I was still teaching', he admits in 1999, 'it was a permanent requirement to be recognized as a philosopher because I was under the pressure of the atheistic trend of French philosophy'.[59] This 'atheistic trend' meant that, in order to be 'recognised as a philosopher', Ricœur had to hide the place God had in his philosophy, simply by not writing about it.

Secondly, if Thévenaz's thought leaves us with an unresolved ambiguity, as most commentators agree, Greisch has rightly noted that Ricœur's philosophy perfectly follows the second way left open by Thévenaz: that of human reason in the presence of God, seeking by its intellectual efforts, not to take the place of God, but to humbly respond to God's call.[60] What Ricœur means, then, by a 'philosophy without absolutes', is a humble philosophy in the presence of God, a philosophy that knows its beliefs are only ever provisional.

Both these suggestions are evidenced by the fact that in Ricœur's explicitly Christian writings he is perfectly comfortable speaking about 'the absolute' (and as we have seen, he himself notes that 'the absolute' can only be spoken about in theology if it is first possible in philosophy). The clearest example is in his 1972 article 'The Hermeneutics of Testimony', which begins: 'What sort of philosophy makes a problem of

---

[57] Paul Ricœur, 'Réponses aux critiques', in *'Temps et récit' de Paul Ricœur en débat*, ed. Christian Bouchindhomme and Rainer Rochlitz (Paris: Éditions du Cerf, 1990), 211; Ricœur, 'Intellectual Autobiography', 13; Ricœur, *Réflexion faite*, 26.

[58] My translation: 'Quel poids accorder à cet aveu?' (Jean Greisch, *Paul Ricœur: l'itinérance du sens* [Grenoble: Millon, 2001], 431).

[59] Paul Ricœur and Questioners, 'Roundtable Discussion', in *Memory, Narrativity, Self and the Challenge to Think God: The Reception within Theology of the Recent Work of Paul Ricœur*, ed. Maureen Junker-Kenny and Peter Kenny (Münster: LIT, 2004), 203.

[60] Greisch, *Paul Ricœur*, 433.

testimony? I answer: A philosophy for which the question of the absolute is a meaningful question.'[61] There can be hardly any more direct rejection of the first interpretation of Thévenaz than this, even if it only appears in his confessionally Christian writings.

CONCLUSION

Thévenaz's conception of human finitude is such that philosophy can have no absolute, because any absolute that the human mind might claim to attain would be both idolatry God and self-divinisation. For Thévenaz, philosophy's proper task is strictly limited to investigation of 'the human condition' alone. However, Thévenaz has noticed something important that hasty advocates of a cosy relation between philosophy and theology often fail to observe. Thévenaz has pointed to a connection between a philosophy with a *conception* of God and a philosophy which aspires to the *position* of God. This shows us that the *prima facie* simple idea that there is a God, but we are not God, seems to contain some hidden problems, because in order to be able to conceive the infinite, we must have something of the infinite inside ourselves. Therefore to assert human finitude as the starting point of philosophy leads, in many cases, to asserting the impossibility of *conceiving* God without transgressing those boundaries.

Ricœur's gentle but devastating 'questions' to Thévenaz at the end of his preface are sufficient evidence of the large divergence between them. Ricœur responds to Thévenaz by pointing out, first that a philosophy without absolutes ultimately falls apart, and secondly that a philosophy with no place for God cannot *later* recognise God after it is 'converted' to theology, in other words, to belief in the God of historical revelation. But as we shall see, Ricœur agrees with Thévenaz that we must have something of the absolute in us if we are to conceive the absolute. To be human is not, after all, to be nothing but finitude.

But if we are not only finite, what are we instead? What does Ricœur say it means to be human? This is the topic of the next chapter, to which we now turn.

---

[61] Paul Ricœur, 'The Hermeneutics of Testimony', trans. David Stewart and Charles Reagan, *Anglican Theological Review* 61, no. 4 (1979): 435. Translation modified: 'Quelle sorte de philosophie fait du témoignage un problème? Je réponds: une philosophie pour qui la question de l'absolu est une question sensée' (Paul Ricœur, 'L'herméneutique du témoignage', in *Lectures* 3, 104).

4

Finitude and the Infinite

The God of the Philosophers

> God has put eternity into man's heart, yet he cannot find out what God has done from the beginning to the end.
> Ecclesiastes 3:11 ESV

Ricœur, then, in his openness to natural theology, is not entirely Barthian, but in the previous chapter this openness was only in the form of criticisms of the Barthian philosopher Thévenaz. In this chapter we consider Ricœur's positive account of the human condition, which is inextricably bound up with his understanding of the place for God in philosophy.

Thévenaz's basic position, described in the last chapter, that philosophy should concern itself with the human and can have no place for God, is by no means unique. As we shall see, Thévenaz represents the mainstream view and Ricœur is the outlier. Under the influence, not of Barth, but of Martin Heidegger, the majority of twentieth-century French philosophers have maintained that philosophy cannot conceive of any infinite, absolute, or transcendent, because human finitude precludes any possible conception of such; philosophy's only legitimate object, therefore, is 'the human condition' – contingent, standalone, positive, and without any opposite. While Ricœur agrees that the absolute is not a determinate concept, his study of 'the human condition' drives him to insist that it is nonetheless impossible not to think in relation to an implied absolute that, although it cannot be conceived, can still be thought, by means of a *via negativa*, as 'the inconceivable'. Following Jean Nabert, Ricœur calls this absolute the 'Original Affirmation'; following Jaspers he calls it 'Transcendence'; and following Descartes he calls it 'the Infinite'. He never calls it God, to avoid the misunderstanding that he is importing theological concepts into philosophy. But we shall see that Ricœur does equate these terms with all that can be known philosophically about God (Pascal's 'God of the philosophers'), even though this turns out to be only negative, apophatic knowledge of something that is itself fully positive. This negative outline nonetheless serves as the essential philosophical foundation for theology, without which theology could no more speak of God than could philosophy.

A PHILOSOPHICAL ARGUMENT, NOT A THEOLOGICAL PROOF

The very idea of this chapter – that Ricœur made an argument for the existence of God – may seem preposterous to some. As is well known, nobody in the twentieth century was more tirelessly scrupulous than Ricœur in maintaining rigorous boundaries between philosophy and theology. Nobody was more allergic to the accusation of being a Christian apologist, a crypto-theologian, and not a 'real philosopher'. Besides, does Ricœur himself not make it clear? 'We clearly reject', he insists, 'the pretensions of an overly zealous apologetics which would pretend to derive God from nature or from subjectivity by a simple rational implication'.[1] Any claim that Ricœur of all people might have tried to prove God's existence seems an absurdity likely to make the poor philosopher turn in his grave.

I have no intention of problematising Ricœur's boundaries between philosophy and theology, or of accusing him of transgressing those boundaries. But for Ricœur to speak about God philosophically implies no transgression of boundaries, for four reasons. First, God is a legitimate topic for philosophy proper; therefore, there is a way of speaking about God from within philosophy that does not trespass on theology. A *philosophical* argument for a *philosophical* God implies nothing about the 'God of Abraham, Isaac, and Jacob' – that is, of Judaeo-Christian revelation. To make an argument concerning the 'God of the philosophers' is not the same as to argue that this same God is revealed in the Bible, even if Ricœur happened to believe that as well. Similarly, to deny that the God of the Bible can be proven on philosophical grounds is not the same as to deny that the God of the philosophers can be argued for on philosophical grounds, even if the argument is made by someone who happens also to believe for other reasons that the God of the philosophers is revealed in his fullness in the Bible.

[1] Ricœur, *Freedom and Nature*, 468.

Secondly, I do not claim that Ricœur was trying to *prove* the existence of God. An argument is not the same as a proof, in the sense of an apodictic and undoubtable conclusion grounded in rigid rational premises.[2] In his 'Intellectual Autobiography', Ricœur speaks of his lifelong 'resistance that I have opposed to the claim to immediacy, adequation, and apodicticity made by the Cartesian cogito and the Kantian "I think"'.[3] It is only when arguments for God are seen as apodictic that Ricœur, in alarm, swings to the opposite extreme in order to put as much distance as possible between himself and any notion of the so-called proofs associated by many in France with a rigid and inflexible neo-Thomism. 'My mistrust of the proofs of the existence of God', he says in a late interview, 'had led me always to treat philosophy as an anthropology. ... In this case, I am agnostic on the plane of philosophy'.[4] We must understand this statement accurately by putting it in its proper context. While Ricœur does 'treat philosophy as an anthropology' – always starting from the human – we shall see that he does not think philosophy can be true to itself if it is *nothing other* than anthropology. Moreover, he is only 'agnostic' philosophically speaking in regard to the specifically Christian claims of what, in his most famous statement on the topic, he calls 'biblical faith'.[5] His claim is only that his philosophy is agnostic about confessional Christianity, not about God in a generic philosophical sense.

Thirdly, Ricœur's disciplinary boundaries, while always rigorous, were not always the same throughout his life. In his early phase he was more willing to let philosophy and theology dialogue fruitfully with each other. When this changed in the 1960s, it was not because of any change in his philosophical opinions, but for pragmatic reasons of safeguarding his career, as we already saw in Chapter 3. The rise of atheist philosophies led to more and more criticisms of Ricœur for the theological dimension of his work, compelling him to keep strictly within the confines of philosophical anthropology in order to remain a respected voice in the philosophical scene.[6] But this does not mean Ricœur changed his

---

[2] On this point, see John Hughes, 'Proof and Arguments', in *Imaginative Apologetics: Theology, Philosophy and the Catholic Tradition*, ed. Andrew Davison (London: SCM Press, 2011), 3–11.
[3] Ricœur, 'Intellectual Autobiography', 4.
[4] Ricœur, *Critique and Conviction*, 150.
[5] Paul Ricœur, *Oneself as Another*, trans. Kathleen Blamey (Chicago: University of Chicago Press, 1992), 24.
[6] See Olivier Mongin, *Paul Ricœur* (Paris: Éditions du Seuil, 1994), 205–6.

mind, merely that the theological dimension of his philosophy had to be kept underground until after he retired.

Fourthly and finally, it is true that God is not a philosophical concept for Ricœur, in the sense of something fully graspable by the mind, like an object. But this does not mean philosophy cannot speak about God, just as philosophy speaks about other things that are not philosophical concepts. Philosophy may speak about God as long as it does not attempt to import theological ideas given by revelation and then claim that these ideas can be proven philosophically.

NO SUCH THING: TWENTIETH-CENTURY OBJECTIONS TO THE INFINITE

We now turn to consider the broader landscape of philosophy in twentieth-century France. At the heart of French philosophical discourse from the 1940s onwards is the question of finitude, especially the 'finitude of human reason'. As Merleau-Ponty wrote, 'no philosophy can be ignorant of the problem of finitude without thereby being ignorant of itself as a philosophy'.[7] Ricœur is no exception to this general trend. His philosophical anthropology, he says, is an 'anthropology of finitude'.[8] Finitude is *the* central focus (argues Sophie-Jan Arrien) not only in Ricœur's early period but throughout his entire corpus: 'from *Freedom and Nature* (1950) to *The Course of Recognition* (2004), ... the finite human or human finitude is the focus of Ricœur's anthropology in its diverse expressions'.[9]

So what does the concept of 'finitude' entail? The anthropological focus of French philosophy means that the word refers only to *human* finitude, not the finitude of objects in the world. Finitude denotes the structural limits of human existence, the impassable horizon of human thought and knowledge. Most discourses on finitude emphasise the limits imposed by human temporality (meaning both that we cannot think

---

[7] Maurice Merleau-Ponty, *Phenomenology of Perception*, trans. Donald Landes (1945; repr., London: Routledge, 2013), 20.
[8] Ricœur, *Philosophical Anthropology*, 15. 'anthropologie de la finitude' (Ricœur *Anthropologie philosophique*, 40). He also later defines all hermeneutic philosophy as a philosophy of finitude, in contrast to Hegelianism. See Paul Ricœur, 'Hegel aujourd'hu ', *Esprit*, no. 3 (2006): 193.
[9] My translation: 'De *La philosophie de la volonté* (1950) au *Parcours de la reconnaissance* (2004) ... l'homme fini ou la finitude humaine, tel est le foyer de l'anthropologie de Ricœur sous ses figures diverses' (Arrien, 'Introduction', 234).

outside of temporal categories and that our lifetime is temporally limited by birth and death), contingency (meaning both that we are not a necessary part of existence and that we are historically situated), perspectivity (the fact that we only ever see or know things from one point of view), and particularity (the fact that we only have one individual existence). For some philosophers, finitude is a reason to deny any absolute truth, whereas for others, finitude only denies the possibility of absolute *knowledge* for human beings. Similarly, for many, finitude underscores the impossibility of any knowledge of God, while others have found in finitude a helpful contrast of human limitations with God's unlimited knowledge, power, and reality.

Whether or not the word 'finitude' is used, the nature of human limitation and finiteness has been a topic of debate throughout the history of philosophy[10] and theology.[11] Yet nevertheless, the debate found renewed vigour from the 1940s onward in France as a result of the explosive entry of Heidegger into the French intellectual scene. Since then virtually all French discussions of finitude have had Heidegger at their root, whether explicitly or not.[12]

For a short while, Jean-Paul Sartre was Heidegger's foremost French interpreter, and Heideggerian finitude was understood through Sartre's lens.[13] Soon, however, a host of other French philosophers were reading and interpreting Heidegger for themselves. In 1960 an article by Henri Birault sought to dissociate Heideggerian *Endlichkeit* from Sartre's

---

[10] For example, Drew Hyland finds finitude to be a central concern for Plato even though it is never thematised: 'the occasion of philosophy, and perhaps the human occasion altogether, is almost always one in which we are forced to confront a situationally specific form of finitude, limitation, or negation' (Drew A. Hyland, *Finitude and Transcendence in the Platonic Dialogues* [Albany: SUNY Press, 1995], 4).

[11] According to Tarek Dika, 'finitude was a theological concept the origins of which can be traced to Gregory of Nyssa, if not Before' (Tarek R. Dika, 'Finitude, Phenomenology, and Theology in Heidegger's *Sein und Zeit*', *Harvard Theological Review* 110, no. 4 [2017]: 477).

[12] On Heidegger's impact in French philosophy, see, *inter alia*: Tom Rockmore, *Heidegger and French Philosophy: Humanism, Antihumanism, and Being* (London: Routledge, 1995); Dominique Janicaud, *Heidegger in France*, trans. David Pettigrew and François Raffoul (Bloomington: Indiana University Press, 2015); and Dominique Janicaud, *Heidegger en France* (Paris: Albin Michel, 2001). For a more understated account, see Gary Gutting, 'Footnotes to Heidegger?', in *Thinking the Impossible: French Philosophy since 1960* (Oxford: Oxford University Press, 2011).

[13] 'In the post-war period, it was Sartre's redeployment of certain Heideggerian themes that set the terms of the debate' (Edward Baring, 'Theism and Atheism at Play: Jacques Derrida and Christian Heideggerianism', in *The Trace of God: Derrida and Religion*, ed. Edward Baring and Peter E. Gordon [New York: Fordham University Press, 2014], 73).

account of finitude.[14] Sartre's finitude, Birault says, is intrinsically connected to the idea of the Infinite. Under this guise, 'God' haunts Sartre's writings even while Sartre perpetually rejects him. This is because Sartre still sees finitude as a privation, a lack, a sadness at not being infinite, not being God.[15] Therefore, Birault concludes, 'the very idea of finitude is an originally religious and Christian idea.... In this sense, contemporary existentialism [meaning primarily Sartre], insofar as it gravitates around the theme of absolute finitude, is not only an atheist theology, but also an irreligious religion, a de-Christianised Christianity'.[16] By contrast, Birault continues, Heidegger's account of finitude is precisely aimed at needing no 'Infinite' as its opposite, either desired as in Christianity or rejected as in atheism.[17] Birault therefore finds Heideggerian finitude to be more 'radical' because it is a standalone finitude without any ground or any opposite.

Heideggerian 'radical' finitude, whether rightly or wrongly understood, became the norm in French scholarship. Heidegger later abandoned the use of the term *Endlichkeit*, because he saw it as being too closely intertwined with theology and theological concerns. Birault explains that the French word *finitude* is 'a fundamentally theological concept, and Christian even in its profanation of Christianity' and that therefore '[Heideggerian] *Endlichkeit* is not [Sartrean] finitude.'[18] But even so, Heidegger deemed *Endlichkeit* to be a misleading term, because it is too caught up in the traditional metaphysics he wanted to reject. So '[e]ven though the Heideggerian concept of *Endlichkeit* never was the theological-Christian concept of finitude, it no less remains', in Birault's estimation, 'that the idea of finite-being is in itself an ontologically theological idea'.[19]

---

[14] Henri Birault, 'Heidegger et la pensée de la finitude', *Revue Internationale de Philosophie* 14, no. 52 (2) (1960): 135–62.
[15] Birault, 'Heidegger et la pensée de la finitude', 149.
[16] My translation: 'L'idée même de finitude est une idée originellement religieuse et chrétienne.... En ce sens, l'existentialisme contemporain, dans la mesure où il gravite autour du thème de la finitude absolue, n'est pas seulement une théologie athée, c'est encore une religion irréligieuse, un christianisme déchristianisé' (Birault, 'Heidegger et la pensée de la finitude', 155).
[17] Birault, 'Heidegger et la pensée de la finitude', 155–7.
[18] My translation: 'Si la finitude est, comme nous avons essayé de l'établir, un concept foncièrement théologique, et chrétien jusque dans sa profanation du christianisme, alors, l'*Endlichkeit* n'est pas finitude' (Birault, 'Heidegger et la pensée de la finitude', 157).
[19] My translation: 'En effet, si le concept heideggérien d'*Endlichkeit* n'a jamais été le concept théologico-chrétien de la finitude, il n'en demeure pas moins que l'idée de l'être-fini est en elle-même une idée ontologiquement théologique' (Birault, 'Heidegger et la pensée de la finitude', 158).

Heidegger stopped speaking of finitude but the French did not. Indeed, the discourse on human finitude has continued into the twenty-first century and remains a live debate in continental philosophy and theology, with new books and articles published continually.[20]

At the time Ricœur is writing, all debates on finitude have Heidegger as their primary source of inspiration.

How did Heidegger's philosophy of finitude gain so much prominence in France? My suggestion is that it was because Heidegger clothed it in the garb of a philosopher whose stature made him indisputable: Immanuel Kant. The most influential book on finitude was Heidegger's commentary, *Kant and the Problem of Metaphysics*.[21] Nicknamed the *Kantbuch*, this commentary was vastly more popular in France even than Heidegger's *Being and Time*, having been translated into French more than thirty years earlier.[22] It is here that the phrase 'finitude of human reason' appears – not in Kant's writings, but in Heidegger's interpretation of Kant. As Colin McQuillan shows, that is why it is really

---

[20] See, *inter alia* (note also the prevalence of Kant and Heidegger): Arjan Markus, *Beyond Finitude: God's Transcendence and the Meaning of Life* (Frankfurt am Main: P. Lang, 2004); Emmanuel Falque, *Métamorphose de la finitude. Essai philosophique sur la naissance et la résurrection* (Paris: Éditions du Cerf, 2004); Giovanni Pietro Basile, *Trancendance et finitude: la synthèse transcendantale dans la 'Critique de la raison pure' de Kant* (Paris: L'Harmattan, 2005); Quentin Meillassoux, *Après la finitude: essai sur la nécessité de la contingence* (Paris: Éditions du Seuil, 2006); J. Colin McQuillan, 'Beyond the Analytic of Finitude: Kant, Heidegger, Foucault', *Foucault Studies*, 2016, 184; André Gravil, *Philosophie et finitude* (Paris: Éditions du Cerf, 2007); Jan-Olav Henriksen, *Finitude and Theological Anthropology: An Interdisciplinary Exploration into Theological Dimensions of Finitude* (Leuven: Peeters, 2011); Oren Magid, 'Heidegger on Human Finitude: Beginning at the End', *European Journal of Philosophy* 25, no. 3 (2017): 657–76; Dika, 'Finitude, Phenomenology, and Theology in Heidegger's *Sein und Zeit*'; Bruce Ellis Benson and B. Keith Putt, eds., *Evil, Fallenness, and Finitude* (Cham: Palgrave Macmillan, 2017); Robert D. Stolorow, 'Phenomenological Contextualism and the Finitude of Knowing', *The Humanistic Psychologist* 46, no. 2 (2018): 204–10; Güçsal Pusar, 'Heidegger on Kant, Finitude, and the Correlativity of Thinking and Being', *The Journal of Speculative Philosophy* 32, no. 3 (2018): 400; Peter J. Adams, *Navigating Everyday Life: Exploring the Tension between Finitude and Transcendence* (Lanham: Lexington Books, 2018); Ruth Jackson Ravenscroft, *The Veiled God: Friedrich Schleiermacher's Theology of Finitude* (Leiden: Brill, 2019); and Christina M. Gschwandtner, *Welcoming Finitude: Toward a Phenomenology of Orthodox Liturgy* (New York: Fordham University Press, 2019).

[21] Martin Heidegger, *Kant and the Problem of Metaphysics* (Bloomington: Indiana University Press, 1962), 27. 'Endlichkeit menschlicher Erkenntnis … Endlichkeit der Vernunft' (Martin Heidegger, *Kant und das Problem der Metaphysik* [Bonn: Friedrich Cohen, 1929], 19).

[22] See J. Colin McQuillan, 'Kant, Heidegger, and the In/Finitude of Human Reason', *CR: The New Centennial Review* 17, no. 3 (2017): 82.

Heidegger who is behind the widespread 'idea that Kant is a defender of "transcendental" or "radical" finitude, even when he [Heidegger] is not named and *Kant and the Problem of Metaphysics* is not cited'.[23]

Through Heidegger, Kant became celebrated as the inaugurator of an era of philosophy that acknowledges its own finitude, and Heidegger's reading of Kantian finitude reigned supreme.[24] But did Heidegger interpret Kant correctly? McQuillan's close comparison of the *Kantbuch* and Kant's *Critique of Pure Reason* leads him to the conclusion that Heidegger has violently projected his own views onto Kant, and therefore that the *Kantbuch* 'more closely resembles a work of philosophical ventriloquism, in which one philosopher is made to say what another philosopher thinks', than any faithful representation.[25] McQuillan's own reading of the first *Critique* argues that 'Kant actually displays a remarkable ambivalence about the "finitude" of human reason, so much so that he could be said to affirm the finitude and the infinity of human reason at the same time.'[26]

Nonetheless, under the influence of the Heideggerian reading of Kant, philosophers produced two major objections to the possibility of thinking transcendence. The first objection (which we already saw in Thévenaz) is that finitude is not a limit (*Grenze*) but a limitation (*Schranke*) that cannot, by definition, be transgressed. The second objection is that finitude is a positive standalone category, defined by itself and not as a lack or negation of the Infinite, and does not imply infinitude as its dialectical opposite.

To understand the first objection, we must distinguish these two Kantian terms. As Tenje Sparby puts it, 'limitation [*Schranke*] is a development of the concept of limit [*Grenze*] in that the limitation is a limit that is posited as essential'.[27] In other words, a *Grenze* (limit) may perhaps be transgressed, but a *Schranke* (limitation) cannot be transgressed by its very nature. For the mainstream of French thought, finitude is seen as an essential limitation (*Schranke*) and not a simple limit (*Grenze*) because it has to do with our human constitution. As Alan Renaut writes, this makes the limitation of finitude 'a question of structure and not of

---

[23] McQuillan, 'Kant, Heidegger, and the In/Finitude of Human Reason', 83.
[24] 'A number of French philosophers attribute to Kant the discovery of "transcendental" finitude, a finitude so "radical" that it shook the foundations of traditional metaphysics' (McQuillan, 'Kant, Heidegger, and the In/Finitude of Human Reason').
[25] McQuillan, 'Kant, Heidegger, and the In/Finitude of Human Reason', 84.
[26] McQuillan, 'Kant, Heidegger, and the In/Finitude of Human Reason', 94.
[27] Terje Sparby, *Hegel's Conception of the Determinate Negation* (Leiden: Brill, 2014), 204.

degree'.²⁸ For example, a tree is limited in height – this is a question of degree because it could have been taller. But the colour red cannot have any height: its height limitation is part of its nature. A book may have a limited number of pages (question of degree), but it cannot have legs (question of structure).

This structural/essential limitation means, as Jean Greisch puts it, that 'the absolute [that is, God] is not thinkable as a "horizon inaccessible by definition"'. It is this unsurpassable limitation of human finitude that turns 'the metaphysical question … into the anthropological question'.²⁹ Human beings can only think about human beings, because human beings can only know human beings, because all knowledge and all thought must become human by passing into the human mind. In this view, the human mind is structurally, or essentially, incapable of thinking transcendence. This philosophical position led to what McQuillan calls 'the growing anthropologization of philosophy', behind which 'the Heideggerian thinking … is very much present'.³⁰ Philosophy turned from a metaphysical discourse into a confined investigation of 'the human condition' which pretended to be metaphysically neutral.

The second objection to conceptions of the Infinite is that finitude is a standalone category, not to be understood as a lack or incompletion in relation to the Infinite. This objection usually takes the form of a reaction to a famous passage of Descartes's *Meditations* in which he asserts the priority of the Infinite over the finite:

And I must not imagine that I do not conceive the infinite by means of a true idea, but only by the negation of the finite …; for, on the contrary, I see manifestly that there is more reality in the infinite substance than in the finite, and hence that I have in me in some way the notion of the infinite, before that of the finite, that is to say the notion of God, before that of myself.³¹

---

²⁸ My translation: 'question de structure, non de degré' (cited in Jean Greisch, *L'arbre de vie et l'arbre du savoir: le chemin phénoménologique de l'herméneutique heideggérienne (1919–1923)* [Paris: Éditions du Cerf, 2000], 18).
²⁹ My translation: '[que] l'absolu n'est pensable comme un "horizon par définition inaccessible" … la transformation de la question métaphysique … en la question "anthropologique"' (Greisch, *L'arbre de vie et l'arbre du savoir*).
³⁰ McQuillan, 'Kant, Heidegger, and the In/Finitude of Human Reason', 82.
³¹ René Descartes, *Discourse on Method and the Meditations*, trans. F. E. Sutcliffe (London: Penguin, 1968), 124. 'Nec putare debeo me non percipere infinitum per veram ideam, sed tantùm per negationem finiti, ut percipio quietem & tenebras per negationem motûs & lucis; nam contrà manifeste intelligo plus realitatis esse in substantiâ infinitâ quàm in finitâ, ac proinde priorem quodammodo in me esse perceptionem infiniti quàm finiti, hoc est Dei quàm meî ipsius' (René Descartes, *Meditationes de prima philosophia* [apud Iohannem Blaeu, 1644], 24).

No Such Thing: Twentieth-Century Objections to the Infinite 95

We shall return to this quotation later when considering how Ricœur appropriates it, but its present significance is in the widespread reaction against it that took place in twentieth-century France. Following Jean Greisch, we discern three formulations of this objection in Jean Nabert, Heidegger, and Foucault. First, 'we cannot but follow Nabert's judgment', says Greisch, that

> the attempt to understand finitude by its correlation to an opposite is philosophically somewhat deceptive. Whether it is the finite-infinite couple, or particular-universal, whole-part, endless-finite duration, contingent-necessary etc., we may simply evoke the suffering of the loss of a loved one, or the 'feeling of the self's inadequacy to itself which escapes us, but which haunts every act' to discover that 'it [the feeling of finitude] is something more profound than that'.[32]

The quotations come from Nabert's *Le désir de Dieu*, which notably has a preface by Ricœur.[33] In other words, Ricœur is clearly aware of this objection.

Secondly, for Heidegger a proper understanding of finitude is not an immediately negative one, defined as absence or lack compared with the fullness of the Infinite. Heidegger is keen that the word 'finite' refer not to a cessation (in contrast to the infinite which would never cease) but to a completion. The word 'end' (*fin* in French) has this ambiguity – meaning either that something has stopped or that something has reached its *telos*, the latter being the preferred meaning to 'finite' for Heidegger.[34] Similarly Joan Stambaugh states that 'finitude is never simply a limited, "negative" characteristic for Heidegger, especially since the "positive" counterpart, infinity, is totally absent from his thought'.[35]

Thirdly, Foucault's conception of human finitude is likewise one that needs no Infinite (God) to make sense of its own reality. Foucault situates himself in opposition to 'the Cartesian solution', and instead 'excludes all recourse to the fully positive idea of divine infinity in the light of which

---

[32] My translation: 'On ne peut que souscrire au jugement de Nabert qu'une tentative de comprendre la finitude par sa corrélation à un opposé est philosophiquement assez décevante. Qu'il s'agisse du couple fini-infini, particulier-universel, tout-partie, durée sans fin-durée finie, contingent-nécessaire, etc., il suffit d'évoquer l'épreuve de la perte d'un être aimé, où "le sentiment d'une inadéquation de soi à soi qui nous fuit, mais qui hante chaque acte", pour découvrir que "cela est autre chose et plus profond"' (Greisch, *L'arbre de vie et l'arbre du savoir*, 13–14).
[33] Jean Nabert, *Le désir de Dieu* (Paris: Éditions du Cerf, 1996).
[34] Jean Greisch, *Ontologie et temporalité: esquisse d'une interprétation intégrale de 'Sein und Zeit'* (Paris: Presses universitaires de France, 1994), 325.
[35] Joan Stambaugh, *The Finitude of Being* (Albany: SUNY Press, 1992), 3.

alone finite being can understand itself'. Here 'we are in the presence of a "fundamental finitude which rests only on its own fact"'.[36]

THE UNIQUENESS OF RICŒUR'S PHILOSOPHICAL ANTHROPOLOGY

When considered in its historical context, what stands out as exceptional in Ricœur's account is that, in his own words 'we must speak of infinitude as much as of human finitude'.[37] In stark contrast to Heidegger and his followers, Ricœur shows that one cannot give an adequate account of 'the human condition' while bracketing out the question of God: the two belong inseparably together. He does this by arguing that 'the human condition' is not purely and solely finitude. Following Descartes and a new, non-Heideggerian reading of Kant, Ricœur defines the human as both finitude and infinitude, inseparably and indivisibly united. As we shall see, this 'infinitude' which is also part of the human condition renders possible, even necessary, a discourse on the inconceivable Infinite that lies beyond the limits of human reason.

To show the possibility of conceiving transcendence, and thus speaking of God philosophically, Ricœur must develop a completely different philosophical anthropology, showing by means of a very focus on 'the human condition' that it cannot avoid bringing in the question of transcendence. He does not erect his new anthropology of finitude in opposition to the great Kant, but as a different interpretation of Kant to that offered by Heidegger.[38] As Greisch notes, Ricœur's philosophical anthropology is 'directly grafted onto a re-reading of Kant'.[39] Ricœur's

---

[36] My translation: 'à la différence de la solution cartésienne ... exclut tout recours à l'idée pleinement positive de l'infinité divine à la lumière de laquelle seul l'être fini peut se comprendre lui-même.... Nous sommes alors en présence d'une "finitude fondamentale qui ne repose que sur son propre fait"' (Greisch, *L'arbre de vie et l'arbre du savoir*, 19).

[37] Paul Ricœur, *Fallible Man*, trans. Charles A. Kelbley (New York: Fordham University Press, 1986), 4. 'qu'on doive parler d'infinitude autant que de finitude humaine' (Paul Ricœur, *Finitude et culpabilité*, Philosophie de la volonté 2 [Paris: Éditions Points, 2009], 40).

[38] Jean-Luc Amalric is astute enough to notice that even though *Fallible Man* never mentions the *Kantbuch*, it is nonetheless 'a direct critique of the Heideggerian ontology of finitude that is outlined, in particular, in his *Kantbuch*' (Jean-Luc Amalric, 'Finitude, Culpability, and Suffering: The Question of Evil in Ricœur', in Davidson, *A Companion to Ricœur's 'Fallible Man'*, 189). Ricœur also explicitly criticises the *Kantbuch* in *Philosophical Anthropology*, 9; Ricœur, *Anthropologie philosophique*, 32.

[39] My translation: 'se greffe aussi directement sur une relecture de Kant' (Greisch, *L'arbre de vie et l'arbre du savoir*, 26).

Fallible Man, the main source for understanding Ricœurian finitude, is called by Anderson 'Ricœur's most overtly Kantian book'.[40] Indeed, what is at stake here is the right way to understand Kant: whether he ruled out any talk of the infinite, or whether, as McQuillan suggests, he sees the human as both finite and infinite at the same time.

In order to show how unique Ricœur is, and how he stands alone like a solitary lighthouse against the great wave of Heideggerian thought, let us look at two typologies of twentieth-century philosophy. First, Emmanuel Falque shows that Ricœur's interpretation of Kant is one of three in the twentieth century, the other two being Heidegger and Jean-Luc Marion.[41] But since Marion's account of finitude is built on a Heideggerian foundation, the primary contrast remains the one between Heidegger and Ricœur. Secondly, Greisch catalogues what he considers to be the three most influential recent conceptions of finitude: in Michel Foucault (1926–1984), Heidegger, and finally Ricœur. Ricœur is the only one, Greisch notes, who takes the 'Cartesian paradox of the finite/infinite human' as a starting point, that is to say, the only one who does not use human finitude in order to rule out the possibility of infinitude.[42] Indeed, says Greisch, Ricœur wants to 'shatter the great imperative which almost all contemporary anthropologies seem to respect', that of defining the human exclusively and solely by finitude.[43] We might strengthen Greisch's account by pointing out that Foucault's philosophy of finitude is itself Heideggerian in inspiration, even if it is not identical to Heidegger's. Especially in his early period, Foucault's 1966 *The Order of Things*[44] builds on Heidegger's conception of finitude.[45] This means that again there are really only two rival philosophies of finitude in the twentieth century: Heidegger and Ricœur. As Jérôme Porée rightly observes, when it comes to the relation between finitude and transcendence, Ricœur's 'adversary in all cases is Heidegger'.[46]

---

[40] Anderson, *Ricœur and Kant*, 10.
[41] Emmanuel Falque, 'The Extra-Phenomenal', *Diakrisis Yearbook of Theology and Philosophy* 1 (22 May 2018): 9–28; Emmanuel Falque, 'Hors phénomène', *Revue de métaphysique et de morale* 99, no. 3 (2018): 323.
[42] Greisch, *L'arbre de vie et l'arbre du savoir*, 27.
[43] My translation: 'briser le grand impératif que semblent respecter presque toutes les anthropologies contemporaines' (Greisch, *L'arbre de vie et l'arbre du savoir*, 26).
[44] Michel Foucault, *The Order of Things* (London: Routledge, 2018); Michel Foucault, *Les mots et les choses: une archéologie des sciences humaines* (Paris: Gallimard, 2014).
[45] See the convincing argument for this in McQuillan, 'Beyond the Analytic of Finitude'.
[46] My translation: 'L'adversaire commun dans tous les cas est Heidegger' (Jérôme Porée, 'Finitude et transcendance: une philosophie à deux foyers', in Jack Verheyden, Theo Hettema, and Pieter Vandecasteele, eds., *Paul Ricœur: Poetics and Religion* [Leuven: Uitgeverij Peeters, 2011], 190).

THE NEED FOR TRANSCENDENCE

In spite of Ricœur's uniqueness, he does not operate without precedent. Ricœur's initial sources of inspiration for an alternative anthropology are, unsurprisingly, his two mentors. At the beginning of his 1948 *Gabriel Marcel et Karl Jaspers*, Ricœur explains why he chose these two to write about instead of Sartre and Heidegger. It is because, while all four focus on 'the human condition', Jaspers/Marcel understand the human only in light of transcendence. Sartre/Heidegger, by contrast, treat 'the human condition' in isolation. Ricœur sees no possible point of comparison between two such radically different philosophies:

> It is not possible to superimpose reflections on man belonging to a philosophy without divine transcendence – as with Heidegger and Sartre – and those of a philosophy where freedom [that is, the human] and transcendence are polar opposites, as with Jaspers and Marcel.[47]

Nor does Ricœur remain neutral about which approach is superior. He briefly puts his cards on the table and argues in favour of the choice made by Marcel/Jaspers: 'The problem of the human is always that of the confines [*confins*] of the human and thus eventually of the meaning of transcendence.'[48] Thus, the question of transcendence simply cannot be ignored or even postponed, because it affects everything:

> The self is not the final word of philosophy; existence – incarnate existence, free, dialogical – is not Transcendence; existence is only through Transcendence. This conviction, we know, is the common soul of the philosophy of Marcel and Jaspers. These are both bifocal philosophies, as opposed to Heidegger and Sartre.[49]

Focussing in on the contrast between Jaspers and Heidegger, he writes:

> Who has not understood that for Heidegger and Jaspers the meaning of the world is controlled by a different meaning of Transcendence? As someone said, Heidegger's philosophy is from beginning to end a 'discourse on the absence of God'.

---

[47] My translation: 'Il n'est pas possible de superposer les réflexions sur l'homme appartenant à une philosophie sans Transcendance divine, – comme chez Heidegger et Sartre – et celles d'une philosophie où la liberté et la Transcendance sont polairement opposées, comme chez K. Jaspers et G. Marcel' (Ricœur, *Marcel et Jaspers*, 18).

[48] My translation: 'Le problème de l'homme est toujours celui des confins de l'homme et donc finalement du sens de la Transcendance' (Ricœur, *Marcel et Jaspers*).

[49] My translation: 'Le moi n'est pas le dernier mot de la philosophie; l'existence – l'existence incarnée, libre, dialogante – n'est pas la Transcendance; l'existence n'est que par la Transcendance. Cette conviction, nous le savons, est l'âme commune de la philosophie de G. Marcel et de celle de K. Jaspers. Ce sont toutes deux des philosophies à deux foyers, à l'encontre de Heidegger et de Sartre' (Ricœur, *Marcel et Jaspers*, 265).

[For Heidegger] human reality is Transcendence; for Jaspers it is *in the presence of Transcendence.*[50]

This criticism reveals that Ricœur considers Heidegger to be far from religiously and metaphysically neutral, despite Heidegger's own claims. While Ricœur concedes that *Being and Time* claims to be only the first part of a longer philosophical project, and 'we must retain the possibility of a further development of [Heidegger's] as yet unfinished œuvre', he immediately adds a caveat: 'Nonetheless it remains that Heidegger believed it possible to successfully complete an analysis of the human without taking the problem of God into account'.[51]

To 'analyse the human without taking God into account' – this is precisely what Ricœur believes impossible. It is instructive to compare the methodology of Heidegger's *Being and Time*, as Ricœur understands it, with Ricœur's methodology in *Freedom and Nature*. These two great philosophical treatises have much in common, and at first sight Ricœur seems to do the very thing for which he criticises Heidegger, because at the beginning he states that he aims to describe the human will in abstraction from transcendence.[52] But a closer look reveals the true distance between the two methodologies. Ricœur expresses great hesitation about abstracting transcendence, because of 'how difficult this abstraction is to sustain and how much equivocation it leaves in the doctrine of

---

[50] My translation: 'Qui n'a compris que le sens du monde est commandé chez Heidegger et Jaspers par un sens différent de la Transcendance? Comme quelqu'un l'a dit, la philosophie de Heidegger est de bout en bout un "discours sur l'absence de Dieu". La réalité humaine est la Transcendance; pour Jaspers, elle est *devant* la Transcendance' (Dufrenne and Ricœur, *Karl Jaspers et la philosophie de l'existence*, 367).

[51] My translation: 'Il faut réserver la possibilité d'un développement ultérieur de l'œuvre encore inachevée; il reste que Heidegger ait cru possible de mener à bien l'analyse de l'homme sans mettre en jeu le problème de Dieu' (Dufrenne and Ricœur, *Karl Jaspers et la philosophie de l'existence*, 367, n. 47). To illustrate this Ricœur quotes from Heidegger's *Vom Wesen des Grundes*: 'The ontological interpretation of Dasein as being-in-the-world decides neither positively nor negatively concerning a possible being toward God. Presumably, however, the elucidation of transcendence first achieves an *adequate concept* of *Dasein*, and with respect to this being it can then be *asked* how things stand ontologically concerning the relation of *Dasein* to God' (Martin Heidegger, *Pathmarks*, ed. and trans. William McNeill [Cambridge: Cambridge University Press, 1998], 371, n. 62). 'Durch die ontologische Interpretation des Daseins als In-der-Welt-sein ist weder positiv noch negativ über ein mögliches Sein zu Gott entschieden. Wohl aber wird durch die Erhellung der Transzendenz allererst ein *zureichender Begriff* des *Daseins* gewonnen, mit Rücksicht auf welches Seiende nunmehr *gefragt* werden kann, wie es mit dem Gottesverhältnis des Daseins ontologisch bestellt ist' (Martin Heidegger, *Wegmarken*, vol. 9, Gesamtausgabe [Frankfurt am Main: Vittorio Klostermann, 1976], 159, n. 56).

[52] Ricœur, *Freedom and Nature*, 29ff; Ricœur, *Le volontaire et l'involontaire*, 31ff.

subjectivity'.⁵³ For him it is only an approximation, attempted for the sake of focussing on one specific element of the human, and by no means any claim to completeness. In fact, he immediately adds that 'completion of the ontology of the subject demands a new change of method, *moving on to a kind of "Poetics" of the will*'.⁵⁴ The key word here is 'completion'. In Chapter 7 we will consider all the implications of this, as well as what Ricœur means by 'poetics'.⁵⁵ For now it is only important to note that the 'poetic' methodology removes the brackets around transcendence, which Ricœur says will provide 'completion' to philosophical anthropology.

In brief, while Heidegger and Ricœur both labour in the field of philosophical anthropology, the great difference between the two lies in the larger frame of reference from which the human is seen. Ricœur argues, *contra* Heidegger, that this larger frame of reference can never be neutral and is implied in everything else we say about the human.

Ricœur's position is now clear. It remains to be seen how he argues for it in his own constructive philosophical work, to which we now turn.

FINITE PERSPECTIVE, INFINITE AWARENESS

The heart of Ricœur's philosophical anthropology is the 1960 *Fallible Man*, the slender first volume of the second part of *Philosophy of the Will*. 'Numerous scholars have taken *Fallible Man* as the key to understanding Ricœur', Anderson informs us; additionally, 'in 1986 Ricœur himself admits that this book is the one he favors the most of all his works'.⁵⁶ Although it explores numerous aspects of the finite-infinite nature of the human (myth, reason, ethics, action, and feeling), to avoid repetition I shall focus only on his depiction of reason, which is Ricœur's philosophical point of departure and the place where the argument is clearest.

Fallible Man begins with a frank acknowledgement of its own uniqueness for its context: 'we dissociate ourselves to some extent from the contemporary tendency to make finitude the global characteristic of

---

⁵³ Ricœur, *Freedom and Nature*, 29. 'On ne saurait dire pourtant combien cette abstraction est difficile à soutenir et combien elle laisse d'équivoque dans la doctrine de la subjectivité' (Ricœur, *Le volontaire et l'involontaire*, 32).
⁵⁴ Ricœur, *Freedom and Nature*, 30. Italics original: 'L'achèvement de l'ontologie du sujet exige un nouveau changement de méthode, l'*access à une sorte de "Poétique"* de la volonté' (Ricœur, *Le volontaire et l'involontaire*, 32).
⁵⁵ See Chapter 7 below, the section titled 'Ricœurian Poetics: Creative Discourse about Creation'.
⁵⁶ Anderson, *Ricœur and Kant*, 10.

human reality'.⁵⁷ Nor is finitude the starting point of rational reflection, but something revealed to us by reflection: 'the initial guiding concept of [philosophical] anthropology is not and cannot be that of finitude'; rather, 'finitude is the result and not the origin'.⁵⁸

To reveal our finitude to us, Ricœur invites us to reflect on the nature of *perspective*: 'primal finitude consists in perspective or *point of view*'.⁵⁹ If we reflect on perception we discover that it is only ever one-sided. When we perceive an object, we perceive it 'inadequately', that is to say, incompletely (if 'adequate' or 'complete' would mean all-encompassing perception of the whole of an object). Perception is being used here as a synecdoche for all mental life; knowledge and thought are perspectival by nature, inflected by the orientation of the knowing subject. Our viewpoint on the world, both physical and mental, comes *from somewhere* geographical, somewhere historical, which for us is the zero-point of departure we call 'here'. Reflection on our perspective reveals to us that 'it belongs to the *essence* of perception to be inadequate'.⁶⁰

This is the least controversial part of Ricœur's argument. Next, however, Ricœur invites us to consider what it means that we can be aware of our own finitude.

> It is finite man *himself* who speaks of his *own* finitude. A statement on finitude testifies that this finitude knows itself and expresses itself. Thus it is of the nature of human finitude that it can experience itself only on the condition that there be a 'view-on' finitude, a dominating look which has already begun to transgress this finitude.⁶¹

Ricœur is not, by this observation, adding a second step to reflection on finitude, as if we first discovered our finitude and later our awareness of it. No: 'In one and the same movement, in a single flash', he says, 'the

---

57 Ricœur, *Fallible Man*, 3. 'Nous nous séparons quelque peu de la tendance contemporaine à faire de la finitude la caractéristique globale de la réalité humaine' (Ricœur, *Finitude et culpabilité*, 39).
58 Ricœur, *Fallible Man*, 136. 'Le premier concept directeur d'une telle anthropologie n'est pas, et ne peut être celui de finitude. Dans cette dialectique, la finitude est résultat et non origine' (Ricœur, *Finitude et culpabilité*, 187).
59 Ricœur, *Fallible Man*, 24. Italics original: 'La finitude originaire consiste dans la *perspective* ou *point de vue*' (Ricœur, *Finitude et culpabilité*, 61).
60 Ricœur, *Fallible Man*, 23. Italics original: 'Il appartient à l'*essence* de la perception d'être inadéquate' (Ricœur, *Finitude et culpabilité*, 60).
61 Ricœur, *Fallible Man*, 24. Italics original: 'C'est l'homme fini *lui-même* qui parle de sa *propre* finitude. Un énoncé sur la finitude atteste que cette finitude se connaît et se dit elle-même; il appartient donc à la finitude humaine de ne pouvoir s'éprouver elle-même que sous la condition d'une "vue-sur" la finitude, d'un regard dominateur qui a déjà commencé de la transgresser' (Ricœur, *Finitude et culpabilité*, 61-2).

act of existing becomes embodied and transcends its embodiment.... We become *aware of our finitude by going beyond it*.[62]

This observation nullifies all arguments about finitude as a total barrier or *Schranke*. What Ricœur argues in *Fallible Man*, Greisch says, is that 'the human is a being of transcendence, insofar as he/she is not enclosed in bounded limits (*Schranke*, in Kant's terminology)'.[63] Greisch recognises, then, that for Ricœur we are enclosed in bounded limits in some ways, but *insofar as* we are not, we have access to transcendence by participating in it. Ricœur does not reject the structural restrictions of finitude, but only the way they have been universalised to exclude everything else. Developing Hegel's famous argument that to know a limit is already to have gone beyond it, Ricœur argues that if we were nothing but finitude, we could never know it. We would be like animals, without consciousness of ourselves. Our awareness of our finitude is proof that finitude is only *part* of our ontological being, not the *whole* of it. 'Every description of finitude', he says, is 'incomplete, if it neglects to account for the transgression that makes discourse on finitude possible. The complete discourse on finitude is a discourse on the finitude and the infinitude of man'.[64] What makes us distinctively human is our awareness of the finite nature of our perspective, which does not and cannot come from that finite perspective itself. 'All perception is perspectival', says Ricœur. 'But how could I recognize a perspective, in the very act of perceiving, if *in some way* I did not escape from my perspective?'[65]

Not everyone has found this argument persuasive. Falque calls it 'far from self-evident', adding that it 'derives from a postulate of spirituality'.[66] A flippant response might be that neither is Heideggerian finitude

---

[62] Ricœur, *History and Truth*, 306. 'D'un seul mouvement, d'un seul jet, l'acte d'exister s'incarne et déborde son incarnation.... Nous prenons *conscience de notre finitude en la dépassant*' (Ricœur, *Histoire et vérité*, 379).

[63] My translation: 'L'homme est un être de transcendance, dans la mesure où il n'est pas enfermé dans les limites bornées (*Schranke*, dans la terminologie de Kant.' (Greisch, *Paul Ricœur*, 56).

[64] Ricœur, *Fallible Man*, 25. 'Toute description de la finitude est ... incomplète, si elle omet de rendre compte de la transgression qui rend possible le discours même sur la finitude. Ce discours complet sur la finitude est un discours sur la finitude et sur l'infinitude de l'homme' (Ricœur, *Finitude et culpabilité*, 62).

[65] Ricœur, *Fallible Man*, 26. 'Toute perception est perspectiviste. Mais comment connaîtrai-je une perspective, dans l'acte même de percevoir, si *en quelque façon* je n'échappais à ma perspective?' (Ricœur, *Finitude et culpabilité*, 63).

[66] Falque, 'The Extra-Phenomenal', 22. 'un présupposé qui selon nous est loin d'aller de soi sinon dans nombre de discours immédiatement dérivés du postulat de la spiritualité' (Falque, 'Hors phénomène', 338).

Language as Transcendence of Perspective 103

(which Falque is most influenced by) 'self-evident', although due to its prevalence it is often assumed to be so. A more adequate and less flippant response might be to suggest that Ricœur is pointing, in Kantian fashion, to the 'conditions for the possibility' of a discourse on finitude. Heidegger believes that his depiction of finitude applies, not just to himself, but to all human beings. Yet what guarantees the 'postulate' that no human being has ever existed whose being-in-the-world is fundamentally different to how Heidegger describes it? By claiming universality, however implicitly, for his analytic of Dasein, Heidegger claims to transcend the finitude of his own horizon and say something that is true for all human beings, always. But he can only do this by employing language, and it is reflection on language that forms the centrepiece of Ricœur's argument, to which we now turn.

LANGUAGE AS TRANSCENDENCE OF PERSPECTIVE

How do we transgress our finitude? By *language*, Ricœur tells us: 'the transgression of the point of view is nothing else than speech as the possibility of expressing'.[67] When we name an object, we name it as it is *in itself*, not as we see it from our point of view. We name it such that others can identify and recognise the thing we name, in spite of their irremediably different perspective: 'As soon as I speak, I speak of things in their absence and in terms of their non-perceived sides'.[68]

Ricœur finds human infinitude and transcendence in the very nature of language. This is already evident from the two titles of *Fallible Man*'s chapter subsections: 'Finite Perspective' and 'Infinite Verb'. Perception, which is finite, is only one aspect of the human condition. Human knowledge is not only perception but also speech. The human condition must be understood, not only as perspectival knowledge, but as communication through language in a shared world. By reflecting on how language relates to perception, we acquire a fuller account of the human condition: 'The dialectic of "name" and "perspective", therefore, is the very dialectic of infinitude and finitude.'[69]

---

[67] Ricœur, *Fallible Man*, 26. 'La transgression du point de vue n'est pas autre chose que la parole en tant que possibilité de dire' (Ricœur, *Finitude et culpabilité*, 64).
[68] Ricœur, *Fallible Man*, 27. 'Dès que je parle, je parle des choses dans leurs faces non perçues et dans leur absence' (Ricœur, *Finitude et culpabilité*, 64).
[69] Ricœur, *Fallible Man*, 29. 'La dialectique du "nom" et de la "perspective" est ainsi la dialectique même de l'infinitude et de la finitude' (Ricœur, *Finitude et culpabilité*, 67).

Finitude and the Infinite: The God of the Philosophers

It is by means of the transcendent nature of language that the characteristics of truth explored in Chapters 1 and 2 – unity and universality – become accessible to the human. First, philosophy, although tied to a historical situation, transcends that situation through language and aims at universal truths. Philosophy is not trying to hide its historicity, says Ricœur, by not referring to it; it merely 'wishes to express something different. It asks: what is real? What is *physis*? What is an idea? What is transcendence? In this the philosopher is silent as to his situation.... His question dissimulates his situation ... because it surpasses and transcends'.[70]

Secondly, language reveals the *unity* of the human discourse on truth as more foundational than the perspectival differences between us. To focus on perspective is to focus only on what divides; but language is what unites perspectives in a common vision. Ricœur explains that 'the otherness of consciousness is relative to a primordial identity and unity that makes possible the understanding of language'.[71] This insight concerning the deep connection between language and unity can unlock the meaning of the biblical myth of Babel:

> And the LORD said, 'Look, they are one people, and they have all one language; and this is only the beginning of what they will do; nothing that they propose to do will now be impossible for them. Come, let us go down, and confuse their language there, so that they will not understand one another's speech.' So the LORD scattered them abroad from there over the face of all the earth, and they left off building the city.[72]

Ricœur's argument, that language presupposes a prior unity grounded in transcendence, parallels this biblical text, in which the 'one' people are held together by the 'one' language which enables them to attain to divinity. The abolition of this 'one' language denies them divinity at the same moment as dividing them.[73]

---

[70] Ricœur, *History and Truth*, 72. 'C'est autre chose qu'elle veut dire. Elle se demande qu'est-ce qui est réel? qu'est-ce que la *physis*? qu'est-ce qu'une idée? qu'est-ce que la transcendance? En cela la philosophie est muette sur sa situation ... sa question dissimule sa situation ... parce qu'elle dépasse, parce qu'elle transcende' (Ricœur, *Histoire et Vérité*, 85).

[71] Ricœur, *Fallible Man*, 138. 'L'altérité des consciences est relative à une identité et à une unité primordiales qui rendent possible la compréhension du langage' (Ricœur, *Finitude et culpabilité*, 190).

[72] Genesis 11:6–8 NRSV.

[73] In a later book Ricœur will both expand and problematise this point when he discusses relevance of the Babel myth for the problem of translation. If languages do not have a common origin but are radically heterogeneous, then translation is impossible; but if

Language as Transcendence of Perspective

The transcendent nature of language is also the key to resolving the paradoxes and difficulties left behind by Thévenaz, Jaspers, and Marcel, as well as being a response to Heidegger. Let us look at each of these in turn.

First, Thévenaz's systematic efforts to abolish all absolutes lead him, in the end, to the abolition of language. We cannot posit a 'real absolute' without divinising ourselves, but the only alternative is a 'relative absolute', which, Thévenaz observes, 'explodes language'.[74] Language is left in mid-air, because it has been denied its only possible basis by Thévenaz's conception of the human as pure finitude without any infinite aspect. The brutal consistency of Thévenaz's thought unveils the necessarily transcendent dimension to language; but instead of conceding the possibility of a real absolute, Thévenaz opts instead to leave language 'exploded'.

Secondly, language is the stumbling block for Jaspers's theory of the radical particularity and uniqueness of each human individual. As we saw in Chapter 2,[75] Jaspers noticed that language simply will not let you treat each human as radically unique: 'I speak also of the many selves and of their Existenz; but I cannot mean it that way, because the many do not exist as cases of a universal.'[76] Language generalises by its very nature. Jaspers is forced to choose: either language is inherently misleading or generalisations are part of reality. He opts for the former: 'All statements about historicity would thus be bound to become untrue if taken literally and logically; for they will always be made in general form – the only form in which we can think and speak – while the original being of historic consciousness

---

translation is possible, then 'we must establish its rightful possibility through an inquiry into the origin' (Paul Ricœur, *On Translation*, trans. Eileen Brennan [London: Routledge, 2006], 14; 'il faut en établir la possibilité de droit par un enquête sur l'origine' [Paul Ricœur, *Sur la traduction* (Paris: Bayard, 2004), 26]). He wants us to push past these 'ruinous' theoretical alternatives to the practical fact of translation. To do this, he reinterprets the Babel myth as resulting from finitude, rather than sin. Its message is that the one original language is a divine thing beyond the reach of finite humans; therefore the diversity of languages is a simple fact, and 'starting from this fact of life, let us translate!' (Ricœur, *On Translation*, 20; 'à partir de cette réalité de la vie, traduisons!' [Ricœur, *Sur la traduction*, 37]).

[74] My translation: 'Parler d'absolu relatif, c'est faire sauter le langage' (Thévenaz, 'La philosophie sans absolu', 199).

[75] See Chapter 2 above, the section titled 'Karl Jaspers: Radical Flight to the Individual'.

[76] Jaspers, *Philosophy*, 1969, 2:16. 'Existenzerhellung spricht weiter von den vielen Selbst als den Existenzen: sie kann es aber so nicht meinen, da es die Vielen als Exemplare eines Allgemeinen nicht gibt' (Jaspers, *Philosophie*, 307–8).

itself depends upon its singularity.'[77] But Ricœur opts for the latter. As we saw in Chapter 2, Ricœur replied to Jaspers that communication by language is only possible if particularity and universality are held together by a doctrine of similitude.[78] This lends support for Alan Olson's suggestion that Ricœur's linguistic turn seems to emerge from a desire to make transcendence more tangible than did Jaspers: 'It was as though Ricœur were exploring every possible development in philosophy of language and linguistics as preparation for the task of speaking – and more definitively than Jaspers – the meaning of the nature and reality of Transcendence.'[79]

Thirdly Marcel, because of his abhorrence for abstractions, is unable to see that language is inherently abstract. Ricœur himself did not comment on this directly, though he does critique Marcel's overly negative posture towards abstractions and objectivity.[80] Doubtless, we can stray into unreality through the use of abstractions, as Marcel clearly saw. But abstractions are nonetheless our only way of communicating to one another. Words like 'tree', 'dog', 'happy', 'eating' are already generalisations that hide the important differences between the concrete objects/feelings/activities described, yet to refrain from abstractions for this reason is to refrain from speaking. Marcel's philosophy, 'if taken seriously, sh[oul]d reduce him and us to perfect silence', as C. S. Lewis put it.[81]

Finally, anyone who knows Heideggerian terminology will recognise the following as a rejection of Heidegger's anthropology of pure finitude. Ricœur writes that the transcendent nature of language means that 'I am not wholly defined by my status of being-in-the-world: my insertion in the world is never so total that I lose the distance [*recul*] of signifying, of intending, the principle of expression. This distance [*recul*] is the very root of reflection on point of view as point of view.'[82]

---

[77] Jaspers, *Philosophy*, 1969, 2:116. 'Alle Aussagen über Geschichtlichkeit müßten daher wörtlich und logisch genommen unwahr werden; denn sie haben immer die Form des Allgemeinen — nur in ihr läßt sich denken und sprechen — , während das geschichtliche Bewußtsein selbst nur in seiner Einzigkeit ursprünglich ist' (Jaspers, *Philosophie*, 409).
[78] Dufrenne and Ricœur, *Karl Jaspers et la philosophie de l'existence*, 334.
[79] Olson, *Transcendence and Hermeneutics*, 156–7.
[80] See Chapter 2 above, the section titled 'Paul Ricœur: A Mediating Philosophy of Similitude'.
[81] C. S. Lewis, *The Collected Letters of C. S. Lewis*, vol. 3: *Narnia, Cambridge, and Joy, 1950–1963* (New York: HarperCollins, 2009), 24.
[82] Ricœur, *History and Truth*, 309. Translation modified: 'Autrement dit, je ne suis pas entièrement défini par mon statut d'être-au-monde: mon insertion au monde n'est jamais si totale que je ne conserve le recul du singulier [*sic*], du vouloir-dire, principe du dire. Ce recul est le principe même de la réflexion sur le point de vue comme point de vue' (Ricœur, *Histoire et Vérité*, 382).

However, Ricœur is not divinising language. Language, like human nature, is both finite and infinite at the same time. 'The spoken word [*la parole*]', he says, 'is also human; it too is a mode of finitude. It is not, as is pure contemplation, the transcending of the human condition; it is not the Word of God, the creative word, but the word of man'.[83] In fact, he observes, the ability to say something false or incoherent is both the sign of our finitude and the greatest evidence of language's infinite nature in contrast to the finitude of perception. Perception cannot be right or wrong; it is simply 'how things are seen'. But the fact that speech can be false testifies to its possibility to be true in a way that transcends perception. The 'absurd signification', Ricœur says, 'reveals the property that all meaning has of exceeding every present perceptive fulfilment: I say more than I see when I signify'.[84] Language can both reach higher and fall further, just as humans can be both better and worse than animals because of their closer proximity to the divine.[85]

'In the sign', concludes Ricœur, 'dwells the transcendence of the λόγος of man'.[86] *Fallible Man* thus stands at the threshold of Ricœur's entry into the realm of language and semiotics. Ricœur has passed into a conception of the role of language which surpasses that of his mentors, paving the way for a rich two decades of reflection on language, text, and interpretation which precipitated Ricœur's rise to world renown.

TRANSCENDENCE BY MEANS OF NEGATION

The biggest difficulty with Ricœur's anthropology of 'finite/infinite disproportion' could be that it returns to the arrogance of nineteenth-century philosophies which assume a divine 'absolute' viewpoint on reality. Ricœur anticipates this objection. 'How can we avoid', he writes, 'setting

---

[83] Ricœur, *History and Truth*, 200. 'La parole aussi est humaine; elle aussi est un mode de la finitude; elle n'est pas, comme la contemplation pure, l'au-celà de la condition humaine; elle n'est pas la parole de Dieu, la parole créatrice, mais la parole de l'homme' (Ricœur, *Histoire et Vérité*, 241).

[84] Ricœur, *Fallible Man*, 28. 'La signification absurde ne fait que révéler, par l'impossibilité d'être remplie, le propre de toute signification d'excéder tout remplissement perceptif actuel: je dis plus que je ne vois quand je signifie' (Ricœur, *Finitude et culpabilité*, 66).

[85] Henriksen puts it this way: 'Ricœur stresses how language is located in between the finite situation and something that transcends it. In this way, language points toward a dialectical relationship between the finite and the infinite' (Henriksen, *Finitude and Theological Anthropology*, 21).

[86] Ricœur, *Fallible Man*, 28. 'Dans le signe réside la transcendance du λόγος de l'homme' (Ricœur, *Finitude et culpabilité*, 65).

up this idea of non-perspective as a new point of view, which would be, as it were, an overview of the other points of view, a sweep over the centers of perspective? Finitude signifies that such a non-situated view or *Übersicht* does not exist. But if reflection upon point of view is not a point of view, then what is its nature?'[87]

The answer, for Ricœur, is to remember the way in which this 'infinite' point of view was discovered: through a *negation* of the human possibility of an infinite point of view. I picture other points of view like my own in an imagined neutral space which we all occupy, and in which my zero-point which I call 'here' is *not* absolute. I picture myself as from above, in a room with other people looking at an object from perspectives other than my own. As soon as I wish to name the object *as* an object, and not as a two-dimensional impression on my own perception, I 'judge of the entire thing by going beyond its given side into the thing itself. This transgression is the intention to signify. Through it I bring myself before a sense which will never be perceived anywhere by anyone, which is not a superior point of view, which is not, in fact, a point of view at all but an inversion into the universal of every point of view'.[88]

The so-called superior perspective, Ricœur is saying, is only an 'inversion', a pointing to what I do not have. The 'universal point of view' that denies all 'universal points of view' is not a self-contradiction because the former is defined *negatively*, an inside-out universal. Finitude is surpassed and transcendence attained only by means of *negation*. 'I cannot *express* my transcendence over my perspective', Ricœur says, 'without expressing myself negatively'.[89]

This negative road to transcendence is explicitly left open as a possibility by Heidegger, if not directly in regard to infinity, then at least in respect of eternity. When speaking of the philosophical impossibility of conceiving a divine eternity that is something more than an endless

---

[87] Ricœur, *Fallible Man*, 26. 'Comment ne pas ériger cette idée de la non-perspective en un nouveau point de vue, qui serait en quelque sorte vue plongeante sur les points de vue, survol des centres perspectivistes? La finitude signifie qu'une telle vue non située, qu'une telle *Uebersicht* n'existe pas. Si la réflexion sur le point de vue n'est pas point de vue, qu'est son acte?' (Ricœur, *Finitude et culpabilité*, 63).

[88] Ricœur, *Fallible Man*, 26. Translation modified: 'Je juge de la chose même en transgressant la face de la chose dans la chose elle-même. Cette transgression, c'est l'intention de signifier par elle, je me porte au-devant du sens qui ne sera jamais perçu de nulle part ni de personne, qui n'est pas un super-point de vue, qui n'est pas du tout point de vue, mais inversion dans l'universel de tout point de vue' (Ricœur, *Finitude et culpabilité*, 64).

[89] Ricœur, *History and Truth*, 311. Italics original: 'Je ne puis *dire* ma transcendance à ma perspective sans m'exprimer négativement' (Ricœur, *Histoire et vérité*, 385).

temporality, Heidegger remarks: 'whether the way afforded by the *via negationis et eminentiae* is a possible one, remains to be seen'.[90]

The *via negationis*, I argue, is precisely the way Ricœur took. His sustained reflection on negation has revealed it as the way to transcendence and the infinitude in the heart of the human. Our ability to grasp the infinite is 'the negative in which my transcendence consists'.[91] To borrow a metaphor from painting, the Absolute/Infinite is a sort of 'negative space' that is only visible by the contours of absence that define it. We conceive it negatively as a reality that lies beyond all conception. In this way the 'universal point of view' against which so much twentieth-century thought reacted becomes inextricably connected to the very ability to deny it. At the same time, it avoids the dangers, associated with the nineteenth-century, of claiming a universal point of view, because what is claimed is a *negative* universal, a transcendent perspective which reveals to us our own limitations.

It is no accident that negation should be the lynchpin of Ricœur's argument. Recent archival research by Alison Scott-Baumann has brought to light the exhaustive decades-long study that Ricœur made of the concept of negation. 'For about 20 years', Scott-Baumann tells us – starting from after World War II – Ricœur 'lectured not only on negation but also on related themes such as finitude and infinity, nothingness and apophatic theology'.[92] Ricœur considered negation to be the dominant theme of the philosophies of his time; as he did with all other philosophical trends, he went the 'long route' of carefully incorporating it into his own thought. Ricœur published almost nothing on negation, in spite of this intense decades-long focus.[93] But the Ricœur archives are full of lecture notes organising negation into themes, categories, and historical moments.

Ricœur found in the manifold forms of negation a fruitful avenue for philosophical thought because it pushes continually at the limits of what can be known. One of these limits is revealed by negating finitude as what we are, creating an open space for conceiving transcendence as

---

[90] Martin Heidegger, *Being and Time*, trans. John Macquarrie and Edward Robinson (Bodmin: Blackwell, 1962), 499. 'Ob hierzu die via negationis et eminentiae einen möglichen Weg bieten könnte, bleibe dahingestellt' (Martin Heidegger, *Sein und Zeit* [Tübingen: Niemeyer, 1967], 427).
[91] Ricœur, *History and Truth*, 311. 'Le négatif en quoi consiste ma transcendance' (Ricœur, *Histoire et vérité*, 385).
[92] Scott-Baumann, *Ricœur and the Negation of Happiness*, 5.
[93] Scott-Baumann, *Ricœur and the Negation of Happiness*, 4.

what we cannot conceive. Negativity becomes the way out of solipsistic idealism into the free air of realities beyond the mind's ability to grasp.

We note, furthermore, how far this argument is from defining finitude as merely a 'lack' or an 'absence' in the way Heidegger and Foucault were so opposed to. Indeed, for Ricœur, a finite thing can be positive regardless of whether or not it is contained by an infinite. We must beware of Hegel's famous 'bad infinite' which warns against imagining the infinite as another finite quantity that somehow competes with the finite for space.[94] When we make the finite and the infinite *exclude* one another, then 'an equal dignity of permanence and independence is ascribed to the finite and to infinite. The being of the finite is made an absolute being'.[95] This, however, contradicts the very nature of finitude, which is to be relative.

Rather, for Ricœur 'the finite and the infinite do not limit each other but are present to each other and in each other'.[96] The true infinite is not a *threat* to the positivity of finitude. Nonetheless, this positivity is further underscored by Ricœur in two ways. First, by noting that the 'finite perspective' is what is concretely and positively known, whereas the 'infinite verb' is a negation of this fundamental positivity, an unknown, a non-point-of-view: 'what is finite is altogether positive; only the infinite *lacks* an outline'.[97] Ricœur's second way is by contrasting finitude with a true

---

[94] 'Dualism, in putting an insuperable opposition between finite and infinite, fails to note the simple circumstance that the infinite is thereby only one of two, and is reduced to a particular, to which the finite forms the other particular. Such an infinite, which is only a particular, is co-terminous with the finite which makes for it a limit [*Grenze*] and a barrier [*Schranke*]: it is not what it ought to be, that is, the infinite, but is only finite' (Georg Wilhelm Friedrich Hegel, The Logic of Hegel, trans. William Wallace, 2nd ed. [Oxford: Oxford University Press, 1892], 176–7; 'Der Dualismus, welcher den Gegensatz von Endlichem und und [sic] Unendlichem unüberwindlich macht, macht die enfache Betrachtung nicht, daß auf solche Beise sogleich das Unendliche nur das Eine der Beiden ist, daß es hiemit zu einem nur Besondern gemacht wird, wozu das Endliche das andere Besondere ist. Ein solches Unendliches, welches nur ein Besonderes ist, neben dem Endlichen ist, an diesem eben damit seine Schranke, Gränze hat, ist nicht das, was es seyn soll; nicht das Unendliche, sondern ist nur endlich' [G. W. F. Hegel, *Encyclopädie der philosophischen Wissenschaften im Grundrisse*, 3rd ed. (Heidelberg: Oßwald (C. F. Winter), 1830), 110]).

[95] Hegel, *Hegel's Logic*, 177. 'wird dem Endlichen die gleiche Würde des Bestehens und der Selbständigkeit mit dem Unendlichen zugeschrieben; das Seyn des Endlichen wird zu einem absoluten Seyn gemacht' (Hegel, *Encyclopädie der philosophischen Wissenschaften im Grundrisse*, 110–11).

[96] Ricœur, *Freedom and Nature*, 369. 'Le fini et l'infini ne se bornent pas l'un l'autre, mais sont présents l'un à l'autre, l'un dans l'autre' (Ricœur, *Le volontaire et l'involontaire*, 346).

[97] Ricœur, *Freedom and Nature*, 447. Italics original: 'Ce qui est fini est tout positif; seul l'infini *manque* de contour' (Ricœur, *Le volontaire et l'involontaire*, 420).

negative: evil. Expounding the significance of this contrast will be the task of Chapter 5.

TRANSCENDENCE AS ORIGINAL AFFIRMATION

Neither the finite nor the infinite is negative itself. Negativity is neither the end nor the beginning: it is only the *way*. For Ricœur, we discover transcendence by negation, but transcendence itself is not negativity, not emptiness, but unbounded fullness. It is the originary source of all positivity, all reality, all true substance. It is the Original Affirmation.

The way in which negation reveals an underlying positivity is explained in Ricœur's 1956 article 'Negativity and Primary Affirmation'.[98] There are several reasons for considering this the single most important text for understanding Ricœur's early philosophy. First, it is one of Ricœur's only published works which deals with negation, the topic which was Ricœur's obsession for so many years. Secondly, it is in one scholar's words the 'transition point which leads from the first volume [or Part] of Philosophy of the Will (*The Voluntary and the Involuntary*) to the second volume (*Finitude and Guilt*)', published right between these two.[99] Thirdly, its title conjoins negativity with the other most significant concept in Ricœur's early work. The term 'Original/Primary Affirmation' (*affirmation originaire*) is taken from the French reflexive philosopher Jean Nabert, who Ricœur later claimed 'was to have a decisive influence on me in the 1950s and 1960s' – notably the exact same decades as those of his intense study of negation.[100] Pierre Colin argues that Ricœur's early writing 'would not have remained authentically philosophical except through its faithfulness to the guidelines laid down by Nabert'.[101] The notion of Original Affirmation in particular, Jean-Luc Amalric argues, is the 'guiding thread' of both *Freedom and Nature* and *Fallible Man*'s philosophical anthropology.[102] Everything, then, points to this article as

---

[98] Now found at the end of Ricœur *History and Truth*; Ricœur, *Histoire et vérité*.
[99] My translation: 'marque de transition qui conduit du premier volume de la Philosophie de la Volonté (*Le volontaire et l'involontaire*, 1950) au deuxième volume (*Finitude et culpabilité*, 1960)' (Cristina Amaro Viana Meireles, 'Paul Ricœur et l'idée d'une Affirmation Originaire', *Revista Contemplação* 0, no. 10 [24 July 2015]: 107).
[100] Ricœur, 'Intellectual Autobiography', 6. 'Jean Nabert devait m'influencer de façon plus décisive dans les années cinquante et soixante' (Ricœur, *Réflexion faite*, 15).
[101] My translation: 'ne demeurait authentiquement philosophique que par sa fidélité aux lignes directrices tracées par Nabert' (Colin, 'Herméneutique et philosophie réflexive', 16).
[102] My translation: '*L'homme faillible* ... trouve son principal fil conducteur dans la notion d'affirmation originaire, héritée de Nabert' (Jean-Luc Amalric, 'Affirmation

revealing the very heart of Ricœur's early thought, and its significance cannot be overestimated.

This text begins with the same argument we followed in *Fallible Man*: that the fact that we are aware of our finitude means that we transcend this very finitude (revealing an 'infinitude' in the human constitution), but that such transcending is negative in character. However, Ricœur now takes this argument one step further. We discover our infinitude by negating our finitude, but before this, we discover our finitude by negating a positive infinitude. Just as Thévenaz said that philosophy began with the discovery that our point of view is not absolute, so finitude begins with the discovery that we are not infinite. Therefore infinitude is in fact found by means of a double negation, or a 'denegation' which, because it negates itself, is actually affirmation. 'Before the denegation or negation of transcendence', Ricœur summarises, 'there is a primal negation which is the negation of finitude'.[103]

The final step in Ricœur's argument is to show that *all* negation conceals a prior affirmation, thus showing that the denegation of transcendence unveils a fundamental positivity. Ricœur does this by seeking a hidden positivity in the most intrinsically negative human activities, 'indignation, protestation, recrimination, and revolt'.[104] His source of inspiration for this idea is, unexpectedly, Albert Camus's book *The Rebel*. Camus begins by asking: 'What is a rebel? a man who says no, but whose refusal does not imply a renunciation. He is also a man who says yes, from the moment he makes his first gesture of rebellion.'[105] One cannot rebel against something without believing in something else. Rebellion against one order can only be motivated by a positive vision of an alternative order. That positive vision might be vague and

---

originaire, attestation et reconnaissance: Le cheminement de l'anthropologie philosophique ricœurienne', *Études Ricœuriennes / Ricœur Studies* 2, no. 1 [10 June 2011]: 13). See also Jean-Luc Amalric, 'Act, Sign and Objectivity: Jean Nabert's Influence on the Ricœurian Phenomenology of the Will', in *A Companion to Ricœur's 'Freedom and Nature'*, ed. Scott Davidson (Lanham: Lexington Books, 2018).

[103] Ricœur, *History and Truth*, 316. 'Ma thèse est donc limitée: avant la dénégation ou négation de transcendance, il y a la négation primaire qui est la négation de finitude' (Ricœur, *Histoire et vérité*, 391).

[104] Ricœur, *History and Truth*, 322. 'L'indignation, la protestation, la récrimination, la révolte' (Ricœur, *Histoire et vérité*, 399).

[105] Albert Camus, *The Rebel: An Essay on Man in Revolt*, trans. Anthony Bower (London: Vintage, 1991), 13. 'Qu'est-ce qu'un homme révolté? Un homme qui dit non. Mais s'il refuse, il ne renonce pas: c'est aussi un homme qui dit oui, dès son premier mouvement' (Albert Camus, *L'homme révolté*, 30th ed. [Paris: Gallimard, 1954], 25).

confused; it might be unviable in reality; it might even be little more than to be rid of an annoyance or to gain superiority over others. It might (at the most perverted extreme) be the destruction of all things – 'some people just want to watch the world burn', as the film *The Dark Knight* puts it. But it is always there, implied in every rejection of the status quo.

'Camus', he says, 'so rightly expressed it, without perceiving all the *metaphysical* implications of it'.[106] In this rare use of the word 'metaphysical', Ricœur shows his commitment to the impossibility of separating philosophical anthropology and metaphysics. What Camus applied only to the field of anthropology, Ricœur transposes into metaphysical discourse. Ricœur is at his most Platonic here, and it is no surprise that he invokes Plato's *Sophist* three times in this essay including a long concluding quotation. He is arguing that every negative gesture presupposes a positive value, and that even though that value may never be realised in the physical world, it is still positive and substantial, because the physical world is not the only thing that is real. 'Shall we say', he asks, 'that the object of adhesion [of the rebel] is precisely what does not exist?' No, we shall not, he replies, because 'the adhesion which foments rebellion is the testimonial of an "I am" beyond factual being'.[107]

Similarly, with uncharacteristic decisiveness, Ricœur comes out in support of Descartes's famous prioritisation of the infinite over the finite. 'Descartes was correct', Ricœur writes, 'when he said that the idea of the infinite was wholly positive and identical to being *plane et simpliciter*, and that the finite was at fault with respect to being'. He then quotes the passage from Descartes that we saw above, including the last line, which states that 'I have in me the notion of the infinite before that of the finite, the notion of God before that of myself.'[108] Descartes, we read, was *correct* in putting the positive notion of the infinite before that of the finite, and in identifying 'the infinite' with 'God'.

---

[106] Ricœur, *History and Truth*, 323. 'comme le disait si justement Camus, sans en apercevoir toutes les implications métaphysiques' (Ricœur, *Histoire et vérité*, 399).
[107] Ricœur, *History and Truth*, 323. 'Dira-t-on que l'objet de l'adhésion, c'est précisément ce qui n'est pas? ... l'adhésion qui fomente la révolte est l'attestation d'un "je suis" par-delà l'être-donné' (Ricœur, *Histoire et vérité*, 299).
[108] Ricœur, *History and Truth*, 315. 'C'est Descartes qui avait raison lorsqu'il disait que l'idée d'infini était tout entière positive et identique à l'être *plane et simpliciter* et que le fini était en défaut par rapport à l'être.... j'ai en quelque façon premièrement en moi la notion de l'infini, que du fini, c'est-à-dire de Dieu, que de moi-même' (Ricœur, *Histoire et vérité*, 389–90).

WHY RICŒUR'S ARGUMENT IS NOT APOLOGETICS

'The Infinite', then, is clearly a philosophical name for God in Descartes's philosophy. Furthermore, 'Original Affirmation' is Nabert's philosophical term for God, as Ricœur makes explicit in a late interview.[109] However, the fact that Ricœur quotes Descartes with approval does not amount to Ricœur himself identifying the philosophical term 'the Infinite' with the Judaeo-Christian God. The kind of apologetics from which Ricœur always kept a careful distance was the kind that attempted to prove, on philosophical grounds, the truths of the Christian faith that are given only by revelation, starting by identifying the 'God of the philosophers' with the Judaeo-Christian God. But as we have already seen, Ricœur makes no attempt to prove anything, nor does his argument have any intrinsic relation to theology. Ricœur is careful never to 'identify' the 'God of the philosophers' and the 'God of the Bible' as if there were nothing in the latter that was not already there in the former. In a third late interview, Ricœur explains: 'I ... resist the identification of a God who is named and who is prayed to in the *Psalms* and in the prophecies, with the word "God" in philosophy.'[110] This identification forgets that 'what we name "God" in philosophy is not somebody to whom we can pray, it is not somebody with whom we can enter into a personal relation, but a *concept*'.[111] However, this caution of Ricœur does not compel us to set up a radical either/or alternative between the 'God of the philosophers' and the 'God of the Bible'. In a 2003 interview, Ricœur says with careful phrasing that he is 'not sure about the absolute irreconcilability between the God of the Bible and the God of Being (understood with Jean Nabert as "primary affirmation" ...)'.[112] Between the two extremes of 'identity' and 'irreconcilability' there lies the middle road of an 'overlap', or an inclusion, where one thing contains elements of the other without the two coinciding exactly. Ricœur is claiming just this: that in the heart of the human condition is an openness to transcendence that is acquired by a participation in that same transcendence. Whether that transcendence will turn out also to have personality, or any of the other features

---

[109] 'the God of Being (understood with Jean Nabert as 'primary affirmation' ...)' (Richard Kearney, *On Paul Ricœur: The Owl of Minerva* [London: Taylor & Francis, 2017], 169).
[110] Yvanka Raynova and Paul Ricœur, 'All That Gives Us to Think: Conversations with Paul Ricœur', in *Between Suspicion and Sympathy: Paul Ricœur's Unstable Equilibrium*, ed. Andrzej Wierciński (Toronto: Hermeneutic Press, 2003), 686.
[111] Raynova and Ricœur, 'All That Gives Us to Think'. Italics original.
[112] Kearney, *On Paul Ricœur*, 169.

commonly associated with the Christian God, is an entirely different question that forms no part of the argument.

The apophatic nature of Ricœur's argument means that he by no means aims to form a determinate concept of God which could be used to ground a philosophical system, in a move Heidegger rightly condemned as ontotheological. The type of infinite or absolute we find in Ricœur is one that is only apprehended, not comprehended. In this sense I agree with Christina Gschwandtner's argument that 'God' in Ricœur's philosophy is a 'symbol'.[113] A symbol is Ricœur's name for something from outside philosophy that can never be absorbed by philosophy, that is, turned into a determinate concept that can be fully grasped by the human mind. We saw above that Ricœur described the philosophical God as a 'concept'. But what is it a concept of? The answer is found in Ricœur's favourite Jaspersian maxim: it is a concept of that which cannot be conceived.[114]

It is only by refusing to determine God philosophically that Ricœur can hold open the possibility that religious revelation might supplement the negative picture of God provided by philosophy. But it would be a great mistake to think that theology determines what is left undetermined by philosophy. Ricœur remains close to his mentor Marcel, for whom 'the theology which philosophy leads us to is an essentially negative theology'.[115] What this means is that once philosophy has established the ungraspability of transcendence as a matter of principle due to human finitude, it has laid foundations that are never revoked by theology. The Christian God remains the Ungraspable One. Biblical revelation for Ricœur does not lead to any determinate concept of God, but, by means of tensions and apparent contradictions, holds open the incomprehensibility of the object of its discourse:

> [In the Bible,] the word 'God' does not function as a philosophical concept, whether this be being either in the medieval or in the Heideggerian sense of being. Even if one is tempted to say – in the theological meta-language of all these pretheological languages – that 'God' is the religious name for being, still the word 'God' says more.... To understand the word 'God' is to follow the direction of the meaning of the word ... I mean its double power to gather all the

---

[113] Christina M. Gschwandtner, 'Ricœur's Hermeneutic of God', *Philosophy and Theology* 13, no. 2 (2001): 287–309.

[114] As discussed in Chapter 3, Karl Jaspers wrote that 'it is conceivable that there are things which are not conceivable' (Jaspers, *Philosophy*, 1969, 3:35). Ricœur quotes this little maxim more often than anything else by Jaspers.

[115] Marcel, *Being and Having*, 122.

significations that issue from the partial discourses and to open up a horizon that escapes from the closure of discourse.[116]

Even in theology, the word 'God' 'escapes from the closure of discourse', says Ricœur. It is 'not a philosophical concept' because it 'says more' than what philosophy can pin down or determine. Philosophy can only point, by means of negation, to the infinitude which is implied in any discourse on finitude; to the Original Affirmation that precedes any possible negation. Whether this Original Affirmation will turn out to be a person to whom one can pray – that is a question that this philosophical method cannot answer.

CONCLUSION

What is significant about Ricœur's approach is that it begins, not with metaphysics, but with a focus on the human condition. Ricœur finds the infinite as the source of all positivity, not by ignoring human finitude, but by offering, in Kantian style, a critique of the 'conditions for the possibility' of any discourse on finitude, something we might suggest is somewhat lacking in Heidegger. Ricœur's philosophical anthropology answers a demand made by one theologian, that: 'if we are to find God in the world again, shall we not have to revise our conception of man?'[117]

Ricœur's essay 'Negativity and Primary Affirmation' is a concise apophatic natural theology, a *via negativa* by which God is approached in darkness and mystery. God cannot be conceived except as the Inconceivable,[118] or grasped except as the Ungraspable, or known except as the Unknowable. In this way, Ricœur follows the heart of the Christian tradition, for which, in Aquinas's words, 'we cannot know what God is, but rather what He is not'.[119] Let us review the steps of how Ricœur does this.

In Chapter 3 we saw how Thévenaz represents the Barthian rejection of the possibility of any 'God of the philosophers', which he identifies with 'the Absolute'. Thévenaz's argument is that any attempt to conceive God ends in claims to absolute knowledge which only God himself could

---

[116] Ricœur, *Figuring the Sacred*, 45–6.
[117] Ansfridus Hulsbosch, *God's Creation: Creation, Sin, and Redemption in an Evolving World*, trans. Martin Versfeld (London, New York: Sheed and Ward, 1965), 6.
[118] Recall Ricœur's favourite phrase of Jaspers discussed above: 'It is conceivable that there is the inconceivable.'
[119] 'De Deo scire non possumus quid sit, sed quid non sit' (St Thomas Aquinas, *Summa Theologiae*, trans. Laurence Shapcote [New York: Benziger Brothers, 1911], Ia, Q.3, intro.).

have. In thinking the Absolute, the philosopher makes him- or herself absolute, which amounts to a self-divinisation and thus to idolatry. What is lacking in Thévenaz's account is any concept of the *imago Dei*, which Ricœur (speaking in this case of freedom) calls 'the infinite [in the human] of which Descartes says that it makes us like God'.[120] But for Ricœur's two mentors, Jaspers and Marcel, things are not so simple. Jaspers's very investigation of 'the human condition' leads him to conclude that it is impossible not to think the absolute, but that it must be conceived as that which cannot be conceived. Marcel likewise notices that one cannot deny our ability to take an absolute standpoint without somehow participating in that very absolute standpoint, even if only by negation.

The Barthian rejection of metaphysics represented by Thévenaz, and the Heideggerian notion of finitude as a *Schranke*, form a strange alliance when it comes to understanding the nature of philosophy.[121] We have seen how Heideggerian finitude, taken up by the majority of twentieth-century French philosophers, refuses to define itself negatively as lack of a prior infinitude, both because finitude is positive in itself and has no opposite, and because finitude is an unsurpassable barrier which by its very structure and essence blocks access to the infinite, or transcendence. The task of philosophy can therefore be nothing more than an investigation of 'the human condition'.

We have seen, finally, how Ricœur develops a robust philosophical anthropology that sees the human, not as pure finitude, but as a paradox of both finitude and infinitude For Ricœur, if the human were only finite, we should never have known it. Our knowledge of our finitude reveals an infinitude within us, and thus our transcendence. This transcendence is known only by a *via negativa* whereby we discover the infinite through negation of the finite. What negation uncovers, however, is not itself negative but an Original Affirmation which is a philosophical term for God. Ricœur shows us how we cannot investigate 'the human condition' or understand our own finitude except by reference to a transcendent Infinite in which we participate but that we can never know as a determinate concept. The question of what it means to be human cannot be separated from the question of God.

---

[120] Ricœur, *Freedom and Nature*, 22. 'cet infini dont Descartes disait qu'il nous rend semblable à Dieu' (Ricœur, *Le volontaire et l'involontaire*, 27).

[121] In this sense, it is perhaps not as difficult as Milbank suggests (speaking about Jean-Luc Marion), to 'be both Barth and Heidegger at once' (John Milbank, 'Only Theology Overcomes Metaphysics', *New Blackfriars* 76, no. 895 [1995]: 325).

5

Finitude and Evil

The Crucial Distinction

> The basic mistake of many conceptions about creation lies in the fact that finitude is felt to be a flaw, a hurt which as such should not really have been one of the features of this world.... Finitude is thought to be improper, an ailment, even sinfulness or apostasy, a flaw in the existence of mankind and the world.
> Edward Schillebeeckx[1]

Are evil, guilt, and failure an inevitable part of human reality? Although most philosophies of his time answer 'yes' to this question, Ricœur boldly opts for a negative answer. Unlike his contemporaries, Ricœur insists that 'the human condition' cannot be properly understood if guilt is made an essential part of us. He argues that to understand evil properly is to see it as a historical accident, a contingent event, in asymmetrical relation to the original created goodness that lies at the heart of the human. For Ricœur, our finitude not as in itself a flaw, but a positive good. The 'confusion of guilt and finitude', he asserts, 'appears to me to be one of the gravest confusions of contemporary *"existential"* philosophy'.[2]

The previous chapter examined how Ricœurian finitude points to an infinite, or transcendence, accomplished by means of a complex *via negativa*, whereby finitude is negated once in order to discover infinitude and then again to discover the 'Original Affirmation' of infinitude that underpins all

---

[1] Edward Schillebeeckx, *God among Us: The Gospel Proclaimed*, trans. John Bowden (London: SCM, 1983), 92.
[2] Paul Ricœur, 'The Relation of Jaspers' Philosophy to Religion', in *The Philosophy of Karl Jaspers*, ed. Schilpp, 632. Italics original: 'La confusion de la culpabilité et de la finitude me paraît être une des plus redoutables confusions de la philosophie existentielle contemporaine' (Paul Ricœur, 'Philosophie et religion chez Karl Jaspers', *Revue d'histoire et de philosophie religieuses* 37, no. 3 [1957]: 227).

things and in which all things participate. This chapter and the next focus on Ricœurian finitude's other 'opposite': evil, which appears in human life as suffering, sin, and guilt.

PREVIOUS SCHOLARSHIP ON RICŒUR'S DISTINCTION

Ricœur's unique way of distinguishing finitude and evil/sin/guilt has received almost no attention in secondary literature, despite the fact that it is Ricœur's central concern in writing the two volumes that comprise Part II of *Philosophy of the Will*. This lacuna is all the more surprising if we consider the large amount of attention that scholars have devoted to Ricœur's work on evil.[3] For example, in a recent edited volume, *Evil, Fallenness, and Finitude*, three essays are devoted to the problem of evil in Ricœur's philosophy.[4] Yet even though finitude is a term in the book's title, not one of these essays observes that Ricœur's initial concern with evil arises from his project to distinguish it from finitude, let alone discusses the distinction itself. Elsewhere the topic receives a brief mention from Charles Courtney when he addresses Ricœur's criticisms of Karl Jaspers. Courtney observes that 'At the level of eidetic reflection on human being Ricœur finds fallibility (finitude) and only the possibility of fault (guilt). The reality of guilt appears only when philosophy addresses, at the level of empirics, actual human experience.'[5] Jan-Olav Henriksen's book, which contains a section dealing with the conflation of finitude and guilt, only mentions in a footnote that this is 'commented upon by Ricœur', but does not employ the resources available in Ricœur for addressing the problem.[6] A more satisfactory account can be found in Petruschka Schaafsma's

---

[3] See, *inter alia*: John S. Tanner, '"Say First What Cause": Ricœur and the Etiology of Evil in Paradise Lost', *PMLA* 103, no. 1 (1988): 45–56; Monika Chorab, 'Understanding Evil in the Philosophy of Paul Ricœur, Jean Nabert, and Gabriel Marcel', *Rocznik Teologii Katolickiej* 10 (2011): 221–31; D. Dixon Sutherland, 'A Theological Anthropology of Evil: A Comparison in the Thought of Paul Ricœur and Teilhard de Chardin', *Neue Zeitschrift für Systematische Theologie und Religionsphilosophie* 34, no. 1 (1992): 85–100; and Geoffrey Dierckxsens, 'The Ambiguity of Justice: Paul Ricœur on Universalism and Evil', *Études Ricœuriennes / Ricœur Studies* 6, no. 2 (2015).
[4] Benson and Putt, *Evil, Fallenness, and Finitude*. See in this volume: Marius-Daniel Ban, 'Paul Ricœur on Mythic-Symbolic Language: Towards a Post-Theodical Understanding of the Problem of Evil' (169–84); Michael Funk Deckard and Mindy Makant, 'The Fault of Forgiveness: Fragility and Memory of Evil in Volf and Ricœur' (185–202), Mathew Yaw, '*Circulus Vitiosus Existentiae*: Ricœur's Circular Hermeneutics of Evil' (203–20).
[5] Courtney, 'Reading Ciphers with Jaspers and Ricœur'.
[6] Henriksen, *Finitude and Theological Anthropology*, XV.

article.[7] To explain why Ricœur gives priority to philosophical anthropology over ethics, Schaafsma notes that for Ricœur, ethics begins too late and does not penetrate to the fundamentals of being human, a penetration which 'is the precondition for speaking about evil in a meaningful way'.[8] But Schaafsma's focus in the article is not primarily on this Ricœurian distinction, which in fact only takes up a few paragraphs.

Only one article stands out as an exception to this general blindness about Ricœur's explicit aim. Jean-Luc Amalric points out that 'the originality of [*Philosophy of the Will*] resides in its decision to develop an approach to evil and the bad will which categorically rejects any reduction of evil to finitude', and that 'the central thesis of the book is to affirm the existence of a fundamental discontinuity between *finitude and guilt*'. Amalric also notes that, although the entire philosophical tradition 'has always tried to *reduce evil to finitude*', Ricœur places the blame for the contemporary confusion at the feet of Kierkegaard.[9] But the article's main purpose is to delineate Ricœur's conception of evil, so Amalric does not investigate Ricœur's distinction beyond observing that 'the whole methodical arrangement of the *Philosophy of the Will* can ... be construed as an attempt to dissociate finitude and guilt'.[10]

This chapter and the next fill the lacuna in scholarship by gathering all the early Ricœur has to say about distinguishing finitude and evil. I argue that for Ricœur, finitude must be grasped in its primordial essence, prior (ontologically, not temporally) to its corruption, if either finitude or evil is to be understood. Ricœur's method for distinguishing them is twofold. First, he appeals to the ideal implied every time a situation is criticised as evil or wrong, an ideal retrieved by the productive power of the imagination in discovering the real. We could not call something bad unless we could imagine how it should be instead. Second, he appeals to the experience of guilt as containing, in its very essence, the feeling that we could have done otherwise. This feeling reveals the freedom at the root of every evil act.

A brief prefatory note about terminology. At times I will treat the words 'evil', 'sin', and 'guilt' as if they were synonymous. While their nuances are important at certain points, Ricœur himself often uses them

---

[7] Petruschka Schaafsma, 'Philosophical Anthropology against Objectification. Reconsidering Ricœur's Fallible Man', *International Journal of Philosophy and Theology*, 75, no. 2 (2014): 152–68.
[8] Schaafsma, 'Philosophical Anthropology against Objectification', 156–7.
[9] Amalric, 'Finitude, Culpability, and Suffering', 179, 184, 185–6.
[10] Amalric, 'Finitude, Culpability, and Suffering', 187.

interchangeably,[11] because his focus is zoomed out to what they have in common: the idea that something is wrong. This is clear because he will occasionally use an umbrella term for all three, 'the fault' (*la faute*). Concerning this, one of his translators writes: 'this term reflects Ricœur's basic intuition of a world out of kilter, of basic disruption marking all existence. In conversation Ricœur has stated that he had sought the most neutral term which would express this sense of radical disruption which means that all is not right with humanity'.[12] In addition to this definition, we must note that *la faute*, like 'finitude', 'existence', and 'ontological', has a strictly anthropological meaning in Ricœur, in keeping with the philosophical conventions of the period. It refers only to evil found in the human subject, not to evil encountered or experienced in the world independently of human interaction.

Although terms like 'evil' and 'guilt' have a theological origin, they were widely used in philosophical discourse in Ricœur's time without reference to their theological dimension. It is in fact part of Ricœur's project to highlight all that is necessarily implied when philosophers casually use these words, and their unavoidable theological connotations. But for Ricœur this does not disqualify them as philosophical terms; rather, he insists that philosophy must treat them as 'symbols', a concept I shall explain in Chapter 7.[13] For now suffice it to define a symbol as: an idea from outside philosophy that nourishes philosophical thought.

TYPOLOGY OF CONFUSION

'More than any other notion', Ricœur writes, 'finitude is that to which guilt tends to be reduced'.[14] Before expounding Ricœur's own way of distinguishing the two, we shall survey the confusion as he sees it. Not only will this enable us to understand the problem to which Ricœur is responding, it will also provide its own valuable insights into Ricœur's own perspective.

---

[11] Consider, for example, the book titles: *Finitude and 'Guilt'*, and *The Symbolism of 'Evil'*, the latter of which is one part of the former.
[12] 'Translator's Introduction', in Ricœur, *Freedom and Nature*, xxxv.
[13] See the section on 'Ricœurian Symbols: How Theology Inspires Philosophy' in Chapter 7 below.
[14] Paul Ricœur, *Husserl: An Analysis of His Phenomenology*, trans. Edward Ballard and Lester Embree (Evanston: Northwestern University Press, 1967), 231. 'La finitude est par priorité la notion sur laquelle tend à se rebattre la culpabilité' (Paul Ricœur, *À l'école de la phénoménologie* [Paris: Vrin, 1998], 83–4).

How and why, then, is finitude confused with sin, evil, and guilt? Throughout the 1940s and 1950s Ricœur identifies a number of types of confusion without ever thematising them. I argue that his criticism takes four overlapping but distinct forms:

1) Philosophy, wishing to construct a pure ontology of unchanging essences, makes sin *ontologically essential* rather than *historically contingent*.
2) Philosophy, seeking an excuse for failure, makes sin an inevitable feature of human existence, thereby assimilating evil to finitude.
3) Philosophy, disappointed by its epistemological limitations, attributes these to fault, thereby assimilating finitude to evil.
4) Philosophy, perceiving problems in the world, blames them on something naturally good, confusing its corruption with its essence.

Although these categories are in no particular order, certain subgroupings are possible. The first two have different *motivations* but lead to the same *result*: evil is made a part of finitude. The same applies to the last two in which finitude is made a part of evil. Ultimately, however, all these types of confusion 'arrive at the same point' for Ricœur.[15]

CONFUSION 1: 'ONTOLOGICAL GUILT'

The first source of the conflation between finitude and evil lies in philosophy's desire to understand everything in light of the unchanging structures of being, and its resistance to anything historical or accidental ('ontic' in Heideggerian terminology) that would contaminate these structures. A historical 'fall' which introduces guilt into human reality as an accidental feature is in this sense a contamination of the desired methodological purity. According to Ricœur,

> Philosophy would very much like to … extract a purely rational understanding from [the experience of guilt] which would equate fault or error with suffering and death and even reabsorb it into finitude by assimilating it as a 'limit-situation'…. Philosophy tends to reduce the event of guilt to a structure homogenous with other structures of the voluntary and the involuntary.'[16]

---

[15] My translation: 'À une époque où d'autres réduisent le mal à la finitude, la confusion inverse ne ramène-t-elle pas au même point?' (Ricœur, *Lectures 2*, 248).

[16] Ricœur, *Husserl*, 229–30. 'La philosophie voudrait bien … extraire une compréhension purement rationnelle qui alignerait la faute sur la souffrance et la mort, et même la résorbait dans la finitude, en l'assimilant à une "situation-limite"; … la philosophie tend à *réduire* l'aspect événementiel de la culpabilité à une structure homogène aux autres structures du volontaire et de l'involontaire' (Ricœur, *À l'école de la phénoménologie*, 82).

Confusion 1: 'Ontological Guilt'

That is why 'classical existentialism' (as Ricœur puts it) makes guilt ontological, a structural element of 'the human condition', essential and not accidental to human nature.

Ricœur's parade example of this problem is his great mentor, Karl Jaspers; in fact, arguably all his other disagreements with Jaspers have their root here. He criticises Jaspers for making 'the fault' one of many 'limit situations' that mark the ontological relation between human existence (Existenz) and Transcendence: 'In contrast to the whole Christian tradition, which conceives guilt only as *fall*, that is to say, as a debasement with respect to ..., as a *lost* primordial innocence, Jaspers derives guilt from the primitive, unfathomable, unchosen constitution of Existenz. Guilt is that very limitation of Existenz which is espoused by freedom.'[17]

In addition to Jaspers, Ricœur finds this essentialisation of guilt in Jean-Paul Sartre's book *Being and Nothingness*, because Sartre makes guilt an unavoidable consequence of the existence of other people. Since there are always other people – I am born into a world which always already contains others – and since I am superfluous (*de trop*) to them, my existence is always already a guilty existence, and I feel it as such in the light of the gaze of the Other:

It is before the Other that I am *guilty*. I am guilty first when beneath the Other's look I experience my alienation and my nakedness as a fall from grace which I must assume. This is the meaning of the famous line from Scripture: 'They knew that they were naked.' Again I am guilty when in turn I look at the Other, because by the very fact of my own self-assertion I constitute him as an object and as an instrument, and I cause him to experience that same alienation which he must now assume. Thus original sin is my upsurge in a world where there are others; and whatever may be my further relations with others, these relations will be only variations on the original theme of my guilt.[18]

---

[17] Ricœur, 'The Relation of Jaspers' Philosophy to Religion', 632. 'Contrairement à toute la tradition chrétienne, qui ne pense la faute que comme *chute*, c'est-à-dire comme déchéance à partir de ..., comme innocence primordiale *perdue*, Jaspers tire la faute du côté de la constitution primitive insondable, non choisie, de l'existence. La faute c'est la limitation même de l'existence, assumée par la liberté' (Ricœur, 'Philosophie et religion chez Karl Jaspers', 227).

[18] Jean-Paul Sartre, *Being and Nothingness: An Essay on Phenomenological Ontology* (London: Methuen, 1957), 410. Italics original: 'C'est en face de l'autre que je suis *coupable*. Coupable d'abord lorsque, sous son regard, j'éprouve mon aliénation et ma nudité comme une déchéance que je dois assumer; c'est le sens du fameux: "Ils connurent qu'ils étaient nus" de l'Ecriture. Coupable en outre, lorsque, à mon tour, je regarde autrui, parce que, du fait même de mon affirmation de moi-même, je le constitue comme objet et comme instrument, et je fais venir à lui cette aliénation qu'il devra assumer. Ainsi, le péché originel, c'est mon surgissement dans un monde où il y a l'autre et, quelles que

Sartre appears to take no interest in the narrative context of the cited biblical passage. Later we shall explore Ricœur's retrieval of that context as emphasising the *event-like* nature of guilt, establishing a time before Adam and Eve 'knew they were naked'. For now, let us merely note that guilt, for Sartre, is an essential and not an accidental feature of human existence.

Ricœur's engagement with Sartrean guilt is found in two places: an article originally published in 1951, and the unpublished manuscript of a series of lectures given in English at Union Theological Seminary in 1958, titled 'Anthropology of Religion in the Philosophy of Existence'.[19] In the manuscript, when introducing *Being and Nothingness* to his students, Ricœur refers to Sartre's above quoted passage as positing a 'fundamental guilt', that is, an irreducible element of being human. For Sartre (Ricœur says), 'as I am always under the look of the other … I am always guilty. The ultimate implication of this atheism is the guilt without any forgiveness, which is a kind of return to the tragic interpretation of guilt'.[20] However, Sartre's description of the gaze is reductive; it 'does not express the essence of every gaze; it supposes that it is always a stranger who interrupts my solitude'.[21] Sartre's account is not and could not be pure description of the gaze, because 'pure description cannot but clarify a deeper revealing intention'.[22] Other people are only an unavoidable source of guilt for Sartre because he has no sense of a fraternity between human beings that comes from the Christian doctrine that we are children of God. Because we are 'not created as sons of the same father … the presence of the other is the beginning of my fall in the world, and thus of

---

soient mes relations ultérieures avec l'autre, elles ne seront que des variations sur le thème originel de ma culpabilité' (Jean-Paul Sartre, *L'être et le néant: essai d'ontologie phénoménologique* [Paris: Gallimard, 1943], 450). On Sartre's use here of the term 'original sin' and its debt to Augustine, see Kate Kirkpatrick, *Sartre on Sin: Between Being and Nothingness* (Oxford: Oxford University Press, 2017).

[19] Archives Ricœur / Fonds Ricœur, Inventaire 1, dossier 27, 'Anthropology and Religion in the Philosophy of Existence', Lectures at Union Theological Seminary (1958), feuillets 4057–101. We shall return to these lectures in more detail in Chapter 8 below.

[20] Archives Ricœur / Fonds Ricœur, Inv. 1, dossier 27, 'Anthropology and Religion in the Philosophy of Existence', Lectures at Union Theological Seminary (1958), f. 4098-b.

[21] My translation: 'n'exprime pas l'essence de tout regard; elle suppose que c'est toujours un étranger qui fait irruption dans ma solitude' (Paul Ricœur, 'Note sur l'existentialisme et la foi chrétienne', *Revue de Théologie et de Philosophie* 56, no. 4 [2006]: 312).

[22] My translation: 'La description ne peut qu'éclairer une intention révélante plus profonde' (Ricœur, 'Note sur l'existentialisme et la foi chrétienne').

my guilt'.[23] Guilt emerges through our relationship with others because others are seen only as competitors, not as brothers and sisters. In short, 'with Sartre, the description of the gaze is inseparable from a general project of a world without God. If human beings are absolutely discontinuous centres of existence that no creation reconnects, the mutual gaze can only be a battle'.[24]

CONFUSION 2: AN ALIBI FOR FAILURE

A second cause of the finitude/guilt conflation, for Ricœur, is the tendency to treat failure as if it was an inevitable result of our finitude. Both Jaspers and Ricœur agree in seeing this tendency as common throughout the history of philosophy. When responding to Ricœur's critique, Jaspers willingly accepts that he himself 'connect[s] guilt with man's finite nature'; but he defends himself by saying that in so doing he is 'in harmony with the entire philosophical tradition'.[25] But for Ricœur this is not proof of validity; rather, this connection within the tradition is an *aberration* to which philosophy is inclined. Existentialists like Jaspers, he writes, 'proceed no differently than Plotinus and Spinoza: for them also finitude is the ultimate philosophical alibi for guilt, a temptation which seems inherent in a philosophical treatment of the notion of guilt'.[26]

Greek tragedy is another example of treating failure as built into the human constitution. In tragic dramas, Ricœur explains, the gods have inflicted on humans a flawed attitude that leads to 'predestination to evil'.[27] Protagonists are led astray in a way that 'is not a punishment for

---

[23] Archives Ricœur / Fonds Ricœur, inv. 1, dossier 27, 'Anthropology and Religion in the Philosophy of Existence', Lectures at Union Theological Seminary (1958), f. 4098-b.
[24] My translation: 'Chez Sartre, la description du regard est inséparable du projet général d'un monde sans Dieu. Si les êtres humains sont les centres d'existence absolument discontinus que ne relie nulle création, le regard mutuel ne peut être qu'une lutte' (Ricœur, 'Note sur l'existentialisme et la foi chrétienne', 312).
[25] Karl Jaspers, 'Reply to My Critics', in *The Philosophy of Karl Jaspers*, ed. Schilpp, 780. Jaspers denies rather that he 'veil[s guilt] as unavoidable and therefore as innocent necessity' (Jaspers, 'Reply to My Critics'). We need not arbitrate between Ricœur and Jaspers here.
[26] Ricœur, *Husserl*, 230. 'procèdent pas autrement que Plotin et Spinoza: pour elles aussi la finitude est l'ultime alibi philosophique de la culpabilité; cette tantation [sic] paraît inhérente à un traitement philosophique de la notion de culpabilité' (Ricœur, *À l'école de la phénoménologie*, 82).
[27] Paul Ricœur, *The Symbolism of Evil*, trans. Emerson Buchanan (Boston: Beacon, 1969), 218. 'prédestination au mal' (Ricœur, *Finitude et culpabilité*, 43c).

some fault; it is the fault itself, the origin of the fault'.[28] They fail because the gods wanted them to fail, which is why their failure evokes from the audience not condemnation, but pity.

But for Ricœur, it is a violation of the principle of human freedom if we attempt to excuse guilt on the basis of finitude. Guilt is understood only through the feeling of *remorse*, whose basis is the knowledge that 'I could have acted and been otherwise'. This 'conviction of a possibility of innocence each time *lost*' is the very 'meaning of guilt'.[29] That is why Greek tragedy is in fact philosophically unthinkable in the end, a spectacle rather than speculation. 'If the ethical moment in evil is to appear', Ricœur writes, 'there must be at least an indication of a dawn of responsibility, of avoidable fault, and guilt must begin to be distinguished from finitude. But this distinction tends to be muted, annulled by predestination'.[30]

Ricœur blames Kierkegaard, existentialism's greatest precursor, as the modern origin of this 'distortion' (*gauchissement*) of the idea of sin.[31] The true meaning of guilt as the result of a free choice, he says, is 'obscured already in Kierkegaard, a little more in Jaspers, and completely in Heidegger'.[32] Indeed, it is one of the greatest points of similarity between Jaspers and Heidegger that guilt becomes 'inevitable, constitutive'; it therefore 'loses its *moral* character of degradation and takes on an *ontological* significance; sin is limitation itself, the narrowness of existence; but since existence only deepens itself by limiting itself, freedom and fault become indistinguishable'.[33] Without its '*moral* meaning' which is 'its relation to the will', guilt 'inevitably tends to become a misfortune of existence'.[34]

---

[28] Ricœur, *Symbolism of Evil*, 214. 'pas une punition de la faute, mais la faute même, l'origine de la faute' (Ricœur, *Finitude et culpabilité*, 426).

[29] My translation: 'j'aurais pu agir et être autrement ... la conviction d'une possibilité d'innocence chaque fois *perdue* ... sens de la culpabilité' (Ricœur, *Marcel et Jaspers*, 144).

[30] Ricœur, *Symbolism of Evil*, 222. 'Pour qu'apparaisse le moment éthique du mal; il faut au moins que s'esquisse une aube de responsabilité, de faute évitable, et que la culpabilité commence de se distinguer de la finitude; mais cette distinction tend a [*sic*] être amortie, annulée par la prédestination' (Ricœur, *Finitude et culpabilité*, 435).

[31] Ricœur, *Marcel et Jaspers*, 143.

[32] My translation: 'oblitéré déjà chez Kierkegaard, un peu plus chez Jaspers, et tout à fait chez Heidegger' (Ricœur, *Marcel et Jaspers*, 144).

[33] My translation: 'inévitable, constitutive ... perd son caractère *moral* de déchéance pour assumer une signification *ontologique*; le péché est la limitation même, l'étroitesse de l'existence; mais comme l'existence ne s'approfondit qu'en se limitant, la liberté et la faute deviennent indiscernables' (Ricœur, *Marcel et Jaspers*).

[34] My translation: 'son sens *moral*, c'est-à-dire son rapport avec la volonté ... elle tend invinciblement à devenir un malheur de l'existence' (Dufrenne and Ricœur, *Karl Jaspers et la philosophie de l'existence*, 191).

CONFUSION 3: LIMITATIONS AS FAULT

A third confusion Ricœur identifies makes the opposite mistake; instead of seeing failure as part of our finitude, it sees our finitude as already a failure. 'A long philosophic tradition', Ricœur writes, 'which attained its most perfect expression in Leibniz, would maintain that the limitation proper to creatures is the occasion of moral evil. Considered as the occasion of moral evil, this limitation would even merit the name of metaphysical evil'.[35] Now, there is a sense in which this is undeniable: if we fail, it is because we are finite. But *Fallible Man* is aimed precisely at avoiding this over-generalisation according to which finitude itself becomes *blamed* for failure. 'Our whole preceding analysis', Ricœur writes in the conclusion, 'tends to rectify this ancient proposition in a precise way: the idea of limitation as such cannot bring us to the threshold of moral evil'.[36] The sheer fact that we have limits is not a fault; simply not-being-God is not an offence. By contrast, the particular limitation unique to human beings (the 'finite/infinite disproportion' that we investigated in Chapter 4) is the cause not of failure, but of its possibility, which Ricœur names 'fallibility'.

Ricœur once again turns to Jaspers's philosophy to illustrate this problem. Jaspers makes it a fault that we inevitably fail to attain universal and timeless truth. But for Ricœur, that we will never have total knowledge or a perfect philosophical system is due, not to our failings, but to our finite nature, the fact that we are not God. However, this does not deny the epistemological effect of sin. Sin intensifies to the point of distortion what was originally only an incompletion, says Ricœur: 'the fault redoubles (without constituting) the limits from which Existenz suffers, bounded by its position in the world'.[37] Employing a beautiful French pun, he adds: 'the fault makes biased [*partial*] what might have been merely incomplete [*partiel*]', namely, our philosophical worldview.[38]

---

[35] Ricœur, *Fallible Man*, 133. 'Une longue tradition philosophique, qui a atteint son expression la plus parfaite avec Leibniz, veut que la limitation des créatures soit l'occasion du mal moral' (Ricœur, *Finitude et culpabilité*, 184).

[36] Ricœur, *Fallible Man*, 133. 'Toute notre analyse antérieure tend à corriger cette proposition ancienne en un sens précis: l'idée de limitation, prise comme telle, est insuffisante pour approcher du seuil du mal moral' (Ricœur, *Finitude et culpabilité*, 184).

[37] My translation: 'La faute redouble (sans les constituer pourtant) les limites dont souffre l'existence, bornée par son poste même dans le monde' (Dufrenne and Ricœur, *Karl Jaspers et la philosophie de l'existence*, 377).

[38] My translation: 'La faute rend partiel ce qui eût pu n'être que partiel' (Dufrenne and Ricœur, *Karl Jaspers et la philosophie de l'existence*).

Ricœur is not alone in refusing to equate finitude with failure. In fact, here we find him joining in the chorus of twentieth-century accounts of finitude which we surveyed in Chapter 4, for which it was very important not to define finitude primarily as lack or negation of the infinite.[39] However, Ricœur has his own way of underscoring what Emmanuel Falque calls the 'positiveness of finitude'[40] without needing to resort to a denial of the human's access to – and participation in – the infinite. Finitude is undoubtedly positive for Ricœur, a natural good ('What is finite is altogether positive; only the infinite *lacks* an outline'[41]). But for him this does not demand an affirmation of Foucault's 'fundamental finitude which rests only on its own fact'.[42] To say that finitude is positive need not imply it is a standalone category without any inherent relation to the infinite. Why should positivity imply self-sufficiency? Why should a *dialectical relation* to the infinite imply *imperfection*? The positive reality of finitude is not nullified by any infinite to which it is related, any more than the positive reality of the world is nullified when it is seen as created by God.

What we learn from Ricœur is that philosophy may think the infinite without thereby seeing the finite as a lack or an incompleteness, as if the very existence of an infinite threatened the integrity of the finite. Ricœur agrees with all those who, following Heidegger, see finitude as having its own positivity. But why should this mean there is no infinite? Why can the finite not be satisfied with its finitude while at the same time recognising the presence of an infinite that enfolds it? As I have said elsewhere, 'A positive finite number in mathematics does not, by its positivity, abolish a positive infinite number. On the contrary, an infinite number may contain any finite number without destroying either its own positivity or the positivity of the finite number. Why should the two be seen as a threat to each other's internal consistency?'[43] The existence of an infinite in no way

---

[39] See Chapter 4 above, section headed 'No Such Thing: Twentieth-Century Objections to the Infinite'.

[40] Emmanuel Falque, *The Metamorphosis of Finitude: An Essay on Birth and Resurrection* (New York: Fordham University Press, 2012), 18; 'la *positivité de la finitude*' (Emmanuel Falque, *Triduum philosophique: le passeur de Gethsémani. Métamorphose de la finitude. Les noces de l'agneau* [Éditions du Cerf, 2016], 195).

[41] Ricœur, *Freedom and Nature*, 447. Italics original: 'Ce qui est fini est tout positif; seul l'infini *manque* de contour' (Ricœur, *Le volontaire et l'involontaire*, 420).

[42] My translation: 'finitude fondamentale qui ne repose que sur son propre fait' (cited in Greisch, *L'arbre de vie et l'arbre du savoir*, 19).

[43] Barnabas Aspray, 'Transforming Heideggerian Finitude? Following Pathways Opened by Falque', in Martin Koci and Jason Alvis, eds., *Transforming the Theological Turn: Phenomenology with Emmanuel Falque* (Lanham: Rowman & Littlefield, 2020), 170.

implies that finitude must be seen as a lack or an incompletion. Finitude may have its own kind of completion that is different from the completion of infinity. This is precisely the kind of finitude that belongs to creation in Christian theology, about which Chapters 7, 8, and 9 shall expound in more detail.

CONFUSION 4: BLAMING THE NATURALLY GOOD

The third confusion, that of calling 'limitations as such' an evil, is one instance of the fourth and final confusion identified by Ricœur, which is critiqued in the Latin phrase *abusus non tollit usum* ('The abuse does not abolish the use'), and the English expression 'throwing the baby out with the bathwater'. It consists in mistaking the *corruption* of a thing for the *thing itself*, and thus condemning the thing as if it was bad in essence. Consider these examples: the existence of a bad government does not mean it would be better to have no government; alcoholism does not mean all consumption of alcohol is bad; an Islamic terrorist is not representative of Islam.

I contend that Ricœur's entire philosophical career can be characterised as the effort to seek the good essence behind the corrupt appearance. He rarely dismisses any philosophy in its totality, but with remarkable consistency engages it in depth to retrieve the positive insight at its core. He did this with Freudian psychoanalysis, structuralism, analytic philosophy, Marxism, and many others. In Chapters 1 and 2 we saw him do it with French reflexive philosophy and existentialism. It is this impulse which makes him the famous mediator between seemingly opposing philosophies, rather than a polemicist siding with one against the other.

To begin with, Ricœur faults Kant for failing to seek the positive origin of the distinctively human passions: the lusts for *possession*, *power*, and *glory*. Kant began to reflect on these passions as already corrupted, seeing them only in their historical reality as the cause of violence. But Ricœur, convinced that these passions must be distortions of originally good desire, insists on going upstream. Where Kant 'puts himself at once before the *fallen* forms of human affectivity', Ricœur says, 'a philosophical anthropology must be more demanding; it must attempt to restore the primordial state that is at the root of the fallen'.[44]

---

[44] Ricœur, *Fallible Man*, 111. 'Kant se place d'emblée en face des figures déchues de l'affectivité humaine ... une anthropologie philosophique doit être plus exigeante; elle doit procéder à la restauration de l'originaire qui est à la racine du déchu' (Ricœur, *Finitude et culpabilité*, 159).

With the lust for possession first of all, Ricœur writes: 'we must first try to understand the passions of having – greed, avarice, envy, etc. – by reference to a possibly innocent quest for having'.[45] Ricœur also criticises his early mentor Gabriel Marcel for this confusion. Marcel's book *Being and Having* was motivated largely from a polemics against the lust to 'have' things, including ideas and knowledge, in favour of the receptive willingness to 'be' constituted by them in a non-controlling or possessive way.[46] Although Ricœur does not mention Marcel, it is hard not to hear a gentle criticism when he writes: 'it should be possible to draw a dividing line that cuts not between being and having, but between unjust having and a just possession'.[47] Employing the productive faculty of the imagination, Ricœur says that 'having' cannot be intrinsically bad because 'I cannot *imagine* a suspension of having that would be so radical as to deprive the I of any anchorage in the "mine".'[48]

Secondly, in the desire for power, Ricœur admits it is hard not to see an unambiguous evil and the cause of enormous suffering throughout history. Furthermore, the abuse of authority found in all institutions is among the ills to which our age is most sensitive. But, Ricœur insists, we cannot call these things 'abuses' if we are unable to identify their rightful 'use' in an originally good relation: 'authority is not bad in itself.... I could not understand power as evil if I could not imagine an innocent destination of power by comparison to which it is fallen'.[49]

Thirdly, in the case of desiring honour or glory, Ricœur admits, 'nowhere is it more difficult to distinguish the perverse form from the constituting intention', because it seems to have nothing but vanity behind it; yet he still insists: 'nowhere, however, is it more necessary to summon the alienated modalities of the I to its primordial essence'.[50] What lies behind

---

[45] Ricœur, *Fallible Man*, 113. 'Je dois donc d'abord tenter de comprendre les passions de l'avoir – avidité, avarice, envie, etc. – par référence à une requête d'avoir qui eût pu être innocente' (Ricœur, *Finitude et culpabilité*, 161).

[46] Marcel, *Being and Having*; Marcel, *Être et avoir*.

[47] Ricœur, *Fallible Man*, 115. 'Une ligne de partage doit pouvoir être tracée, qui passe non entre l'être et l'avoir, mais entre l'avoir injuste et une juste possession' (Ricœur, *Finitude et culpabilité*, 163–4).

[48] Ricœur, *Fallible Man*, 115. Italics original: 'Je ne puis *imaginer* une suspension de l'avoir si radicale qu'elle ôterait tout point d'appui du moi dans le mien' (Ricœur, *Finitude et culpabilité*, 163).

[49] Ricœur, *Fallible Man*, 118–20. 'L'autorité n'est pas en soi mauvaise.... Je ne comprendrais pas le pouvoir comme mal si je ne pouvais imaginer une destination innocente du pouvoir à partir de quoi il est déchu' (Ricœur, *Finitude et culpabilité*, 166–9).

[50] Ricœur, *Fallible Man*, 120. 'Nulle part il n'est plus difficile de distinguer la figure perverse de l'intention constituante.... Nulle part pourtant il n'est plus nécessaire d'en appeler des modalités aliénées à l'essence originaire' (Ricœur, *Finitude et culpabilité*, 169–70).

the distortion is the simple need for mutual recognition and respect. In a passage that foreshadows his Gifford Lectures given twenty-six years later,[51] Ricœur writes: 'My existence for myself is dependent on this constitution in another's opinion. My "self", it may be said, is received from the opinion of others that establishes it.'[52]

Ricœur finds a fourth example of mistaking the abuse for the essence in the opposite errors of Karl Jaspers and Jean Nabert concerning the classical philosophical problem of the 'one and the many' (one of only two core problems in philosophy, Ricœur once told a prospective student).[53] It is a fact that human beings do not all see the world in the same way, even though we inhabit the same world. Thus the 'oneness' of truth is multiplied through the diversity of perspectives on reality. But in addition to diversity of viewpoints there is also disagreement over mutually exclusive beliefs, leading to conflict and opposition. For Jaspers, the *evil of disagreement* is absorbed into finitude; universal truth becomes impossible to attain, and each individual is left to find his or her own truth without attempting to correlate it to the truths found by others. But for Jean Nabert, the *innocent finitude of diversity* is absorbed into evil; the multiplicity of minds, perspectives, cultures, races, and religions becomes itself a sign of fallenness. 'In contrast to the many doctrines [like Jaspers's] which reduce evil to finitude', Ricœur says, 'Jean Nabert tends rather to reduce finitude to evil'.[54]

However, for Ricœur, the fact that there are diverse perspectives on the world contains elements of both evil and finitude that must be disentangled from one another, something both Jaspers and Nabert have failed to do in different ways. 'A philosophy of evil', he declares, must distinguish between 'the original plurality of personal vocations *and* the jealousy that isolates and opposes consciousnesses'.[55] That is, it must

---

[51] Ricœur, *Oneself as Another*; Paul Ricœur, *Soi-même comme un autre* (Paris: Éditions du Seuil, 2015).
[52] Ricœur, *Fallible Man*, 121. 'Mon existence pour moi-même est tributaire de cette constitution dans l'opinion d'autrui ; mon "Soi" – si j'ose dire – je le reçois de l'opinion d'autrui' (Ricœur, *Finitude et culpabilité*, 170).
[53] 'Listen, little one, philosophy is very simple. There are two problems: the one and the many, and the same and the other' (My translation: 'Écoute, petit, la philosophie, c'est très simple. Il y a deux problèmes: l'un et le multiple, et le même et l'autre' [Dosse, *Paul Ricœur*, 254]).
[54] My translation: 'A l'inverse de tant de doctrines qui réduisent le mal à la finitude, Jean Nabert tendrait plutôt à réduire la finitude au mal' (Ricœur, *Lectures 2*, 244).
[55] My translation: 'C'est une tâche de la philosophie du mal de distinguer ... la pluralité originaire des vocations personnelles *et* la jalousie qui isole et oppose les consciences' (Ricœur, *Lectures 2*, 248).

distinguish 'between the "original" – and originally good – principle of the *difference* of consciousnesses *and* the "historical" principle by which this difference "suddenly" becomes each consciousness's *preference* for itself by which it pursues the death of the other'.[56] This distinction would lead to the insight that the uniqueness of every individual philosophy is due *both* to finitude *and* sin in different degrees: first to finitude 'because [a philosophy] is the work of a person whose life is short, whose character gives shape to everything, and whose information is limited'; and secondly to sin 'because their passions give a pretext for altering faith by opinion and confusing the more-than-reason with the less-than-reason'.[57] Note that, according to Ricœur, there are truths above even uncorrupted finite reason, but that sin confuses these with irrationality.

Ricœur seems to be unique in this approach, at least in his own understanding. Every one of his typical interlocutors seems subject to this accusation of his, even those who were his greatest influences. Marcel escapes with the lightest criticism, but Ricœur does not derive the idea for this distinction between finitude and evil from Marcel, since Marcel wrote nothing about it. We therefore appear to be looking at an element of Ricœur's thought which is without precedent.

In summary, what have we learned about Ricœur's view of finitude by attending to his critiques of other philosophies? First, that to be guilty is not part of human nature as such; rather, guilt is superadded. Secondly, sin must be committed freely or it is not sin; ethics implicitly presupposes a will free to 'do otherwise'. Thirdly, to be a limited, finite being is not itself a fault or the punishment for a fault; finitude is naturally good and positive. Fourthly, the corruption of something always masks an originally good essence. Everything in Ricœur's philosophy is therefore bent on seeing evil as an aberration and not part of the natural order. Finitude in all its aspects, including limitation, is *originally good*, and any guilt it now carries is a result of *free choice*. Evil is a parasitic, unnecessary deviation which cannot be rationalised into a fundamental ontology or called inevitable because it is a distortion or a corruption of something more basically good.

---

[56] My translation: ' entre le principe "originaire" – et originairement bon – de la *différence* des consciences *et* le principe "historique" par lequel cette différence devient "soudain" la *préférence* que chaque conscience a pour soi et à partir de laquelle elle poursuit la mort de l'autre' (Ricœur, *Lectures 2*, 249).

[57] My translation: 'parce qu'elle est l'œuvre d'un homme dont la vie est courte, le caractère impérieux et l'information bornée, et parce que ses passions prennent prétexte de son corps même pour altérer la foi par l'opinion et confondre le plus que raison avec le moins que raison' (Dufrenne and Ricœur, *Karl Jaspers et la philosophie de l'existence*, 378).

OBJECTIONS TO THE POSSIBILITY OF DISTINGUISHING THEM

Finitude and evil must be distinguished because in Ricœur's eyes they are almost ubiquitously confused by twentieth-century philosophers. But more importantly, they must be distinguished in order for ethical discourse based on an idea of the Good to begin. 'A philosophy of evil', Ricœur wrote, 'is tasked with distinguishing evil *and* finitude'.[58] Although Ricœur's radical and innovative proposal is mentioned in many of his early writings, the 'task' he sets himself takes fullest form in Part II of his *Philosophy of the Will*, to which he gives the title *Finitude and Guilt*. Ten years later he explains the reason for this title:

> My problem was to distinguish between finitude and guilt. I had the impression, or even the conviction, that these two terms tended to be identified in classical existentialism at the cost of both experiences.... This is why I chose *Finitude and Guilt* as a general title for the two volumes of which I spoke and the problem was that of their difference and of their connection.[59]

However, an objection immediately imposes itself: on what basis can philosophy reliably describe a perfect primordial finitude of which we have no experience, in order to identify what in us is due to evil and contrast it to what would be the case even if, in a hypothetical universe, we had never sinned? In other words, is Ricœur's task feasible?

Ricœur has no illusions about the difficulty of the project. The entry of sin into the world, he says, means that 'the greatness *and* the guilt of man are inextricably mingled, so that it is impossible to say: here is the primordial man, there is the evil result of his contingent history'.[60] Therefore to attempt to 'reverse engineer' sinful humanity, separating evil aspects from good, is like trying to separate the ingredients of a soup that has been blended. Worse still, our fallenness brings a blindness of confusion, meaning that the flaw itself impairs our ability to understand it. We are like an insane person trying to distinguish sane from insane thoughts.

---

[58] My translation: 'C'est une tâche de la philosophie du mal de distinguer mal *et* finitude' (Ricœur, *Lectures 2*, 248).
[59] Paul Ricœur, 'Appendix: From Existentialism to the Philosophy of Language', in *The Rule of Metaphor: Multi-Disciplinary Studies of the Creation of Meaning in Language*, trans. David Pellauer (London: Routledge, 1978), 372–3. Original French not available.
[60] Ricœur, *Symbolism of Evil*, 247. Italics in translation: 'La grandeur et la culpabilité de l'homme sont inextricablement mêlées sans qu'on puisse dire: ici est l'homme originaire, là est le maléfice de son histoire contingente' (Ricœur, *Finitude et culpabilité*, 461).

I shall consider four overlapping objections to Ricœur's project from both philosophy and theology, before turning to examine Ricœur's anticipated response to each.

First, according to Jacques Ellul, a French Protestant theologian and Ricœur's contemporary, what Ricœur proposes is impossible from a Christian perspective. There is no trace of non-sinful finitude left in us, Ellul claims, because if there was, we would not be in need of God's saving grace – which would diminish the central importance of Jesus' death on the cross. '*Is* the world with which we are familiar the world created as God willed it?' he asks; 'Ricœur explains the nonexistence of the fall for man, but the Bible tells us about a total damage to the creation.... We find no answer in Ricœur.'[61] The effects of the fall must be total in order for the grace of God in Christ to be total. Ellul continues:

> The whole doctrine of Ricœur, like all the doctrines which minimize the seriousness of the fall and of man's evil, minimizes the work of Jesus Christ by the same token.... If the fall and evil were not totally serious, would God have gone to the extreme of this unthinkable sacrifice of his Son? ... Hence, there is no longer any antecedent innocence remaining in existence, for that innocence permits some economy in God's work.[62]

We shall see later that Ellul's reading of Ricœur is inaccurate, since Ricœur neither 'explains the nonexistence' nor 'minimises the seriousness' of the fall (why else would he write an entire book on it?). Ellul also seems to have forgotten that Ricœur is writing philosophy, not theology. Nonetheless Ellul's fundamental objection, that total depravity denies the possibility of any non-sinful remainder, deserves attention because if it is true theologically, then it is true for Christians also philosophically. Theology would thus impose limits on what can be achieved from philosophy.

---

[61] Jacques Ellul, *To Will & to Do: An Ethical Research for Christians*, trans. C. Edward Hopkin (Philadelphia: Pilgrim Press, 1969), 40. Italics original: '*Est-ce que* le monde que nous connaissons *est* le monde créé tel que Dieu l'a voulu? Ricœur explique l'inexistence de la chute pour l'homme, mais la Bible nous parle d'une dégradation totale de la création.... Nous ne trouvons chez Ricœur aucune réponse' (Jacques Ellul, *Le vouloir et le faire: une critique théologique de la morale* [Geneva: Labor et Fides, 2013], 59).

[62] Ellul, *To Will & to Do*, 41. 'Toute la doctrine de Ricœur, comme toutes celles qui minimisent la chute et la gravité du mal de l'homme, minimise par là l'œuvre de Jésus-Christ.... Croit-on que si la chute et le mal n'avaient pas eu la gravité la plus totale, Dieu aurait été jusqu'à cet impensable sacrifice de donner son Fils? ... Il n'y a donc plus aucune innocence antécédente qui subsiste, car cette innocence-là permet de faire l'économie de la réalité de l'œuvre de Dieu' (Ellul, *Le vouloir et le faire*, 59).

A second Barthian objection focuses on the *epistemological* aspect of total depravity, making it impossible to have any innate understanding of unfallen existence. Ricœur describes this attitude in one of his earliest articles, published when he was only twenty-four years old.[63] After outlining two typical approaches to relating philosophy and theology, which he labels 'Thomist' and 'Barthian', Ricœur argues that the underlying cause of the difference between them is 'the problem of sin and the fall':

> The Bible teaches that God made man in his image, and that a resemblance, a similitude, a conformity to God, a 'deiformity' existed before the fall (whatever meaning one might give to this 'before'). The question is thus to know to what extent the fall altered this resemblance of man to God. 'Radically', respond Jansenists, Calvinists, Barthians: nature is totally perverted.[64]

While the focus of this passage is access to God, it implies that for 'Jansenists, Calvinists, Barthians' knowledge of pre-fallen humanity is equally impossible. The total corruption of the human by sin leaves no foothold by which we might grasp an imagined primordial paradise any more than the God who created us in that paradise. Ricœur refuses, in this article, to give a preference for one or the other position, observing merely that the question is the 'very point of rupture between the Reformation and Catholicism'.[65] But we note that even at this early stage he was asking himself how total were the effects of sin, and connecting this question to that of how philosophy and theology relate.

A third objection comes from Pierre Thévenaz, the French Swiss Barthian and friend of Ricœur's whose 'philosophy without absolutes' we encountered in Chapter 3. Thévenaz is a philosopher by trade, and explores philosophically the question of uncorrupted finitude that would be the true human 'normal'. However, as a Barthian he does not believe that philosophy can offer us any stable or meaningful answers, which

---

[63] Paul Ricœur, 'Note sur les rapports de la philosophie et du Christianisme', *Le Semeur* 38, no. 9 (1936).
[64] My translation: 'La Bible enseigne que Dieu fit l'homme à son image, et qu'il existait avant la chute (quel que soit le sens que l'on puisse donner à cet "avant") une ressemblance, une conformité, avec Dieu, une "deiformité". La question est alors de savoir jusqu'à quel point la chute a altéré cette ressemblance de l'homme avec Dieu. "Radicalement", répondent jansénistes, calvinistes, barthiens: la nature est totalement pervertie' (Ricœur, 'Note sur les rapports de la philosophie et du Christianisme', 554–5).
[65] My translation: '*au point même de rupture de la Réforme et du catholicisme*' (Ricœur, 'Note sur les rapports de la philosophie et du Christianisme', 555).

means that he intentionally leaves us with nothing but aporias and dead-ends. Although he does not reference Ricœur, his stance is worth noting since it is the philosophical counterpart to Ellul's.

In his last public address before his death in 1955, Thévenaz was asked to speak on the topic of 'the normal human' (*l'homme normal*), and to say what philosophy can teach us about 'norms' (ethical, social, etc.) for human behaviour. His response is essentially that there are no norms for human behaviour, and that it is not philosophy's job to provide them. He ridicules the idea that 'we should call for the philosopher, for the theologian, who can serve you with norms'.[66] No, he answers, 'here we venture into a field where the notion of normal no longer has *any meaning*.'[67] 'The notion of normal', he declares, 'does not interest the philosopher at all',[68] because to speak of a 'normal human' presupposes 'a human essence which would be stable, which we can access because it is eternal, we have it within us, it is only covered by a sort of envelope of imperfection, but, if we scratch it a little, we can make it reappear; and that would mean that our task is to conform ourselves to this primitive human essence'.[69] This leads, he says, to a conformism which flattens diversity, without which some of the greatest minds in history would not have been what they are. Furthermore, to speak of 'ideal norms' implies a vision of what 'should be but is no longer' (primordial paradise); but 'the philosopher is interested in what *is*, both in the domain of facts, and then in the domain beyond facts, of a fundamental metaphysical reality'.[70] And in the domain of facts, the notion of 'normal' is not philosophical but 'medical. "Pathological" is the positive notion; *it is "abnormal" which is the positive notion that responds to facts*. You can diagnose an

---

[66] My translation: 'Appelons le philosophe, appelons le théologien, qui vont vous servir des normes' (Pierre Thévenaz, 'L'homme normal', *Revue de Théologie et de Philosophie* 25, no. 3 [1975]: 207).

[67] My translation (italics original): 'Ici nous nous aventurons alors sur un plan où la notion de normal n'a plus *aucun sens*' (Pierre Thévenaz, 'L'homme normal', 208).

[68] My translation: 'La notion de normal n'intéresse absolument pas le philosophe' (Pierre Thévenaz, 'L'homme normal', 206).

[69] My translation: 'La notion d'homme normal suppose ... une essence de l'homme qui serait stable, et qu'alors nous pourrions rejoindre, parce qu'elle est éternelle, nous la portons en nous, elle est simplement couverte d'une certaine gangue de déformation, mais, en grattant un peu, nous pourrions la faire réapparaître; et alors ça voudrait dire que notre tâche est de nous conformer à cette essence primitive de l'homme' (Pierre Thévenaz, 'L'homme normal', 209).

[70] My translation: 'doit être, qui n'est pas encore.... Le philosophe s'intéresse à ce qui *est*, à la fois dans le domaine des faits, et puis dans un domaine au-delà des faits qui est celui d'une réalité métaphysique fondamentale' (Pierre Thévenaz, 'L'homme normal', 210).

illness, an illness is a fact.... It is by absence that one will define the normal, by the absence of the pathological'.[71]

In this text Thévenaz does not give reasons for rejecting the idea of a 'primitive human essence' or of 'metaphysical reality' beyond concrete facts, but it is clear, both from the context and from what we saw of his rejection of absolutes in Chapter 3, that he is no advocate of either concept. Thévenaz thus presents us with a philosophy for which the idea of a 'normal' human has no meaning, except negatively as the absence of medical or psychological anomalies. The world of illness and abnormality is the 'real' world of the 'facts', compared with which any idea of normality is an imagined chimera that makes no philosophical sense.

Finally, we turn to an objection by Heidegger, not to the possibility of the project as such, but to its possibility *as philosophy*. When Heidegger introduces his own concept of fallenness, he distinguishes it sharply from the Christian idea of moral corruption: 'Neither must we take the fallenness of *Dasein* as a "fall" from a purer and higher "primal status". Not only do we lack any experience of this ontically, but ontologically we lack any possibilities or clues for Interpreting it.'[72] The key words here are 'experience' (*Erfahrung*) and 'Interpreting' (*Interpretation*). Heidegger's objection turns on two points: the absence of any experience of a supposed innocence prior to the current state of things (note Heidegger also avoids giving any moral judgement on the current state of things), and the absence of criteria for any alternative interpretation than the one given in plain experience. For Heidegger, philosophy which sticks only to this experience can have no recourse to different 'states' of being human, past or future, primordial or eschatological. Therefore (in Jean Greisch's words), 'Heidegger underlines that only a theological anthropology seems capable of reflecting on the different "states" of the human: original innocence, fall, redemption, beatific vision.'[73]

---

[71] My translation (italics mine): 'médicale. "Pathologique", c'est la notion positive: c'est "anormal" qui est la notion positive qui répond à des faits – on peut constater la maladie, la maladie est un fait ... simplement l'indication d'une absence de symptômes maladifs.... En effet, c'est par l'absence qu'on va définir le normal, par l'absence du pathologique' (Pierre Thévenaz, 'L'homme normal', 206).

[72] Heidegger, *Being and Time*, 220. 'Die Verfallenheit des Daseins darf daher auch nicht als "Fall" aus einem reineren und höheren "Urstand" aufgefaßt werden. Davon haben wir ontisch nicht nur keine Erfahrung, sondern auch ontologisch keine Möglichkeiten und Leitfäden der Interpretation' (Heidegger, *Sein und Zeit*, 176).

[73] My translation: 'comme le souligne Heidegger, que seule une anthropologie théologique semble être à même de réfléchir sur les différents "états" de l'homme: innocence originelle, chute, rédemption, vision béatifique' (Greisch, *Paul Ricœur*, 53).

RICŒUR'S RESPONSE: WHY THE DISTINCTION IS POSSIBLE

Ricœur anticipates all these objections in his work, and as we shall see, insists that the distinction between finitude and sin not only *can* but *must* be attempted, indeed is already implicit in all ethical judgements. To know we are insane is to have still a grain of sanity left; to call anything evil is to rely, in spite of ourselves, on an understanding, however vague and undefined, of what is good. Employing the Kantian distinction between knowledge and thought, Ricœur insists that the 'first Adam' cannot be *known*, but he nonetheless insists that he can be *thought*. 'Innocence', he says, 'plays the role of the Kantian thing-in-itself: it is thought of to the extent of being posited, but it is not known'.[74]

In the introduction to *Freedom and Nature*, Part I of *Philosophy of the Will*, when Ricœur announces that he is going to 'bracket the fault' and describe the human will without evil, guilt, or morality, he raises the above objections himself. 'We could object', he begins, that such a description 'pretends to describe an innocent existence which is not accessible to us'.[75] However, he replies, he does not intend to depict a primordial sinless humanity, but to analyse human features that are true with or without sin: 'it is not the lost paradise of innocence which we propose to describe, but the structures which are the fundamental possibilities offered equally to innocence and to the fault as a common keyboard of human nature on which mythical innocence and empirical guilt play in different ways'.[76]

Anticipating Ellul's objection, he asks: 'if corruption seizes the *whole* man, voluntary and involuntary, how can we describe possibilities apart from innocence or the fault?'[77] In his answer, Ricœur locates himself in a more 'Thomist' than 'Barthian' camp (to employ the terms he used in his early essay mentioned above):

---

[74] Ricœur, *Symbolism of Evil*, 250. 'L'innocence joue ici le rôle de la chose en soi dans le kantisme: on la pense suffisamment pour la poser, mais on ne la connaît pas' (Ricœur, *Finitude et culpabilité*, 465).

[75] Ricœur, *Freedom and Nature*, 25. 'On objectera alors que l'eidétique prétend décrire une existence innocente, laquelle nous est inaccessible' (Ricœur, *Le volontaire et l'involontaire*, 28).

[76] Ricœur, *Freedom and Nature*, 26. 'Ce n'est pas le paradis perdu de l'innocence que nous prétendons décrire, mais des structures qui sont des possibilités fondamentales offertes à la fois à l'innocence et à la faute, comme le clavier commun d'une nature humaine sur lequel jouent de façon différente l'innocence mythique et la culpabilité empirique' (Ricœur, *Le volontaire et l'involontaire*, 28–9).

[77] Ricœur, *Freedom and Nature*, 26. 'Si la faute s'empare de *tout* l'homme volontaire et involontaire, comment décrire des possibilités en deçà de l'innocence ou de la faute?' (Ricœur, *Le volontaire et l'involontaire*, 29).

We need to understand that a fundamental nature subsists even within the most complete fault. The fault happens to freedom; the guilty will is a freedom in bondage and not a return to an animal or mineral nature from which freedom is absent.... If man ceased being this power to decide, to act, and to consent, he would cease to be a man, he would be an animal or a stone.[78]

Contrary to Ellul's reading, Ricœur affirms that sin affects the whole person. The lesson of Genesis 1–3, he says, is that '*Every* dimension of man – language, work, institutions, sexuality – is stamped with the twofold mark of being destined for the good and inclined toward evil.'[79] Sin certainly affects every part of a human, but – this is the key point – without erasing their humanity. 'Difficult though it is', Ricœur explains, 'we must in some sense think of the fundamental nature of freedom and its bondage as superimposed. Man is not part free and part guilty; he is totally guilty, in the very heart of a total freedom ... I *am* free *and* this freedom *is* unavailable'.[80] To be 'totally' guilty is not the same as to be no longer human: 'evil, however positive, however seductive, however affective and infective it may be, cannot make a man something other than a man; infection cannot be a defection'.[81] Sin's effect was total but not irrevocable: 'The fall is a caesura cutting across everything that makes man human; everything – sexuality and death, work and civilization, culture and ethics – depends on both a primordial nature, lost but yet [*contra* Ellul/Thévenaz] still lying there underneath, and an evil which, although radical, is nonetheless contingent.'[82]

---

[78] Ricœur, *Freedom and Nature*, 25. 'Il nous faudra comprendre qu'une nature fondamentale subsiste dans une faute pourtant totale, la faute arrive à une liberté; la volonté coupable est une liberté serve et non pas le retour à une nature animale ou minérale d'où la liberté serait absente.... Si l'homme cessait d'être ce pouvoir de décider, de mouvoir et de consentir il cesserait d'être homme, il serait bête ou pierre' (Ricœur, *Le volontaire et l'involontaire*, 29).

[79] Ricœur, *Symbolism of Evil*, 246. Italics mine: 'Toute dimension de l'homme – langage, travail, institution, sexualité – porte en surimpression la double marque de la destination au bien, du penchant au mal' (Ricœur, *Finitude et culpabilité*, 460).

[80] Ricœur, *Freedom and Nature*, 26. 'Il nous faut donc, aussi difficile et paradoxal que cela soit, penser en quelque façon en surimpression la nature fondamentale de la liberté et son esclavage. L'homme n'est pas à moitié libre et à moitié coupable; il est totalement coupable, au cœur même d'une liberté ... Je *suis* libre *et* cette liberté *est* indisponible' (Ricœur, *Le volontaire et l'involontaire*, 29).

[81] Ricœur, *Symbolism of Evil*, 156. 'Le mal, aussi positif, aussi séduisant, aussi affectant et infectant soit-il, ne saurait faire de l'homme autre chose qu'un homme, l'infection ne peut être une défection' (Ricœur, *Finitude et culpabilité*, 366).

[82] Ricœur, *Symbolism of Evil*, 250. 'La chute est-elle une césure à travers toute l'humanité de l'homme: tout – sexualité et mort, travail et civilisation, culture et éthique – relève à la fois d'une nature originaire perdue et pourtant toujours sous-jacente, et d'un mal qui, pour être radical, n'en est pas moins contingent' (Ricœur, *Finitude et culpabilité*, 464).

However, can we access this primordial nature enough to describe it? Ricœur admits that 'we have access to the primordial only through what is fallen'.[83] Nonetheless,

> if the fallen denotes nothing about that *from which* it has fallen, no philosophy of the primordial is possible, and we cannot even say that man is fallen. For the very idea of downfall involves reference to the loss of a certain innocence that we understand sufficiently to name it and to designate the present condition as a lapse, a loss or a fall. I cannot understand treason as evil without judging it by an idea of trust and loyalty in relation to which it is evil.[84]

In other words, at the very core of our experience of evil is the feeling, 'this ought not to be' – a sense of corruption, distortion, and disorder where there was supposed to be order. If we analyse this feeling, we see that it presupposes that we are able to imagine an ideal world without that evil element. The concept of evil has no meaning if it does not entail failure compared with something else, namely, a world without evil. 'Consequently', Ricœur summarises, 'to say that man is so evil that we no longer know what his goodness would be is really to say nothing at all; for if I do not understand "good", neither do I understand "evil".'[85] We cannot speak of evil except in light of a prior idea of the good.

Powerful as this argument is, does it overturn the final objection from Heidegger, that we have no experience of any other human 'state' than the one we are in, and that therefore we have no criteria for interpreting it? How can we say anything about that of which we have no experience?

The strength of this difficulty, most clearly articulated by Heidegger, leads Ricœur to emphasise the productive function of the *imagination* for philosophy, an idea he acquires from Kant's *Critique of the Power of*

---

[83] Ricœur, *Fallible Man*, 76. 'Nous n'avons pas d'autre accès à l'originaire que le déchu' (Ricœur, *Finitude et culpabilité*, 120).

[84] Ricœur, *Fallible Man*, 76. 'Si le déchu ne donne pas d'indication sur *ce dont* il est déchu, aucune philosophie de l'originaire n'est possible et on ne peut pas même dire que l'homme est déchu; car l'idée même de déchéance comporte référence à la perte de quelque innocence que nous comprenons suffisamment pour la nommer et pour désigner la condition présente comme écart, comme perte ou comme chute. Je ne peux comprendre la trahison comme mal sans la mesurer à une idée de la confiance et de la fidélité par rapport à quoi la trahison est le mal' (Ricœur, *Finitude et culpabilité*, 120).

[85] Ricœur, *Fallible Man*, 145. 'Dès lors, dire que l'homme est si méchant que nous ne savons plus ce que serait sa bonté, c'est proprement ne rien dire du tout; car si je ne comprends pas le "bon", je ne comprends pas non plus le "méchant"' (Ricœur, *Finitude et culpabilité*, 198).

Judgement.⁸⁶ Ricœur admits that 'it is always "*through*" the fallen that the primordial shines through', that our experience is only one of a fallen world. But he insists despite this that we can 'isolate this representation of the primordial ... but only in *imaginary* mode'.⁸⁷

Ricœur introduces the role of the imagination as part of his argument for the legitimacy – even the reality – of the human ideal of the good, even when this ideal cannot be perceived through the bodily senses. Although he has Kant in support of this argument, it seems that the philosophy of Ricœur's time was suspicious of the potential flights of fancy that the imagination could go on, and Ricœur feels compelled to defend his use of the imagination at some length. Appealing to precedent, he writes: 'all the great philosophers have had to deal with this power of the imagination, whether they be Kant, Schelling, Hegel, Bergson, or Heidegger'.⁸⁸ He also underlines: 'There is in this imagination nothing scandalous for philosophy; Imagination is an indispensable mode of the investigation of the possible.'⁸⁹ Moreover, the fact that it investigates the 'possible' does not mean it cannot find the 'real' buried therein. 'Imagination is not a fanciful dream,' he insists: it 'manifests the essence by breaking the prestige of the fact. In imagining another state of affairs or another kingdom, I perceive the possible, and *in the possible, the essential*'.⁹⁰ In

---

⁸⁶ The imagination later became one of Ricœur's hallmarks and the subject of numerous studies. See, *inter alia*: Saulius Geniusas, 'Between Phenomenology and Hermeneutics: Paul Ricœur's Philosophy of Imagination', *Human Studies* 38, no. 2 (2015): 223–41; Lior Levy, 'Sartre and Ricœur on Productive Imagination', *The Southern Journal of Philosophy* 52, no. 1 (2014): 43–60; Michaël Fœssel, 'Action, normes et critique: Paul Ricœur et les pouvoirs de l'imaginaire', *Philosophiques* 41, no. 2 (2014): 241–52; George H. Taylor, 'Ricœur's Philosophy of Imagination', *Journal of French and Francophone Philosophy* 16, no. 1/2 (1 January 2006): 93–104; Thomas Busch, 'Sartre and Ricœur on Imagination', *American Catholic Philosophical Quarterly* 70, no. 4 (1996): 507–18; Jean-Luc Amalric, *Paul Ricœur, l'imagination vive: une genèse de la philosophie ricœurienne de l'imagination* (Paris: Editions Hermann, 2013).
⁸⁷ Ricœur, *Fallible Man*, 144. Italics original: 'C'est toujours "à travers" le déchu que l'originaire transparaît ... mais seulement sur un mode *imaginaire*' (Ricœur, *Finitude et culpabilité*, 144).
⁸⁸ Ricœur, *Philosophical Anthropology*, 150. 'Les grands philosophes ont tous eu à faire avec cette puissance de l'imagination, qu'ils s'appellent Kant, Schelling, Hegel, Bergson ou Heidegger' (Ricœur, *Anthropologie philosophique*, 239).
⁸⁹ Ricœur, *Fallible Man*, 145. 'Cette imagination n'a rien de scandaleux pour la philosophie; l'imagination est un mode indispensable d'investigation du possible' (Ricœur, *Finitude et culpabilité*, 197–8).
⁹⁰ Ricœur, *Fallible Man*, 112. Italics mine: 'Cette imagination n'est pas un rêve fantastique; c'est une "variation imaginative", pour parler comme Husserl, qui manifeste l'essence, en rompant le prestige du fait: en imaginant un autre fait, un autre régime, un autre règne, j'aperçois le possible et dans le possible l'essentiel' (Ricœur, *Finitude et culpabilité*, 159–60).

brief, imagination can reveal aspects of reality that can be known in no other way.

To see imagination as supplying a cognitive mediation of all experience reveals, *contra* Heidegger, the ambiguity in all appeals to the category of 'experience'. The term 'experience' is vague and should not be too quickly taken as determinative, because experience is always already interpreted, mediated, by the time it is described. 'I have vigorously resisted the word "experience" throughout my career', Ricœur will say much later, 'out of a distrust of immediacy, effusiveness, intuitionism'.[91] Human understanding is rooted not only in experience but in the *necessarily* imaginative way such experience is interpreted. Ricœur argues persuasively that even to give the label 'evil' to an experience is already to interpret it in light of an ethical paradigm rooted, however vaguely, in an understanding of the Good. This explains why Heidegger is forced to bracket ethics out of consideration if he is to succeed in describing 'the human condition' in its current state without implying a prior state of innocence. Even though by doing so Heidegger's philosophy remains consistent, Ricœur's alternative allows ethics to be born in the midst of philosophical anthropology.[92]

Indeed, throughout Ricœur's three-part *Philosophy of the Will* we find a repeated insistence on the priority of good over evil, of order over disorder, of the normal over the abnormal, both ontologically in the sense that the latter is derivative of the former, and epistemologically in the sense that we only recognise the latter starting from the former. 'We fail to understand a function', he argues, 'if we start from its disorders. Only the normal is intelligible'.[93] Ricœur is unlikely to be responding directly to Thévenaz's rejection of '*l'homme normale*' and his claim that the abnormal is the reality and the normal merely the absence of defects. The sentiment was prevalent at the time, due to psychoanalysis's approach to understanding the human via the pathological. That is why what Ricœur writes is a response not only to Thévenaz but to psychoanalysis more broadly: 'we are led to reject any inherent intelligibility

---

[91] Ricœur, *Critique and Conviction*, 139. 'J'ai beaucoup résisté au mot "expérience" dans mon trajet, par méfiance à l'égard de l'immédiateté, de l'effusion, de l'intuitionnisme' (Ricœur, *La critique et la conviction*, 211–12).

[92] On the connection between ethics and anthropology in Ricœur, see Schaafsma, 'Philosophical Anthropology against Objectification. Reconsidering Ricœur's Fallible Man'.

[93] Ricœur, *Freedom and Nature*, 229. 'On échoue à comprendre une fonction à partir de ses dérèglements; seul le normal est intelligible' (Ricœur, *Le volontaire et l'involontaire*, 214).

of the pathological';[94] 'We must vigorously insist that the pathological forms ... are *understood* only in relation to its non-pathological and truly constitutive forms.'[95]

Not only *can* finitude and evil be distinguished, but Ricœur makes the stronger claim that they *must* if we are to have any understanding of either. 'It is *necessary* to proceed in this way', Ricœur writes (when seeking the primordial goodness of the quests for possession, power, and glory): 'although we *know* these fundamental quests only *empirically* through their hideous and disfigured visages, in the form of greed and the passions of power and vanity, we *understand* these passions in *their essence* only as a perversion of ....'[96] This final ellipsis is the imaginative space for that 'of which' the passions are a perversion, and for Ricœur this alone can bring clarity to ethics.[97]

As for whether this imaginative capacity diminishes the importance of Christ's saving work, as Ellul suggests, Ricœur does not address this because to do so would be to stray too far from his philosophical concerns. One theological response to Ellul, however, might be as follows. By pointing to a trace of original goodness in humanity, Ricœur would only be diminishing Christ's saving work if humanity was to be given the credit for that original goodness. If, rather, God the Creator is responsible for all the original goodness of his creatures, which we hope Ellul would agree, then the original goodness of humanity is only a diminution

---

[94] Ricœur, *Freedom and Nature*, 5. 'On est ... conduit à refuser tout intelligibilité propre au pathologique' (Ricœur, *Le volontaire et l'involontaire*, 9).

[95] Ricœur, *Fallible Man*, 125. Italics original: 'Il faut dire avec force que l'on ne *comprend* les formes pathologiques de l'estime de soi qu'à partir de ses formes non-pathologiques et proprement constituantes' (Ricœur, *Finitude et culpabilité*, 175).

[96] Ricœur, *Fallible Man*, 111–12. 'Il *faut* procéder ainsi: car bien que nous ne *connaissons empiriquement* ces requêtes fondamentales que sous leur visage défiguré et hideux, sous la forme de l'avidité, des passions du pouvoir et de la vanité, nous ne *comprenons dans leur essence* ces passions que comme perversion de ...' (Ricœur, *Finitude et culpabilité*, 159).

[97] Ricœur defines the word 'passion' differently from Descartes. For Descartes, 'passion is simply opposed to action', whereas for Ricœur passion is a more specific word to describe the corruption of the will: 'passion is not a degree of emotion: emotion belongs to a fundamental nature which is the common keyboard serving both innocence and fault. Passions show the ravages wrought at the core of this essential nature by a principle which is at the same time active and belonging to nothingness' (Ricœur, *Freedom and Nature*, 20–1; 'Chez Descartes passion s'oppose simplement à action.... Mais la passion n'est pas un degré dans l'émotion: l'émotion appartient à une nature fondamentale qui est le clavier commun de 'innocence et de la faute; les passions marquent les ravages opérés au sein de cette nature fondamentale par un principe à la fois actif et apparenté au néant' [Ricœur, *Le volontaire et l'involontaire*, 23–4]).

of Christ's work to the extent that Christ's work (salvation) and God's work (creation) were in some kind of competition with one another, such that to increase the importance of one decreases the importance of the other. And this would only be the case if Christ were only a historical figure, without also being the one 'by whom all things were created' and 'in whom all things hold together' (Cf. Col. 1:16–17).

CONCLUSION

In the midst of a cacophony of confusion about finitude and evil, and over against an abundance of objections that they cannot be distinguished, Ricœur insists that a distinction is implied in the very notion of evil as what-ought-not-to-be. Yet when we look at the world around us, we find what-ought-not-to-be happening everywhere throughout history. If evil is not part of the natural human condition, how did it get to be so prevalent? Ricœur is not blind to this simple and practical question. Although he must first establish that evil is contingent, that is not the end of his project. He must then go on to show the right way of understanding the relation between finitude and evil, which it is the task of the next chapter to unfold.

6

Rightly Relating Evil and Finitude

The last chapter showed that, according to Ricœur, finitude is more originary than evil; where finitude is ontological, evil is contingent and accidental. The question which poses itself as this point is: if everything was originally good, how did it go wrong? This question, a common variant of the perennial *unde malum*, is also central to Ricœur's project. So far, we have exclusively focussed on how Ricœur *separates* finitude from evil. However, Ricœur was only concerned to separate them in order to recast their relation: 'the problem', we recall, 'was that of their difference *and of their connection*'.[1] He is not content to paint a beautiful picture of the primordial goodness of finitude, but seeks the entry point of evil, the reason evil is now among us.

This chapter considers three ways Ricœur cautiously reconnects finitude and evil. First, Ricœur does not merely say that evil is historical and good ontological. On the one hand, ontology must at least contain the possibility of evil for any evil to have occurred, and on the other hand, there is more to history than a narrative of human errors, which would turn salvation into nothing more than a return to the Garden of Eden. Ricœur has a positive role for history as the necessary path of humanity's growth, which would have taken place even if there had been no sin. Secondly, evil is not entirely and solely a result of human freedom for Ricœur. On the contrary, he criticises this 'Pelagian' view because it fails to explain our experience of being always part culprits, part victims, in

---

[1] Ricœur, 'Appendix: From Existentialism to the Philosophy of Language', 372–3. Italics mine. Original French not available.

every evil act. Our sinful inclinations are both the result of captivity to what he calls a sinful 'quasi-nature' and also point beyond to a mysterious force of darkness that precedes us. Ricœur finds a mysterious inevitability to sin that defies philosophical clarification, leading him to the threshold of recognising an evil 'other' in the universe, mythically represented as the serpent in the biblical narrative. Thirdly, despite Ricœur's reticence to make metaphysical judgements, he argues against the traditional privative understanding of evil. I will argue, first, that this is inconsistent, and second, that if we keep the focus on Ricœur's philosophical anthropology, he does indeed affirm that evil is a privation of the will, which is not insignificant in light of the stated limits of his discourse.

FROM POSSIBILITY TO REALITY

Before showing the ways finitude is related to evil in Ricœur, it is worth summarising the argument of *Finitude and Guilt*. As Part II of his *Philosophy of the Will* project, it has itself two parts which address the question of evil at two different levels. The first volume, *Fallible Man*, remains at the level of evil's *possibility* in the human will, to which Ricœur gives the name 'fallibility'.[2] Ricœur recognises that even if there is no essential or inevitable guilt in human ontology, the possibility of evil must be latent in human nature or else evil would never have become reality. Ricœur calls 'fallibility' this human capacity for evil, sourcing it in what he calls the finite/infinite 'disproportion' that we examined in Chapter 4.[3] We are not simply animals, unaware of our own finitude, satisfied with nothing more than the fulfilment of our physical needs. An animal cannot fail morally, and it is moral failure Ricœur means in this context. Human existence is unlike any other kind of existence because it is caught between a finite particularity and an infinite intention, both in intellect and feeling. We are capable of an infinite knowledge and an infinite desire which constitutes what Ricœur, borrowing a phrase from Jean Nabert, calls our 'non-coincidence of self to self'.[4] It is this disproportion that 'makes man *capable* of failing'.[5]

---

[2] Ricœur, *Fallible Man*, xliv; Ricœur, *Finitude et culpabilité*, 28.
[3] See Chapter 4 above, the section titled 'Language as Transcendence of Perspective'.
[4] Ricœur, *Fallible Man*, 141. 'non-coïncidence de soi à soi' (Ricœur, *Finitude et culpabilité*, 193).
[5] Ricœur, *Fallible Man*, 145. Italics original: 'rend l'homme *capable* de faillir' (Ricœur, *Finitude et culpabilité*, 198).

The second part of *Finitude and Guilt* is called *The Symbolism of Evil*. Here Ricœur transitions from evil's *possibility* to its *reality*, which famously demands what he calls a 'revolution in method, represented by the recourse to a hermeneutics',[6] about which much has already been written and which need not detain us here.[7] Although Ricœur's fully fledged hermeneutics only appears after his engagement with Freudian psychoanalysis, the initial impulse towards hermeneutics begins because Ricœur sees no rational connection between evil's possibility and its reality, no 'logical transition ... between the fundamental reality of man and his present existence, between his ontological status as a being created good and destined for happiness and his existential or historical status'.[8] In the absence of a logical transition, Ricœur is compelled to take an altogether different philosophical starting point; no longer abstract reflection on fundamental ontology, but interpretation of symbolic and mythological language that comes from outside philosophy.

The first half of *The Symbolism of Evil* examines three ancient symbols for evil: defilement or stain, where evil is seen to infect a person from the outside; sin or deviation, characterised as objectively missing the mark; and guilt, which individualises and subjectivises sin as a personal experience. All three are symbols because they depend on physical language but refer to a reality beyond the physical.

In the second half Ricœur presents a typology of Western myths of the origin of evil, which he classifies into four basic variations:

1) For the 'theogonic' myth, evil is more original than good, since creation is the emergence of order out of a chaos that preceded it, a result of a cosmic war of the gods. Evil is thus in creation from the beginning, not superadded but part of the very structure of being.
2) The 'tragic' myth differs from the 'theogonic' in that evil is joined eternally to good in the figure of a god who is beyond good and evil. It is a myth of 'divine blinding' where failure is built into the

---

[6] Ricœur, *Fallible Man*, xliv. 'une révolution de méthode représentée par le recours à une herméneutique' (Ricœur, *Finitude et culpabilité*, 28).
[7] On the beginnings of Ricœur's famous 'hermeneutical turn' in *The Symbolism of Evil*, see, *inter alia*: Richard Kearney, 'On the Hermeneutics of Evil,' in David Kaplan, ed., *Reading Ricœur* (Albany: SUNY Press, 2008), 71–88; Ihde, *Hermeneutic Phenomenology*; Colin, 'Herméneutique et philosophie réflexive'.
[8] Ricœur, *Symbolism of Evil*, 163. 'Il n'y a pas de déduction, de transition logique, entre la réalité fondamentale de l'homme et son existence actuelle, entre son statut ontologique de créature bonne et destinée au bonheur et son état existentiel ou historique' (Ricœur, *Finitude et culpabilité*, 373).

human constitution. It is man's destiny to fail, and so he is not blamed but only pitied for his failure.
3) The 'Adamic' myth makes evil an aberration that enters into a world originally good. It is both anthropological and ethical in a way the other myths are not, because free human choice is the entry point for evil.
4) The 'Orphic' myth is dualistic, seeing the soul as the true self and the body as a punishment for the soul's prior transgression. Finitude, understood as the limits of being in a body, is 'both an effect of evil and a new evil'.[9]

For Ricœur it is insufficient simply to describe these four myths, presenting the internal coherence of each: 'One cannot rest here; for the question of *truth* has not yet been posed.'[10] There comes a moment when one must commit one's own life and thought to one of them, when one must 'leave the comparativist point of view aside' and 'become implicated in the life of one symbol, one myth'.[11] His own chosen myth, to which he gives his allegiance and on the basis of which his philosophical anthropology proceeds, is the 'Adamic myth' recounted in the first chapters of the Hebrew Scriptures. For him, 'only the "Adamic" myth is strictly anthropological', because only there is finitude fully distinguished from guilt.[12]

One may object that to proceed on the basis of a myth is to cease doing philosophy, because surely philosophy must be free of such unfounded presuppositions. We must wait until Chapter 7 for a full answer to this objection. To summarise here, Ricœur is using the myth as a stimulus for philosophical thought, not as an authoritative declaration to which philosophy must submit. An idea may have its origin outside philosophy and yet bring new insights without compromising the philosophical method.

This simple sketch of Ricœur's account of evil would be misleading by itself because it makes it sound as if Ricœur sees no intermingling at all between finitude and evil. The reality involves complications which it

---

[9] Ricœur, *Symbolism of Evil*, 284. 'à la fois effet du mal et nouveau mal' (Ricœur, *Finitude et culpabilité*, 500).
[10] Ricœur, *Conflict of Interpretations*, 297. Italics original: 'On ne peut y demeurer; car la question de la *vérité* n'est pas encore posé' (Ricœur, *Conflit des interprétations*, 293).
[11] Ricœur, *Conflict of Interpretations*, 298–9. 'Cela n'est possible que si, quittant le point de vue comparativiste, je m'engage ... dans la vie d'un symbole, d'un mythe' (Ricœur, *Conflit des interprétations*, 294).
[12] Ricœur, *Symbolism of Evil*, 233. 'Seule le mythe "adamique" est proprement anthropologique' (Ricœur, *Finitude et culpabilité*, 445).

is the task of the rest of this chapter to investigate. We begin with what I have dubbed Ricœur's 'Irenaean moment'.

CONNECTION 1: THE IRENAEAN MOMENT AND ADAM'S IMMATURITY

When speaking about evil, Ricœur continually returns to the theme of its *historicity,* calling it a *contingent event,* having no place in the ontological structure of the human. In contrast to the philosophical anthropologies of Jaspers and Sartre considered above, Ricœur insists that evil is 'not an element of fundamental ontology.... It can be conceived only as an accident, an interruption, a fall.... The fault remains an alien body in the essential structure of man'.[13] Moreover, Ricœur abstracts evil from his description of the structures of the will in order to highlight its historical nature: 'only a pure description of the voluntary and the involuntary apart from the fault can reveal the fault as a fall, as loss, as absurdity'.[14]

However, in banishing evil from the realm of the eternally real, Ricœur has created an unbridgeable gap (like Lessing's 'ugly ditch') between history and ontology. We are left with what he calls 'the discordance between the fundamental reality – state of innocence, status of a creature, essential being – and the current modality of man, as defiled, sinful, guilty'.[15] This discordance is expressed in the pressing question: how did evil enter the world? Anything that happens in history must be possible at the ontological level or else it could not have happened by definition. The drama of history cannot be radically disconnected from the ontological framework on which it is based; on the contrary, all historical occurrences are manifestations of what is true at the ontological level. In short, 'what we have done' reveals 'what we are'. Ricœur's analysis therefore urgently leads to the question: if 'what we have done' is evil,

---

[13] Ricœur, *Freedom and Nature* 24. 'La faute n'est pas un élément de l'ontologie fondamentale ... Elle ne peut être pensée que comme irruption, accident, chute.... La faute reste un corps étranger dans l'eidétique de l'homme' (Ricœur, *Le volontaire et l'involontaire,* 27).
[14] Ricœur, *Freedom and Nature,* 27. 'Seule une description pure du volontaire et de l'involontaire en deçà de la faute peut faire apparaître la faute comme chute, comme perte, comme absurdité' (Ricœur, *Le volontaire et l'involontaire,* 30).
[15] Ricœur, *Symbolism of Evil,* 163. Translation modified: 'la discordance entre la réalité fondamentale – état d'innocence, statut de créature, être essentiel – et la modalité actuelle de l'homme, en tant que souillé, pécheur, coupable' (Ricœur, *Finitude et culpabilité,* 373).

what does this reveal about 'what we are'? Furthermore, such a sharp division between history and ontology can lead to the idea that history has no greater significance than that of the terrain on which evil plays out its disastrous narrative, and therefore that redemption is nothing more than a return to the Garden of Eden as if nothing had ever happened.

Nothing could be further from Ricœur's intentions. History, like everything else for Ricœur, is originally good and has an originally good purpose. However much primordial finitude is good and however much sin is a subsequent interruption, it would be a confusion to say that primordial finitude is therefore *perfect*. Ricœur never calls our original pre-fallen state *perfect*; on the contrary, he criticises this very appellation:

> All the speculations on the supernatural perfection of Adam before the fall are adventitious contrivances which profoundly alter the original naïve, brute meaning; they tend to make Adam superior and hence a stranger to our condition, and at the same time they reduce the Adamic myth to a genesis of man from a primordial superhumanity.[16]

Rather, Ricœur calls our primordial state one of *innocence* and insists that this means a state without sin, without guilt, without flaw or blemish. Ricœur makes the distinction explicit between innocence and perfection in a brief allusion to 'the destination of man' which, he says, is 'projected in the image of *primordial innocence* and *final perfection*'.[17]

This subtle point of Ricœur's is easy to miss because of the popular use of the word 'perfect', so a brief excursus may clarify Ricœur's approach. In everyday language we tend to think of perfection as flawlessness, revealing a static ontology without any concept of the goodness of change and growth. But the Greek for 'perfect' – '*teleos*' – does not mean simply 'flawless'; it refers to an Aristotelian final causality according to which a thing has a 'teleological' dimension, that is to say, exists for a particular purpose. Something is '*teleos*' only if it has reached the goal of its existence, has come to the end of its journey, is 'finished' in the profoundest and most beautiful sense of the word. In fact, '*teleos*' can be translated

---

[16] Ricœur, *Symbolism of Evil*, 233. 'Toutes les spéculations sur la perfection surnaturelle d'Adam avant la chute sont des arrangements adventices qui en altèrent profondément la signification originelle, naïve et brute; elles tendent à rendre Adam supérieur et donc étranger à notre condition et du même coup ramènent le mythe adamique à une genèse de l'homme à partir d'une surhumanité primordiale' (Ricœur, *Finitude et culpabilité*, 445–6).

[17] Ricœur, *Symbolism of Evil*, 165. Italics mine: 'la destination de l'homme, projetée dans l'imagination de l'innocence originaire et de la perfection finale' (Ricœur, *Finitude et culpabilité*, 375).

Connection 1: The Irenaean Moment

as either 'perfect' or 'mature'. The technically accurate English word for flawlessness without perfection is 'immature'. This word usually implies something that is supposed to be mature and is flawed in being behind its growth schedule. But a thing can be immature yet flawless if it is *in process*, like an acorn, which may have nothing wrong with it and yet not reach perfection until it has become a flourishing oak tree; or like a child, who is not to blame for lacking the maturity of an adult; or like a beginner in a language class who receives a 'perfect' exam score, in spite of the fact that he or she is nowhere near fluent.

This distinction between flawlessness and perfection, yielding the concept of innocence as a 'flawless immaturity', has a long pedigree in Christian theology. According to the second-century Church Father Irenaeus, Adam and Eve were 'immature', which is why they were susceptible to temptation even though they were without sin.[18] They were *flawless yet fallible*. Thus Irenaeus' conception of an evil *possible* but not yet *real* in the heart of humanity captures precisely the domain of Ricœur's *Fallible Man*, in which we are depicted as fragile, disproportionate in regard to ourselves, and this without reference to the presence or absence of guilt.

Ricœur finds in Irenaeus an affirmation of the goodness of humanity's history. Rejecting the overly individualistic conception of what it means to be created in 'the image of God' that would apply only to separate persons, Ricœur turns to Irenaeus for a richer idea that 'the image of God is humanity, indivisibly collective and individual', in other words, humankind as a whole, continually developing and evolving from its created beginnings to its glorified end.[19] History, for Ricœur, is a part of God's ongoing process of creation in which humanity participates: 'We should see the image of God not as the residual trace of a craftsman who has abandoned his work to the ravages of time, but as a continuous act in the creative movement of history and duration.'[20] Even after the fall, 'history remains a creation of God' and therefore remains fundamentally good.[21]

---

[18] Denis Minns, *Irenaeus: An Introduction* (London: Continuum, 2010), 75.
[19] Ricœur, *History and Truth*, 111. Translation modified: 'L'image de Dieu c'est l'Homme, indivisément collectif et individuel' (Ricœur, *Histoire et vérité*, 129).
[20] Ricœur, *History and Truth*, 110–11. 'Nous cherchions dans l'image de Dieu ... non comme une trace laissée par un ouvrier qui abandonne son ouvrage à l'usure du temps, mais comme un acte continué dans le mouvement créateur de l'histoire et de la durée' (Ricœur, *Histoire et vérité*, 128).
[21] My translation: 'L'histoire reste une création de Dieu' (Paul Ricœur, 'Vérité: Jésus et Ponce Pilate', *Le Semeur* 44, no. 5 [1946]: 391).

This same idea, namely, that created immaturity is to be fulfilled in history, is the reason why, for Ricœur, the 'Adamic myth' is not complete in itself without an eschatological vision as its counterpart. The 'symbol of the beginning ... is a *retrospective* symbol closely bound up with a whole historical experience turned toward the *future*'.[22] Such a future is in no manner a simple return to the Garden of Eden, making history nothing but a meaningless digression. The coming Kingdom of God, already in the Hebrew Scriptures, is 'not at all the regret for a lost golden age, but the expectation of a perfection the like of which will not have been seen before'.[23]

We are led by Ricœur, then, and by Irenaeus, to the idea that the risk of the possibility of evil is a necessary moment in the fullness of humanity's development. In order for humankind to pass from created innocence to glorified perfection, we had to undergo some sort of test or trial, symbolised in the Bible as the temptation in the Garden of Eden. 'When the Gnostics tried to embarrass them with the problem of evil, the Fathers did not hesitate to include in the grandeur of creation the creativity of a free man capable of disobeying. For them, the risk of evil was thus included in the coming to maturity of the whole of creation.'[24]

However, Ricœur does not stop at the *possibility* of evil as a necessary feature of human freedom: he also posits the *necessity* of evil as playing an indispensable role in the full glorification of humanity. In doing this he subscribes to the ancient doctrine known as '*felix culpa*' (the happy fault), according to which the good that God brings from evil is greater than the good that would have been without evil. Ricœur finds evidence for such a view in Romans 5:12–21, where the apostle Paul famously compares Adam with Christ considered as a 'second Adam'. Interpreting this passage, Ricœur notes that:

The apostle, by means of the similitude [between Adam and Christ], brings to light a progression: 'But not as the fault, so also the gift. For if by the fault of one

---

[22] Ricœur, *Symbolism of Evil*, 260. Italics original: 'symbole du commencement ... est un symbole *rétrospectif*, solidaire de toute une expérience historique tournée vers l'*avenir*' (Ricœur, *Finitude et culpabilité*, 475).

[23] Ricœur, *Symbolism of Evil*, 265. 'Cette image du Règne à venir n'exprime aucunement le regret d'un âge d'or aboli, mais l'attente d'une perfection inédite' (Ricœur, *Finitude et culpabilité*, 480).

[24] Ricœur, *History and Truth*, 128. 'Lorsque les gnostiques les embarrassaient avec le problème du mal, ils n'hésitaient pas à inclure dans la grandeur de la création la production de l'homme libre capable de désobéir; le risque du mal était ainsi inclus à leurs yeux dans cette venue à maturité de la création tout entière' (Ricœur, *Histoire et vérité*, 148–9).

many died, *how much more* the grace of God and the gift conferred by the grace of one man, Jesus Christ, have abounded unto many' (5:15). This 'how much more' ... excludes the possibility that the 'gift' should be a simple restoration of the order that prevailed before the 'fault'.[25]

Therefore, Ricœur summarises, 'evil itself is a part of the economy of superabundance. Paraphrasing Saint Paul, I dare to say: Wherever evil "abounds", there hope "superabounds".'[26]

This is more than saying that God can use evil for his own good purposes. It is more than saying that the temptation in the Garden of Eden was necessary as a test for freedom to reach its maturity. It is rather to say that not only the temptation, but also succumbing to it, was necessary for humanity to be able to reach its perfection in the image of God. Ricœur calls this 'likeness to gods by means of transgression'.[27] His idea seems to be based on the fact that the Genesis account uses the phrase 'likeness to God' twice; first at the creation of Adam and Eve, and secondly after they have succumbed to the temptation.[28] 'Why not take seriously', he asks, 'this affirmation that, in acquiring discernment, man effectively realized his likeness to God, which remained dormant, as it were, in his innocence?'[29]

This final step, making evil necessary for full flourishing, is problematic and cuts across the rest of Ricœur's work. I shall turn first to two difficulties identified by Ellul before offering my own critique. First, Ellul points out that Ricœur's interpretation of the Pauline 'how much more?' 'ends in justifying the sin instead of the sinner'.[30] Secondly, Ellul

---

[25] Ricœur, *Symbolism of Evil*, 272. Italics original: 'L'apôtre, par le moyen de la similitude, fait apparaître une progression: "Mais il n'en va pas du don comme de la faute. Si, par la faute d'un seul la multitude est morte, *combien plus* la grâce de Dieu et le don conféré par la grâce d'un seul homme, Jésus-Christ, se sont-ils répandus à profusion sur la multitude". Ce "combien plus"... exclut que le "don" soit une simple restauration de l'ordre antérieur à la "faute"' (Ricœur, *Finitude et culpabilité*, 487–8).

[26] Ricœur, *Conflict of Interpretations*, 439. 'Le mal lui-même fait partie de l'économie de la surabondance. Paraphrasant saint Paul, j'ose dire: là où le mal "abonde", l'espérance "surabonde"' (Ricœur, *Conflit des interprétations*, 429).

[27] Ricœur, *Symbolism of Evil*, 253. 'ressemblance aux dieux par le moyen de la transgression' (Ricœur, *Finitude et culpabilité*, 468).

[28] 'The man has become like one of us in knowing good and evil' (Gen 3:22 ESV).

[29] Ricœur, *Symbolism of Evil*, 253. 'Pourquoi ne pas prendre au sérieux cette affirmation qu'en accédant au discernement l'homme a effectivement réalisé sa similitude avec Dieu, qui restait comme en sommei dans l'innocence?' (Ricœur, *Finitude et culpabilité*, 468, n.10).

[30] Ellul, *To Will & to Do*, 272, n.9. 'conduit à justifier non pas le pécheur mais le péché' (Ellul, *Le vouloir et le faire*, 30, n.9).

critiques the idea that the image of God is realised in humanity through the fall: 'one cannot help being surprised at the idea that the man created by God had not been the true man, and that man will only come into being through disobedience, pardon, and a resurrection at the very end of human history'.[31] This latter criticism slightly misses the mark, because as we have seen, Ricœur gives a positive role to human history as God's *ongoing* creation of humanity independently of sin, so 'the man created by God' is more properly understood as the glorified humanity at the end of all things than the innocent humanity in its beginnings.

Though inaccurate in itself, Ellul's criticism nevertheless offers a clue to a problematic assumption Ricœur makes. He treats the two references to 'likeness to God' as if they were both desirable likenesses that are appropriate and good for the created human state. But might not the 'likeness to God' of created humanity be equivocal to the 'likeness to God' acquired by means of the fall, and might not the latter likeness be one that is not fitting for finite creatures? Ricœur ought to know this, since he himself denounces the bad kind of 'likeness to God' in philosophies that claim a God's-eye view on reality, as we saw in Chapter 1.

But the biggest problem with Ricœur making evil necessary for human growth is that it contradicts everything else he has done to make evil *unnecessary*, an aberration and an accident. As we saw, Ricœur masterfully shows that the *possibility* of evil is inscribed in the heart of human freedom and thus temptation is necessary for freedom to reach full maturity. He also highlights the great chasm between the *possibility* of evil in ontology, which is rational, and the *reality* of evil in history, which is irrational and absurd. Why, then, does he blithely cross the line from possibility to reality by affirming the *felix culpa*? He himself showed us that evil must be *possible* because of human freedom, but it can never be *necessary* without ceasing to be what it is by definition: an irruption of the ought-not in the is. As Jérôme Porée puts it, 'Evil is not necessary: a different history is possible.'[32]

Although I believe Ricœur's affirmation of the *felix culpa* to be a mistake, I also find resources in Ricœur's own work to provide a more satisfactory response to the difficulty. As part of his attack on the idea of

---

[31] Ellul, *To Will & to Do*, 272, n.9. 'On est contraint de s'étonner à l'idée que l'homme créé par dieu n'ait pas été le vrai homme, et que c'est seulement au travers de la désobéissance, du pardon et de la résurrection, au terme de l'histoire humaine que l'homme sera' (Ellul, *Le vouloir et le faire*, 30, n.9).

[32] My translation: 'Le mal n'est pas nécessaire: une autre histoire est possible' (Porée, 'Finitude et transcendance: une philosophie à deux foyers', 205).

Adam's 'perfection before the fall', Ricœur places the blame partly on the imagery of 'fall' itself: 'The very word "fall", which is foreign to the biblical vocabulary, is contemporaneous with the elevation of the "Adamic" condition above the present human condition; only what has first been elevated falls.'[33] Instead he invites us to see Adamic myth, in keeping with the Hebrew concept, as 'a myth of "deviation", or "going astray", rather than a myth of the "fall"'.[34] If we combine this Hebrew image of sin as 'going astray' with the Irenaean image of history as humanity's journey towards maturity (an image Ricœur found so fruitful), it becomes clear that sin cannot be an advancement on that journey. A digression is not a progression, even if by God's grace humanity can return to the true path and find its destiny in him. Sin has no *necessary* part to play, however much God may weave it into his purposes, using it for good so seamlessly that we, situated within history, cannot see how the good could have been achieved in any other way.

Ricœur's 'Irenaean moment' has explained why evil must remain a possibility for Adam and Eve, and has given a dignity and value to history by connecting it to God's ongoing creation of humankind progressing from innocent immaturity to final perfection. In Ricœurian spirit but against the letter, we can say that this progression happens despite, not because of, the 'deviation' of sin, and in this way we preserve Ricœur's careful separation of possibility and reality that he himself gives us in the form of the two separate books that comprise *Finitude and Guilt*.

CONNECTION 2: FREEDOM, THE SERPENT, AND THE ANTERIORITY OF EVIL

Ricœur qualifies his contention that guilt is only understandable as a function of freedom in two ways. First, he finds in the doctrine of original sin a paradoxical recognition that we are not radical 'first causes' of evil with absolute freedom, that our complicity in an evil act is not the same as total responsibility. Secondly, he finds in the idea of the 'anteriority of evil' a mysterious reference to a non-human creature who provided

---

[33] Ricœur, *Symbolism of Evil*, 233. 'Le mot même de chute, étranger au vocabulaire biblique, est contemporain de cette surélévation de la condition "adamique" au-dessus de la condition humaine actuelle; ne tombe que ce qui a été d'abord élevé' (Ricœur, *Finitude et culpabilité*, 446).

[34] Ricœur, *Symbolism of Evil*, 233. 'plutôt un mythe de "l'écart" qu'un mythe de la "chute"' (Ricœur, *Finitude et culpabilité*, 446).

the opportunity for Adam's failure, a creature depicted in the Genesis account as a serpent.

Against all assertions, both philosophical and theological, that sin is predestined or inevitable, Ricœur emerges as a champion of freedom. That for him, freedom is the heart of what it means to be human, and our humanity shines forth primarily in responsible choice, is shown in his interchangeable use of the word 'freedom' with 'the human', 'existence' and 'subjectivity'.[35] Freedom is one of the deepest motivations of his entire project to distinguish finitude from guilt, because evil loses its meaning if it is detached from freedom in his eyes. 'To affirm freedom', he writes, 'is to take upon oneself the origin of evil. By this proposition, I affirm a link between evil and freedom which is so close that the two terms imply one another mutually'.[36] Even more strongly, 'evil is an invention of freedom'.[37] This is because to confess guilt is to reveal an 'awareness that one could have done otherwise', which, he says, is 'closely linked to the awareness that one *should* have done otherwise', or as Kant succinctly put it, 'you must, therefore you can'.[38] Evil cannot be blamed on circumstances, third parties, or even God. It is we human beings who are the cause of evil and who bear the responsibility for it.

However, we would dramatically misunderstand Ricœur's philosophy of freedom if we remained at this level, where freedom is prioritised in order to explain evil. Although Ricœur never revokes or retracts this first stage, he does not see it as sufficient by itself. He calls it the 'ethical vision

---

[35] See, *inter alia*: Ricœur, *Marcel et Jaspers*, 18; Ricœur, *Freedom and Nature*, 19, 23; Ricœur, *Le volontaire et l'involontaire*, 22, 26. Ricœurian freedom is not of a Sartrean kind, unhinged from motivations, moral constraints, and character. James Marsh has demonstrated that Ricœur's *Freedom and Nature* is a critical correction to Sartre's overly voluntarist understanding of freedom, aimed precisely at demonstrating '*the reciprocity of the involuntary and the voluntary*', in other words, the way in which 'freedom and nature' presuppose each other like two sides of the same coin ([Ricœur, *Freedom and Nature*, 4]; '… réciprocité de l'involontaire et du volontaire' [Ricœur, *Le volontaire et l'involontaire*, 8]). See James Marsh, 'Ricœur's Phenomenology of Freedom as an Answer to Sartre' in Kaplan, *Reading Ricœur*.
[36] Ricœur, *Conflict of Interpretations*, 431. 'Affirmer la liberté, c'est prendre sur soi l'origine du mal. Par cette proposition, j'atteste un lien si étroit entre mal et liberté que ces deux termes s'impliquent mutuellement' (Ricœur, *Conflit des interprétations*, 422).
[37] Ricœur, *Conflict of Interpretations*, 300. 'Le mal est une invention de la liberté' (Ricœur, *Conflit des interprétations*, 297).
[38] Ricœur, *Conflict of Interpretations*, 432-3. 'La conscience d'avoir pu faire autrement est très étroitement liée à celle d'avoir *dû* faire autrement: … on sait l'usage que Kant a fait de cette affirmation: tu dois, donc tu peux' (Ricœur, *Conflit des interprétations*, 423).

of the world',[39] and attributes it variously to Pelagius and to Kant. 'For the Pelagians', Ricœur explains, 'freedom is without any acquired nature, without habit, without history and encumbrances. It is a freedom that in each one of us would be a unique and isolated instance of the absolute indetermination of creation'.[40] The problem is that the 'ethical vision of the world' in which I am fully and solely responsible for my actions can lead to an overwhelming sense of guilt that condemns us without mercy, a paralysing weight of responsibility in which I 'bear the burden of evil in the world alone'.[41] Such a burden, besides being unbearable, would not fit our experience that 'every individual finds evil *already there*; nobody begins it absolutely'.[42]

But this Kantian/Pelagian 'ethical vision of the world', is only the first of 'several stages of reflection' for Ricœur, a stage in which we discover the nature of evil by confessing our complicity in it.[43] 'Who does not see', he asks, that if we see this Pelagian moral vision as the last word, 'we triumph, in a way, in emptiness? The price of clarity is the loss of depth'.[44] 'What is lacking', he asks, 'in the ethical vision of evil? What is lacking, what is lost, is the darksome experience of evil which surfaces in different ways ... and which constitutes properly speaking the "tragic" aspect of evil'.[45]

The 'darksome experience of evil' to which Ricœur refers is the feeling that, however complicit we are in evil, we are also victims of a seduction. Perhaps only retrospectively, after we have committed an evil deed, do we have the feeling that we were led astray by a force that confused our

---

[39] Ricœur, *Fallible Man*, xlvi. 'vision éthique du monde' (Ricœur, *Finitude et culpabilité*, 30).
[40] Ricœur, *Conflict of Interpretations*, 279. ' l'idée pélagienne d'une liberté sans nature acquise, sans habitude, sans histoire et sans bagages, qui serait en chacun de nous un point singulier et isolé d'absolue indétermination de la création' (Ricœur, *Conflit des interprétations*, 275).
[41] Ricœur, *Symbolism of Evil*, 205. Translation modified: 'seul porter le poids du mal dans le monde' (Ricœur, *Finitude et culpabilité*, 417).
[42] Ricœur, *Symbolism of Evil*, 256. Italics original: 'Chacun trouve le mal *déjà là*; nul ne le commence absolument' (Ricœur, *Finitude et culpabilité*, 472).
[43] Ricœur, *Conflict of Interpretations*, 431. 'plusieurs moments de réflexion (Ricœur, *Conflit des interprétations*, 422)
[44] Ricœur, *Conflict of Interpretations*, 303. 'Qui ne voit pas qu'au moment même où nous disons cela, nous triomphons en quelque sorte dans le vide? Le prix de la clarté, c'est la perte de la profondeur' (Ricœur, *Conflit des interprétations*, 299–300).
[45] Ricœur, *Conflict of Interpretations*, 304. 'Qu'est-ce qui ne passe pas dans la vision éthique du mal? Ce qui ne passe pas, ce qui est perdu, c'est cette ténébreuse expérience du mal qui affleure de diverses façons ... et qui constitue à proprement parler le "tragique" du mal' (Ricœur, *Conflit des interprétations*, 300). By 'tragic', Ricœur is referring to the second myth in his typology, in which the human is predestined to commit evil.

thoughts and drew us forward by the overwhelming pull of a temptation coming from within. In this experience, Ricœur says, 'man ... appears *no less a victim than guilty*'.⁴⁶

This admission is the greatest paradox of ethics. It seems to contradict our point of departure. We began by saying: evil is what I *could have* not done; and this remains true. But at the same time I claim: evil is this prior captivity, which makes it so that I *must do* evil. This contradiction is interior to my freedom; it marks the nonpower of power, the nonfreedom of freedom.⁴⁷

Ricœur does not think this paradox can be resolved from within philosophy: 'we do not know how it is possible that freedom could be enslaved'.⁴⁸ Philosophy can only point to the contradiction wherein we are both free and captive at the same time. But this need not be the end of reflection. If philosophy draws on ancient mythologies, it may find ideas that stimulate further thought and illuminate the human condition without ever providing full rational clarity. This is precisely the premise of Ricœur's project in *The Symbolism of Evil*, and the reason he turns to symbols as ideas beyond the limits of philosophy. 'Why this recourse to a prior symbolism?' he asks; 'Because the paradox of a captive free will – the paradox of a *servile will* – is insupportable for thought'.⁴⁹ To end without full rational clarity is not a problem for Ricœur only because of his stance towards the finite limitations of philosophical investigation.⁵⁰ While we strive for rational coherence as we think *from* symbols, we can never achieve total transparency to our philosophy precisely because of our finitude.⁵¹

---

⁴⁶ Ricœur, *Fallible Man*, xlix. Italics mine: 'L'homme ... ne paraît pas moins victime que coupable' (Ricœur, *Finitude et culpabilité*, 34).
⁴⁷ Ricœur, *Conflict of Interpretations*, 436. Italics original: 'Cet aveu est le plus grand paradoxe de l'éthique. Il semble contredire notre point de départ: nous avons commencé en disant: le mal c'est ce que j'*aurais pu* ne pas faire; et cela reste vrai; mais en même temps j'avoue: le mal est cette captivité antérieure qui fait que je *ne peux pas ne pas faire le mal*. Cette contradiction est intérieure à la liberté, elle marque le non-pouvoir du pouvoir, la non-liberté de la liberté' (Ricœur, *Conflit des interprétations*, 426).
⁴⁸ Ricœur, *Conflict of Interpretations*, 439. 'Nous ne savons pas d'où a pu venir que la liberté se soit rendue serve' (Ricœur, *Conflit des interprétations*, 429).
⁴⁹ Ricœur, *Symbolism of Evil*, 152. Italics original: 'Pourquoi ce recours à la symbolique antérieure? Parce que le paradoxe d'un libre arbitre captif – le paradoxe d'un *serf-arbitre* – est insupportable pour la pensée' (Ricœur, *Finitude et culpabilité*, 362).
⁵⁰ For Ricœur's approach to finitude and truth, see Chapters 1 and 2.
⁵¹ This is why John Hick's criticism reveals a basic misunderstanding of Ricœur's whole project. In a review of *The Symbolism of Evil*, Hick complains that Ricœur gives us no reason 'why we should suppose that the pre-rational responses expressed in primitive mythologies are to be trusted in preference to scientific investigation and philosophical

Connection 2: Freedom, the Serpent, & Anteriority of Evil 159

Because of sin's paradoxical, non-conceptualizable nature, Ricœur rejects the traditional Christian doctrine of original sin as a coherent concept, considering it to be contaminated by the philosophical drive to achieve rational clarity. He accuses Augustine, who first formulated original sin theologically, of trying to rationalise what can only remain a mystery for thought. As a doctrine, Ricœur says, original sin is 'false knowledge' that 'compresses in an inconsistent notion a juridical category of debt and a biological category of inheritance'.[52]

But although he rejects original sin as a comprehensible doctrine, Ricœur retains it as a 'symbol' in which Christians can believe if they disclaim complete conceptual mastery of it. Even in its conceptual incoherence the doctrine preserves something of the truth about evil. Ricœur explains this with reference to Augustine's rational formulation, both denying evil a nature and then incorporating in the will a 'quasi-nature of evil':[53]

> There is something desperate here from the viewpoint of conceptual representation and something very profound from the metaphysical viewpoint. It is in the will itself that there is something of a quasi-nature. Evil is a kind of involuntariness at the very heart of the voluntary, no longer facing the voluntary but within the voluntary; and it is this which is the servile will.[54]

This is why, in Ricœur's view, the doctrine of original sin comes closer to the truth after all than the bloodless 'ethical vision of the world' of Kant and Pelagius.

> I do not hesitate to say that Pelagius can be right a thousand times against the pseudo-concept of original sin. Nevertheless, Saint Augustine transmits with this

---

reflection' (John Hick, 'The Symbolism of Evil, by Paul Ricœur', *Theology Today* 24, no. 4 [1968]: 522). But Ricœur gives countless reasons, all of which have to do with the limits of philosophical discourse and the need for philosophy to attend, not only to 'scientific investigation', but to all non-philosophical sources of reflection. Hick remains trapped in an Enlightenment positivist worldview that almost any of Ricœur's writings reveal to be insufficient.

[52] Ricœur, '"Original Sin": A Study in Meaning' in *Conflict of Interpretations*, 270. ' faux savoir qui bloque dans une notion inconsistante une catégorie juridique de dette et une catégorie biologique d'héritage' ('Le "Péché originel": étude de signification' in Ricœur, *Conflit des interprétations*, 266).

[53] Ricœur, *Conflict of Interpretations*, 285. 'incorporer à cette volonté une quasi-nature du mal' (Ricœur, *Conflit des interprétations*, 281).

[54] Ricœur, *Conflict of Interpretations*, 286. 'Il y a quelque chose de désespéré au point de vue de la représentation conceptuelle et de très profond au point de vue métaphysique: c'est dans la volonté même qu'il y a de la quasi-nature; le mal est une sorte d'involontaire au sein même du volontaire, non plus en face de lui, mais en lui, et c'est cela le serf-arbitre' (Ricœur, *Conflit des interprétations*, 281).

dogmatic mythology something essential that Pelagius completely misunderstood. Perhaps Pelagius is correct in his quarrel with the mythology of original sin, and principally with the Adamic mythology. But it is Augustine who remains right, through and in spite of this Adamic mythology.[55]

In brief, for Ricœur the metaphysics of inherited guilt is a 'contamination by pseudo-philosophy',[56] but it points towards the mystery of the captive will to which both the biblical accounts and our own experience witness.

The symbol of original sin is not the only way evil is anterior to freedom. We now turn to consider the second 'source' of evil prior to freedom that Ricœur locates in the figure of the serpent in Genesis 3. Just as the symbol of original sin makes each individual 'part victim, part guilty' due to an evil that precedes them, so the biblical references to an evil being prior to the fall mean that humanity as a whole is also 'part victim, part guilty'. Adam and Eve find their own 'anterior evil' in the serpent. In Ricœur's words: 'evil comes into the world insofar as man *posits* it, but man posits it only because he *yields* to the siege of the Adversary'.[57] This doctrine 'contributes ... pity for human beings'[58] by relieving us of the crushing burden of *total* responsibility for evil. The serpent 'represents the aspect of evil that could not be absorbed into the responsible freedom of man'.[59]

That the serpent does not rationally explain the origin of evil, Ricœur is well aware. This would be to fall prey to what has been called 'homunculus fallacy' in which one has the illusion of solving a problem but

---

[55] Ricœur, *Conflict of Interpretations*, 281. 'Je n'hésite pas à dire que Pélage peut avoir mille fois raison contre le pseudo-concept de péché originel, saint Augustin fait passer à travers cette mythologie dogmatique quelque chose d'essentiel que Pélage a entièrement méconnu; Pélage a peut-être toujours raison contre la mythologie adamique, mais c'est Augustin qui a toujours raison à travers et malgré cette mythologie adamique' (Ricœur, *Conflit des interprétations*, 277). In fact, Ricœur's position is closer to Augustine than he realises, and his disagreement with Augustine is a result of a misreading. See Bochet, *Augustin dans la pensée de Paul Ricœur*. On the 'Lutheran' inflection of Augustine in Ricœur, see Daniel Frey, 'On the Servile Will', in Scott Davidson, ed., *A Companion to Ricœur's 'The Symbolism of Evil'* (Lanham: Lexington Books, 2020), 53.
[56] Ricœur, *Symbolism of Evil*, 5. ' contamination par la pseudo-philosophie' (Ricœur, *Finitude et culpabilité*, 206).
[57] Ricœur, *Fallible Man*, xlix. Italics original: 'Le mal entre dans le monde en tant que l'homme le pose, pais l'homme ne le *pose* que parce qu'il *cède* à l'investissement de l'Adversaire' (Ricœur, *Finitude et culpabilité*, 34).
[58] Ricœur, *Symbolism of Evil*, 322. 'la pitié pour l'homme' (Ricœur, *Finitude et culpabilité*, 540).
[59] Ricœur, *Symbolism of Evil*, 258. 'Il figure cette face du mal qui ne peut être reprise dans la liberté responsable de l'homme' (Ricœur, *Finitude et culpabilité*, 473).

in reality has only pushed it back a stage.⁶⁰ To explain human evil by recourse to prior, angelic evil, leaves unexplained where this prior evil came from. 'The serpent signifies', says Ricœur, not the ultimate source of evil, but only 'that man does not begin evil. He finds it. For him, to begin is to continue'.⁶¹ The meaning of the serpent is not to provide a theodicy; it is to say 'that man is not the absolute evil one, but the evil one of second rank'.⁶²

There are thus two witnesses to an evil that exists 'prior' to freedom: the servile will and the serpent. These add a paradoxical element to the otherwise simplistic 'ethical vision of the world'. At the individual level, I find myself in bondage to a sinful quasi-nature. And at the global level, the human race finds itself in bondage as a consequence of yielding to the temptation of an evil 'other' that preceded us. But in spite of these two caveats, freedom does not cease to be freedom for Ricœur, and therefore remains partly responsible for sin. As Peter Kemp puts it, 'Sin and guilt, according to Ricœur's analysis in *The Symbolism of Evil*, includes both an external power and the responsibility of the self for yielding to evil'.⁶³

CONNECTION 3: EVIL AS PRIVATION

Finally, we turn to consider the extent to which Ricœur's distinction between finitude and evil lends support to the classical theistic doctrine of evil as a 'privation of being' or a 'privation of the good'.⁶⁴

In addressing this question, we must remember that Ricœur's project is philosophical anthropology, not metaphysics; he seeks to describe not being qua being but the human will. Even if, as I have shown, he does not believe anthropology can be totally unhinged from any implied

---

⁶⁰ See Dov Rosen Shlomo, 'Between the Homunculus Fallacy and Angelic Cognitive Dissonance in Explanation of Evil: Milton's Poetry and Luzzatto's Kabbalah', in *Evil, Fallenness, and Finitude*, ed. Bruce Ellis Benson and B. Keith Putt (Cham: Palgrave Macmillan, 2017), 57–75.
⁶¹ Ricœur, *Conflict of Interpretations*, 295. 'Le serpent signifie que l'homme ne commence pas le mal. Il le trouve. Pour lui, commencer, c'est continuer' (Ricœur, *Conflit des interprétations*, 291).
⁶² Ricœur, *Symbolism of Evil*, 259. 'que l'homme n'est pas le méchant absolu; il n'est que le méchant en second' (Ricœur, *Finitude et culpabilité*, 474).
⁶³ Peter Kemp, 'Narrative Ethics and Moral Law in Ricœur', in John Wall, William Schweiker, and David Hall, eds., *Paul Ricœur and Contemporary Moral Thought* (New York: Routledge, 2002), 44.
⁶⁴ See, for example, Rowan Williams, 'Insubstantial Evil', in *On Augustine* (London: Bloomsbury, 2016), 79–105.

metaphysics, he still wants to avoid metaphysical speculation as far as possible.[65] Moreover, he sees in the Bible no encouragement to engage in metaphysical speculation. When he speaks, for example, of the biblical symbol of 'Sin as Nothingness', he qualifies what he means by this: 'Of course, a culture that has not worked out the idea of being does not have a concept of nothingness either; but it may have a symbolism of negativity'.[66] There is no privative doctrine of evil in the Hebrew scriptures, for Ricœur, because he believes that these scriptures do not have any metaphysics at all.

This does not mean Ricœur has nothing to say about the classical doctrine of evil as privation. He describes it, in its historical context, as belonging to the doctrine of original sin, and strangely associates it with the 'ethical vision of the world' that denies the mysterious anteriority of evil. When describing this ethical stage, he writes, '"Original sin" first of all means one thing: that evil is not something that exists, that evil has no being, no nature, because it comes from us, because it is the work of freedom'.[67] 'For when we speak later on', he continues, referring to the second stage, of 'a quasi-nature for evil', this 'must not budge us from refusing evil a nature or a substance'.[68]

We may think that this statement amounts to Ricœur affirming the privative view of evil. But when Ricœur moves on from the 'ethical stage' of his argument, he also criticises the privative view of evil as an 'impossible concept' which does not 'account for the positive power of evil'.[69] It ignores, he says, the paradox of the servile will, which points to the 'externality' of evil.

---

[65] In a 2003 interview, Ricœur states: 'I no longer subscribe to the typically anti-metaphysical Protestant lineage of Karl Barth (though it is true that in early works like *The Symbolism of Evil* I was still somewhat under his influence).' Kearney, *On Paul Ricœur*, 166.

[66] Ricœur, *Symbolism of Evil*, 74. 'Certes, une culture qui n'a pas élaboré l'idée d'être n'a pas non plus un concept du néant; mais elle peut avoir un symbolisme de la négativité' (Ricœur, *Finitude et culpabilité*, 280).

[67] Ricœur, *Conflict of Interpretations*, 272. 'Le "péché originel" signifie une première chose: que le mal n'est rien qui soit, n'a pas d'être, pas de nature, parce qu'il est de nous, parce qu'il est œuvre de liberté' (Ricœur, *Conflit des interprétations*, 268).

[68] Ricœur, *Conflict of Interpretations*, 272. 'Car, quand nous parlerons tout à l'heure de *peccatum originale* ou *naturale*, il ne faudra pas que la réintroduction d'une quasi-nature du mal nous ramène en deçà de ce refus du mal-nature, du mal-substance' (Ricœur, *Conflit des interprétations*, 268).

[69] Ricœur, *Conflict of Interpretations*, 275, 302. 'Concept impossible'; 'Il n'est pas sûr que le concept trop négatif ... rende compte de la puissance positive du mal' (Ricœur, *Conflit des interprétations*, 271, 298).

Connection 3: Evil as Privation

Ricœur seems to think that the Christian tradition only affirmed a privative view of evil in order to protect human freedom. Therefore the question of whether evil has 'substance' appears in Ricœur's thought when he speaks of evil's 'externality' or 'anteriority' to freedom. This leads to a strange confusion whereby Ricœur thinks that evil cannot be purely privative because evil is accounted for not by freedom but by something 'exterior' to it (in both original sin and the figure of the serpent). For example, he points to the symbol of defilement as biblical evidence that 'evil is not nothing; it is not a simple lack, a simple absence of order; it is the power of darkness; it is posited; in this sense it is something to be "taken away": "I am the Lamb of God who takes away the sins of the world"'.[70] Ricœur admits that defilement is only a symbol, but, contrary to his normal rule for symbols to indicate something opaque to thought, this time he reveals what lies behind the symbol: 'defilement ... signifies the servile will'.[71] As we saw above, the servile will testifies to evil's positivity and reveals the insufficiency of a purely privative doctrine of evil. Therefore, when Ricœur speaks of the 'positive power of evil', he means the two 'anterior evils' described above, that is to say, any evil that does not originate in the human will.

Ricœur thus denies evil as privation because of the 'externality' and 'positivity' of evil outside human freedom. In other words, because the Devil (the serpent according to Christian tradition) is a positive substance, and the Devil is the personification of evil, evil cannot be privative.

This points to an inconsistency in Ricœur's thought. On the one hand, he claims that he is only doing philosophical anthropology, not metaphysics. His description of evil, he says, 'is by no means a decision concerning the root origin of evil, but is merely the description of the place where evil appears and from where it can be seen'.[72] Any judgement about evil in the metaphysical categories of being and nothingness 'needs a *Poetics* of freedom and of the being of man which exceeds the possibilities of a philosophical anthropology' which 'can neither posit nor

---

[70] Ricœur, *Symbolism of Evil*, 155. 'Le mal n'est pas rien; il n'est pas simple défaut, simple absence d'ordre; il est la puissance des ténèbres; il est "posé"; en ce sens il est quelque chose à "ôter": "Je suis l'Agneau de Dieu qui ôte les péchés du monde"' (Ricœur, *Finitude et culpabilité*, 365).

[71] Ricœur, *Symbolism of Evil*, 155. 'La souillure ... signifie seulement le serf-arbitre' (Ricœur, *Finitude et culpabilité*, 365).

[72] Ricœur, *Fallible Man*, xlvi. 'n'est aucunement une décision sur l'origine radicale du mal, mais seulement la description du lieu où le mal apparaît et d'où il peut être vu' (Ricœur, *Finitude et culpabilité*, 31).

take away the right of an absolute genesis of being, to which evil would belong primordially'.[73]

On the other hand, despite the stated limits of his analysis, Ricœur criticises Augustine's metaphysics of privation, as if it only pertained to an anthropology of freedom. This perhaps shows more clearly than anything else the futility of attempts to describe 'the human condition' in abstraction from metaphysical questions, a futility Ricœur readily observes in his critiques of Heidegger and Sartre.[74] The traditional Christian metaphysics of privation was not primarily about anthropology or the Devil. That is why it is not contradicted by the anteriority of evil. Rather, it was about the doctrine of creation, according to which evil cannot have substance because all substance is created by God and is therefore good. This includes the serpent, humanity's 'anterior evil'. Ricœur ought to have taken note of this. That the serpent is also a creature in the biblical story he calls a 'capital point',[75] but he bypasses its significance. If the serpent is a creature, then it is originally good and its 'positive power' to do evil is a created gift which it abuses because of its freedom, just as we commit evil because we abuse the created gift of our human freedom.[76] Thus the existence of the serpent prior to Adam and Eve has nothing to do with the question of whether or not evil is privative, because the 'power of darkness' is no less created, originally good, and subsequently corrupted, than our own human powers.

Setting aside this inconsistency, we find a much clearer affirmation of evil-as-privation in Ricœur if we turn instead to his description of evil from the point of view of philosophical anthropology, which is in keeping with Ricœur's own stated limits for his work. At this anthropological level Ricœur is much happier to speak of evil as non-being, and does so regularly. For example, when describing the paradox of the 'servile will', he states that the will's bondage has *less reality* than its freedom: 'In the

---

[73] Ricœur, *Symbolism of Evil*, 327–8. 'relève d'une "*Poétique*" de la liberté et de l'être-homme qui excède les possibilités d'une anthropologie philosophique'; 'ne peut ainsi ni poser ni déposer le droit d'une genèse absolue de l'être à quoi le mal appartiendrait originairement' (Ricœur, *Finitude et culpabilité*, 545–6). On the meaning of 'poetics' in Ricœur, see Chapter 7 below, the section titled 'Ricœurian Poetics: Creative Discourse about Creation'.

[74] See Chapter 4 above, the section titled 'The Need for Transcendence'.

[75] Ricœur, *Symbolism of Evil*, 255. '[La Bible] dit seulement – et c'est capital – qu'il est lui aussi une créature' (Ricœur, *Finitude et culpabilité*, 470).

[76] As Thomas Weinandy puts it, 'Satan and the other fallen angels ... are not ontologically evil as such.... The good of their intellect and will remains even if they use these goods only to do evil' (*Does God Suffer?* [Edinburgh: T&T Clark, 2000], 152).

phrase ... "I *am* free and this freedom *is* unavailable", the word to be is not on the same level: freedom is more fundamental than the fault'.[77] Just as evil is parasitic on the good, bondage depends on freedom for its own reality. Similarly, the 'passions' are not substantive emotions, but corruptions of the will in Ricœur's vocabulary.[78] That is why Ricœur can describe the will without speaking about the passions. The passions, he says, are not aspects of the will or the body: they do not belong in the human condition at all because they are not part of its most basic constitution. Instead, they reveal

> a specific non-being of the will, an ontological deficiency belonging to the will. The privileged experience of this non-being, in spite of its negative turn, is already an ontological dimension; it is, so to speak, the negative proof of being, the empty ontology of lost being.[79]

Elsewhere he adds that 'passions show the ravages wrought at the core of this essential nature by a principle which is at the same time active and belonging to nothingness'.[80] That is why guilt, for Ricœur, is ultimately not something *added* to the human constitution like a foreign body or burden. Although 'retrospectively, from the point of view of sin', it can seem like this, in fact 'goodness is altogether positive; it is sin that is the nothingness of vanity'.[81]

CONCLUSION

The way Ricœur handles finitude and evil is analogous to his handling of philosophy and theology. In both cases, it is only by rigorously distinguishing the two that the true connections between them can be brought

---

[77] Ricœur, *Freedom and Nature*, 27. Italics original: 'Dans la phrase ...: je *suis* libre et ma liberté *est* indisponible, le mot être n'est pas au même niveau: la liberté est plus fondamentale que la faute' (Ricœur, *Le volontaire et l'involontaire*, 30).
[78] On Ricœur's understanding of 'passion', see footnote 48 above.
[79] Ricœur, *Husserl*, 228. ' un *non-être* spécifique de la volonté, une déficience ontologique propre à la volonté; l'expérience privilégiée de ce non-être, malgré son tour négatif, est déjà de dimension ontologique; elle est, si l'on peut dire, l'épreuve négative de l'être, l'ontologie en creux de l'être perdu' (Ricœur, *À l'école de la phénoménologie*, 80).
[80] Ricœur, *Freedom and Nature*, 20-1. 'La passion n'est pas un degré dans l'émotion: l'émotion appartient à une nature fondamentale qui est le clavier commun de l'innocence et de la faute; les passions marquent les ravages opérés au sein de cette nature fondamentale par un principe à la fois actif et apparenté au néant' (Ricœur, *Le volontaire et l'involontaire*, 24).
[81] Ricœur, *Symbolism of Evil*, 251. 'vue rétrospectivement à partir du péché'; 'bonté est toute positive; c'est le péché qui est le néant de la vanité' (Ricœur, *Finitude et culpabilité*, 465).

to light. Where the previous chapter explored how Ricœur drew the *distinction*, this chapter has seen how he redraws the *relation* between finitude and evil.

We have seen first of all how the possibility of evil is inscribed in the nature of finitude, making it not necessarily fallen, but necessarily fallible. Yet this is only at the beginning of history. Even had there been no evil, no sin, no 'Fall', there would have been a progression from immaturity to perfection, and this progression remains a part of human history, an epic narrative which does not need evil to be capable of development.

Next, we saw how Ricœur complicates his strong insistence on freedom by discerning an unfree element in the human condition, something which leads to the brink of the theological doctrines of original sin and the Devil. To be human is to be part guilty, part victim. These two elements are the two ways in which evil is 'anterior' to human freedom and conditions it.

Finally, we saw how Ricœur affirms the nothingness of evil in his anthropology, even if he is unwilling to do so in his metaphysics. Unfortunately, Ricœur breaks his own rule about metaphysical speculation by rejecting the metaphysics of evil as privation – because, of course, to reject something metaphysical is to have a metaphysical opinion about it. Yet even if Ricœur did not remain within the limits of his anthropological project, we may still do so.

Ricœur's 'anthropology of privation' should not be surprising in light of the themes we have encountered throughout this chapter, in which he continually contrasts the historical contingency of evil with the ontological priority of the good. Everywhere we see Ricœur arguing that what is good is more basic, more *real*, than what is evil, and this leads him to seek the original goodness behind all manifestations of evil, revealing what Ricœur's biographer calls his 'original asymmetry in favour of the Good'.[82]

Ricœur's fundamentally positive view of human finitude is rigorously philosophical, because he argues for it philosophically without drawing on any revealed authority to support his argument. And yet it is nonetheless based on his conviction that humans are fundamentally good because they are created by a good Creator. It is to this underlying source of inspiration that we now turn.

---

[82] My translation: 'dissymétrie initiale en faveur du Bien' (Dosse, *Paul Ricœur*, 15).

7

The Poetic Symbol of Creation

> It is creation as a whole that names God.
> Paul Ricœur[1]

That the biblical account of creation is the source of inspiration for his philosophical anthropology Ricœur never tries to hide. For example, he writes that his first major project, *Philosophy of the Will*, 'depends on the concrete myth of innocence' as 'what gives us the desire to know man apart from his fault'. He adds that this myth 'sustains' – not only the never-completed third part of a poetics, but already the first part in/and its 'eidetic description of the voluntary and the involuntary'.[2] Ricœur openly acknowledges, therefore, that his entire project is both *sustained by* and *depends upon* an originally good human nature more fundamental than any subsequent corruption. While Chapter 5 presented Ricœur's philosophical argument for this fundamental goodness, the present chapter reveals its subterranean 'pre-philosophical' roots in biblical notions of creation.

---

[1] André LaCocque and Paul Ricœur, *Thinking Biblically: Exegetical and Hermeneutical Studies*, trans. David Pellauer (Chicago: University of Chicago Press, 2003), 299.
[2] Ricœur, *Freedom and Nature*, 28. 'L'inspection des possibilités fondamentales de l'homme s'appuie en fait sur ce mythe concret de l'innocence. C'est lui qui donne le *désir* de connaître l'homme en deçà de sa faute. ... Le mythe d'innocence est le désir, le courage, et l'expérience imaginaire qui soutiennent la description eidétique du volontaire et de l'involontaire' (Ricœur, *Le volontaire et l'involontaire*, 31).

PREVIOUS SCHOLARSHIP ON CREATION IN RICŒUR

Although many have pointed to the theological dimension of Ricœur's early 'poetics',[3] and some of these have noted the significance of creation as a symbol,[4] the extent to which creation underlies Ricœur's early thought is less frequently mentioned.[5] Some scholars even argue the opposite, claiming that creation – as something distinct from and somehow predating the problem of evil – is problematically absent in Ricœur's philosophical anthropology. William Schweiker claims that 'theological ethics cannot be satisfied with Ricœur's understanding' of the self,[6] because Ricœur 'collapses what counts as a sufficient account of the content of the good into answering the problem of the self, the aporia of happiness and duty'.[7] By contrast, he argues that 'grace, not violence, is the primordial origin of our sense of ourselves as responsible beings. Creation and not the fall is the fundamental backing of our moral claims'.[8] Similarly, Paul van Tongeren argues that Ricœur's early work is focussed on the fall and salvation, and that only in the writings of his last few years did Ricœur shift his focus on creation.[9] This is the reason, van Tongeren surmises, that Ricœur only completes the 'poetics' – originally planned as the third part of his early project – in his

---

[3] See, for example: John Wall, 'Ricœur, Poetics, and Religious Ethics' in Erfani, *Paul Ricœur*, 48; Verheyden, Hettema, and Vandecasteele, eds., *Paul Ricœur: Poetics and Religion*; Domenico Jervolino, 'In Search of a Poetics of the Will', in *Paul Ricœur: Honoring and Continuing the Work*, ed. Farhang Erfani, trans. Amin Erfani and Carrie Golden (Lanham: Lexington Books, 2011).

[4] See, for example, Luca M. Possati, *Ricœur face à l'analogie: entre théologie et déconstruction* (Paris: Éditions L'Harmattan, 2012). Mark Wallace has also observed, in the introduction to *Figuring the Sacred*, that for Ricœur 'the biblical teaching that forms the background of this dialectic between love and justice is that all human beings are codependent members of an originary and ongoing creation'; Wallace also speaks of Ricœur's 'creation-centred approach to the tension between love and justice' which 'harks back to his earlier ecological exegesis of Gen 1:1-2:4a' (Ricœur, *Figuring the Sacred*, 31).

[5] Creation is not even mentioned in Dan Stiver's *Ricœur and Theology*.

[6] William Schweiker, 'Imagination, Violence, and Hope: A Theological Response to Ricœur's Moral Philosophy', in David E. Klemm and William Schweiker, eds., *Meanings in Texts and Actions: Questioning Paul Ricœur* (Charlottesville: University Press of Virginia, 1993), 206.

[7] Schweiker, 'Imagination, Violence, and Hope', 220.

[8] Schweiker, 'Imagination, Violence, and Hope', 222.

[9] Cf. Paul J. M. van Tongeren, 'Salvation and Creation: On the Role of Forgiveness in the Completion of Paul Ricœur's Philosophy', *International Journal of Philosophy and Theology* 75, no. 2 (15 March 2014): 181.

penultimate publication: *Memory, History, Forgetting*.[10] It is only here that 'the primacy of the religious notion of creation has helped him to fulfil his promise of a poetics'.[11]

Five scholars have recognised the impulse of creation underlying Ricœur's early work. First, Lucca Possati has seen how creation is what underlies Ricœur's 'poetics'.[12] Second, Douglas Earl understands Ricœur's philosophy as 'expressive of a doctrine of creation in which the world is a place that is "graced", is "meaningful" and able to symbolize the divine'.[13] Third, Kevin Vanhoozer notes that for Ricœur the poetry of creation 'evokes visions of a reconciliation between humanity and nature, thereby revealing the basis of their profound unity. Since Kant, of course, knowledge of Creator and Creation is not open to us. But thanks to poetic language we may continue to think beyond the limits of reason alone'.[14] Fourth, Daniel Frey claims that Ricœur's early philosophy is based on a 'return to Edenic innocence'. As we saw in Chapter 6, this is not quite accurate, since Ricœur acknowledges a progression of maturity since Eden apart from sin.[15] But Frey means simply to point to how foundational creation is for Ricœur's thought. For Frey, a Barthian, this is the severest criticism. From a Barthian perspective, the Christian cannot 'proceed, like the philosopher, from the bottom up [Frey cites Barth]: 'A sword of fire bars him from the way taken by the philosopher"'.[16] This is a reference to the sword of fire held by the cherubim to prevent Adam and Eve from returning to Eden (Genesis 3:24). Frey then invokes Ellul's criticism (which we examined in Chapter 5) to conclude that Ricœur's 'starting point ... outside of Christology inevitably constitutes it as an alternative to theological discourse, even as an adversary'.[17] We have already seen Ricœur's response

---

[10] Paul Ricœur, *Memory, History, Forgetting*, trans. David Pellauer and Kathleen Blamey (Chicago: University of Chicago Press, 2004); Paul Ricœur, *La mémoire, l'histoire, l'oubli* (Paris: Éditions du Seuil, 2004).
[11] Tongeren, 'Salvation and Creation', 181.
[12] Possati, *Ricœur face à l'analogie*, 60.
[13] Douglas S. Earl, *Reading Joshua as Christian Scripture* (Winona Lake: Pennsylvania State University Press, 2010), 28.
[14] Kevin Vanhoozer, *Biblical Narrative in the Philosophy of Paul Ricœur: A Study in Hermeneutics and Theology* (Cambridge: Cambridge University Press, 1990), 280.
[15] See Chapter 6 above, section titled 'Connection 1: The Irenaean Moment and Adam's Immaturity'.
[16] Frey, 'On the Servile Will' in Davidson, *A Companion to Ricœur's 'The Symbolism of Evil'*, 63.
[17] Frey, 'On the Servile Will', 61.

to these sorts of objections;[18] here they serve only as further evidence that Ricœur was never particularly Barthian.

Building on these scholars, I contend that the doctrine of creation is not only present in Ricœur's early work, but is the driving force behind his insights about human finitude. Creation is a 'poetic symbol' for Ricœur, theological in origin but yielding insights that can be argued for philosophically. We have already explored some of these insights: in Chapter 1, creation is both the content of hope in the final unity of being, and the reason for our inability to unify being completely in a closed philosophical system. In Chapter 4 we saw that finitude (the human creature) cannot be thought except in relation to the infinite (the creator). In Chapter 5 we surveyed how his belief in the goodness of all created things inspires him to argue that finitude must be distinguished from evil because evil was not part of the original creation. The next three chapters will build on these hints, using the symbol of creation as a heuristic lens to collect the scattered signs of transcendence in Ricœur's early philosophical anthropology. This chapter first explains what Ricœur means by the words 'poetic' and 'symbol'. Chapter 8 then shows how creation functions as Ricœur's overarching category for the unity of reality beyond what we can see or conceive. Finally, in Chapter 9 we turn to the ethical function of creation for Ricœur, showing how by this symbol he contends for the original goodness of every created thing.

The use of creation as a poetic symbol will draw attention to the significant yet largely unrecognised impact of Kant's *Critique of the Power of Judgement* on Ricœur's thought.[19] While Ricœur's great indebtedness to Kant is hard to miss and is frequently acknowledged, secondary literature tends to focus on how Ricœur uses either Kant's ethics or his *Critique of Pure Reason* to furnish an account of the free thinking subject.[20] The only full-length monograph on Kant's relation to Ricœur barely refers to the third *Critique* at all, except to mention that Ricœur got the phrase 'the symbol gives rise to thought' from it.[21] But as we shall

---

[18] See Chapter 5 above, section titled 'Ricœur's Response: Why the Distinction Is Possible'.

[19] Notable exceptions include: Scott-Baumann, *Ricœur and the Hermeneutics of Suspicion*, 73–4; Denis Thouard, 'Kant et l'herméneutique', *Archives de Philosophie* 61, no. 4 (1998): 629–58.

[20] See, *inter alia*: Laurent Jaffro, 'La conception ricœurienne de la raison pratique: Dialectique ou éclectique?', *Études Ricœuriennes/Ricœur Studies* 3, no. 1 (2012): 156–71; James Carter, *Ricœur on Moral Religion* (Oxford: Oxford University Press, 2014), 44–55, 80–8; and Gregor, *Ricœur's Hermeneutics of Religion*, 44–55, 80–8.

[21] Anderson, *Ricœur and Kant*, 66. In fairness, Anderson's topical focus is their understanding of the will, which does not feature prominently in the third *Critique*.

see, not only symbols, but the power of the imagination, the ontological dimension of poetry, and the idea of creation as a source of inspiration for philosophy – all these major Ricœurian themes have their origin in the third *Critique*.

RICŒURIAN SYMBOLS: HOW THEOLOGY INSPIRES PHILOSOPHY

Before considering the many connections between Ricœur's account of finitude and the Christian doctrine of creation, we must address an obvious methodological difficulty: Is it not a betrayal of philosophy to base it on a theological idea? How can philosophy claim to be autonomous, that is to say, truly philosophical, when it depends on a theological concept for its reflective insights? Do not confessional beliefs contaminate the purity of philosophy as rationally accessible to anyone?

By arguing that creation, a theological concept, underpins Ricœur's philosophy, I do not mean to suggest that Ricœur confused the two disciplines. His scrupulousness in keeping to the limits of autonomous philosophical discourse is exemplary, as has been noted by both philosophers and theologians.[22] The limits he recognises are those defined by Kant, and it is within the framework of Kantianism that Ricœur develops his concept of 'poetics' and 'symbols', by which he uses creation, like Kant, as a heuristic lens through which the human condition is powerfully illuminated.

One key way in which Ricœur establishes a relationship between philosophy and theology, but without confusing them or absorbing one into the other, is with his concept of the symbol. In Ricœurian terminology, a symbol is not merely a sign pointing to something else that might also be seen. Rather, a symbol stands for something (a theological idea, for instance) that can never be 'seen', that is to say, clearly grasped by philosophy. It is beyond the limits of philosophy, itself ungraspable as a determinate concept and opaque to reason, but it inspires philosophical thought nonetheless, 'opening our eyes' to dimensions of what it means to be human of which we were previously unaware, but which can subsequently be argued for on their own merits.

---

[22] See, for example, Dominique Janicaud, 'The Theological Turn of French Phenomenology', in *Phenomenology and the 'Theological Turn': The French Debate*, trans. Bernard Prusak (New York: Fordham University Press, 2000); Dominique Janicaud, *Le tournant théologique de la phénoménologie française* (Paris: Éditions de L'Éclat, 1991).

At the beginning of *Freud and Philosophy* Ricœur recounts the history of the development of his concept of symbols, showing that it began, before his hermeneutic interest, with his commitment to hold together 'the rich words of symbols and myths' and the seemingly contradictory demands of 'the tradition of rationality of philosophy' by which he primarily meant the French reflexive school.[23] In order to hold together these two, and making use of Kant's canonical status as a philosopher for French reflexion, he took 'a phrase from Kant's *Critique of Judgement*': 'symbols give rise to thought'.[24] Let us briefly examine this idea in its original Kantian context.

For Kant, a symbol (which he also calls an aesthetic idea) is an 'indirect presentation' of a concept by means of analogy with an 'object of sensible intuition'.[25] It is indirect because it 'occasions much thinking though without it being possible for any determinate thought, i.e. concept, to be adequate to it, which, consequently, no language fully attains or can make intelligible'.[26] A symbol can never become a concept (as Kant understands concepts) with full rational clarity, but this does not mean it has no rational value. When using a symbol 'the imagination is creative, and sets the faculty of intellectual ideas (reason) into motion, that is, at the instigation of a representation it gives more to think about than can be grasped and made distinct in it'.[27] The symbol gives rise to thought through the productive capacity of the imagination. 'Our language is full of such indirect presentations', Kant adds, 'in accordance with an analogy, where the expression does not contain the actual schema for the

---

[23] Ricœur, *Freud and Philosophy*, 38. 'Je jurais d'une part d'*écouter* la riche parole des symboles et des mythes qui précède ma réflexion, l'instruit et la nourrit, d'autre part de continuer ... la tradition de rationalité de la philosophie' (Ricœur, *De l'interprétation: essai sur Freud*, 48).

[24] Ricœur, *Freud and Philosophy*, 38. 'Le symbole donne à penser, disais-je, reprenant un mot de Kant dans la *Critique du jugement*' (Ricœur, *De l'interprétation: essai sur Freud*, 48).

[25] Immanuel Kant, *Critique of the Power of Judgment*, ed. Paul Guyer, trans. Paul Guyer and Eric Matthews (Cambridge: Cambridge University Press, 2000), 226. 'indirekte Darstellung ... Gegenstand einer sinnlichen Anschauung' (Immanuel Kant, *Kritik der Urteilskraft*, ed. Karl Vorländer [Leipzig: F. Meiner, 1922], 212 [5:352]).

[26] Kant, *Critique of the Power of Judgment*, 192. 'diejenige Vorstellung der Einbildungskraft, die viel zu denken veranlaßt, ohne daß ihr doch irgendein bestimmter Gedanke, d.i. Begriff, adäquat sein kann, die folglich keine Sprache völlig erreicht und verständlich machen kann' (Kant, *Kritik der Urteilskraft*, 168 [5:314]).

[27] Kant, *Critique of the Power of Judgment*, 193. 'So ist die Einbildungskraft hierbei schöpferisch und bringt das Vermögen intellektueller Ideen (die Vernunft) in Bewegung, mehr nämlich bei Veranlassung einer Vorstellung zu denken' Kant, *Kritik der Urteilskraft*, 169 (5:315).

concept but only a symbol for reflection'.[28] In a tantalising aside, Kant gives Ricœur great encouragement to think more about symbols: 'this business', he says, 'has as yet been little discussed, much as it deserves a deeper investigation; but this is not the place to dwell on it'.[29] A 'deeper investigation' of this 'business' is precisely what we find in Ricœur.

Ricœur's earliest publication that discusses symbols dates from 1959.[30] But long before then his thought already contained ideas that evidence Ricœur both using this Kantian stimulus and going beyond it. The first sign of this is where he addresses the influence of theology on philosophy in the broadest sense. In doing so he was probably inspired by Karl Jaspers. Although not religious, Jaspers freely acknowledged that philosophy had been inspired to find philosophical truth by the impetus of religious thought, but the truth was no less philosophical for having a non-philosophical origin. In Jaspers' case the notion in question is freedom, which, he says, 'without St. Paul, St. Augustine, and Luther, would perhaps not have come so clearly into our consciousness'.[31] Following this principle of a religious inspiration for philosophy, Ricœur applies it to the word 'sin', which, we recall from Chapter 5, he frequently uses in his philosophical writings. 'Might not the philosopher take exception', he asks concerning his descriptions of evil, sin, and guilt, that they are 'dictated by a Christian theology of original sin'?[32] In response, he distinguishes between a *philosophical insight*, argued philosophically, and its *source*, which need not be philosophical. If an idea can be developed and defended rationally, he asserts, its origin outside philosophy does not invalidate it. Ideas should be judged, not by where they came from, but by their ability to clarify our understanding: 'if theology opens our eyes to an obscure segment of human reality, no

---

[28] Kant, *Critique of the Power of Judgment*, 226. 'Unsere Sprache ist voll von dergleichen indirekten Darstellungen nach einer Analogie, wodurch der Ausdruck nicht das eigentliche Schema für den Begriff, sondern bloß ein Symbol für die Reflexion enthält' Kant, *Kritik der Urteilskraft*, 212 (5:352).
[29] Kant, *Critique of the Power of Judgment*, 226. 'Dies Geschäft ist bis jetzt noch wenig auseinandergesetzt worden, so sehr es auch eine tiefere Untersuchung verdient; allein hier ist nicht der Ort, sich dabei aufzuhalten' Kant, *Kritik der Urteilskraft*, 212 (5:352).
[30] Paul Ricœur, 'The Symbol: Food for Thought', *Philosophy Today* 4, no. 3 (Fall 1960): 196–207; Paul Ricœur, 'Le symbole donne à penser', *Esprit*, no. 275 (7/8) (1959): 60–76.
[31] Jaspers, 'Reply to My Critics', 780.
[32] Ricœur, *Freedom and Nature*, 25. 'Le philosophe récusera-t-il ... sous prétexte qu'elle est commandée par une théologie chrétienne du péché originel?' (Ricœur, *Le volontaire et l'involontaire*, 27).

methodological *a priori* should prevent the philosopher from having his eyes opened and henceforth reading man, his history, and civilization, under the sign of the fall'.[33]

The idea that philosophy can be stimulated by an encounter with non-philosophy would not be controversial, if the goal was that philosophy should absorb the non-philosophy into itself. But the Kantian/Ricœurian symbol is more challenging than that, because in itself it remains opaque and is never fully clarified by philosophical reflection. Therefore in order for symbols to be considered philosophically valid, Ricœur has to develop symbolic thought beyond the embryonic form in which Kant left it, and connect it to the twentieth-century insistence that philosophy can never have the complete rational transparency it desires. Ricœur accomplishes this in two ways: by denying the possibility of neutral or presuppositionless philosophy, and by challenging the assumption that philosophy is best expressed in univocal language.

First, Ricœur suggests that we cannot understand why symbols are valid philosophical material while holding to the belief that philosophy can be presuppositionless: 'One must have experienced the deception that accompanies the idea of a presuppositionless philosophy to enter sympathetically into the problematic we are going to evoke.'[34] Everyone does philosophy from a certain presuppositional standpoint: in this the religious thinker is no different to the atheist or the agnostic. Ricœur will later say of hermeneutics that it 'puts us on guard against the illusion or pretention of neutrality' and that by neutrality he means 'being free from presuppositions'.[35] The impossibility of a neutral standpoint means that 'nobody interrogates from nowhere. It is a great illusion to think

---

[33] Ricœur, *Freedom and Nature*, 25. 'Obscure' in this context means not 'irrelevant' but 'unclear'. 'Si la théologie ouvre les yeux à une zone obscure de la réalité humaine, nul à priori de méthode ne pourra faire que le philosophe n'ait eu les yeux ouverts et ne lise désormais l'homme, son histoire et sa civilisation, sous le signe de la chute' (Ricœur, *Le volontaire et l'involontaire*, 27–8). Ricœur maintained this basic idea throughout his life, and fifty years later we find him using the same language, 'distinguishing "motivation" from "argumentation"' (Ricœur and Questioners, 'Roundtable Discussion', 203).

[34] Ricœur, *Conflict of Interpretations*, 287. 'Il faut peut-être avoir éprouvé la déception qui s'attache à l'idée de philosophie sans présupposition pour accéder à la problématique que nous allons évoquer' (Ricœur, *Conflit des interprétations*, 283).

[35] Ricœur, *Hermeneutics and the Human Sciences: Essays on Language, Action and Interpretation*, 3. 'La présentation qui suit n'est donc pas neutre, au sens où elle serait dénuée de présupposition. Aussi bien l'herméneutique elle-même met-elle en garde contre cette illusion ou cette prétention' (Paul Ricœur, 'La tâche de l'herméneutique', in *Exegesis: problèmes de méthode et exercices de lecture*, ed. François Bovon and Grégoire Rouiller [Neuchâtel: Delachaux & Niestlé, 1975], 179–80).

that one could make himself a pure spectator, without weight, without memory, without perspective, and regard everything with equal sympathy'.[36] Therefore, 'it is necessary to renounce the chimera of a philosophy without presuppositions'.[37]

Secondly, Ricœur argues that we cannot grasp the need for symbols while maintaining that univocal language is the only valid way to speak philosophically. In October 1962 Ricœur made his first visit to the University of Cambridge, at the invitation of Donald MacKinnon, who had recently been appointed Norris-Hulse Professor at the Faculty of Divinity. He spent six weeks (the bulk of the Michaelmas term) in Cambridge giving a series of eight lectures on hermeneutics. During that time he wrote to Gabriel Marcel that in his lectures he was finding it necessary to 'confront logical positivism'. 'I am struggling to show', he wrote, 'that there is an intelligence that *deciphers* and that this intelligence refuses the alternative: either the logic of univocal discourse or nonsense'.[38] He argues instead, in a published article, that symbols provide a greater richness to philosophical discourse: 'In the very age in which our language is becoming more precise, more univocal, more technical, ... it is in this age of discourse that we wish to recharge language, start again from the *fullness* of language'.[39] By 'fullness' Ricœur means discourse that uses language in a non-univocal way. While opaque in itself, a symbol 'has a way of *revealing* things that is not reducible to any translation from a language in cipher to a clear language'.[40]

---

[36] Ricœur, *Symbolism of Evil*, 306. Translation modified: 'Nul n'interroge de nulle part. ... C'est une grande illusion de croire que l'on pourrait se faire pur spectateur, sans poids, sans mémoire, sans perspective, et tout regarder avec une égale sympathie' (Ricœur, *Finitude et culpabilité*, 523).

[37] Ricœur, *Symbolism of Evil*, 19. 'Il faut renoncer à la chimère d'une philosophie sans présuppositions' (Ricœur, *Finitude et culpabilité*, 222).

[38] My translation (italics original): 'Je suis ici sur l'invitation de M. Donald MacKinnon .... Je donne une série de 8 leçons sur la notion d'herméneutique; je dois faire face au positivisme logique et m'efforce de montrer qu'il y a une intelligence qui *déchiffre* et que cette intelligence refuse l'alternative: ou la logique du discours univoque ou le non-sens' (Paul Ricœur, 'Paul Ricœur to Gabriel Marcel', 1 November 1962, Fonds Gabriel Marcel, Bibliothèque Nationale de France, Paris).

[39] Ricœur, *Conflict of Interpretations*, 288. Italics original: 'C'est à l'époque même où notre langage se fait plus précis, plus univoque, plus technique en un mot, ... c'est à cette même époque du discours que nous voulons recharger notre langage, que nous voulons repartir du plein du langage' (Ricœur, *Conflit des interprétations*, 284).

[40] Ricœur, *Symbolism of Evil*, 163. Italics original: 'Le mythe [a type of symbol] a une façon de *révéler*, irréductible à toute traduction d'un langage chiffré en un langage clair' (Ricœur, *Finitude et culpabilité*, 374).

The next stage in Ricœur's development of symbols comes from the inspiration Ricœur draws from Jaspers's concept of the 'ciphers' of transcendence, unfolded climactically in the final chapter of Jaspers's *Philosophy*, the book that was Ricœur's companion while a prisoner of war.[41] While there is no evidence that Jaspersian ciphers are derived from Kantian symbols, it would not be surprising given the overall significance of Kant for Jaspers.[42] A cipher, for Jaspers, is a species of symbol pointing to something that can never itself be seen, a visible manifestation of the invisible, an intellectually graspable notion that reveals the ungraspable.[43] Jaspers classifies ciphers into three levels or stages: experiential, mythical, and speculative.[44] At the final speculative level, a cipher is 'thinking that drives us to think the unthinkable'.[45] It is a revelation of transcendence which cannot be rendered in philosophically objective language:

> In the cipher script the symbol is inseparable from that which it symbolizes. Ciphers bring transcendence to mind, but there is no interpreting them. To interpret, I would have to split what is only in union. I would compare a cipher with transcendence, but transcendence only appears to me in the cipher script; it is not the cipher script. ... The cipher is what it is; it cannot be clarified again by something else.[46]

---

[41] 'It is difficult for me to express today,' testifies Ricœur in 1994, 'to what extent I was fascinated, [not only during World War II but] in the 1950s, by Jaspers's great trilogy, most specifically by the final chapter of the third volume devoted to the "ciphers" of Transcendence: was not the "deciphering" of these ciphers the perfect model of a philosophy of Transcendence that would be at the same time a poetics?' (Ricœur, 'Intellectual Autobiography', 13). 'Je ne saurais dire aujourd'hui à quel point j'étais fasciné, dans les années cinquante, par la trilogie – *Philosophie* – de Jaspers et plus précisément par le dernier chapitre du tome III consacré aux "chiffres" de la Transcendance: le "déchiffrement " de ces chiffres ne constituait-il pas le modèle parfait d'une philosophie de la transcendance qui serait en même temps une poétique?' (Ricœur, *Réflexion faite*, 25).

[42] See, *inter alia*: Jaspers, *Philosophy*, 1969, 1:2; Jaspers, *Philosophie*, vi; Jaspers, 'On My Philosophy', 137.

[43] Ricœur admits that a Jaspersian cipher is unlike any other kind of symbol (Ricœur, *Marcel et Jaspers*, 425). But the same is true of Ricœur's particular use of the word 'symbol' in these early writings. He expressly identifies the two concepts in one essay, speaking of Jaspers's 'ciphers, which I am calling symbols' (Ricœur, *Philosophical Anthropology*, 114); ('chiffres, que j'appelle symboles' [Ricœur, *Anthropologie philosophique*, 185]).

[44] Jaspers, *Philosophy*, 1969, 3:113–19; Jaspers, *Philosophie*, 786–92.

[45] Jaspers, *Philosophy*, 1969, 3:119. 'Spekulation ist ... ein Denken, das denkend über das Denkbare hinaustreibt' (Jaspers, *Philosophie*, 791).

[46] Jaspers, *Philosophy*, 1969, 3:124. 'In der Chiffreschrift ist Trennung von Symbol und dem, was symbolisiert wird, unmöglich. Sie bringt Transzendenz zur Gegenwart, aber sie ist nicht deutbar. Wollte ich deuten, müßte ich, was nur zusammen ist, wieder trennen: ich würde sie mit der Transzendenz vergleichen, welche mir doch nur in ihr erscheint, aber sie nicht ist.... Chiffreschrift aber ist als sie selbst und kann nicht noch einmal klar werden durch ein Anderes' (Jaspers, *Philosophie*, 796–7).

In Ricœur's first article on symbols he adopts Jaspers's threefold classification with approval, renaming the first two as 'primary symbols' (sin as defilement, water as cleansing) and 'secondary symbols' which have narrative form and are more commonly called myths.⁴⁷ Regarding the third, speculative level, the Ricœurian symbol shares with the Jaspersian cipher the feature that it cannot be 'translated' into pure conceptuality: it 'presents its meaning in the opaque transparency of an enigma and not by translation'.⁴⁸

However, due to his greater faithfulness to Kant, Ricœur's symbols also depart from the Jaspersian cipher in a way that reflects the difference (analysed in Chapter 2) between Jaspers's individualism and Ricœur's more Kantian reach towards universal truth. Jaspers has no criteriology of ciphers: each individual is alone in choosing to take something for a cipher or not, and their choice cannot be validated by any universal criteria. Because of this, ciphers do not bring greater clarity to philosophical discourse; they are simply a mediator between the individual human (Existenz) and transcendence.⁴⁹ For Ricœur, on the other hand, not all symbols are equal. While not rationally transparent, their adequacy can be measured by their capacity to illuminate one another and the world.

Already in 1936, Ricœur shows a rich understanding of the illuminating function of religious symbols on philosophy. In this case, he is speaking of faith, describing it as 'a certain *paradox*' that, if embraced,

---

⁴⁷ Ricœur, 'The Symbol', 201; Ricœur, 'Le symbole donne à penser', 67.
⁴⁸ Ricœur, *Symbolism of Evil*, 16. 'Le symbole donne son sens .. dans la transparence opaque de l'énigme et non par traduction' (Ricœur, *Finitude et culpabilité*, 219). That is why I disagree with Gschwandtner that Ricœur ultimately wants to bring the symbol into full conceptual clarity (see Christina Gschwandtner, 'Wagering for a Second Naïveté? Tensions in Ricœur's Account of the Symbolism of Evil', in Davidson, *A Companion to Ricœur's The Symbolism of Evil*, 87–101). She bases this on Ricœur's claim that philosophy that learns from symbols must 'yet be fully rational', and that 'the question of truth is unceasingly eluded' (cited on page 90). But by 'fully rational' Ricœur does not mean that the symbol itself becomes clear, only that philosophy must reason to its limits about the symbol. Similarly, he says that the question of truth is eluded when one simply describes symbols as a 'disinterested spectator' (as Mircea Eliade does), without wagering on the truth of one of them as he intends to do (see Ricœur, *Symbolism of Evil*, 353–4; Ricœur, *Finitude et culpabilité*, 573–4).
⁴⁹ 'As in consciousness at large it is the experiment that mediates between subject and object, so it is the cipher that mediates between Existenz and transcendence' (Jaspers, *Philosophy*, 1969, 3:120; 'Wie im Bewußtsein überhaupt das Experiment der Mittler zwischen Subjekt und Objekt ist, so die Chiffre zwischen Existenz und Transzendenz' [Jaspers, *Philosophie*, 793]).

becomes 'the enlivening of a whole way of thinking that finds itself suddenly illuminated': faith is 'something that can only ever be *clarifying, never clarified in itself*'.⁵⁰ If it remains itself paradoxical, faith is valid when it brings rational clarity to *other* things, to our concepts and to the world around us.

That is why, for Ricœur, to abandon presuppositionless philosophy does not leave us with a relativistic or fideistic *impasse* where nobody's starting point is better or worse than anyone else's. One's choice of symbol is not immune to philosophical critique. Instead, Ricœur develops criteria to evaluate the truth of a symbol by means of its ability to illuminate areas of philosophy that would otherwise have been darkness: the symbol is 'revealed insofar as it is revealing.... It calls for verification of its revealed origin by its revealing power'.⁵¹ It opens our eyes to aspects of reality that we would not otherwise have known: 'the symbol, used as a means of detecting and deciphering human reality, will have been verified by its power to raise up, to illuminate, to give order to [a] region of human experience'.⁵² An image may help illustrate what Ricœur means. When defending mysticism, G. K. Chesterton writes: 'The one created thing which we cannot look at is the one thing in the light of which we look at everything. Like the sun at noonday, mysticism explains everything else by the blaze of its own victorious invisibility'.⁵³ A Ricœurian symbol is heliotropic, explaining other things even as it remains itself unexplained.

The explanatory power of a symbol cannot be proven universally beyond doubt. If it could, then it would have the status of complete clarity and would no longer be a symbol. While Ricœur agrees with Jaspers in rejecting any universal *provability* of the truth of a symbol, he insists in a Kantian manner that a philosophy starting from symbols can be *argued for*. Ricœur explains the difference between a proof and an argument by speaking of one's position as a *wager* which is won or lost depending on the explanatory power the symbol gives to those who base their thinking on it:

---

⁵⁰ My translation (italics original): 'un certain *paradoxe* ... vivification de toute une pensée qui se trouve brusquement illuminée, quelque chose qui ne saurait être qu'*éclairant* mais jamais *éclairé en soi*' (Ricœur, 'Note sur les rapports', 549).
⁵¹ Ricœur, *Symbolism of Evil*, 308. 'révélée en tant que révélante. ... Il appelle la vérification de son origine révélée par son pouvoir révélant' (Ricœur, *Finitude et culpabilité*, 525).
⁵² Ricœur, *Symbolism of Evil*, 355. 'Le symbole, employé comme détecteur et déchiffreur de la réalité humaine, aura été vérifié par son pouvoir de susciter, d'éclairer, d'ordonner cette région de l'expérience humaine' (Ricœur, *Finitude et culpabilité*, 575).
⁵³ G. K. Chesterton, *Orthodoxy* (London: John Lane, 1908), 48–9.

I wager that I shall have a better understanding of man and of the bond between the being of man and the being of all things if I follow the *indication* of symbolic thought. That wager then becomes the task of *verifying* my wager and saturating it, so to speak, with intelligibility. In return, the task transforms my wager: in betting *on* the significance of the symbolic world, I bet at the same time *that* my wager will be restored to me in the power of reflection, in the element of coherent discourse.[54]

From this 'philosophy that thinks from symbols' emerges a new dimension of the relationship between philosophy and theology. Theology, says Ricœur, is thinking about the symbol itself and seeking an internal agreement between symbols: 'The theologian testifies to the agreement of the Adamic myth with Christology'.[55] Philosophy, on the other hand, is the attempt to make sense of the rest of reality in light of symbols: 'The philosopher verifies what is revealed by that which reveals'.[56] Theology looks *at* the symbol, proclaiming the revealed truth that cannot be reduced to pure reason; philosophy looks *through* the symbol at the world illuminated by it, wagering on the greater understanding gained by the symbol's lens.

But the use of symbols is not peculiar to religious philosophers, Ricœur claims. He sees himself as simply following what all philosophers do when they are prompted to think philosophically on the basis of an event or expression from outside philosophy: 'I am not any worse off than anyone else. No one is the master of the origin of his thoughts'.[57] Even Heidegger uses symbols: 'it would be easy to show that all of Heidegger's "existentials" have their origin in the sphere of symbols. They are symbols interpreted philosophically; starting from symbols results in comprehension of human reality'.[58]

---

[54] Ricœur, *Symbolism of Evil*, 355. Italics original: 'Je parie que je comprendrai mieux l'homme et le lien entre l'être de l'homme et l'être de tous les étants si je suis l'*indication* de la pensée symbolique. Ce pari devient alors la tâche de *vérifier* mon pari et de le saturer en quelque sorte d'intelligibilité; en retour cette tâche transforme mon pari: en parlant *sur* la signification du monde symbolique, je parie en même temps *que* mon pari me sera rendu en puissance de réflexion, dans l'élément du discours cohérent' (Ricœur, *Finitude et culpabilité*, 574).

[55] Ricœur, *Symbolism of Evil*, 310. 'Le théologien atteste la convenance du mythe adamique à la christologie' (Ricœur, *Finitude et culpabilité*, 527).

[56] Ricœur, *Symbolism of Evil*, 309. 'Le philosophe vérifie le révélé par le révélant' (Ricœur, *Finitude et culpabilité*, 527).

[57] Reagan, *Paul Ricœur*, 125. 'Je ne suis pas plus mal placé que quiconque. Personne n'est le maître de l'origine de ses pensées' (Charles Reagan, 'Interview avec Paul Ricœur', *Journal of French and Francophone Philosophy* 3, no. 3 [1992]: 158).

[58] Ricœur, 'The Symbol', 207. 'Il serait aisé de montrer que les "existentiaux" de Heidegger sont tous issus de la sphère symbolique. Ce sont des symboles philosophiquement interprétés; à partir de la sphère des symboles, une compréhension de la réalité humaine est ouverte' (Ricœur, 'Le symbole donne à penser', 75).

Such is Ricœur's justification for the theological origin of his philosophical project. 'I hold', he proclaims, 'that no symbol *qua* opening and uncovering a truth of man is foreign to philosophical reflection'.[59]

RICŒURIAN POETICS: CREATIVE DISCOURSE ABOUT CREATION

For Ricœur, therefore, anything that comes from outside philosophy and inspires philosophical thought is a symbol. But why is the particular symbol of the biblical creation narrative so important for him? The answer, as we shall see, is that his entire *Philosophy of the Will* was oriented towards unfolding human reality in light of its status as created by a good Creator. Creation is the ultimate symbol that inspires Ricœur's philosophy, not as an event in the past but as a reality in the present, a reality that speaks of the fundamental goodness of all things.

Nonetheless, Ricœur begins his *Philosophy of the Will* project by bracketing both symbols, sin and creation (or evil and transcendence), out of his analysis. *Freedom and Nature* aims to describe the human condition in abstraction from either of these dimensions. But he never meant to stop there. Each of the three projected parts of *Philosophy of the Will* was to have its own method. The first he calls an 'eidetics', pure description in double brackets. The second he labels an 'empirics', a method that removes the brackets around evil/sin by considering its historic manifestations. But a description of the human will is not complete, he informs us, until both brackets have been removed and the human condition has been examined in light of transcendence. To this third and final methodology he gives the title 'poetics'. 'The completion of the ontology of the subject', he writes, 'demands a new change of method, *moving on to a kind of "Poetics" of the will*'.[60]

Why does Ricœur call this third method a 'poetics'? My contention is that Ricœur's use of the word 'poetics' is an expansion of Kant's understanding of the metaphysical function of poetry. For Kant, only poetry has the power to make invisible things visible. Kant gives poetry 'the highest rank of all' the arts, because it allows the mind to judge 'independently of determination by nature, in accordance with points of view

---

[59] Ricœur, *Conflict of Interpretations*, 305. 'Je tiens que nul symbole en tant qu'ouvrant et découvrant une vérité de l'homme n'est étranger à la réflexion philosophique' (Ricœur, *Conflit des interprétations*, 301).

[60] Ricœur, *Freedom and Nature*, 30. Italics original: 'L'achèvement de l'ontologie du sujet exige un nouveau changement de méthode, l'*access à une sorte de "Poétique"* de la volonté' (Ricœur, *Le volontaire et l'involontaire*, 32).

that nature does not present by itself in experience either for sense or for the understanding, and thus to use it for the sake of and as it were as the schema of the supersensible'.[61] In other words, only poetry enables thought to soar beyond its own finite limits and imagine reality in light of the 'supersensible'. Poetry is not merely *belles-lettres*, but uses the imagination to speak about things beyond the boundaries of knowledge that can never become determinate philosophical concepts. Poetic ideas 'strive toward something lying beyond the bounds of experience'.[62] It is significant that when Kant turns to examples of this poetic function, they are all drawn from religion and theology. 'The poet', he writes, 'ventures to make sensible rational ideas of invisible beings, the kingdom of the blessed, the kingdom of hell, eternity, creation, etc'.[63] All this is made possible by the productive capacity of the imagination.

Expanding on this Kantian understanding of poetry, Ricœur gives the name 'poetics' to a philosophical method which removes the brackets around transcendence and completes his trilogy by describing human reality from a theological ('supersensible') point of view. Ricœurian 'poetics' refers to creation in two senses: (1) linguistic creations of the human order that employ the creativity of imagination through language; and (2) divine creation that is revealed by this linguistic creation. John Wall notes that 'Ricœur's earliest notion of poetics is in fact a religious one'.[64] In his later works Ricœur focusses only on the first sense of 'poetics' as human linguistic creativity, apparently dropping the more metaphysical/religious sense.[65] But in Ricœur's early work both senses are

---

[61] Kant, *Critique of the Power of Judgment*, 204. '§53. Vergleichung: des ästhetischen Werts der schönen Künste untereinander. Unter allen behauptet die Dichtkunst ... den obersten Rang. Sie ... stärkt das Gemüt, indem sie es sein freies, selbsttätiges und von der Naturbestimmung unabhängiges Vermögen fühlen läßt, die Natur, als Erscheinung, nach Ansichten zu betrachten und zu beurteilen, die sie nicht von selbst, weder für den Sinn noch den Verstand in der Erfahrung darbietet, und sie also zum Behuf und gleichsam zum Schema des Übersinnlichen zu gebrauchen' (Kant, *Kritik der Urteilskraft*, 183 [5:326–7]).
[62] Kant, *Critique of the Power of Judgment*, 192. 'Sie zu etwas über die Erfahrungsgrenze hinaus Liegendem wenigstens streben' (Kant, *Kritik der Urteilskraft*, 168 [5:314]).
[63] Kant, *Critique of the Power of Judgment*, 192. 'Der Dichter wagt es, Vernunftideen von unsichtbaren Wesen, das Reich der Seligen, das Höllenreich, die Ewigkeit, die Schöpfung u. dgl. zu versinnlichen' (Kant, *Kritik der Urteilskraft*, 168 [5:314]).
[64] John Wall, 'Ricœur, Poetics, and Religious Ethics' in Erfani, *Paul Ricœur*, 48.
[65] Cf. his description of poetics in *Lectures 3*, 301. On the term 'poetics' in Ricœur, see also: Verheyden, Hettema, and Vandecasteele, *Paul Ricœur*; and Olivier Abel, 'Paul Ricœur's Hermeneutics: From Critique to Poetics', in *Between Suspicion and Sympathy: Paul Ricœur's Unstable Equilibrium*, ed. Andrzej Wierciński (Toronto: Hermeneutic Press, 2003), 11–21; Serge Meitinger, 'Entre "intrigue" et "métaphore": la poétique de P. Ricœur devant la spécificité du poème', in *Paul Ricœur: les métamorphoses de la raison herméneutique*, ed. Jean Greisch and Richard Kearney (Paris: Éditions du Cerf, 1991).

present, in a subtle play on words. 'Poetry', Ricœur writes, 'is the art of *conjuring up the world as created*. It is in effect the *order of creation* which [the "eidetics"] holds in suspension' (and by implication, which the 'poetics' no longer suspends).[66] Poetry, then, is creative language that speaks about creation, a description of the world from the imaginative viewpoint of seeing it as created.[67]

But Ricœur never wrote his projected third part, the 'poetics' of the will. After publishing *The Symbolism of Evil* (which removed the brackets around evil) he became increasingly occupied with linguistic, hermeneutic, and psychoanalytic questions.[68] This does not mean, however, that it is impossible to examine Ricœur's poetics. Thankfully, glimpses of the poetics shine through the extant two parts. Ricœur was aware of this, seeing it not as a result of sloppy methodology but of the fact that no philosophy can fully erase all trace of its presuppositions. We see evidence of this in a letter Ricœur wrote to Gabriel Marcel in June 1950, narrating the events of his doctoral examination by Jean Wahl and René Le Senne[69] (the thesis published as *Freedom and Nature*). Ricœur reports that Wahl detected the belief that humans are created by a good God and are therefore originally good like a lingering scent on the pages of *Freedom and Nature*: 'Jean Wahl, whose critique was the most perceptive at my examination, reproached me with an implicit use of a *certain feeling of good creation*, which was at odds with my declaration of method'.[70] Ricœur

---

[66] Ricœur, *Freedom and Nature*, 30. Italics mine: 'Au sens radical du mot, la poésie est l'art de conjurer le monde de la création. C'est en effet l'ordre de la création qui est tenu en suspens par la description' (Ricœur, *Le volontaire et l'involontaire*, 32).

[67] While Ricœurian poetics has been much discussed, only Possati has noticed the wordplay in Ricœur's use of the term: 'Semantic innovation remains under tension in relation to the biblical idea of creation: it is separated, but not cut off from it. In describing the creation of language and creative language we describe divine creation' (My translation: 'L'innovation sémantique … reste sous tension par rapport à l'idée de création biblique: elle est séparée, mais pas coupée de celle-ci. En décrivant la création du langage et le langage créatif nous décrivons la création divine' [Possati, *Ricœur face à l'analogie*, 61]).

[68] He does, however, claim much later that some aspects of his poetics were achieved in subsequent writings: '*The Symbolism of Evil*, *The Rule of Metaphor*, *Time and Narrative* do aspire in several ways to the title of poetics' (Ricœur, 'Intellectual Autobiography', 14). '*La symbolique du mal*, *la Métaphore vive*, *Temps et récit*, se réclament à plusieurs égards d'une poétique' (Ricœur, *Réflexion faite*, 26).

[69] There may have been more people present, but these are the only two Ricœur mentions.

[70] My translation (italics mine): 'Jean Wahl, qui a été le plus perspicace dans la critique à ma soutenance, m'a reproché un usage implicite d'un certain sentiment de la création bonne, en rupture avec ma déclaration de méthode' (Paul Ricœur, 'Paul Ricœur to Gabriel Marcel', 16 June 1950, Fonds Gabriel Marcel, Bibliothèque Nationale de France, Paris).

admits that Wahl was probably correct about the lingering scent of creation, but defends himself this way:

> I am not at all claiming to have taken a starting point 'without presuppositions'; at the origin, eidetics, empirics, and poetics are all simultaneous. ... So it is not surprising that the Poetics could and must 'seep through' ... because the bracketing is not an existential doubt, but a methodological neutralisation demanded by the rigour of eidetic analysis.[71]

Ricœur then reports that René Le Senne made the opposite criticism to Wahl, saying that the abstraction of transcendence left humanity with an inherent brokenness and sadness. This accusation, however, Ricœur rejected entirely, telling Marcel: 'I am completely convinced to the contrary and I find Wahl's criticism much more appropriate, of having a "haunting transcendence" that justifies the joyful overtones of the living pact between freedom and nature'.[72]

Wahl's 'reproach' is the first of a chorus of voices who agree that Ricœur's 'poetics' continually 'seeps through' in the two published parts of his early trilogy. 'Even postponed', writes Théoneste Nkéramihigo, the '*Poétique* underlies the currently available work from Ricœur.... We acknowledge the diffuse presence and the guiding function of the *Poétique* explicitly absent from Ricœur's writing.'[73] Loretta Dornisch agrees: 'since the adventure of the poetics was and is never far from Ricœur's current project, references are sprinkled throughout most of his writings from the beginning'.[74] Timo Helenius goes further, claiming

---

[71] My translation: 'Je ne prétends nullement avoir pris un point de départ "sans présupposé"; à l'origine, eidétique, empirique, poétique sont simultanées. ... Il n'est donc pas étonnant que la Poétique puisse et doive "sourdre" ... car la parenthèse n'est pas un doute existentiel, mais une neutralisation méthodologique exigée par la rigueur de l'analyse eidétique' (Ricœur, 'Paul Ricœur to Gabriel Marcel', 15 June 1950).

[72] My translation: 'Je suis bien convaincu du contraire et je trouve plus juste le reproche de Wahl d'avoir une "transcendance honteuse" pour justifier l'accent joyeux du pacte vital entre la liberté et la nature' (Ricœur, 'Paul Ricœur to Gabriel Marcel', 16 June 1950).

[73] Cited in Jervolino, 'In Search of a Poetics of the Will', 161 n. 3. See Théoneste Nkéramihigo, *L'homme et la transcendance: essai de poétique dans la philosophie de Paul Ricœur* (Rome: Pontificia Universitas Gregoriana, 1984). We must note the dissenting voice of Robert Jacques, however, who objects strongly to Nkéramihigo's portrayal, calling it apologetic, and offers instead what Possati calls an 'immanentist reading' of Ricœur's work in which transcendence is nothing to do with God but is merely the human Other. See Robert Jacques, 'Corps et transcendance: une mise en relation dans le volontaire et l'involontaire de Paul Ricœur', *Revue de Théologie et de Philosophie* 127 (1995): 235–49; Possati, *Ricœur face à l'analogie*, 36–7.

[74] Loretta Dornisch, *Faith and Philosophy in the Writings of Paul Ricœur* (Lewiston: Edwin Mellen Press, 1990), 365.

that '*all* of Ricœur's work is to be understood as a series of incomplete approximations into the "poetics of being and of the will in being"'.[75] But of these voices only Possati identifies creation as Ricœur's poetic symbol *par excellence*: 'The traces of analogy in *The Voluntary and the Involuntary* [the French title of *Freedom and Nature*] point in the direction of an idea of creation, of a poetics of creation ... understood as the act of God who gives life to the universe'.[76] Although sin is also a symbol, creation is the primary symbol that drives Ricœur's philosophy, because (as we saw in Chapter 5[77]) the idea of something gone wrong implies a prior idea of what would be right: 'a myth of fall is possible only within the context of a myth of creation and innocence'.[78] Similarly, 'there will perhaps never be an empirical approach to the fault without a mythical approach to innocence'.[79] Sin depends on creation for its meaning.

Why did Ricœur abandon the project of a poetics of the will? Jervolino is probably right that Ricœur later thought it was 'too closely related to what can be called a "triumphant ontology"'.[80] It would have brought too much conceptual closure to Ricœur's philosophy, which was not available to finite human thought in his view. Poetics is a horizon from which to think, but to conceptualise it in a determinate way would be to draw the horizon too close and to claim too much for philosophy. It is the very nature of poetic symbols that they cannot become 'determinate concepts' (to use Kantian terminology). Poetics may influence philosophy but may not be absorbed by it. Ricœur himself later says that the last sentence of *Freedom and Nature* ('to will is not to create') pointed prophetically to the 'abandonment of the great project' because it 'placed creation, in the biblical sense, outside the field of philosophy'.[81] Ricœur neither wished nor considered himself competent to do 'theology proper'.

---

[75] Helenius, 'Ricœur's Kierkegaard', 13. Italics mine.
[76] My translation: 'Les traces de l'analogie dans *Le volontaire et l'involontaire* pointent en direction d'une idée de création, d'une poétique de la création ou des créatures, ... entendue comme acte de Dieu qui donne la vie à l'univers' (Possati, *Ricœur face à l'analogie*, 60).
[77] See Chapter 5, section titled, 'Ricœur's Response: Why the Distinction is Possible'.
[78] Ricœur, *Fallible Man*, 145. 'Un mythe de chute n'est possible que dans le contexte d'un mythe de création et d'innocence' (Ricœur, *Finitude et culpabilité*, 198).
[79] Ricœur, *Freedom and Nature*, 28. 'L'empirique de la faute ne va peut-être jamais sans la mythique de l'innocence' (Ricœur, *Le volontaire et l'involontaire*, 31).
[80] Jervolino, 'In Search of a Poetics of the Will', 156.
[81] My translation: 'Aussi bien les derniers mots du *Volontaire et de l'involontaire* n'étaient-ils pas: vouloir n'est pas créer? Et ce mot n'était-il pas prémonitoire de l'abandon ultérieur du grand projet, dans la mesure où il mettait la création au sens biblique hors du champ de la philosophie?' (Ricœur, *Réflexion faite*, 26). Strangely, this last clause does not appear in the English translation (see Ricœur, 'Intellectual Autobiography').

CONCLUSION

Before Ricœur had any idea that his philosophy would become hermeneutical in nature, his concept of symbols was a way of bringing theological ideas into philosophy without compromising the boundaries between the two. What prevents such a compromise – indeed, what prevents Ricœur's thought from becoming theology – is that the religious symbol is never brought to full conceptual clarity, never explained without remainder; rather, it fertilises philosophy, enabling it to produce thought that nourishes and sustains. For Ricœur, the most fertile of all symbols is the doctrine of creation, which is the foundation for his never-written 'poetics' of the will. Nonetheless, throughout Ricœur's early work we see glimpses and clues of the way the symbol of creation underpins his philosophy.

In what ways, then, does the poetics of creation shine through? That is the topic of the next two chapters.

8

The Mysterious Unity of Creation

> The mysterious unity of being is primary.
> Paul Ricœur[1]

In Chapter 1 we saw the tension in Ricœur between the problems he sees in closed philosophical systems and his Kantian commitment to unity as a demand of philosophy. Because of his belief in final unity, Ricœur distanced himself from the non-systematic nature of Marcel's philosophy. By means of 'ontological hope' he enabled philosophy to keep searching for unity without finding it, stimulated by the hope that reality *is* united even if that unity will never be fully discovered before the end of all things.[2] It is now time to supplement that point by showing that Ricœur was enabled to make hope central by means of the doctrine of creation, a doctrine which (as he learned from Kant) posits the unity of being (because all of reality has in common its created status in relation to a single Creator), while denying the possibility of proving that unity in a totalising philosophical system due to the finite limits of the creaturely perspective.

This chapter focusses on the way creation supplies a language to express the ultimate unity of being – particularly the radically different kinds of being known as subject and object, freedom and nature – yet at the same

---

[1] My translation: 'L'unité mystérieuse de l'être est première' (Ricœur, 'Paul Ricœur to Gabriel Marcel, Le Chambon s/Lignon', 25 November 1945, Fonds Gabriel Marcel, Bibliothèque Nationale de France, Paris).

[2] See Chapter 1 above, section headed 'Paul Ricœur: The Unity of the System as Eschatological Hope'.

Immanuel Kant: Teleology That Unifies Freedom and Nature

time preventing us from the presumption of thinking we have attained that unity in philosophy in any complete sense. In spite of Marcel's aversion to systems, Ricœur's commitment to unity finds inspiration in his own time from Marcel's concept of mystery, especially in contrast to Kierkegaard and Jaspers and their philosophies of paradox. In Ricœur's view, philosophies that end in paradox are impoverished by the absence of a doctrine of creation that would safeguard a transcendent unity. Although paradox rightly captures our own inability to achieve a final synthesis, it also has a tendency to project itself beyond the mind and make reality itself appear torn and conflictual. In contrast to this, Marcel gives Ricœur a way of avoiding totalising systems that does not end with paradox: the concept of mystery. Lastly, this chapter asks whether Ricœur believed in the classical doctrine of creation *ex nihilo*; the answer is that this question oversteps the boundaries of Ricœur's chosen profession as a philosopher.

Before expounding Ricœur, however, we shall present the Kantian backdrop to Ricœur's search for philosophical unity and the use of the category of creation as part of that search. Although Ricœur does not refer to Kant directly in these discussions, the many parallels between Kant's third *Critique* and Ricœur's never-written third part of *Philosophy of the Will*, not to mention the more explicit influence of Kant on symbols and poetics, make it clear that Kant is in the background of Ricœur's thought. Both Kant's and Ricœur's 'thirds' are attempts to bring unity and closure to the preceding two, and both base this unity on the non-philosophical idea of creation without making creation a fully comprehensible philosophical concept.

IMMANUEL KANT: TELEOLOGY THAT UNIFIES FREEDOM AND NATURE

We saw in Chapter 1 how important it is for Ricœur to posit the unity of reality as a condition for the possibility of philosophising. But where does Ricœur get the idea that to construe reality as *created* can help bring unity to its seemingly disparate elements, especially freedom/subjectivity and nature/objectivity? I suggest that this philosophical move is already present *in nuce* in Kant's third *Critique*. As Christopher Insole shows, 'Kant deals extensively and continuously with the question of the precise causal joint between God and the creation.'[3] In the *Critique of the Power*

---

[3] Christopher Insole, *The Intolerable God: Kant's Theological Journey* (Grand Rapids: Eerdmans, 2016), 54.

of Judgment Kant construes creation as a 'regulative idea' that is intrinsic to teleological judgement, that is to say, the necessary recognition of an 'objective purposiveness' in nature. By means of the teleological judgement of objective purposiveness in nature, Kant 'attempts to unify the theoretical and practical parts of his philosophical system', bringing about 'the unity of nature and freedom'.[4]

Kant summarises his first two critiques in this way: 'the critique of pure theoretical reason … yielded the laws of nature, the critique of practical reason the law of freedom'.[5] The problem is that 'there is an incalculable gulf fixed between' these two domains of being.[6] But Kant is committed to seeing philosophy as a system that demands unity. He is not happy with an ultimately fragmented philosophy. Therefore a third critique is called for, which would be a 'means for combining the two parts of philosophy into one whole'.[7] 'There must', he writes, 'be a ground for the unity of the supersensible that grounds nature with that which the concept of freedom contains practically'.[8] Unity is a condition for the possibility of experience, without which our sensations would remain forever fragmented beyond possible cognition. Nature must, therefore, 'contain … a lawful unity, not fathomable by us but still thinkable, in the combination of its manifold into one experience possible in itself'.[9] This unity is found by means of the human faculty of teleological judgement which mediates between theoretical and practical reason by attributing an 'objective purposiveness' to nature, seeing nature as designed by an intelligence.

---

[4] Michael Rohlf, 'Immanuel Kant', in *The Stanford Encyclopedia of Philosophy*, ed. Edward N. Zalta, Summer 2018 (Stanford University: Metaphysics Research Lab, 2018), https://plato.stanford.edu/archives/sum2018/entries/kant/.

[5] Kant, *Critique of the Power of Judgment*, 8. 'Die Kritik der reinen theoretischen Vernunft, welche den Quellen alles Erkenntnisses a priori (mithin auch dessen, was in ihr zur Anschauung gehört) gewidmet war, gab die Gesetze der Natur, die Kritik der praktischen Vernunft das Gesetz der Freiheit' (Immanuel Kant, *Einleitung in die Kritik der Urteilskraft* [Leipzig: F. Meiner, 1914], 15 [20:202]).

[6] Kant, *Critique of the Power of Judgment*, 63. 'eine unübersehbare Kluft' (Kant, *Kritik der Urteilskraft*, 11 [5:175]).

[7] Kant, *Critique of the Power of Judgment*, 64. 'Verbindungsmittel der zwei Teile der Philosophie zu einem Ganzen' (Kant, *Kritik der Urteilskraft*, 12 [5:176]).

[8] Kant, *Critique of the Power of Judgment*, 63. 'Also muß es doch einen Grund der Einheit des Übersinnlichen, welches der Natur zum Grunde liegt, mit dem, was der Freiheitsbegriff praktisch enthält, geben' (Kant, *Kritik der Urteilskraft*, 63 [5:176]).

[9] Kant, *Critique of the Power of Judgment*, 70. 'eine für uns zwar nicht zu ergründende, aber doch denkbare gesetzliche Einheit in der Verbindung ihres Mannigfaltigen zu einer an sich möglichen Erfahrung' (Kant, *Kritik der Urteilskraft*, 20 [5:183–4]).

This is not a philosophical proof for the existence of God, Kant underlines. The idea that the unity of nature, conceived through its purposiveness, can be 'thought' but not 'fathomed' is a respectful acknowledgement that there are things beyond the possibility of the human mind to grasp. Kant resists making God simply a piece of the physical laws of the universe as an explanation for certain phenomena, in a way that after Heidegger would be called 'ontotheological'. 'If one brings the concept of God', Kant writes, 'into natural science and its context in order to make purposiveness in nature explicable', this leads to a 'mix-up between natural science and the occasion that it provides for the teleological judging of its objects' on the one hand, 'and the consideration of God, and thus a theological derivation' on the other.[10] Therefore, 'we must carefully and modestly restrict ourselves to the expression that says only exactly as much as we know, namely that of an end of nature', without drawing hasty conclusions about whether this 'end' is a divine purpose or not.[11] He concludes that 'Physical teleology certainly drives us to seek a theology, but it cannot produce one.'[12]

One of the things Ricœur most respects about Kant is his rigour in remaining within the limits of what can be known philosophically.[13] Kant is a transcendental idealist, not an absolute idealist; he maintains the idea of a thing-in-itself which can be 'thought' as an 'idea' but cannot be 'known' as a 'concept'. By this means Kant points towards a necessary unity in reality that transcends the human mind's determinate grasp. Although we cannot comprehend it in a totalising philosophical system, a purposiveness in nature points to something beyond the limits of thought, the idea of a single intelligent cause of nature whose purposiveness is a guarantee of the final unity of reality. This 'something' is a regulative idea for Kant, a heuristic lens that helps explain phenomena without thereby proving itself to be real.

[10] Kant, *Critique of the Power of Judgment*, 253. 'Wenn man also für die Naturwissenschaft und in ihren Kontext den Begriff von Gott hineinbringt, um sich die Zweckmäßigkeit in der Natur erklärlich zu machen, ... um Naturwissenschaft und die Veranlassung, die sie zur teleologischen Beurteilung ihrer Gegenstände gibt, nicht mit der Gottesbetrachtung und also einer theologischen Ableitung zu vermengen' (Kant, *Kritik der Urteilskraft*, 245 [5:381]).
[11] Kant, *Critique of the Power of Judgment*, 253. 'Man muß ... sich sorgfältig und bescheiden auf den Ausdruck, der gerade nur soviel sagt, als wir wissen, nämlich eines Zwecks der Natur, einschränken' (Kant, *Kritik der Urteilskraft*, 245 [5:382]).
[12] Kant, *Critique of the Power of Judgment*, 307. 'Die physische Teleologie treibt uns zwar an, eine Theologie zu suchen; aber kann keine hervorbringen' (Kant, *Kritik der Urteilskraft*, 310 [5:440]).
[13] 'I have always recognized in [Kant] the philosopher who joins a precise architectonic of the power of thought to an intransigent sense of the limits involved' (Ricœur, 'My Relation to the History of Philosophy', 8). Originally in English.

Because Ricœur respects the boundaries of philosophical discourse set by Kant, he also makes use of creation as an 'idea' rather than a 'concept', meaning that it can be thought but not grasped with any sort of conceptual closure. Creation in Ricœur is analogous to a 'regulative idea' in that, without being conceivable itself, it brings coherence to what can be conceived.

PAUL RICŒUR: THE SUPERIORITY OF MYSTERY TO PARADOX

However, Ricœur finds himself in a philosophical milieu which is quite different from that in which Kant lived. Stimulated by the anti-systematic nineteenth-century philosophies of Kierkegaard and Nietzsche, the twentieth century saw a rise in paradoxical philosophies that did not seek a final unity, but rather posited a radical brokenness to thought. In the wake of the absolute idealism that succeeded Kant, this brokenness was often extended to include reality itself, because the difference between thought and reality had become erased.

The first signs of Ricœur's suspicion of paradox appear in a letter to Marcel, written from the prisoner-of-war camp in 1943. When informing Marcel of his project to write a book on Jaspers (with co-prisoner Mikel Dufrenne), Ricœur expresses doubt that Jaspers sufficiently 'escapes intellectualism',[14] by which he seems to mean that his philosophy is overly focussed on the mind's internal structures at the cost of reflection on reality itself. Ricœur then asks, 'is the paradox of the abstract "I think" and the concrete "I am" a lazy solution?'[15] In other words, should we end with paradox? At that time, Ricœur was not sure.

Two years later, having returned to Paris after his release, Ricœur writes to Marcel again, more confident about the inadequacy of paradox as a final resting point. Prompted by a re-reading of Jean Wahl's *Kierkegaardian Studies*,[16] Ricœur confesses his growing 'distrust' of Kierkegaard's thought:[17]

---

[14] My translation: 'je doute qu'on dépasse l'intell[ectualisme]' (Paul Ricœur, 'Paul Ricœur to Gabriel Marcel', 2 May 1943, Fonds Gabriel Marcel, Bibliothèque Nationale de France, Paris).

[15] Ricœur, 'Paul Ricœur to Gabriel Marcel', 2 May 1943.

[16] Jean Wahl, *Études Kierkegaardiennes* (Paris: Vrin, 2012).

[17] This reservation about Kierkegaard is an important supplement to Timo Helenius's otherwise comprehensive and helpful analysis of the influence of Kierkegaard on Ricœur (Helenius, 'Ricœur's Kierkegaard'). Helenius indicates (p. 10) that he tried without success to access the archive materials in the Fonds Ricœur. If he had gained access to the archives, he might have revised his claim that: 'Ricœur may have been suppressing the Kierkegaardian elements [in his thought] in order to distinguish himself from

Paul Ricœur: The Superiority of Mystery to Paradox

[Kierkegaard's] mistake seems to me more and more that of putting paradox above mystery. In the end, there is nothing more intellectual than paradox. Perhaps paradox is the highest expression of mystery, but only its expression: it would be the failure of understanding in the presence of the participation which truly unifies it.[18]

This passage also shows Ricœur's growing appreciation of Marcel's concept of mystery – which, we recall from Chapter 2,[19] cannot be comprehended or overcome because it concerns something we stand inside and participate in, and therefore cannot see objectively. Like Ricœurian symbol, Marcellian mystery is not a refusal to think, but a source of inexhaustible thought.

Ricœur goes on to express doubt that paradox can be consistently maintained to the end. 'Paradox', he tells Marcel, 'would dissolve into ruinous contradiction if I did not have a prior sense of union, i.e. of love; only mystery is ontological; paradox remains on the level of discourse'.[20] In other words, however much paradox may express an *epistemological* (or 'intellectual') truth, Ricœur is not willing to make it *ontological*.

Three years later, in 1948, Ricœur published *Gabriel Marcel et Karl Jaspers*, in which he characterises Marcel's thought as founded on mystery and Jaspers's as founded on paradox.[21] He chose to compare these two in particular, he says, because of their similarities: both emphasise a 'critique of knowledge',[22] opposed to the totalising systems of

---

Kierkegaard who is simply a bit too much like Ricœur' (p. 11) These letters to Marcel are evidence that early on Ricœur became cautious of Kierkegaardian paradox. Another corrective is found in *Marcel et Jaspers*, 143, where Ricœur blames Kierkegaard for the 'distortion' by which finitude is conflated with guilt, as we saw in Chapter 3. Neither of these elements is marginal in either Ricœur's or Kierkegaard's philosophy.

[18] My translation: 'La faute me paraît de + en + de mettre le paradoxe au-dessus du mystère. Il n'y a rien de plus intellectuel que le paradoxe finalement. Peut-être que le paradoxe est l'expression suprême du mystère, mais seulement son expression: ce serait l'échec de l'entendement devant la participation qui elle unit vraiment' (Ricœur, 'Paul Ricœur to Gabriel Marcel, Le Chambon s/Lignon', 25 November 1945, Fonds Gabriel Marcel, Bibliothèque Nationale de France, Paris).

[19] See Chapter 2 above, section headed 'Gabriel Marcel: Universal Truth is not Universal Proof'.

[20] My translation: 'le paradoxe se dissoudrait en contradiction ruineuse si je n'avais un pressentiment de l'union c.à.d. de l'amour; seul le mystère est ontologique; le paradoxe reste sur le plan du discours' (Ricœur, 'Paul Ricœur to Gabriel Marcel, Le Chambon s/Lignon', 25 November 1945, Fonds Gabriel Marcel, Bibliothèque Nationale de France, Paris).

[21] Ricœur, *Marcel et Jaspers*.

[22] My translation: 'critique du savoir' (Ricœur, *Marcel et Jaspers*, 38).

nineteenth-century absolute idealism; and both have an openness to transcendence that is lacking in Heidegger and Sartre (as we saw in Chapter 4).[23] But beyond these substantial agreements Ricœur discerns some significant divergences that hang on the difference between mystery and paradox. 'Shall we say,' he asks, 'that Jaspersian paradox is only a more sophisticated expression, in the language of understanding, of a mystery that Marcel suggests ...?'[24] No, he concludes, because while Marcel ultimately believes in unity, Jaspers's thought is ambiguous about the relation of the mind to reality, showing that it has not fully escaped the trappings of absolute idealism. At times Jaspers claims that paradox is only in thought,[25] but at other times his work exhibits paradoxes that are 'no longer only at the level of discourse but of being itself, as its separation or brokenness'.[26] This is evidence for Ricœur that in Jaspers's philosophy 'the fracture is in some way ontological and not only methodological'.[27] We saw in Chapter 1 how this position of Jaspers's gives a tragic flavour to philosophy, in which our minds cannot escape the demand for a unity that does not exist.[28] It is also another instance of Jaspers conflating finitude with evil that we saw in detail in Chapter 5, because it makes an inevitable failure out of the mind's limitations.[29] This means, Ricœur concludes, that we 'can no longer consider [Jaspersian] paradox as a simple mode of expression, like the broken language of an indivisible experience; for such a philosophy paradox is the flourishing, at the level of expression, of a fracture in being'.[30]

Ricœur concedes one good thing about paradox: it is 'humbled logic; it confesses its poverty that tends to be masked by the apparatus of the

---

[23] Ricœur, *Marcel et Jaspers*, 18. See Chapter 4 above, section titled 'The Need for Transcendence'.

[24] My translation: 'Dira-t-on que le paradoxe est seulement chez K. Jaspers une expression plus raffinée ...?' (Ricœur, *Marcel et Jaspers*, 206).

[25] Ricœur, *Marcel et Jaspers*, 129.

[26] My translation: 'La tension ... s'oriente chez K. Jaspers vers une ontologie paradoxale où le paradoxe n'est plus seulement au niveau du discours mais de l'être même, comme sa déhiscence ou sa déchirure' (Ricœur, *Marcel et Jaspers*, 131).

[27] My translation: 'La déchirure soit en quelque façon ontologique et non pas seulement méthodologique' (Ricœur, *Marcel et Jaspers*, 349).

[28] See Chapter 1 above, section headed 'Paul Ricœur: The Unity of the System as Eschatological Hope'.

[29] See Chapter 5 above, section headed 'Confusion 3: Limitations as Fault'.

[30] My translation: 'Une telle philosophie ne peut plus considérer le paradoxe comme un simple mode d'expression, comme le langage brisé d'une expérience indivise; le paradoxe est pour elle l'affleurement au plan de l'expression d'une déchirure de l'être' (Ricœur, *Marcel et Jaspers*, 40).

system'.[31] But he argues, as he did in the letter to Marcel, that nobody can consistently maintain a paradoxical philosophy to the end: 'it is on the basis of a perceived unity, a unity sensed and recognised by the "heart", that reason tries to express by systematic paradox what cannot be expressed and rests uncharacterizable'.[32] This 'assurance' of unity 'is not yet or no longer philosophy.... That is why philosophy is paradoxical'.[33] But he insists that we can never be satisfied with paradox: 'probably a definitively fractured philosophy is impossible and paradox always has as its backdrop a union and a participation'.[34] Even more strongly, he contends that the very *possibility of philosophy* depends on the primacy of conciliation over fragmentation'.[35]

These remarks point to a narrow road between a *permanent* paradox that for Ricœur would destroy philosophy, and a premature synthesis that would lead to the 'totalising systems' towards which twentieth-century philosophy was so hostile. Ricœur does not think that Jaspers has walked that narrow road: for him paradox remains final. But for Ricœur, '*Paradox is the intellectual envelope of mystery*'.[36] Ricœur prefers Marcellian mystery because by it we may follow Kant in holding to the ultimate unity of reality, while at the same time insisting that such unity is not fully graspable by the finite human mind.

What is the mystery that unifies reality beyond thought? For Ricœur it is the mystery of creation. Introducing his own concept of 'consent' (which the next chapter expounds), Ricœur writes to Marcel: 'By consent I return to the *mysterious unity of creation*; I reinstate the union of soul

---

[31] My translation: 'Le paradoxe est la logique humiliée; il confesse son indigence que l'appareil du système tend à masquer' (Dufrenne and Ricœur, *Karl Jaspers et la philosophie de l'existence*, 386).

[32] My translation: 'C'est à partir d'une unité devinée, pressentie, reconnue par le "cœur", que la raison tente d'exprimer par une systématique du paradoxe ce qui en peut être dit et qui reste incaractérisable' (Dufrenne and Ricœur, *Karl Jaspers et la philosophie de l'existence*, 385).

[33] My translation: 'Cette assurance n'est pas encore ou n'est plus une philosophie.... C'est pourquoi la philosophie est paradoxale' (Dufrenne and Ricœur, *Karl Jaspers et la philosophie de l'existence*, 386).

[34] My translation: 'peut-être qu'une philosophie définitivement déchirée est impossible et que le paradoxe a toujours pour toile de fond une *union* et une participation' (Dufrenne and Ricœur, *Karl Jaspers et la philosophie de l'existence*, 379).

[35] My translation (italics original): 'La *possibilité de la philosophie* dépend de la primauté de la conciliation sur la déchirure' (Dufrenne and Ricœur, *Karl Jaspers et la philosophie de l'existence*, 388).

[36] My translation (italics original): '*Le paradoxe est l'enveloppe intellectuelle du mystère*' (Dufrenne and Ricœur, *Karl Jaspers et la philosophie de l'existence*, 385).

and body.... The mysterious unity of being is primary.'[37] Here we see creation take centre stage for Ricœur as the mystery that unifies being.

Ricœur joins together Marcel's notion of mystery as something we cannot grasp because we are part of it, and Kant's use of creation as the category that unifies freedom and nature, subject and object, in a unity that transcends the limits of the mind's ability to conceive. Kierkegaardian/Jaspersian paradox, on the other hand, remains locked in an absolute idealist prison in Ricœur's view, which is why it cannot overcome the division between subject and object, mind and body, freedom and transcendence, and why it ends by fracturing not only thought but reality.

In *Freedom and Nature* Ricœur demonstrates what it looks like to walk the fine line between affirming paradox temporarily and denying it permanently. On the one hand, he refuses to bring conceptual closure to the synthesis of subjectivity (freedom) and objectivity (nature) whose reciprocity is the book's primary theme. It is 'the paradox of freedom and nature', that 'there is no logical procedure by which nature could be derived from freedom (this involuntary from the voluntary), or freedom from nature. There is no *system* of nature and freedom'.[38] On the other hand, he does not stop with paradox. As he said concerning Jaspers, nobody can think paradox to the end because thought ultimately demands unity: 'a paradoxical ontology is possible only if it is covertly reconciled'.[39] One can never *see* this reconciliation as a philosophical concept, but it is nonetheless the invisible foundation 'on the basis of which the great contrasts of freedom and nature are articulated'.[40]

What is the invisible foundation that reconciles subjectivity and objectivity? It is beyond philosophy's *present* capacity to say, whatever may be its *future* capacity, Ricœur replies. His position here is extremely

---

[37] My translation (italics mine): 'Par le consentement je repasse sur l'unité mystérieuse de la création; je réinstaure l'union de l'âme et du corps.... L'unité mystérieuse de l'être est première' (Ricœur, 'Paul Ricœur to Gabriel Marcel, Le Chambon s/Lignon', 25 November 1945, Fonds Gabriel Marcel, Bibliothèque Nationale de France, Paris).

[38] Ricœur, *Freedom and Nature*, 19. 'le paradoxe qui culmine comme paradoxe de la liberté et de la nature.... Il n'y a pas de procédé logique par lequel la nature procède de la liberté, (l'involontaire du volontaire), ou la liberté de la nature. Il n'y a pas de système de la nature et de la liberté' (Ricœur, *Le volontaire et l'involontaire*, 22).

[39] Ricœur, *Freedom and Nature*, 19. 'Une ontologie paradoxale n'est possible que secrètement réconciliée' (Ricœur, *Le volontaire et l'involontaire*, 22).

[40] Ricœur, *Freedom and Nature*, 19. Translation modified: 'La jointure de l'être est aperçue dans une intuition aveuglée qui se réfléchit en paradoxes; elle n'est jamais ce que je regarde, mais cela à partir de quoi s'articulent les grands contrastes de la liberté et de la nature' (Ricœur, *Le volontaire et l'involontaire*, 22).

Paul Ricœur: The Superiority of Mystery to Paradox

nuanced and needs to be spelled out clearly. He first asks whether there is any category or language that envelops subjectivity and objectivity, encompassing both in a higher unifying whole: 'Does there exist a universe of discourse which would be "neutral" with respect to objectivity and subjectivity?'[41] He replies that, 'to this ultimate question we believe we have to answer *negatively, at least provisionally*',[42] because 'subjects and objects do not fit together: nature as a totality of objects and subjects is a contradictory idea'.[43] We end in paradox, but provisionally.

Why is Ricœur's negative answer only a provisional one? Because his philosophy is currently still rooted in an 'eidetic' method that places the self in the centre in Cartesian fashion and from which one must eventually arrive at paradox. But for a brief moment charged with significance, Ricœur lifts the curtain on a future possibility:

> A different unity might exist between the subjectivity of willing and life and the objectivity of natural knowledge. The unity of *creation* might bring together all the forms of being beyond all fragmenting knowledge. A unity of creation might be discovered by an entirely different dimension of consciousness than that which proceeds to a 'regional eidetics' of the Cogito and of nature. I am also a reader of ciphers, as Jaspers puts it. It is not accidental that a unity of inspiration animates the great medieval cosmologies: it is a unique desire which starts with God and returns to God through all the degrees of being.[44]

'This unity', he concludes, 'lost as knowledge, must be rediscovered in some other way in the "poetics" of the will'.[45] In other words, it would

---

[41] Ricœur, *Freedom and Nature*, 423. 'Existe-t-il un univers du discours qui soit "neutre" par rapport à l'objectivité et à la subjectivité?' (Ricœur, *Le volontaire et l'involontaire*, 398).

[42] Ricœur, *Freedom and Nature*, 423. Italics original: 'A cette ultime question nous croyons devoir répondre *négativement, du moins provisoirement*' (Ricœur, *Le volontaire et l'involontaire*, 398).

[43] Ricœur, *Freedom and Nature*, 424. 'Les sujets et les objets ne font pas addition la nature comme totalité des objets et des sujets est une idée inconsistante' (Ricœur, *Le volontaire et l'involontaire*, 398).

[44] Ricœur, *Freedom and Nature*, 425. Translation modified (italics original): 'Une autre unité peut exister entre la subjectivité du vouloir et de la vie et l'objectivité de la connaissance naturelle. Une unité de *création* peut rassembler toutes les formes d'êtres par-delà tout savoir brisé. Une unité de création peut être surprise par une toute autre dimension de la conscience que celle qui procède aux "eidétiques régionales" du Cogito et de la nature. Je suis aussi lecteur de chiffres, selon le mot de Jaspers. Ce n'est pas par hasard qu'une unité de souffle ou d'inspiration anime les grandes cosmologies médiévales: c'est un unique désir qui procède de Dieu et fait retour à Dieu à travers tous les degrés de l'être' (Ricœur, *Le volontaire et l'involontaire*, 399).

[45] Ricœur, *Freedom and Nature*, 425. 'Cette unité perdue comme savoir devra être retrouvée d'une autre façon dans la "poétique" de la volonté' (Ricœur, *Le volontaire et l'involontaire*, 399).

have been the task of Ricœur's never-completed third part to rediscover a harmonious reality that sees both subjectivity and objectivity as united in the overarching category of 'created'.

JEAN-PAUL SARTRE: AN INSUPERABLE DUALISM

Ricœur applies his insight – that freedom and nature can be reconciled only by the overarching category of creation – in his critiques of the anti-religious polemics of Jean-Paul Sartre. Creation is a category that Sartre often mentions as part of his rejection of religion, because he sees it as incompatible with freedom.[46] By showing the compatibility of creation with freedom, Ricœur undermines Sartre's favourite argument against religion.

Sartre's rejection of God arises from his ontology, according to which there are two kinds of being: in-itself and for-itself, which are roughly equivalent to objectivity and subjectivity respectively. The for-itself is defined entirely by freedom, which he calls a nothingness at the heart of being. The for-itself can have no 'nature' because that would make it in-itself. Without a nature to constrain its actions, the for-itself is entirely free by definition. If we were not wholly free we would not be the for-itself, therefore man is 'wholly and forever free or he is not free at all'.[47] The idea of God is of a something at once for-itself and in-itself in a contradictory synthesis of being and nothingness, therefore God does not exist.[48]

Already in the introduction to *Being and Nothingness*, Sartre begins his polemic against creation by giving two possible understandings of it and rejecting them both. First, 'the theory of perpetual creation' suggests that all things are sustained by God at all moments.[49] But this 'makes it [creation] disappear in the divine subjectivity'.[50] Creation is not really different from God and thus there is no creation. Alternatively, 'if being exists as over against God, it is its own support; it does not preserve the least trace of divine creation. In a word, even if it had been created,

---

[46] Crittenden observes that creation is a category to which Sartre frequently returns in his early work as central to his polemics against religion. See Paul Crittenden, 'Sartre's Absent God', *Sophia* 51, no. 4 (2012): 495–507.
[47] Sartre, *Being and Nothingness*, 441. 'L'homme ne saurait être tantôt libre et tantôt esclave: il est tout entier et toujours libre ou il n'est pas' (Sartre, *L'être et le néant*, 485).
[48] Sartre, *Being and Nothingness*, 90. Sartre, *L'être et le néant*, 126. See Crittenden, 'Sartre's Absent God', 502.
[49] Sartre, *Being and Nothingness*, lxiv. 'la théorie de la creation continuée' (Sartre, *L'être et le néant*, 31).
[50] Sartre, *Being and Nothingness*, lxiv. 'le fait s'évanouir dans la subjectivité divine' (Sartre, *L'être et le néant*, 31).

being-in-itself would be inexplicable in terms of creation; for it assumes its being beyond the creation'.⁵¹ Sartre concludes: 'This is equivalent to saying that being is uncreated.'⁵²

But Sartre's bigger problem with the idea of creation concerns human subjectivity or freedom, which he considers completely incompatible with the idea that we are created. He argues that to create something is to have a purpose for it, and that purpose constitutes the unchanging essence of the created thing. 'When we think of God as the creator, we are thinking of him, most of the time, as a supernal artisan.'⁵³ This is where the idea of humans having a 'nature' came from: 'man is the realisation of a certain conception which dwells in the divine understanding'.⁵⁴ But if humans are free by definition, they are able to continually create themselves, which means there can be no created human 'nature'. 'There is no human nature, because there is no God to have a conception of it. Man simply is. Not that he is simply what he conceives himself to be, but he is what he wills.'⁵⁵

In his published writings, Ricœur critiques Sartre's ontology from a strictly philosophical perspective, both directly in the essay 'Negativity and Primary Affirmation', and indirectly in *Freedom and Nature*. These critiques have been well and accurately presented in Ricœur scholarship, primarily in two articles. Anthony Cipollone examines Ricœur's *direct* critique, which is essentially that Sartre is too quick to define freedom as the absence of reality: 'Ricœur maintains that Sartre has an inadequate philosophy of being, one which sees being only as factual, thus implying that freedom is no-thing.'⁵⁶ A fuller account of being would see freedom (the for-itself) as just as 'real' as the in-itself: both subjectivity and objectivity have their own distinctive kinds of reality. Additionally, James

---

51 Sartre, *Being and Nothingness*, lxiv. 'Si l'être existe en face de Dieu, c'est qu'il est son propre support, c'est qu'il ne conserve pas la moindre trace de la création divine. En un mot, même s'il avait été créé, l'être-en-soi serait inexplicable par la création, car il reprend son être par delà celle-ci' (Sartre, *L'être et le néant*, 31).
52 Sartre, *Being and Nothingness*, lxiv. 'Cela équivaut à dire que l'être est incréé' (Sartre, *L'être et le néant*, 31).
53 Jean-Paul Sartre, *Existentialism and Humanism*, trans. Philip Mairet (London: Methuen, 1948), 27. 'Lorsque nous concevons un Dieu créateur, ce Dieu est assimilé la plupart du temps à un artisan supérieur' (Jean-Paul Sartre, *L'existentialisme est un humanisme* [Paris: Nagel, 1966], 19).
54 Sartre, *Existentialism and Humanism*, 27. 'Ainsi l'homme individuel réalise un certain concept qui est dans l'entendement divin' (Sartre, *L'existentialisme est un humanisme*, 20).
55 Sartre, *Existentialism and Humanism*, 28. 'Il n'y a pas de nature humaine, puisqu'il n'y a pas de Dieu pour la concevoir' (Sartre, *L'existentialisme est un humanisme*, 22).
56 Anthony P. Cipollone, 'Concrete Human Freedom: Ricœur on Sartre', *Iliff Review* 35, no. 3 (1978): 44.

Marsh draws attention to Ricœur's *indirect* critique of Sartre in *Freedom and Nature*, even though its pages barely mention him.[57] According to Marsh, Sartre's account of freedom is one-sided, and Ricœur's alternative both incorporates and surpasses it, taking it up into a fuller both-and approach based on the reciprocity of freedom and nature:

> The most basic difference between the two thinkers seems to be that between Sartre's identification of consciousness and freedom and Ricœur's sense of the human being as unity of voluntary and involuntary. Freedom runs all the way down into the depths of the human being for Sartre, whereas for Ricœur it is the relationship between voluntary and involuntary that runs all the way down.[58]

But in addition to these two critiques of Sartre in Ricœur's published work, there is a third, more religiously focussed, critique in Ricœur's unpublished lectures given at Union Theological Seminary in 1958, titled 'Anthropology of Religion in the Philosophy of Existence'.[59] Alison Scott-Baumann indicates the existence of these lectures in her excellent work based on archival evidence, yet she only gives a brief summary of their contents, writing that in the first half of the lectures, Ricœur presents the philosophies of Hegel, Kierkegaard, Nietzsche, and Marx, 'the fathers of existentialism', and in the second half he expounds and evaluates the thought of the '"sons": Heidegger, Jaspers, Marcel and Sartre'.[60] What follows is a more detailed exposition of Ricœur's lecture on Sartre, which is material that has never been reviewed before. It is relevant for my purposes because here the category of creation takes centre stage in Ricœur's critique of Sartre.

After presenting Sartre's thought with typical thoroughness, Ricœur begins his critical evaluation by putting a question mark over Sartre's conception of God as the impossible synthesis of in-itself-for-itself that each human being desires but can never attain. He is not sure that Sartre has captured what Christians mean by God: 'is this ideal of man *God*? Sartre has only proved that man cannot be God. I cannot be my own foundation'.[61] Sartre has 'only excluded the false God that man cannot

---

[57] James Marsh, 'Ricœur's Phenomenology of Freedom as an Answer to Sartre', in Kaplan, *Reading Ricœur*, 13–29.
[58] Kaplan, *Reading Ricœur*, 25.
[59] Archives Ricœur / Fonds Ricœur, Inventaire 1, dossier 27, 'Anthropology and Religion in the Philosophy of Existence', Lectures at Union Theological Seminary (1958), f. 4057–4101.
[60] Scott-Baumann, *Ricœur and the Negation of Happiness*, 34.
[61] Archives Ricœur / Fonds Ricœur, Inv. 1, dossier 27, 'Anthropology and Religion in the Philosophy of Existence', Lectures at Union Theological Seminary (1958), f. 4096. Italics are underlinings in manuscript.

become'.⁶² Ricœur then criticises Sartre's radical dichotomy between objectivity and subjectivity that makes it impossible for the two to relate. Ricœur had already noted in his published article that Sartre has made freedom/subjectivity a 'nothingness' which means he is forced to give to objectivity alone the status of 'something':

> We have at the outset a very narrow and crude idea of being, reduced to the status of the *thing*, the brute fact.... [Sartre's] notion of being-in-itself, which serves as a foil to his notion of nothingness, is too flimsy and already 'thingified'.... What he has demonstrated is that in order to be free, one must be constituted as no-thing.... This is the crucial point of his philosophy. His philosophy of nothingness is the consequence of an inadequate philosophy of being.⁶³

In this published text, Ricœur only speaks of being and does not mention creation. But in his unpublished lectures, creation is named as that without which Sartre cannot bring together the for-itself (subjectivity) and the in-itself (objectivity) in any satisfactory way: 'What chance is there of an encounter of freedom [subjectivity] and worldliness [objectivity] if they are not rooted in a common creation?'⁶⁴ What chance have they, in other words, if they are opposed as completely as being and nothingness?

'It is strange', Ricœur says, 'that Sartre rejects the idea of creation'.⁶⁵ If Sartre really understood what creation entails, he would see that freedom may easily be a part of it without ceasing to be free. But Sartre is so resistant to pinning down any part of human reality to the status of necessary 'fact' that for him, to say that we are created would be to deny our freedom by determining our nature. Ricœur summarises Sartre's argument thus: 'If God exists, the man [sic] does not exist, because to be given to myself would to be stolen to [sic – probably "from"] myself; a fact would

---

⁶² Archives Ricœur / Fonds Ricœur, Inv. 1, dossier 27, 'Anthropology and Religion in the Philosophy of Existence', Lectures at Union Theological Seminary (1958), f. 4096-b.
⁶³ Ricœur, *History and Truth*, 324. Translation modified (italics original): 'On se donne au départ une idée étroite et pauvre de l'être, réduit au statut de la *chose*, du donné brut.... Ce point est clair chez Sartre: c'est sa notion de l'être en soi, qui sert de repoussoir à sa notion du néant, qui est trop pauvre et déjà chosé-fiée.... Tout ce qu'il a démontré, c'est que pour être libre il faut se constituer en non-chose; mais non-chose n'est point non-être; *nothing is not not-being*; c'est ici, à mes yeux, le point difficile de sa philosophie, sa philosophie du néant est la conséquence d'une philosophie insuffisante de l'être'. Ricœur, *Histoire et vérité*, 400–1).
⁶⁴ Archives Ricœur / Fonds Ricœur, Inv. 1, dossier 27, 'Anthropology and Religion in the Philosophy of Existence', Lectures at Union Theological Seminary (1958), f. 4098.
⁶⁵ Archives Ricœur / Fonds Ricœur, Inv. 1, dossier 27, 'Anthropology and Religion in the Philosophy of Existence', Lectures at Union Theological Seminary (1958), f. 4097.

be introduced into freedom.'[66] This, however, is inconsistent, because 'finally in the philosophy of Sartre, freedom is a fact'.[67] Sartre cannot avoid positing an unchanging essence of being human even if he reduces it to the bare minimum of simply being free. And why is it impossible that God created us with freedom as our essence, and with the purpose that we be free? For Ricœur that is precisely what creation means: freedom and nature as one created whole.

At the end of his critique, Ricœur offers a sketch of his alternative account. Sartre's poor conception of being (as purely thing-like) compels him to make freedom into *less* than being. But Ricœur says: 'Perhaps [instead] freedom is *no-thing* because it is *more* being than the things are. Perhaps the relative negation of nothing is linked to the absolute affirmation of being. I call *creation* this affirmation of being in one.'[68] In other words, if we start from the point of view that sees all reality as created, we need never end with a radical subject/object dualism: 'In a philosophy of creation nature and freedom are two degrees of being supported by the unity of an Act.'[69] This idea of nature and freedom as 'two degrees of being' is, as Marsh has shown, precisely what *Freedom and Nature* systematically expounds.[70]

CREATION EX NIHILO?

The crucial role played by the doctrine of creation in Ricœur's thought leads inevitably to the question of what he really *means* by saying that reality is created. Contemporary theology is home to a variety of accounts of creation, ranging from the traditional metaphysics of creation *ex nihilo*[71]

---

[66] Archives Ricœur / Fonds Ricœur, Inv. 1, dossier 27, 'Anthropology and Religion in the Philosophy of Existence', Lectures at Union Theological Seminary (1958), f. 4097.

[67] Archives Ricœur / Fonds Ricœur, Inv. 1, dossier 27, 'Anthropology and Religion in the Philosophy of Existence', Lectures at Union Theological Seminary (1958), f. 4097.

[68] Archives Ricœur / Fonds Ricœur, Inv. 1, dossier 27, 'Anthropology and Religion in the Philosophy of Existence', Lectures at Union Theological Seminary (1958), f. 4098. Italics are underlinings in manuscript.

[69] Archives Ricœur / Fonds Ricœur, Inv. 1, dossier 27, 'Anthropology and Religion in the Philosophy of Existence', Lectures at Union Theological Seminary (1958), f. 4098.

[70] James Marsh, 'Ricœur's Phenomenology of Freedom as an Answer to Sartre', in Kaplan, *Reading Ricœur*, 13–29.

[71] See, *inter alia*: David B. Burrell, '*Creatio ex nihilo* Recovered', *Modern Theology* 29, no. 2 (2013): 5–21; Janet Martin Soskice, 'Creation and the Glory of Creatures', *Modern Theology* 29, no. 2 (2013): 172–85; Yonghua Ge, *Creatio ex nihilo and Natural Theology in Aquinas* (Chisinau: Lambert Academic Publishing, 2017); Gary Anderson and Markus Bockmuehl, eds., *Creation ex nihilo: Origins, Development, Contemporary Challenges*

Creation Ex Nihilo?   201

to revisionary rejections of the same.[72] Does Ricœur's understanding of creation contribute to this inner-theological debate?

The answer to this question is similar to the answer to the question about Ricœur's views on 'evil as privation'.[73] While Ricœur is aware that philosophical anthropology is never done in a metaphysically neutral space and metaphysics always 'seeps through' even the most rigorous methodological asceticism, he is nonetheless reluctant to take a stand on any metaphysical questions and avoids discussing them except when absolutely necessary.[74] He rarely mentions creation *ex nihilo* at all and never discusses it in any depth. In *The Symbolism of Evil* he never even refers to it. In his essay on original sin, published the same year, he compares Augustine's concept of the *ex nihilo* of creation and the *nihilo* of evil, saying that the equivocation led to a confusion.[75] In his essay on evil, published decades later, Ricœur again accuses Augustine of transposing his concept of the *ex nihilo* of creation on to the *nihilo* of evil.[76] In his biblical/exegetical writings, he simply comments that the question to which creation *ex nihilo* is an answer was unknown before Judaism's encounter with Hellenism,[77] whereas in the 'biblical Creation narratives … it is never a question of Creation *ex nihilo*'.[78] Four years later he seems to have changed his mind, at least concerning the

---

(Notre Dame: University of Notre Dame Press, 2018); Simon Oliver, *Creation: A Guide for the Perplexed* (London: Bloomsbury, 2017); Ian McFarland, *From Nothing: A Theology of Creation* (Louisville: Westminster John Knox Press, 2014).

[72] Joseph Blenkinsopp, *Creation, Un-Creation, Re-Creation: A Discursive Commentary on Genesis 1–11* (London: T&T Clark, 2011); Terence Fretheim, *God and World in the Old Testament: A Relational Theology of Creation* (Nashville: Abingdon Press, 2005); Thomas Jay Oord, *Theologies of Creation: Creatio ex nihilo and Its New Rivals* (New York: Routledge, 2014).

[73] See Chapter 6, section headed 'Connection 3: Evil as Privation'.

[74] Recall Ricœur's interview with Richard Kearney in 2003: 'I no longer subscribe to the typically anti-metaphysical Protestant lineage of Karl Barth (though it is true that in early works like *The Symbolism of Evil* I was still somewhat under his influence)'. Kearney, *On Paul Ricœur*.

[75] Ricœur, *Conflict of Interpretations*, 275; Ricœur, *Conflit des interprétations*, 271.

[76] Ricœur, 'Evil, A Challenge to Philosophy and Theology', 253; Ricœur, 'Le mal', 218.

[77] LaCocque and Ricœur, *Thinking Biblically*, 34; Paul Ricœur and André LaCocque, *Penser la bible* (Paris: Éditions du Seuil, 1998), 60. Mirela Oliva understands this to mean that Ricœur rejects creation *ex nihilo* (see Mirela Oliva, 'Paul Ricœur's Hermeneutics of Creation', *Revue Roumaine de Philosophie* 54, no. 2 [2010]: 197–204). But this is too hasty. Ricœur only says that the Genesis narratives do not answer the question because they do not ask it. He is very careful not to overstep the boundaries here and make a theological judgement where his goal is only to do exegesis.

[78] LaCocque and Ricœur, *Thinking Biblically*, 49. 'nos récits bibliques de création. D'abord, il n'est jamais question de création *ex nihilo*' (Ricœur and LaCocque, *Penser la bible*, 79).

first creation narrative: 'in Genesis 1 the power of the Word arises, which seems to create from nothing'.[79] But even this is quite non-committal.

Like the question of evil as privation, however, if we examine what Ricœur says within the methodological restrictions he sets for himself, we find evidence, not of a metaphysics of creation *ex nihilo*, but of a certain *phenomenological experience* of having come from nothing, a testimony of the mysterious unthinkability of our own beginning. When writing about the type of finitude revealed by the experience of birth, he says: 'If birth should reveal some negation, would it not be the nothingness of origin from which existence proceeded, the *ex nihilo* of existence?'[80] The Cogito can say nothing about whether physical matter existed eternally, but points humbly to the incontrovertible fact that consciousness has a beginning before which it was not. Nonetheless this 'nothingness-past, nothingness before birth', Ricœur says, 'is not a consistent thought'; it belongs to 'mythical language'.[81] This is because the zero-point at the beginning of our existence is not something we can properly conceive; it is a limit-idea of what must be true beyond the horizon of thought. In other words, creation *ex nihilo* fits the profile of a Ricœurian *symbol*.

If the idea of everything arising *ex nihilo* is a symbol, then it is a symbol to which Ricœur did not devote much time, and so we are left to piece together small clues in order to speculate and develop Ricœur in a Ricœurian vein. One such clue is found in how Ricœur contrasts Plato's theodicy with the Bible's: 'In Book II of the *Republic* [Plato writes]: because God is the Good, he is innocence. But ... Plato concludes: God, then, is not the cause of everything, nor even of the greater part of existing things'; for 'the Jewish thinker', on the other hand, 'God is the cause of everything that is good and man is the cause of everything that is vain'.[82] Here Ricœur clearly denies that Plato held to creation *ex nihilo*,

---

[79] My translation: 'en Genèse I survient la puissance de la Parole, qui semble créer à partir de rien' (Paul Ricœur, 'Interpréter la Bible', *Pardès* 32–3, no. 1 [2002]: 39).

[80] Ricœur, *Freedom and Nature*, 457. Italics in translation: 'Si la naissance doit révéler quelque négation, ne serait-ce point ce néant d'origine d'où l'existence procède, le "ex nihilo" de l'existence?' (Ricœur, *Le volontaire et l'involontaire*, 427).

[81] Ricœur, *Freedom and Nature*, 455. 'Le néant-passé, le néant d'avant la naissance, qui n'est pas une pensée consistante, peut devenir l'expression figurée et, si l'on peut dire, chiffrée de ma contingence.... langage mythique' (Ricœur, *Le volontaire et l'involontaire*, 428).

[82] Ricœur, *Symbolism of Evil*, 240. 'Cette motivation n'est pas sans analogie avec celle de Platon au livre II de la *République*: parce que Dieu est le Bien, il est innocent; mais alors que Platon conclut: donc Dieu n'est pas cause de tout, ni même du plus grand nombre des choses existantes, le penseur juif continuera: Dieu est cause de tout ce qui est bon et l'homme de tout ce qui est vain' (Ricœur, *Finitude et culpabilité*, 453–4).

and then shows the difference between this and the biblical account. In another place, Ricœur claims that 'I do not cease to be a created being unless I cease to be; therefore I do not cease to be good'.[83] How can this be understood in any other way than as a total identification of being, goodness, and createdness? Creation *ex nihilo* seems implied in everything Ricœur said about the goodness of creation. If Ricœur is committed to the belief that creation is through-and-through good, to the point of making it his lifelong calling to seek the good in everything as we saw in Chapter 5, then it seems that the belief in creation *ex nihilo* is implied in this, because without creation *ex nihilo* there is no reason to suppose that all of creation is good. If God created out of pre-existent material, then some of it might be at best morally neutral.

Nonetheless, Ricœur refused to comment on creation *ex nihilo* because doing so would have meant 'crossing the Rubicon'[84] into doctrinal theology. His rigorous commitment to disciplinary boundaries prevented him from taking that step. It is also arguable that to move from creation as myth to creation *ex nihilo* is to turn a symbol into a concept. Ricœur may well have seen it that way. I do not, because the *nihil* is still something that cannot be thought coherently and remains at the limits of what the human mind can conceive. But I can see why Ricœur drew back from discussing a term which forms part of a theological system. He was always keen to distance himself from seemingly scholastic debates with hard doctrinal edges, preferring instead an exploratory and questioning approach. And besides, he knew he was no theologian and tried to avoid pronouncing judgement on things outside his expertise – a modesty many contemporary philosophers and theologians could learn something from.

CONCLUSION

We have seen that, for Ricœur, the symbol of creation is the underpinning hope in the ultimate unity of subjectivity and objectivity, of freedom and nature – in short, of all of reality. We have also seen that Ricœur draws this entire idea – not just symbols, but the symbol of creation as unity – from Kant's third *Critique*.

We have also seen how Sartre begins with an understanding of human finitude that is radically free without the constraints of being created.

---

[83] Ricœur, *Symbolism of Evil*, 251 'Je ne cesse point d'être créé, sous peine de cesser d'être; donc je ne cesse pas d'être bon' (Ricœur, *Finitude et culpabilité*, 465).
[84] See Falque, *Crossing the Rubicon* Falque, *Passer le Rubicon*.

But, Ricœur shows, Sartre's weak concept of being cannot allow freedom to be part of being, and if freedom is not a part of being then it cannot be created. If freedom is not created then it can never be reconciled with nature, leaving freedom and nature, subjectivity and objectivity, forever estranged from one another in an insurmountable dualism. Ricœur faults Sartre not so much for his atheist *conclusions* as for his atheist *presuppositions*: Sartre's 'concluded atheism is finally less important and less noticed than the atheism which is presupposed by all the Sartrean analysis'.[85] This all stems from Sartre's inability to accept that we are *created in our freedom*, and that the world is also created, guaranteeing an underlying unity of freedom and nature. Far from *negating* freedom as Sartre suggests, creation for Ricœur actually *undergirds* freedom as its source of reality in a richer conception of being.

Finally, we have seen that Ricœur's philosophy leads to the brink of the doctrine of creation *ex nihilo*, even though Ricœur never talked about this because that would overstep the boundaries of his expertise. In the next chapter we will look in more depth at how the goodness of creation functions in Ricœur's thought.

---

[85] Archives Ricœur / Fonds Ricœur, Inv. 1, dossier 27, 'Anthropology and Religion in the Philosophy of Existence', Lectures at Union Theological Seminary (1958), f. 4097.

9

The Original Goodness of Creation

And God saw everything that he had made, and behold, it was very good.
Genesis 1:31 ESV

The previous chapter demonstrated how the symbol of creation brings unity to the disparate elements of being. We now turn to another crucial dimension of thought given by the same symbol: the fundamental *goodness* of all things. This is one instance of Ricœur taking up Kant's use of creation as a poetic symbol and developing it beyond Kant's own use. The source of this development clearly lies in Ricœur's understanding of God: if God is good, as Christianity has always held, then all he has created is good. As Ricœur puts it, 'The "goodness" of creation is no other than its status as "creature". All creation is good, and the goodness that belongs to man is his being the image of God.'[1] A logical consequence of creation, in Ricœur's eyes, is that humanity's original goodness is not stifled by the effects of evil and sin – indeed, could not possibly be stifled: 'I do not cease to be a created being unless I cease to be; therefore I do not cease to be good.'[2] Nothing could possibly be evil through and through, because by virtue of its existing at all, everything has an underlying trace of goodness.

---

[1] Ricœur, *Symbolism of Evil*, 251. 'La "bonté" de la création n'est pas autre chose que son statut de "créature"; toute la création est bonne et la bonté propre de l'homme, c'est d'être image de Dieu' (Ricœur, *Finitude et culpabilité*, 465).

[2] Ricœur, *Symbolism of Evil*, 251. 'Je ne cesse point d'être créé, sous peine de cesser d'être; donc je ne cesse pas d'être bon' (Ricœur, *Finitude et culpabilité*, 465).

This chapter begins with Ricœur's criticisms of theology for neglecting creation. We conclude by showing how Ricœur's concept of *consent* draws together all the preceding themes. Consent, for Ricœur, is a chosen stance of *hope in the goodness and unity of created finitude*.

A MISSING ELEMENT IN THEOLOGY

In Chapter 5 we saw how Ricœur argued for the primacy of original goodness over evil against the prevailing philosophies of his time. But what I will now show is that, for Ricœur, this same shortcoming was also prevalent in contemporary *theological* discourse. Theology has also failed to reflect on the goodness of creation, and Ricœur considers it his calling as a philosopher to re-establish this foundational doctrine for theologians. 'There is a philosophical side to a theology of creation', he will say in 1999, 'that allows us (maybe this would be the service of the philosopher?) to help the theologian *not to cover over too quickly* a theology of creation by a theology and christology of redemption'.[3] This desire – to pause and soak up the richness of creation before rushing forward to sin and redemption – is already visible in Ricœur's earliest writings.

Ricœur is a polite interlocutor and rarely names the culprits whom he considers to be lacking a proper theology of creation. But in a private letter to Marcel he points to Kierkegaard, saying that the need to rediscover the 'order of creation ... confirms my idea – against Kierkegaard by the way – that a reflection on *creation* must not be stifled by a reflection on *fault*'.[4] It is no accident that Ricœur's 'idea against Kierkegaard' first appears in a letter to Marcel. It was probably originally inspired by him. In his 1934 *Being and Having*, Marcel writes in no uncertain terms about the importance of seeing God in creation:

My deepest and most unshakable conviction – and if it is heretical, so much that [*sic*] the worse for orthodoxy – is, that whatever all the thinkers and doctors

---

[3] Paul Ricœur, 'Ethics and Human Capability: A Response', in *Paul Ricœur and Contemporary Moral Thought*, ed. John Wall, William Schweiker, and David Hall (New York: Routledge, 2002), 283.
[4] My translation: 'Il nous faut sauver le romantisme et la "Naturphilosophie", en retrouvant en nous l'ordre de la création. Cela me confirme dans cette idée – contre Kierkegaard d'ailleurs – qu'une réflexion sur la *création* ne doit pas être étouffée par une réflexion sur la *faute*' (Ricœur, 'Paul Ricœur to Gabriel Marcel, Le Chambon s/Lignon', 25 November 1945, Fonds Gabriel Marcel, Bibliothèque Nationale de France, Paris).

have said, It is not God's will at all to be loved by us against the Creation, but rather glorified through the Creation and with the Creation as our starting-point. That is why I find so many devotional books intolerable. The God who is set up against the Creation and who is somehow jealous of his own works is, to my mind, nothing but an idol.[5]

Marcel's passionate outburst is directed against a type of finitude/evil confusion that equates the love of any worldly thing with idolatry, seeing it as a distraction from undivided devotion to God, rather than as something *through which* we may encounter and enjoy God. Marcel does not mean that we are never in danger of making an idol out of a created thing, but that this danger must be balanced against another danger, that of seeing *everything only* as a potential idol that competes with God for our attention, rather than as an image that reveals God to us. Far from *avoiding* worship of idols, Marcel suggests that to think in this manner is ironically to turn God himself *into* an idol.

Like Marcel, Ricœur reflects on the idol/image distinction. One of his first post-war publications is an article in a Christian journal, Vérité: Jésus et Ponce Pilate' ('Truth: Jesus and Pontius Pilate'). This article contains some of Ricœur's richest theological insights that reveal the contours of his thinking during this period, and even his understanding of his personal vocation.

In a section of this article, titled 'The Fight against Idols', Ricœur warns against idolatries of truth, for example making science the totality of truth. But in the following section his tone abruptly changes. 'The fight for truth', he says, 'is not only a fight against *idols*, but a fight for *signs*, for the signs of creation in every creature'.[6] The problem with seeing idols everywhere is that they obscure the fact that every creature is also

---

[5] Marcel, *Being and Having*, 135. 'Ma conviction la plus intime, la plus inébranlable – et si elle est hérétique tant pis pour l'orthodoxie – c'est, quoi qu'en aient dit tant de spirituels et de docteurs, que Dieu ne veut nullement être aimé par nous *contre* le créé, mais glorifié à travers le créé et en partant de lui. Voilà pourquoi tant de livres d'édification me sont intolérables. Ce Dieu dressé contre le créé et en quelque sorte jaloux de ses propres ouvrages n'est à mes yeux qu'une idole' (Marcel, *Être et avoir*, 196–7). Admittedly Marcel softened this claim immediately: 'What I wrote yesterday needs to be qualified. It is true of the stage I am in at present, but I know that this stage is still rudimentary' (Marcel, *Being and Having*, 136; 'Ce que j'ai écrit hier demanderait tout de même à être nuancé. C'est vrai au stade où je suis, mais je sais que ce stade est encore rudimentaire' [Marcel, *Être et avoir*, 197]).

[6] My translation (italics original): 'Le combat de la vérité n'est pas seulement un combat contre les *idoles*, mais un combat pour les *signes*, pour les signes de la création en toute créature' (Ricœur, 'Vérité: Jésus et Ponce Pilate', 392).

a 'sign' of creation. 'An idol', he explains, is only 'an *image* substituted for a divine model'.[7] Christians are not fundamentally defined by what they are *against*, by the fight *against* false gods in the world, but by the vocation to be and to point to images of God in the world: 'The *no* of Christianity is not like the no of the sceptic or the desperate person. It is the no in view of a yes and because of the yes. It is the no to *idols*, in view of and because of the yes by which we assent to the *sign* of God.'[8]

Ricœur feels the need to emphasise this because of a 'strange thing' he observes in Christian discourse: that the sense of 'God's infinite holiness' and the sense of 'humanity's sinfulness … have often led us to malign the creation under pretext of lifting God higher and abasing humanity lower'.[9] Christians imagine that they are glorifying God by belittling all that is not God. But this is a gross misunderstanding of how God should be glorified: 'however high we put God, however low sin brings humanity, we do not have the right to malign creation'.[10] As Marcel said, God is not in competition with his creation; it does not glorify him to denigrate what he has made.

In addition to Kierkegaard, Ricœur finds another example of 'reflection on fault stifling reflection on creation' in Barth's interpretation of the *Song of Songs*. Barth interprets this biblical book eschatologically, seeing it as a future restoration of the innocence of sexuality in the Garden of Eden. Barth's point is that we do not have access to any such innocence now. But Ricœur claims that to interpret *Song of Songs* this way is to

> strip it of its most noteworthy feature, which is to sing of the innocence of love within the very heart of everyday life…. The poem, re-read in light of Genesis 2:23 may suggest that *creaturely innocence was not abolished by the Fall*, but that it underlies even the history of evil, which the erotic relation never completely avoids. A theological way of reading the poem would then consist in

---

[7] My translation (italics mine): 'Une idole, c'est une image substituée au modèle divin' (Ricœur, 'Vérité: Jésus et Ponce Pilate', 389).

[8] My translation (italics original): 'Le *non* du christianisme n'est pas comme le non du sceptique ou du désespéré. C'est le non en vue du oui et à cause du oui. C'est le non aux *idoles*, en vue et à cause du oui par lequel nous acquiescons [sic] aux *signes* de Dieu' (Ricœur, 'Vérité: Jésus et Ponce Pilate', 389).

[9] My translation: 'Chose curieuse, des éléments importants de notre vision chrétienne du monde, tels que le sentiment de la sainteté infinie de Dieu qui l'exile du monde et le sentiment du péché de l'homme qui l'exile de Dieu, nous ont conduits bien souvent à calomnier la création sous prétexte de mettre Dieu plus haut et l'homme plus bas' (Ricœur, 'Vérité: Jésus et Ponce Pilate', 390).

[10] My translation: 'Or, aussi haut que nous mettions Dieu, aussi bas que le péché ravale l'homme, il est une chose que nous n'avons pas le droit de faire, c'est de calomnier la création' (Ricœur, 'Vérité: Jésus et Ponce Pilate', 390).

proclaiming and celebrating the indestructibility at the base of the innocence of the creature, despite the history of evil and of victimization.[11]

Ricœur is equally disturbed by the Christian tendency to make an ally out of nihilism, seeing it as a preparation for the gospel. Those who celebrate nihilism imagine that cold descriptions of the hopelessness and absurdity of the world will drive people to God. This strategy, says Ricœur, is a dangerous mistake:

> I am disturbed when I hear from Christians that this or that philosophy of despair or of the absurd is a good introduction to the Christian faith. I fear that the absurd is without return, without counterpart, when it has killed the last vestiges of admiration and an obscure sense of mystery which is also the halo of the sacred around every created thing.[12]

Let us not, Ricœur says, erase the 'halo of the sacred around every created thing', obliterating the traces of God in creation and darkening the world by destroying the human instinct for admiration and wonder. What kind of God is then preached as a solution? He is either not the creator, or if he is, he has abandoned creation and cannot be found there. It is at great peril only that Christians borrow the darkness of nihilism to make the uncreated light shine brighter.

By contrast, Ricœur argues that the goodness of creation is the very frontier between the gospel and nihilism, the first light of dawn of the Christian message. It is only because of creation that we can be sure of the asymmetry between good and evil, the priority, originality, and greater power of good over evil: 'The impassable limit that separates Christianity from a philosophy of the absurd is this creation is more fundamental, more original than original sin.'[13]

---

[11] LaCocque and Ricœur, *Thinking Biblically*, 299. Italics mine: '... on le dépouille peut-être de son trait le plus marquant, qui est de chanter l'innocence de l'amour au cœur même de la quotidienneté des jours. Loin d'en être diminuée, la signification théologique en devient peut-être plus forte: le poème, relu à la lumière de Genèse 2,23, suggérerait que l'innocence créaturelle n'est pas abolie par la chute, mais qu'elle sous-tend l'histoire même du mal, à laquelle n'échappe pas par ailleurs la relation érotique. Une façon de lire théologiquement le poème consisterait alors à proclamer et à célébrer l'indestructibilité du fond d'innocence de la créature et, cela, *en dépit de* l'histoire du mal et de la victimisation' (Ricœur and LaCocque, *Penser la bible*, 470).

[12] My translation: 'je m'inquiète quand j'entends dire par les chrétiens que telle ou telle philosophie du désespoir ou de l'absurde est une bonne introduction à la foi chrétienne, je crains que l'absurde soit sans retour, sans contre-partie quand il a tué les derniers vestiges de l'admiration et un obscur sens du mystère qui est encore le halo du sacré autour de chaque chose créée' (Ricœur, 'Vérité: Jésus et Ponce Pilate', 391).

[13] My translation: 'La limite infranchissable qui sépare le christianisme d'une philosophie de l'absurde est là: la création est plus fondamentale, plus originelle que le péché originel' (Ricœur, 'Vérité: Jésus et Ponce Pilate', 391).

This last sentence is Ricœur's clarion call that he repeats untiringly throughout his career. The same conviction will appear almost unchanged, although with new ethical connotations, over fifty years later: 'As radical as evil may be, it will never be more originary than goodness, which is the *Ursprung* in the field of ethics, the orientation to the good as being rooted in the ontological structure of the human being, or in biblical terms: creation, createdness.'[14]

To say it is Ricœur's clarion call means that it is not merely his own personal conviction, but that he summons all Christian thinkers to the same proclamation. The vocation of the Christian academic, he says, is 'to rediscover the lost meaning of creation. I am in God's creation – that is the assurance that the smallest truth must discuss, confirm, acclaim'.[15] Ricœur's plea to Christian intellectuals is: do not merely denounce evil; do not sweep the good away with the bad; rather, *find the good in everything*, however corrupted or distorted by sin it may be: 'The Bible tells us that vanity has been spread over the whole creation. The service of intelligence is to lift a corner of this covering of vanity and rediscover the signs of this creation of which God said it was good.'[16] Waxing lyrical about creation as analogy of God's goodness, he charges all Christians to do the same as himself:

Our task is to rediscover in every image a parable of the Kingdom. Our fight for the truth must be dominated by this golden rule: seek the truth of things, the truth of the human, the truth of history which will be a sign, an image of God. We must never forget that God is not only the Wholly Other, but the One whose image we are. All our thought must be able to be an imitation of God in the name of the imitation of Jesus Christ. This possibility is drawn in the Bible – it is the parables which run throughout the sacred Book. The Bible does not say only: The Kingdom is not of this world; but: the Kingdom is like ... May all my life be an image, a parable of the Kingdom! May all my truths be an image of the uncreated truth![17]

---

[14] Ricœur, 'Ethics and Human Capability: A Response', 284.
[15] My translation: 'Il faut encore que la raison retrouve le sens perdu de la création. Je suis dans la création de Dieu, voilà l'assurance que la moindre vérité doit commenter, confirmer, acclamer' (Ricœur, 'Vérité: Jésus et Ponce Pilate', 390).
[16] My translation: 'La Bible nous dit que la vanité a été étendue sur toute la création. Le service de l'intelligence est de lever un coin de ce voile de vanité et de retrouver les signes de cette création dont Dieu dit qu'elle était bonne' (Ricœur, 'Vérité: Jésus et Ponce Pilate', 390).
[17] My translation (italics original): 'Notre tâche est de retrouver en toute image la parabole du Royaume. Notre combat pour la vérité doit être dominé sur cette règle d'or: chercher la vérité des choses, la vérité de l'homme, la vérité de l'histoire, qui soit un signe, une image de Dieu. Ne l'oublions pas: Dieu n'est pas seulement le Tout-Autre, mais Celui dont nous sommes l'image. Toute notre pensée doit pouvoir être une imitation de Dieu

CONSENTING TO OUR CREATED FINITUDE

'Finitude', says Ricœur, is for Christians 'the condition of the creature'.[18] If creation is both originally good and intrinsically finite, then finitude must be good despite not being divine. But our human limitations are perhaps the hardest of all things to acknowledge as good. As Chapter 5 showed, we are tempted to see our limitations as either an unbearable constraint, a burden to which we cannot reconcile ourselves, or else as a failure and a cause of inevitable guilt. In opposition to this temptation, Ricœur argues: 'the idea of limitation as such cannot bring us to the threshold of moral evil'.[19] If finitude were a flaw, then God could never have created, because the flawless cannot create that which is flawed.

As we shall see, Ricœur connects the goodness of finitude with humble recognition of our creaturely state by means of the concept of consent. There is a goodness proper to creatures that differs from the goodness of the creator. Finitude, which is the status of not-being-God, is not a flaw or a tragedy, because we are not supposed to be God. It is a mistake to blame finitude for failing to be infinite as if divinity were the unreachable *telos* of our existence. It is equally a mistake to blame God for making us finite, as if being God were the only way to be happy and free. The act by which we accept our finitude as good Ricœur names 'consent', and 'refusal' the opposite act of tragic defiance. Because consent, in light of the poetic symbol of creation, yields a vision of reality as united and of human finitude as good, it is beyond the limits of philosophical discourse to prove, even though there are rational arguments in favour of it. Ultimately it remains a 'metaphysical choice',[20] whose basis is hope in the goodness of creation.

Ricœur elaborates his notion of consent, as a form of willing that transcends the active/passive dichotomy, at the end of *Freedom and Nature*. Marsh calls this book 'one of the great, underappreciated works ... in the

---

au nom de l'imitation de Jésus-Christ. Cette possibilité est dessinée dans la Bible: ce sont les paraboles qui courent à travers le livre sacré. La Bible ne dit pas seulement: le Royaume n'est pas de ce monde; mais le Royaume est semblable à ... Que toute ma vie soit donc une image, une parabole du Royaume! Que mes vérités soient l'image de la vérité incréée!' (Ricœur, 'Vérité: Jésus et Ponce Pilate', 389).

[18] Ricœur, 'The Relation of Jaspers' Philosophy to Religion', 632. 'La finitude ... la condition de créature' (Ricœur, 'Philosophie et religion chez Karl Jaspers', 227).
[19] Ricœur, *Fallible Man*, 133. 'L'idée de limitation, prise comme telle, est insuffisante pour approcher du seuil du mal moral' (Ricœur, *Finitude et culpabilité*, 184). See Chapter 5 above, section headed 'Confusion ; Limitations as Fault'.
[20] Ricœur, *Freedom and Nature*, 465. 'des *options* métaphysiques' (Ricœur, *Le volontaire et l'involontaire*, 439).

history of Continental philosophy in the twentieth century'.[21] Its patient rigour, breathtaking assimilation of material from numerous disciplines, and magisterial balance between the extremes of voluntarism and determinism all make it worthy of the status of philosophical classic. Ricœur argues throughout for the '*reciprocity* of the voluntary and the involuntary' (or freedom and nature, or subjectivity and objectivity), the idea that each implies and depends on the other.[22] The book is in three sections: the first deals with *deciding* and focussed on the reciprocity of voluntary decision to involuntary motivations. The second section concerns *action* or effort on the basis of bodily abilities.

The third and final section of *Freedom and Nature*, and the book's climax, is about *consent*. But is there really a third manifestation of the will besides decision and action? 'At first sight', Ricœur admits, 'it does not seem that there is room for a new practical act in addition to decision ... and effort'.[23] It may seem that consent has nothing to do with freedom and is precisely what we have no choice about. But 'in fact', says Ricœur, 'wise men have always construed the recognition of necessity as a moment of freedom'.[24] Consent is a special type of decision and a special type of action that must be treated in its own category. It is a *decision*, albeit of a unique kind. Like every decision, it 'can be expressed by an imperative: let it be; a strange imperative, to be sure, since its terminus is the inevitable'.[25] Consent is also an *action*, equally unique:

> To consent is still to do.... It is an engagement in being. But ... it is specifically willing without being able, a powerless effort, but one which converts its powerlessness into a new grandeur. When I transform all necessity into my freedom, then that which limits and perhaps breaks me becomes the principle of an entirely new effectiveness, an entirely stripped, disarmed effectiveness.[26]

---

[21] Kaplan, *Reading Ricœur*, 5.
[22] Ricœur, *Freedom and Nature*, 341. Italics original: 'La *réciprocité* de l'involontaire et du volontaire' (Ricœur, *Le volontaire et l'involontaire*, 319).
[23] Ricœur, *Freedom and Nature*. Translation modified: 'Il ne semble pas à première vue qu'il y ait place pour un nouvel acte pratique à côté de la décision ... et à côté de l'effort' (Ricœur, *Le volontaire et l'involontaire*, 321).
[24] Ricœur, *Freedom and Nature*, 344. 'De fait, les sages ont toujours fait de la connaissance de la nécessité un moment de la liberté' (Ricœur, *Le volontaire et l'involontaire*, 322).
[25] Ricœur, *Freedom and Nature*, 344. 'Le consentement ... n'est pas sans analogie en effet avec la décision; comme elle, il peut s'exprimer par un impératif: que cela soit; étrange impératif certes, puisqu'il se termine à l'inévitable' (Ricœur, *Le volontaire et l'involontaire*, 322).
[26] Ricœur, *Freedom and Nature*, 345–6. 'Consentir c'est encore faire, ... c'est un engagement dans l'être. Mais ... il est expressément un vouloir sans pouvoir, un effort impuissant, mais qui convertit son impuissance en une nouvelle grandeur; quand je transforme

Ricœur wants to take seriously the difficulty of consent and the strength of reasons against it. In a section titled 'The Sorrow of Finitude', he writes: 'I suffer from being one finite and partial perspective.... If only I could grasp and embrace everything! – and how cruel it is to choose and exclude.'[27] Why else did all those nineteenth-century totalising philosophies transgress our finite perspective, if not because it is hard to accept that we cannot attain absolute knowledge? We suffer, secondly, from the absence of total transparency of our consciousness, the fact that it arises out of an impenetrable darkness called the unconscious.[28] Finally we suffer from our *contingency*, the fact that we neither chose to exist nor remember our beginning.[29]

Freedom has the unique ability to say 'No!' to these dimensions of finitude in the act of *refusal*, the opposite of consent. This refusal can take the form of arrogance or despair, the two rejections either side of finitude that we examined in Chapter 1. Arrogance means rejecting our finitude without realising we are doing so: 'the disguised form of refusal is the haughty affirmation of consciousness as absolute, that is, as creative or as self-producing'.[30] It means rejecting the origins of consciousness in the unconscious, and positing a total self-transparency that is the heart of idealism: 'all idealism is Promethean and conceals a secret rejection of the human condition.... This philosophical titanism is not aware of itself as refusal: this is either its lie or its illusion'.[31] And arrogance is the refusal of continency in a self-positing consciousness: 'it is intolerable to find oneself existing and not-necessary; we need to *posit* ourselves as existing'.[32] But arrogance can easily flip over into despair because both are rooted in the

---

toute nécessité en ma liberté, alors ce qui me borne et parfois me brise devient le principe d'une efficacité toute nouvelle, d'une efficacité entièrement désarmée et dénuée' (Ricœur, *Le volontaire et l'involontaire*, 323).

[27] Ricœur, *Freedom and Nature*, 447. '"La tristesse du fini" ... Je souffre d'être une perspective finie et partielle sur le monde et sur les valeurs.... Que ne puis-je tout prendre et tout embrasser! et qu'il est cruel d'élire et d'exclure!' (Ricœur, *Le volontaire et l'involontaire*, 420).

[28] Ricœur, *Freedom and Nature*, 448–50; Ricœur, *Le volontaire et l'involontaire*, 421–2.

[29] Ricœur, *Freedom and Nature*, 450–56; Ricœur, *Le volontaire et l'involontaire*, 422–8.

[30] Ricœur, *Freedom and Nature*, 463. 'La forme déguisée du refus, c'est l'affirmation altière de la conscience comme absolu, c'est-à-dire comme créatrice ou comme productrice de soi' (Ricœur, *Le volontaire et l'involontaire*, 436).

[31] Ricœur, *Freedom and Nature*, 464. 'Toute idéalisme est prométhéen et recèle un secret refus de la condition humaine ... Ce titanisme philosophique s'ignore comme refus: c'est son mensonge ou son illusion' (Ricœur, *Le volontaire et l'involontaire*, 436).

[32] Ricœur, *Freedom and Nature*, 464. Italics original: 'Il est intolérable de se trouver soi-même existant non-nécessaire; il faut se *poser* existant' (Ricœur, *Le volontaire et l'involontaire*, 437).

refusal of finitude. Arrogance denies finitude, despair acknowledges it, but grudgingly, as the source of all human woes. 'A philosophy of triumphant consciousness', says Ricœur, 'contains the seeds of a philosophy of despair. All that is needed is to recognize the refusal spread throughout the wish of self-positing as a refusal[,] and the vanity and the breakdown of that wish suddenly transform the claims of this titanic freedom into despair'.[33] Both arrogance and despair have at their core the wish to be like God and the rejection of the goodness of created finitude: the only difference is that one thinks it is possible and the other knows it is impossible.

SARTRE'S PHILOSOPHY OF REFUSAL

It is hard not to see Ricœur's description of refusal as another implicit critique of Sartre. Nor would this be surprising, given the period. Sartre describes human beings as 'haunted' by the frustrated desire to be the God-like synthesis of for-itself and in-itself (which, we remember, he also claims is impossible):

> Human reality is suffering because it rises in being as perpetually haunted by a totality which it is without being able to be it, precisely because it could not attain the in-itself without losing itself as for-itself. Human reality therefore is by nature an unhappy consciousness with no possibility of surpassing its unhappy state.[34]

Furthermore, humans cannot bear to acknowledge their contingency, wishing their existence to be a necessary part of reality: 'it is altogether contingent that I be, for I am not the foundation of my being'.[35]

> Human reality is a passion in that it projects losing itself so as to found being and by the same stroke to constitute the In-itself which escapes contingency by being its own foundation, the *Ens causa sui*, which religions call God. Thus the passion of man is the reverse of that of Christ, for man loses himself as man in order that

---

[33] Ricœur, *Freedom and Nature*, 465–6. 'Une philosophie de la conscience triomphante tient en germe une philosophie du désespoir. Il suffit que le refus dissimulé dans le vœu d'auto-position se connaisse comme refus pour que la vanité et l'échec de ce vœu transforment soudain en désespoir la prétention de cette liberté titanesque' (Ricœur, *Le volontaire et l'involontaire*, 438).

[34] Sartre, *Being and Nothingness*, 90. 'La réalité-humaine est souffrante dans son être, parce qu'elle surgit à l'être comme perpétuellement hantée par une totalité qu'elle est sans pouvoir l'être, puisque justement elle ne pourrait atteindre l'en-soi sans se perdre comme pour-soi. Elle est donc par nature conscience malheureuse, sans dépassement possible de l'état de malheur' (Sartre, *L'être et le néant*, 126–7).

[35] Sartre, *Being and Nothingness*, 308. 'Il est tout à fait contingent que je sois, car je ne suis pas le fondement de mon être' (Sartre, *L'être et le néant*, 347–8).

God may be born. But the idea of God is contradictory and we lose ourselves in vain. Man is a useless passion.[36]

Ricœur argues that to see human beings as forever frustrated in their contingency and in their inability to be God, is simultaneously to *recognise* and *refuse* our finitude, transitioning from pride to despair. '"Black existentialism"', says Ricœur, 'is perhaps only a disappointed idealism and the suffering of a consciousness which thought itself divine and which becomes aware of itself as fallen'.[37] Although he does not believe refusal can be disproven on a purely rational basis, he does try to show that it is not rationally necessary, an inevitable consequence of being finite. In his unpublished lectures, he questions Sartre's assertion that the frustrated desire to be God is really an essential and inescapable part of our humanity: 'Is man this ideal of being God?'[38]

By asking the question, Ricœur shows that Sartre has *assumed* more than *argued* for Godlike 'infinitude' (freedom from finitude) as the human ideal. But Ricœur offers an alternative suggestion. From a Christian perspective, informed by the biblical creation narrative, the frustrated desire for Godlike freedom (Sartre's 'ideal of being God') is not an unavoidable aspect of our humanity, but a result of sin and evil: it is 'precisely the temptation of the serpent.... Sartre himself must call it a *passion*'.[39] By saying we could be 'like God', the serpent undermined the goodness of *not* being like God, which is the goodness proper to finitude. The 'useless passion' Sartre speaks about is precisely the passion of wishing to be God. 'Is not this *passion* the substitute to that of: *being a creature*?' Ricœur asks.[40]

---

[36] Sartre, *Being and Nothingness*, 615. 'Toute réalité-humaine est une passion, en ce qu'elle projette de se perdre pour fonder l'être et pour constituer du même coup l'en-soi qui échappe à la contingence en étant son propre fondement, l'*Ens causa sui* que les religions nomment Dieu. Ainsi la passion de l'homme est-elle inverse de celle du Christ, car l'homme se perd en tant qu'homme pour que Dieu naisse. Mais l'idée de Dieu est contradictoire et nous nous perdons en vain; l'homme est une passion inutile' (Sartre, *L'être et le néant*, 662).

[37] Ricœur, *Freedom and Nature*, 466. '"L'existentialisme noir" n'est peut-être qu'un idéalisme déçu, et la souffrance d'une conscience qui s'est crue divine et qui se connaît déchue' (Ricœur, *Le volontaire et l'involontaire*, 438).

[38] Archives Ricœur / Fonds Ricœur, Inv. 1, dossier 27, 'Anthropology and Religion in the Philosophy of Existence', Lectures at Union Theological Seminary (1958), f. 4096.

[39] Archives Ricœur / Fonds Ricœur, Inv. 1, dossier 27, 'Anthropology and Religion in the Philosophy of Existence', Lectures at Union Theological Seminary (1958), f. 4096. Italics are underlines in manuscript.

[40] Archives Ricœur / Fonds Ricœur, Inv. 1, dossier 27, 'Anthropology and Religion in the Philosophy of Existence', Lectures at Union Theological Seminary (1958), f. 4096. Italics are underlines in manuscript.

[The serpent said:] 'Your eyes shall be opened, and ye shall be as gods, knowing good and evil.' It is in relation to this 'desire' that finitude is insupportable, the finitude which consists simply in being created being. The soul of the serpent's question is the 'bad infinite', which simultaneously perverts the meaning of the limit by which freedom was oriented and the meaning of the finitude of the freedom thus oriented by the limit.[41]

For Christians, the limitations of finite freedom are counted a misfortune only because of sin. Adam and Eve were tempted with the God-like freedom of autonomy; by listening to this temptation they became dissatisfied with their creaturely status, and the limits of finitude appeared miserable to them for the first time. Therefore, far from finitude being *itself* an evil, the evil only appears when we refuse to *accept* our finitude; ironically, to conflate finitude with evil is itself the original evil.[42]

What applies to created *finitude* also applies to *contingency*. Christians believe that God created us out of choice, not out of need or compulsion; therefore we are not a necessary part of reality. The state of being that Sartre calls '*contingent*', Ricœur says, 'was understood by the Christian philosopher as the situation of creation'.[43] Sartre finds a tragic misery in our inability to be our own foundation, that is, the creator. For Ricœur, this desire is only a temptation, not intrinsic to our humanity. Our contingency makes us unhappy only if we succumb to the temptation to *want* to be our own foundation, but 'a being who is a creature lacks his own foundation to the precise extent to which he has a transcendent foundation in his Creator'.[44]

---

[41] Ricœur, *Symbolism of Evil*, 253. Translation modified: '"Vos yeux s'ouvriront, vous serez come des dieux, connaissant le bien et le mal"; c'est par rapport à ce "désir" que la finitude est insupportable, cette finitude qui consiste simplement à être créé; l'âme de l'interrogation du serpent, c'est le "mauvais infini" qui pervertit simultanément le sens de la limite qui orientait la liberté et le sens même de la finitude de cette liberté ainsi orientée par le limite' (Ricœur, *Finitude et culpabilité*, 467).

[42] This point has been made more recently by Emmanuel Falque: 'Humanity's temptation – perhaps also the key temptation of a certain form of contemporary Christian philosophy – is to seek to escape into the unlimited, when, in fact, the human being is desired and considered within the limit.... Where finitude is only observed in philosophy, it is, on the contrary, *sought* and *desired in theology*' (Falque, *Crossing the Rubicon*, 146). Italics original: 'Telle est donc la tentation, de l'homme certes: ... la fuite dans l'illimité quand l'homme est voulu et désiré dans la limite.... Là où la finitude n'est que *constatée* en philosophie, elle est au contraire *voulue* et *désirée* en théologie' (Falque, *Passer le Rubicon*, 186).

[43] Archives Ricœur / Fonds Ricœur, Inv. 1, dossier 27, 'Anthropology and Religion in the Philosophy of Existence', Lectures at Union Theological Seminary (1958), f. 4097. Italics are underlines in manuscript.

[44] Ricœur, *Freedom and Nature*, 462. 'L'être qui est créature manque de fondement en soi, dans la mesure même où il a un fondement transcendant dans son Créateur' (Ricœur, *Le volontaire et l'involontaire*, 435).

CONSENT ROOTED IN HOPE

All of this amounts to a Ricœurian argument that Sartre's approach to finitude is not the only possible one. But to find a full elaboration of his alternative, we must return to *Freedom and Nature*. In contrast to Sartrean 'refusal', Ricœur offers 'consent' rooted in a belief, or more precisely a *hope*, in the goodness of created finitude. Consent is the climax of his account of the reciprocity of freedom and nature because 'What is at stake in consent is the ultimate reconciliation of freedom and nature',[45] the final overcoming of the dualism of subject and object, voluntary and involuntary. Instead of battling with nature as an enemy, we welcome it as our counterpart and completion in a unified whole in which we have our subordinate yet rightful place. Consent means that the human subject is neither everything (arrogance, absolute idealism) nor nothing (despair, nihilism). To articulate this Ricœur resorts once again to creator/creature language: by consent, he says, 'the cogito affirms itself but is not its own creator, reflection attests itself as subject but not as self-positing'[46] He puts this more strongly in his letter to Marcel, as we saw above: 'By consent I return to the *mysterious unity of creation*; I reinstate the union of soul and body.... The mysterious unity of being is primary.'[47]

What are we consenting *to* when we consent in this Ricœurian fashion? To our finitude, to 'limitations', to all that is true of us by the fact of our being created and not the creator.[48] To consent is to say that to be finite is good, in spite of the limitations that cause suffering, that frustrate our will, and that thwart our desires. 'Consent', he summarises, 'is right love of the self and of being in the self'.[49]

---

[45] Ricœur, *Freedom and Nature*, 346 'Nous devinons maintenant quel est l'enjeu du consentement: c'est l'ultime conciliation de la liberté et de la nature' (Ricœur, *Le volontaire et l'involontaire*, 324).

[46] Ricœur, *Freedom and Nature*, 468. 'Le cogito s'affirme, mais n'est pas auto-créateur, la réflexion s'atteste elle-même comme sujet, mais n'est pas auto-position' (Ricœur, *Le volontaire et l'involontaire*, 440).

[47] My translation (italics mine): 'Par le consentement je repasse sur l'unité mystérieuse de la création; je réinstaure l'union de l'âme et du corps.... L'unité mystérieuse de l'être est première' (Ricœur, 'Paul Ricœur to Gabriel Marcel, Le Chambon s/Lignon', 25 November 1945, Fonds Gabriel Marcel, Bibliothèque Nationale de France, Paris).

[48] Ricœur, *Freedom and Nature*, 479. '... consentement aux limites' (Ricœur, *Le volontaire et l'involontaire*, 451). Thus Jacques is right that Ricœur never speaks of 'consenting to Transcendence' (I am not sure the phrase even makes grammatical sense), but wrong to see transcendence as nothing more than the human other. See Jacques, 'Corps et Transcendance', 246.

[49] Ricœur, *Freedom and Nature*, 449. 'Le consentement ... est le droit amour de soi et de l'être dans le soi' (Ricœur, *Le volontaire et l'involontaire*, 422).

Ricœur does not attempt to prove the rational necessity of consent, because to do so depends on a belief in creation which implies a creator, crossing the line into an overly confident apologetic stance. This is the correct context for the quotation we looked at in Chapter 4: 'We clearly reject the pretentions of an overly zealous apologetics which would pretend to derive God from nature ... by a simple rational implication.'[50] Consent is beyond the boundaries of what philosophy can prove or disprove. But between refutation of one thing and proof of another, we are faced with the *choice* of metaphysical frameworks – not an arbitrary choice, but a choice that retains an element of risk; implicit here is what Ricœur articulates ten years later as a *wager*.

What is the nature of this choice, this wager? Here Ricœur admits that he can no longer keep evil and transcendence bracketed out of the discussion: here, 'phenomenology is transcended in metaphysics'.[51] To wager means to make a metaphysical judgement that cannot be proven right on purely philosophical grounds. First of all, we must choose to attribute evil either to our finitude or to our desire for infinitude: it is a tragedy, either that we are finite, or that we cannot accept that we are finite. To consent is to accept our finitude as good, and therefore to see our desire to be God as an evil temptation. But secondly, and more fundamentally, to consent means to say 'yes' to the goodness of reality. 'How can we justify the *yes* of consent', Ricœur asks, 'without passing a value judgement on the totality of the universe, that is, without evaluating its ultimate suitability for freedom?'[52] Because such a value judgement can never have sufficient evidence, 'consent would have its "poetic" root in hope'.[53]

As we saw in Chapter 2, hope is the methodological keystone of Ricœur's whole philosophy. Ricœur now says that without hope consent is impossible, not only because of its rational unprovability, but because of the obvious evils in the world that are suffered by undeserving souls.

---

[50] Ricœur, *Freedom and Nature*, 468. 'Nous récusons clairement les prétentions d'une apologétique trop zélée qui prétendrait tirer Dieu de la nature ou de la subjectivité par simple implication rationnelle' (Ricœur, *Le volontaire et l'involontaire*, 440).

[51] Ricœur, *Freedom and Nature*, 467. 'La phénoménologie se transcende elle-même dans une métaphysique' (Ricœur, *Le volontaire et l'involontaire*, 439).

[52] Ricœur, *Freedom and Nature*, 467. Italics in translation: 'Comment justifier le oui du consentement sans porter un jugement de valeur sur l'ensemble de l'univers, c'est-à-dire sans en apprécier l'ultime convenance à la liberté' (Ricœur, *Le volontaire et l'involontaire*, 439).

[53] Ricœur, *Freedom and Nature*, 467. 'Ainsi le consentement aurait sa racine "poétique" dans l'espérance' (Ricœur, *Le volontaire et l'involontaire*, 439).

Hope points towards a future age in which evil will be no more and consent can be made unreservedly:

Perhaps no one can follow consent to the end. Evil is the scandal which always separates consent from inhuman necessity. Perhaps we need to understand that the way of consent [leads] through hope which awaits *something else*.... Admiration is possible because the world is an analogy of Transcendence; hope is necessary because the world is quite other than Transcendence. Admiration sings of the day, reaches the visible miracle, hope transcends in the night.... Thus hope is not the triumph of dualism but sustenance on the way of conciliation.[54]

The object of hope, Ricœur concludes, is belief in the underlying unity of creation: 'hope wills to convert all hostility into a *fraternal tension* within a unity of creation'.[55]

In summary, the greatest obstacle to affirming the goodness of creation is our unwillingness to accept our finitude, our limitations, our contingency. As we saw in Chapter 5, we are tempted to see these un-Godlike qualities either as an evil suffered or as a moral failure in themselves. For Ricœur, to give in to this temptation is to adopt the stance of *refusal*, either in arrogant Promethean denial of our limitations (idealism) or in bitter despair at the absurdity of life (nihilism). To consent, on the other hand, means accepting our finitude, saying 'yes' to the circumstances we did not choose, thereby bringing unity to freedom and nature and situating ourselves in our rightful place in the unified whole that is God's created order.

CONCLUSION

Creation is not merely a doctrine for Ricœur: it is a personal vocation to a universal message. He challenges all Christian intellectuals to seek the

---

[54] Ricœur, *Freedom and Nature*, 480. 'Nul peut-être ne peut aller jusqu'au bout du consentement. Le mal est le scandale qui toujours sépare le consentement de la cruelle nécessité. Peut-être faut-il comprendre que le chemin du consentement ne passe pas seulement par l'admiration de la merveilleuse nature, résumée dans l'involontaire absolu, mais par l'espérance qui attend *autre chose*.... L'admiration est possible parce que le monde est une analogie de la Transcendance; l'espérance est nécessaire parce que le monde est tout autre que la Transcendance. L'admiration, chant du jour, va à la merveille visible, l'espérance transcende dans la nuit.... Ainsi l'espérance n'est point le triomphe du dualisme, mais le viatique sur le chemin de la conciliation' (Ricœur, *Le volontaire et l'involontaire*, 451–2).

[55] Ricœur, *Freedom and Nature*, 481. Italics original: 'Si une distance évanouissante sépare toujours la liberté de la nécessité, du moins l'espérance veut-elle convertir toute hostilité en une *tension fraternelle*, à l'intérieur d'une unité de création' (Ricœur, *Le volontaire et l'involontaire*, 452).

image of God, meaning the original goodness of things, in all the work they do, thereby bringing truth to light. After telling Christian intellectuals that 'the fight for truth is not only a fight against *idols*, but a fight for *signs*, for the signs of creation in every creature',[56] Ricœur gives his personal testimony as an example. 'For me, who teach philosophy', he tells them, 'I read in the Word and hear throughout its revelation a *call*, a command.'[57] The command he hears is this:

> Testify to the truth of the Father whenever you speak of man, the body, needs, habit, time, the value of science, the will, etc.... You were set free by the truth; now you in turn are to set truths free, truths that are captive to the essential lie exhaled by the father of lies. Set these secondary truths free, which have no other meaning than that of *uncovering the signs of original creation*.[58]

In an essay which is primarily about truth, we learn that truth, for Ricœur, is above all the truth of *creation*, the truth that the world was created good by a good Father.

This vocation overflows into Ricœur's academic life from a personal source of religious conviction. Decades later, in his final two Gifford lectures, Ricœur describes the nature of his religious faith:

> I willingly grant that there exists something like a 'religious experience.' ... For my part, the formulations closest and most familiar to me are: a feeling of absolute dependence, in relation to a creation that precedes me; an ultimate concern at the horizon of all my preoccupations; an unconditional trust, which hopes despite ... everything. These are a few synonyms for what, in the contemporary period, has been termed 'faith'.[59]

The first and foremost experience in this list concerns creation. After borrowing a term from Schleiermacher, Ricœur gives it further precision:

---

[56] My translation (italics original): 'Le combat de la vérité n'est pas seulement un combat contre les *idoles*, mais un combat pour les *signes*, pour les signes de la création en toute créature' (Ricœur, 'Vérité: Jésus et Ponce Pilate', 392).

[57] My translation (italics mine): 'Pour moi, qui enseigne la philosophie, je lis dans la Parole, j'entends dans toute la révélation, un appel, un ordre' (Ricœur, 'Vérité : Jésus et Ponce Pilate', 392).

[58] My translation (italics mine): 'Témoigne de la vérité du Père toutes les fois que tu parles de l'homme, du corps, des besoins, de l'habitude, du temps, de la valeur de la science, de la volonté, etc. C'est ton témoignage *indirect*.... Tu as été délivré par la vérité, délivre à ton tour les vérités captives du mensonge essentiel que souffle le père du mensonge. Délivre les vérités secondes qui n'ont pas d'autre sens que de dépister les signes de la création originelle' (Ricœur, 'Vérité: Jésus et Ponce Pilate', 392-3).

[59] Paul Ricœur, 'The Self in the Mirror of the Scriptures', in *The Whole and Divided Self*, ed. David Edward Aune and John McCarthy (New York: Crossroad Publishing Company, 1997), 206.

the 'absolute dependence' he feels is that of a *creature* dependent on a *creator*. In other words, Ricœur's deepest Christian convictions begin, not from salvation, nor from a desire to escape from the wicked world to God. They are rooted, rather, in a fundamental dependence on the original goodness of all things in a 'creation that precedes me'.

It should not be surprising, then, that we see hope in the goodness of created finitude bursting forth in everything Ricœur writes. Creation undergirds his insistence on the limits of human access to truth (Chapters 1 and 2), his discovery that the human has a natural openness to transcendence (Chapters 3 and 4), his commitment to distinguishing finitude from evil (Chapters 5 and 6), and his hope in the unity of being (Chapter 8). A single Ricœurian quotation binds all these themes together. 'In the end', Ricœur writes, 'it is the *unity of creation* that brings together all the relations of opposition between empirical being and being-in-itself, and all the negative dialectic by which these determinations are overcome in the absolute. *Negative theology* has divine omnipresence as both its starting point and its final conclusion. Such is, in our view, philosophy's moment of birth and act of hope.'[60]

In Chapter 1, we saw that for Ricœur, it is the 'unity of creation' that enables us to trust in the unity of truth beyond paradox and contradiction. Yet our created finitude also stipulates that we are not the creator; we have no universal perspective on the world. Between the presumption of taking a creator-like point of view and the resignation that postulates an absurd universe, Ricœur finds the birthplace of philosophy in an 'act of hope' in our partial yet real grasp of truth.

Chapters 3 and 4 concluded that for Ricœur our created finitude guarantees for us the existence of a creator, an 'infinite' in whom we participate. The creator reveals himself to us through his image in us: the image of an 'infinitude' by which we acknowledge our own point of view. But it is a 'negative theology'; we discover the infinite by means of negation of our own finitude.

Chapters 5 and 6 expounded the way in which it is the *goodness* of our created finitude that enables us to distinguish it from evil, sin, and guilt, for Ricœur. The latter are subsequent and only come about through

---

[60] My translation: 'C'est enfin *l'unité de création* qui porte tous les rapports d'opposition entre l'être empirique et l'être en soi et toute la dialectique négative par laquelle les déterminations se surmontent dans l'absolu: La *theologia negativa* a pour point de départ et pour point d'arrivée l'omniprésence divine. Tel est, selon nous, l'acte de naissance et l'acte d'espérance de la philosophie' (Dufrenne and Ricœur, *Karl Jaspers et la philosophie de l'existence*, 388).

the creator's gift of freedom, by which we most resemble him. It is the goodness of our created finitude that, if we trust in it, prevents us from listening to the temptation of the serpent who tells us that finitude is an evil to be suffered, a gaping lack of being.

And lastly, in Chapter 7 we saw how Ricœur justifies using the theological concept of creation in philosophy by calling it a *symbol*, a non-philosophical light that enlightens philosophical discourse by its revealing power, like the sun that hides itself in incomprehensible brilliance yet illuminates the world. Ricœur's projected third part of the *Philosophy of the Will* would have been a 'poetics', which for him meant a description of the will in light of the symbol of creation. Nonetheless the poetics 'seeps through' his extant published works in numerous ways, through his commitment to the final unity of being, and (in this chapter) to its original goodness, and through the metaphysical choice of consent by which we accept our finite place in the universe.

Conclusion

New Frontiers between Philosophy and Theology

In the Introduction I cited Andrew Davison, who wrote that 'we can be *more philosophical* in order to be *more theological*',[1] and Emmanuel Falque's contention that 'the more one theologizes, the better one philosophizes'.[2] In line with such a vision of the relationship with philosophy and theology, this book shows that Ricœur offers us a way of understanding finitude that is rigorously philosophical and yet provides an abundant wealth of insights for theology. Far from confusing the boundaries of philosophy and theology, the richness of Ricœur's insights is due to his clear grasp of the true nature of each.

God, creation, and evil are the three tiers of Ricœur's metaphysics, stated in theological language. But because Ricœur is a philosopher, he prefers to use the language of finitude (the human condition), infinitude (the absolute, transcendence), and nothing ('the fault', guilt). As we have seen, for the early Ricœur finitude is positive, as Heideggerian finitude also is. But unlike Heidegger, Ricœurian finitude is framed on both sides by the infinite and nothingness. It is framed on one side by God, who exceeds it infinitely and in whom it participates, and on the other side by evil, which is no real part of finitude, being nothing in itself and only a negation of the good. Because they are outside the boundaries of finitude, neither God nor evil can be grasped as a determinate philosophical concept. They remain 'mysteries' in Marcellian language, or 'symbols' in Kantian/Ricœurian language. This does not mean they have no effect

---

[1] Davison, *The Love of Wisdom*, ix. Italics original.
[2] Falque, *Crossing the Rubicon*, 107. Translation modified: '*Plus on théologise, mieux on philosophe*' (Falque, *Passer le Rubicon*, 175).

on philosophy, or that thought which proceeds from them as a point of departure cannot be properly philosophical.

In concluding, I should like to revisit the preceding themes with a focus on what each contributes to a Ricœurian understanding of the relationship between philosophy and theology. This is because, as Michael D'Angeli observes, 'the boundaries between philosophy and religion have for decades been at the center of Ricœur scholarship'.[3] Although those boundaries have not been my focus as such, they have been a common thread running implicitly throughout every chapter. It is time to make that thread explicit.

For the epistemology of finitude outlined in Chapters 1 and 2, the point of intersection between philosophy and theology lies in the ontology of hope, which, I argued, is central to Ricœur's philosophical method. For Ricœur, philosophy in its very essence is a never-ending search for truth, which neither claims falsely to have arrived at the fullness of truth, nor despairingly abandons the search. This search can only be sustained by an eschatological hope that we are moving towards the fullness of truth which will be manifest only at the end of time. Ricœur is aware that philosophers may frown on eschatological hope as 'incurably mythical', just as theologians may denounce his work as 'a relapse into a guilty, natural theology'.[4] But for him, philosophy is what it is only because of hope – there is no contradiction, only a 'living tension'.[5] This tension enables him 'to live Christian hope philosophically as the directive principle of reflection',

---

[3] Michael D'Angeli, '"The Double Privilege of Athens and Jerusalem": The Relationship between Philosophy and Religion in the Works of Paul Ricœur', *Sophia* 56, no. 3 (1 September 2017): 454. Among the large quantity of secondary literature on this question, see, *inter alia*: Albano, *Freedom, Truth, and Hope*; Dornisch, *Faith and Philosophy in the Writings of Paul Ricœur*; Blundell, *Paul Ricœur between Theology and Philosophy*; Christopher Watkin, 'Ricœur and the Autonomy of Philosophy: A Reappraisal', *Philosophy Today* 58, no. 3 (2014): 411–25; James R. Pambrun, 'The Relationship between Theology and Philosophy: Augustine, Ricœur and Hermeneutics', *Theoforum* 36, no. 3 (2005): 293–319; Michael Sohn, 'Paul Tillich and Paul Ricœur on the Meaning of "Philosophical Theology"', *Bulletin of the North American Paul Tillich Society* 39, no. 4 (2013): 23–9; Henry Isaac Venema, 'The Source of Ricœur's Double Allegiance', in *A Passion for the Possible: Thinking with Paul Ricœur*, ed. Brian Treanor and Henry Isaac Venema (New York: Fordham University Press, 2010), 62–76; Harold Wells, 'Theology and Christian Philosophy: Their Relation in the Thought of Paul Ricœur', *Studies in Religion/Sciences Religieuses* 5, no. 1 (1975): 45–56.

[4] Ricœur, *History and Truth*, 6–7. 'Je n'ignore pas que l'eschatologie est incurablement mythique au regard de la conscience philosophique du vrai et qu'en retour toute référence à la rationalité achevée du tout de l'histoire est aux yeux du prédicateur du Dernier Jour chute et rechute à une coupable théologie naturelle' (Ricœur, *Histoire et vérité*, 13).

[5] Ricœur, *History and Truth*, 7. 'J'entrevois néanmoins qu'il est possible de convertir cette mortelle contradiction en vivante tension' (Ricœur, *Histoire et vérité*, 13).

because 'the conviction of the ultimate unity of truth is the very Spirit of Reason'.⁶ However, even while hope connects the two, Ricœur later shows how it maintains their distinction at the same time. Hope does not allow philosophy to appropriate theological truths under the guise of hoping for them: 'Thanks to this active approximation of hope by dialectic, philosophy knows something and says something of the Easter-preaching. But what it knows and what it says remain within the limits of reason alone. In this self-restraint abide both the responsibility and the modesty of philosophy.'⁷

Chapters 3 and 4 bring the tension between the disciplines to its apex because they concern God. God is not a philosophical concept, for Ricœur, in the sense of something fully graspable by the mind, like an object. But this does not mean philosophy cannot speak about God, just as philosophy speaks about other things beyond the limits of thought. Philosophy may speak about God as long as it does not attempt to import religious ideas given by revelation and then claim that these ideas can be proven philosophically. Conversely, if philosophy can say nothing about the absolute, then (Ricœur says responding to Thévenaz) neither can theology, because theology presupposes whatever philosophy has established. Ricœur therefore agrees with Aquinas that philosophy can tell us 'that' God is, but not 'what' God is.

In Chapters 5 and 6 it is the terms 'evil', 'sin', and 'guilt' that straddle philosophy and theology. Ricœur is not the only philosopher of his time to use these terms, but he claims that any philosopher who uses them depends, whether they realise it or not, on an imagined ideal of the good against which evil is being measured. In this way, Ricœur exposes the theological presuppositions of the philosophical debate concerning guilt. This does not mean he implicitly accuses philosophers who speak about evil of failing to be properly philosophical; rather, Ricœur gives philosophy licence to reflect on ideas from outside philosophy, including religious ideas.

What is at stake in Chapters 7, 8, and 9 concerns whether 'creation', as a theological notion, can function as a regulative idea that enlightens philosophical discourse without thereby becoming constitutive and compromising the autonomy of philosophy. In defence of this move, Ricœur invokes Kant's third *Critique*, in which Kant does precisely this while keeping strictly to the limits of philosophical reflection. Theology may

---

⁶ Ricœur, *History and Truth*, 7. 'De vivre philosophiquement l'espérance chrétienne comme raison régulatrice de la réflexion, car la conviction de l'unité finale du vrai, c'est l'Esprit même de la Raison' (Ricœur, *Histoire et vérité*, 13).
⁷ Ricœur, *Figuring the Sacred*, 216.

stimulate philosophical discussion only if its doctrines are received as symbols, that is, as ideas that can be thought but not grasped as determinate concepts.

The productive exchange between philosophy and theology in Ricœur's early work should come as no surprise, since it is widely recognised that at this early stage Ricœur was more willing to engage the religious dimension of philosophy than he became after the mid-1960s.[8] Nevertheless, to draw attention to this feature of the early Ricœur may help qualify the claims of a number of scholars that the boundaries Ricœur maintained were inspired by Karl Barth.[9] These claims find support in a few remarks by Ricœur made decades later, in which he recalls the Barthian influence of his younger years.[10] Barth evidently influenced Ricœur to a degree, but this influence never became the kind of orthodox Barthianism that we find in Thévenaz, for example.[11] In the same interview as one of the aforementioned remarks, Ricœur calls Barth 'antiphilosophical',[12] which – coming from a professional philosopher – can hardly be an endorsement. As Ricœur's reference to a 'guilty natural theology' indicates, he knew well that Barthians would be unhappy with his introduction of 'eschatological hope' into philosophy (Chapter 1). They would be no more comfortable with the more explicit 'natural theology' of Ricœur's philosophy of

---

[8] See, for example: Mongin, *Paul Ricœur*, 205; and Peter Kenny, 'Conviction, Critique and Christian Theology: Some Reflections on Reading Ricœur', in *Memory, Narrativity, Self and the Challenge to Think God: The Reception within Theology of the Recent Work of Paul Ricœur*, ed. Maureen Junker-Kenny and Peter Kenny (Münster: LIT, 2004), 93.

[9] See, for example: Blundell, *Paul Ricœur between Theology and Philosophy*; Possati, *Ricœur face à l'analogie*; Wallace, *The Second Naiveté*; and Dan R. Stiver, *Theology after Ricœur: New Directions in Hermeneutical Theology* (Louisville: Westminster John Knox Press, 2001). Note, however, Kevin Vanhoozer's caution that Ricœur commits the Barthian taboo of engaging in natural theology (Vanhoozer, *Biblical Narrative in the Philosophy of Paul Ricœur*, 181). Pamela Sue Anderson has chronicled the 'great disagreement' that 'has emerged in theological literature' over whether Ricœur was a Barthian. See Anderson, *Ricœur and Kant*, 19–20.

[10] Richard Kearney, *Dialogues with Contemporary Continental Thinkers: The Phenomenological Heritage* (Manchester: Manchester University Press, 1984), 27; Ricœur, *Critique and Conviction*, 150; Ricœur, *La critique et la conviction*, 226; Kearney, *On Paul Ricœur*, 166. Ricœur also expresses his indebtedness to Barth a couple of times in earlier works. See: Ricœur, *Freud and Philosophy*, 525; Ricœur, *De l'interprétation: essai sur Freud*, 547; Paul Ricœur, 'The Critique of Religion and The Language of Faith', *Union Seminary Quarterly Review* 28 (1973): 210.

[11] See Chapter 3 above, and Chapter 5 above, section headed 'Objections to the Possibility of Distinguishing Them'.

[12] Ricœur, *Critique and Conviction*, 6. 'Antiphilosophique' (Ricœur, *La critique et la conviction*, 17).

transcendence (Chapter 4). Finally, the primacy Ricœur gives to the doctrine of creation (Chapters 5, 6, 7, 8, and 9) is significantly unBarthian, as Jacques Ellul points out with force;[13] sin, for Barth, is too deeply ingrained in the human for us to know anything of a prior innocence, and the only creation we can know is the new creation in Christ.

This study also shows in similar fashion that we should not take too seriously Ricœur's occasional references to the relationship between his faith and his philosophy as 'controlled schizophrenia'.[14] While it may have felt sometimes like schizophrenia for Ricœur, this is only a sign of the pressure he felt to keep strictly to the disciplinary boundaries, not a real admission that his philosophy and his faith contradict each other or have no contact at all. Ricœur's biographer, when speaking of 'the way in which [Ricœur] reconciles his Protestant religious convictions and his rational philosophical rigour', rightly judges that 'if [Ricœur] evokes in this regard a certain schizophrenia, this quip comes rather from his sense of humour than a split personality'.[15] In fact, when Ricœur is in a more serious mood, he makes it clear that schizophrenia is far from a good description of his thought. When questioned in 1993 about the religious articles in *History and Truth*, he tells his interviewer: 'I *would be* schizophrenic if I had divided completely in two.'[16] Similarly, in a 1965 television broadcast, he tells Georges Canguilhem that the multiplicity of philosophies is no refutation of truth in philosophy, because 'We have the conviction or the hope that through these finite works of the human mind, this produces the encounter with the same being, without which we *would be* schizophrenic.'[17]

---

[13] See Chapter 5 above, section headed 'Objections to the Possibility of Distinguishing Them'.

[14] Ricœur, *Critique and Conviction*, 2. 'Schizophrénie contrôlée' (Ricœur, *La critique et la conviction*, 10). See also Reagan, *Paul Ricœur*, 132; Reagan, 'Interview avec Paul Ricœur', 168.

[15] My translation: 'sur la façon dont il concilie ses convictions religieuses protestantes et sa rigueur rationnelle philosophique. S'il évoque à ce propos quelque schizophrénie, cette boutade relève davantage de son sens de l'humeur que d'une personnalité clivée' (Dosse, *Paul Ricœur*, 16).

[16] Raynova and Ricœur, 'All That Gives Us to Think: Conversations with Paul Ricœur', 673. Italics mine. 'Je serais schizophrène si je m'étais divisé complètement en deux' (Yvanka Raynova and Paul Ricœur, 'Quo vadis? Un entretien avec Paul Ricœur', *Labyrinth* 2 [2000], http://phaidon.philo.at/~iaf/Labyrinth/2000/ricoeur.html).

[17] My translation (italics mine): 'Nous avons la conviction ou l'espoir qu'à travers ces œuvres finis de l'esprit humain, ce produit la rencontre avec le même être, sans quoi nous serions schizophrène' (Jean Flechet, *Philosophie et vérité*, Documentary, 1965, 24:03–24:18, www.imdb.com/title/tt1094271/).

The truth is that Ricœur's philosophy knows its own limits and thus gives ample permission for his faith to spread its wings, just as his faith also knows its own limits and does not impinge on the autonomous freedom of enquiry, which, for Ricœur, was essential to authentic philosophising. He was a thinker of harmony, not discord. Such harmony begins in his own thought with a philosophy and a faith that know their own place and respective roles in relation to each other.

'No negation without prior Original Affirmation.' This statement, which summarises Ricœur's last article in the collection *History and Truth*,[18] could also serve as a summary for his entire early philosophy as we have surveyed it. For him, as we saw in Chapters 1 and 2, the negation by which our finitude constrains our perspective, preventing us from attaining the fullness of truth, is only on the basis of the Original Affirmation by which we still participate in truth. In Chapter 4 we have seen that for Ricœur, the negation by which finitude discovers the Infinite is only the *via negativa* to the encounter with an Affirmation that envelops and sustains the whole of reality. In Chapter 5 Ricœur has been shown to hold that the negation of evil is parasitic on, and derivative from, the Affirmation of the goodness of being that comes, as Chapters 7, 8, and 9 show, from wagering on the truth of the biblical narrative of creation by a good God. All in all, François Dosse is right to speak of Ricœur's philosophy as revealing an 'original asymmetry in favour of the Good'.[19] Instead of the 'anguish of no', Ricœur's philosophy loudly proclaims the 'joy of yes'.[20]

---

[18] 'Negativity and Primary Affirmation', in Ricœur, *History and Truth*; 'Négativité et affirmation originaire', in Ricœur, *Histoire et vérité*.
[19] My translation: 'Dissymétrie initiale en faveur du Bien' (Dosse, *Paul Ricœur*, 15).
[20] Ricœur, *History and Truth*, 305; Ricœur, *Histoire et vérité*, 378.

Bibliography

Abel, Olivier. 'Paul Ricœur's Hermeneutics: From Critique to Poetics'. In *Between Suspicion and Sympathy: Paul Ricœur's Unstable Equilibrium*, edited by Andrzej Wierciński, 11–21. Toronto: Hermeneutic Press, 2003.

Adams, Peter J. *Navigating Everyday Life: Exploring the Tension between Finitude and Transcendence*. Lanham: Lexington Books, 2018.

Aho, Kevin. *Existentialism: An Introduction*. Cambridge: Polity Press, 2014.

Albano, Peter. *Freedom, Truth, and Hope: The Relationship of Philosophy and Religion in the Thought of Paul Ricœur*. Lanham: University Press of America, 1987.

Allen, Diogenes, and Eric Springsted. *Philosophy for Understanding Theology*. 2nd ed. Louisville: Westminster John Knox Press, 2007.

Amalric, Jean-Luc. 'Act, Sign and Objectivity: Jean Nabert's Influence on the Ricœurian Phenomenology of the Will'. In *A Companion to Ricœur's 'Freedom and Nature'*, edited by Scott Davidson, 17–36. Lanham: Lexington Books, 2018.

Amalric, Jean-Luc. 'Affirmation originaire, attestation et reconnaissance: le cheminement de l'anthropologie philosophique ricœurienne'. *Études Ricœuriennes / Ricœur Studies* 2, no. 1 (2011): 12–34.

Amalric, Jean-Luc. 'Finitude, Culpability, and Suffering: The Question of Evil in Ricœur'. In *A Companion to Ricœur's 'Fallible Man'*, edited by Scott Davidson. Lanham: Lexington Books, 2019.

Amalric, Jean-Luc. *Paul Ricœur, l'imagination vive: une genèse de la philosophie ricœurienne de l'imagination*. Paris: Éditions Hermann, 2013.

Anderson, Gary, and Markus Bockmuehl, eds. *Creation ex nihilo: Origins, Development, Contemporary Challenges*. Notre Dame: University of Notre Dame Press, 2018.

Anderson, Pamela Sue. *Ricœur and Kant: Philosophy of the Will*. Atlanta: Scholars Press, 1993.

Aquinas, St Thomas. *Summa Theologiae*. Translated by Laurence Shapcote. New York: Benziger Brothers, 1911.

Arrien, Sophie-Jan. 'Introduction: Paul Ricœur (1913–2013): méthode et finitude'. *Philosophiques* 41, no. 2 (2014): 233–40.

Bakewell, Sarah. *At the Existentialist Café: Freedom, Being, and Apricot Cocktails*. London: Vintage, 2016.

Baring, Edward. 'Theism and Atheism at Play: Jacques Derrida and Christian Heideggerianism'. In *The Trace of God: Derrida and Religion*, edited by Edward Baring and Peter E. Gordon, 72–87. New York: Fordham University Press, 2014.

Basile, Giovanni Pietro. *Transcendance et finitude: la synthèse transcendantale dans la 'Critique de la raison pure' de Kant*. Paris: L' Harmattan, 2005.

Benson, Bruce Ellis, and B. Keith Putt, eds. *Evil, Fallenness, and Finitude*. Cham: Palgrave Macmillan, 2017.

Birault, Henri. 'Heidegger et la pensée de la finitude'. *Revue Internationale de Philosophie* 14, no. 52 (2) (1960): 135–62.

Blenkinsopp, Joseph. *Creation, Un-Creation, Re-Creation: A Discursive Commentary on Genesis 1–11*. London: T&T Clark, 2011.

Blondel, Maurice. 'The Inconsistency of Jean Paul Sartre's Logic'. *The Thomist* 10, no. 4 (1947): 393–7.

Blundell, Boyd. 'Creative Fidelity: Gabriel Marcel's Influence on Paul Ricœur'. In *Between Suspicion and Sympathy: Paul Ricœur's Unstable Equilibrium*, edited by Andrzej Wierciński, 89–102. Toronto: Hermeneutic Press, 2003.

Blundell, Boyd. *Paul Ricœur between Theology and Philosophy: Detour and Return*. Bloomington: Indiana University Press, 2010.

Bochet, Isabelle. *Augustin dans la pensée de Paul Ricœur*. Paris: Éditions Facultés jésuites de Paris, 2004.

Bonzon, Sylvie. 'Paul Ricœur en Suisse romande: rencontres, liens et héritage'. *Revue de Théologie et de Philosophie* 138, no. 4 (2006): 293–306.

Bourgeois, Patrick L. 'Marcel and Ricœur: Mystery and Hope at the Boundary of Reason in the Postmodern Situation'. *American Catholic Philosophical Quarterly* 80, no. 3 (2006): 421–33.

Bourgeois, Patrick L. 'Ricœur and Marcel: An Alternative to Postmodern Deconstruction'. *Journal of French and Francophone Philosophy* 7, no. 1–2 (2010): 164–75.

Bourgeois, Patrick L., and Frank Schalow. *Traces of Understanding: A Profile of Heidegger's and Ricœur's Hermeneutics*. Amsterdam: Rodopi, 1990.

Boven, Martijn, Eddo Evink, and Gert-Jan van der Heiden. 'Paul Ricœur and the Future of the Humanities'. *International Journal of Philosophy and Theology* 75, no. 2 (2014): 112–14.

Burrell, David B. 'Creatio ex nihilo Recovered'. *Modern Theology* 29, no. 2 (2013): 5–21.

Busch, Thomas. 'Sartre and Ricœur on Imagination'. *American Catholic Philosophical Quarterly* 70, no. 4 (1996): 507–18.

Camus, Albert. *L'homme révolté*. 30th ed. Paris: Gallimard, 1954.

Camus, Albert. *The Rebel: An Essay on Man in Revolt*. Translated by Anthony Bower. London: Vintage, 1991.

Carpenter, Peter. 'Thévenaz and His Philosophy'. *Studies in Religion/Sciences Religieuses* 5, no. 4 (1976): 331–7.

Carter, James. *Ricœur on Moral Religion*. Oxford: Oxford University Press, 2014.
Chesterton, Gilbert K. *Orthodoxy*. London: John Lane, 1908.
Chorab, Monika. 'Understanding Evil in the Philosophy of Paul Ricœur, Jean Nabert, and Gabriel Marcel'. *Rocznik Teologii Katolickiej* 10, no. 1 (2011): 221–31.
Cipollone, Anthony P. 'Concrete Human Freedom: Ricœur on Sartre'. *Iliff Review* 35, no. 3 (1978): 37–47.
Colin, Pierre. 'Herméneutique et philosophie réflexive'. In *Paul Ricœur: les métamorphoses de la raison herméneutique*, edited by Jean Greisch and Richard Kearney, 15–36. Paris: Éditions du Cerf, 1991.
Copleston, Frederick. *19th and 20th Century French Philosophy*. A History of Philosophy 9. London: Continuum, 2003.
Courtney, Charles. 'Reading Ciphers with Jaspers and Ricœur'. *Existenz* 1, no. 1–2 (2006). https://existenz.us/volumes/Vol.1Courtney.html.
Crittenden, Paul. 'Sartre's Absent God'. *Sophia* 51, no. 4 (2012): 495–507.
D'Angeli, Michael. '"The Double Privilege of Athens and Jerusalem": The Relationship between Philosophy and Religion in the Works of Paul Ricœur'. *Sophia* 56, no. 3 (2017): 453–69.
Davidson, Scott, ed. *A Companion to Ricœur's 'The Symbolism of Evil'*. Lanham: Lexington Books, 2020.
Davison, Andrew. *The Love of Wisdom: An Introduction to Philosophy for Theologians*. London: SCM Press, 2013.
DeHart, Paul. *The Trial of the Witnesses: The Rise and Decline of Postliberal Theology*. Oxford: Blackwell, 2006.
Descartes, René. *Discourse on Method and the Meditations*. Translated by F. E. Sutcliffe. London: Penguin, 1968.
Descartes, René. *Meditationes de prima philosophia*. apud Iohannem Blaeu, 1644.
Dierckxsens, Geoffrey. 'The Ambiguity of Justice: Paul Ricœur on Universalism and Evil'. *Études Ricœuriennes / Ricœur Studies* 6, no. 2 (2015): 30–49.
Dika, Tarek R. 'Finitude, Phenomenology, and Theology in Heidegger's *Sein und Zeit*'. *Harvard Theological Review* 110, no. 4 (2017): 475–93.
Dornisch, Loretta. *Faith and Philosophy in the Writings of Paul Ricœur*. Lewiston: Edwin Mellen Press, 1990.
Dosse, François. *Paul Ricœur: les sens d'une vie*. 2nd ed. Paris: La Découverte, 2008.
Dufrenne, Mikel, and Paul Ricœur. *Karl Jaspers et la philosophie de l'existence*. Paris: Éditions du Seuil, 1947.
Earl, Douglas S. *Reading Joshua as Christian Scripture*. Winona Lake: Pennsylvania State University Press, 2010.
Earnshaw, Steven. *Existentialism: A Guide for the Perplexed*. London: Continuum, 2006.
Eliot, George. *Daniel Deronda*. London: Penguin Books, 1993.
Ellul, Jacques. *Le vouloir et le faire: une critique théologique de la morale*. Geneva: Labor et Fides, 2013.
Ellul, Jacques. *To Will & to Do: An Ethical Research for Christians*. Translated by C. Edward Hopkin. Philadelphia: Pilgrim Press, 1969.
Erfani, Farhang, ed. *Paul Ricœur: Honoring and Continuing the Work*. Lanham: Lexington Books, 2011.

Falque, Emmanuel. *Crossing the Rubicon: The Borderlands of Philosophy and Theology*. Translated by Reuben Shank. New York: Fordham University Press, 2016.

Falque, Emmanuel. 'Hors phénomène'. *Revue de métaphysique et de morale* 99, no. 3 (2018): 323.

Falque, Emmanuel. *Métamorphose de la finitude. Essai philosophique sur la naissance et la résurrection*. Paris: Éditions du Cerf, 2004.

Falque, Emmanuel. *Passer le Rubicon: philosophie et théologie: essai sur les frontières*. Paris: Éditions Lessius, 2013.

Falque, Emmanuel. 'The Extra-Phenomenal'. *Diakrisis Yearbook of Theology and Philosophy* 1 (2018): 9–28.

Falque, Emmanuel. *The Metamorphosis of Finitude: An Essay on Birth and Resurrection*. New York: Fordham University Press, 2012.

Falque, Emmanuel. *Triduum philosophique: le passeur de Gethsémani. Métamorphose de la finitude. Les noces de l'agneau*. Éditions du Cerf, 2016.

Farges, Julien. 'L'héritage de Gabriel Marcel: Paul Ricœur et la question des limites de la phénoménologie'. *Philosophie*, no. 132 (2016): 31–43.

Flechet, Jean. *Philosophie et vérité*. Documentary, 1965. www.imdb.com/title/tt1094271/.

Flynn, Thomas. *Existentialism: A Very Short Introduction*. Oxford: Oxford University Press, 2006.

Fœssel, Michaël. 'Action, normes et critique: Paul Ricœur et les pouvoirs de l'imaginaire'. *Philosophiques* 41, no. 2 (2014): 241–52.

Foucault, Michel. *Les mots et les choses: une archéologie des sciences humaines*. Paris: Gallimard, 2014.

Foucault, Michel. *The Order of Things*. London: Routledge, 2018.

Fretheim, Terence. *God and World in the Old Testament: A Relational Theology of Creation*. Nashville: Abingdon Press, 2005.

Gallagher, Kenneth T. *The Philosophy of Gabriel Marcel*. New York: Fordham University Press, 1962.

Ge, Yonghua. *Creatio ex nihilo and Natural Theology in Aquinas*. Chisinau: Lambert Academic Publishing, 2017.

Gedney, Mark. 'Jaspers and Ricœur on the Self and the Other'. *Philosophy Today* 48, no. 4 (2004): 331.

Geniusas, Saulius. 'Between Phenomenology and Hermeneutics: Paul Ricœur's Philosophy of Imagination'. *Human Studies* 38, no. 2 (2015): 223–41.

Grabau, Richard. 'Preface'. In *Philosophy of Existence*, by Karl Jaspers. Philadelphia: University of Pennsylvania Press, 2010.

Gravil, André. *Philosophie et finitude*. Paris: Éditions du Cerf, 2007.

Gregor, Brian. *Ricœur's Hermeneutics of Religion: Rebirth of the Capable Self*. Lanham: Lexington Books, 2019.

Greisch, Jean. *L'arbre de vie et l'arbre du savoir: le chemin phénoménologique de l'herméneutique heideggérienne (1919–1923)*. Paris: Éditions du Cerf, 2000.

Greisch, Jean. *Ontologie et temporalité: esquisse d'une interprétation intégrale de 'Sein und Zeit'*. Paris: Presses universitaires de France, 1994.

Greisch, Jean. *Paul Ricœur: l'itinérance du sens*. Grenoble: Millon, 2001.

Greisch, Jean. 'Préface'. In *Méthode réflexive appliquée au problème de Dieu chez Lachelier et Lagneau*, by Paul Ricœur. Paris: Éditions du Cerf, 2017.

Grump, Eric. 'Between Conviction and Critique: Reflexive Philosophy, Testimony, and Pneumatology'. In *Ricœur as Another: The Ethics of Subjectivity*, edited by Richard A. Cohen and James L. Marsh. Albany: SUNY Press, 2002.

Gschwandtner, Christina M. 'Ricœur's Hermeneutic of God'. *Philosophy and Theology* 13, no. 2 (2001): 287–309.

Gschwandtner, Christina M. *Welcoming Finitude: Toward a Phenomenology of Orthodox Liturgy*. New York: Fordham University Press, 2019.

Gutting, Gary. 'Footnotes to Heidegger?' In *Thinking the Impossible: French Philosophy since 1960*. Oxford: Oxford University Press, 2011.

Hackett, Stuart. 'Philosophical Objectivity and Existential Involvement in the Methodology of Paul Ricœur'. *International Philosophical Quarterly* 9, no. 1 (1969): 11–39.

Hahn, Lewis Edwin, ed. *The Philosophy of Paul Ricœur*. Vol. 22. The Library of Living Philosophers. Chicago: Open Court, 1995.

Hegel, Georg Wilhelm Friedrich. *Die Wissenschaft Der Logic*. Vol. 1. 2 vols. Werke 5. Frankfurt: Suhrkamp, 1970.

Hegel, Georg Wilhelm Friedrich. *Encyclopädie der philosophischen Wissenschaften im Grundrisse*. 3rd ed. Heidelberg: Oßwald (C.F. Winter), 1830.

Hegel, Georg Wilhelm Friedrich. *The Logic of Hegel*. Translated by William Wallace. 2nd ed. Oxford: Oxford University Press, 1892.

Hegel, Georg Wilhelm Friedrich. *The Science of Logic*. Edited and translated by George Di Giovanni. Cambridge: Cambridge University Press, 2010.

Heidegger, Martin. *Being and Time*. Translated by John Macquarrie and Edward Robinson. Bodmin: Blackwell, 1962.

Heidegger, Martin. *Kant and the Problem of Metaphysics*. Bloomington: Indiana University Press, 1962.

Heidegger, Martin. *Kant und das Problem der Metaphysik*. Bonn: Friedrich Cohen, 1929.

Heidegger, Martin. *Pathmarks*. Edited and translated by William McNeill. Cambridge: Cambridge University Press, 1998.

Heidegger, Martin. *Sein und Zeit*. Tübingen: Niemeyer, 1967.

Heidegger, Martin. *Wegmarken*. Vol. 9. Gesamtausgabe. Frankfurt am Main: Vittorio Klostermann, 1976.

Helenius, Timo. 'Ricœur's Kierkegaard'. *International Journal of Philosophy and Theology* 80, no. 4–5 (2019): 356–73.

Henriksen, Jan-Olav. *Finitude and Theological Anthropology: An Interdisciplinary Exploration into Theological Dimensions of Finitude*. Leuven: Peeters, 2011.

Herberg, Will, ed. *Four Existentialist Theologians*. Garden City: Doubleday Anchor Books, 1958.

Hick, John. 'The Symbolism of Evil, by Paul Ricœur'. *Theology Today* 24, no. 4 (1968): 521–22.

Hort, Bernard. 'Une philosophie sans absolu'. *Revue de Théologie et de Philosophie* 120, no. 3 (1988): 353–58.

Hughes, John. 'Proof and Arguments'. In *Imaginative Apologetics: Theology, Philosophy and the Catholic Tradition*, edited by Andrew Davison, 3–11. London: SCM Press, 2011.

Hulsbosch, Ansfridus. *God's Creation: Creation, Sin, and Redemption in an Evolving World*. Translated by Martin Versfeld. London and New York: Sheed and Ward, 1965.

Huskey, R. K. *Paul Ricœur on Hope: Expecting the Good*. New York: Peter Lang, 2009.

Hyland, Drew A. *Finitude and Transcendence in the Platonic Dialogues*. Albany: SUNY Press, 1995.

Ihde, Don. *Hermeneutic Phenomenology: The Philosophy of Paul Ricœur*. Evanston: Northwestern University Press, 1971.

Ille, George. *Between Vision and Obedience – Rethinking Theological Epistemology: Theological Reflections on Rationality and Agency with Special Reference to Paul Ricœur and G. W. F. Hegel*. Cambridge: James Clarke & Co, 2014.

Insole, Christopher. *The Intolerable God: Kant's Theological Journey*. Grand Rapids: Eerdmans, 2016.

Jackson Ravenscroft, Ruth. *The Veiled God: Friedrich Schleiermacher's Theology of Finitude*. Leiden: Brill, 2019.

Jacques, Robert. 'Corps et transcendance: une mise en relation dans le volontaire et l'involontaire de Paul Ricœur'. *Revue de Théologie et de Philosophie* 127, no. 1 (1995): 235–49.

Jaffro, Laurent. 'La conception ricœurienne de la raison pratique: dialectique ou éclectique?' *Études Ricœuriennes / Ricœur Studies* 3, no. 1 (2012): 156–71.

Janicaud, Dominique. *Heidegger en France*. Paris: Albin Michel, 2001.

Janicaud, Dominique. *Heidegger in France*. Translated by David Pettigrew and François Raffoul. Bloomington: Indiana University Press, 2015.

Janicaud, Dominique. *Le tournant théologique de la phénoménologie française*. Paris: Éditions de L'Éclat, 1991.

Janicaud, Dominique. 'The Theological Turn of French Phenomenology'. In *Phenomenology and the 'Theological Turn': The French Debate*. Translated by Bernard Prusak, 16–103. New York: Fordham University Press, 2000.

Jaspers, Karl. *Einführung in die Philosophie*. 2nd ed. Munich: Piper, 1971.

Jaspers, Karl. 'Epilogue 1955'. In *Philosophy*. Translated by E. B. Ashton, Vol. 1, 11–43. Chicago: University of Chicago Press, 1969.

Jaspers, Karl. 'Nachwort (1955)'. In *Philosophie*, 3rd ed., XV–LV. Berlin: Springer-Verlag, 1956.

Jaspers, Karl. 'On My Philosophy'. In *Existentialism from Dostoevsky to Sartre*, edited by Walter Kaufman, 131–57. New York: Meridian Books, 1956.

Jaspers, Karl. 'Philosophical Autobiography'. In *The Philosophy of Karl Jaspers*, edited by Paul Arthur Schilpp, 2nd, augmented ed., 3–75. Library of Living Philosophers. LaSalle: Open Court, 1981.

Jaspers, Karl. *Philosophie*. 2nd ed. Berlin: Springer-Verlag, 1948.

Jaspers, Karl. *Philosophy*. Translated by E. B. Ashton. Vol. 1. 3 vols. 1932. Reprint, Chicago: University of Chicago Press, 1969.

Jaspers, Karl. *Philosophy*. Translated by E. B. Ashton. Vol. 2. 3 vols. Chicago: University of Chicago Press, 1969.

Jaspers, Karl. *Philosophy*. Translated by E. B. Ashton. Vol. 3. 3 vols. Chicago: University of Chicago Press, 1969.

Jaspers, Karl. *Reason and Existenz*. Translated by William Earle. London: Routledge, 1956.

Jaspers, Karl. 'Reply to My Critics'. In *The Philosophy of Karl Jaspers*, edited by Paul Arthur Schilpp, 2nd ed., 748–843. The Library of Living Philosophers. LaSalle: Open Court, 1981.
Jaspers, Karl. *Vernunft und Existenz*. 3rd ed. Bremen: Johs. Storm Verlag, 1949.
Jaspers, Karl. *Way to Wisdom*. New Haven: Yale University Press, 1954.
Jervolino, Domenico. 'In Search of a Poetics of the Will'. In *Paul Ricœur: Honoring and Continuing the Work*, edited by Farhang Erfani, translated by Amin Erfani and Carrie Golden. Lanham: Lexington Books, 2011.
Jervolino, Domenico. 'Pierre Thévenaz et La Condition Humaine de La Raison'. *Revue de Théologie et de Philosophie* 25, no. 3 (1975): 175–84.
Jervolino, Domenico. *The Cogito and Hermeneutics: The Question of the Subject in Ricœur*. Translated by Gordon Poole. Dordrecht and London: Kluwer Academic, 1990.
Junker-Kenny, Maureen, and Peter Kenny, eds. *Memory, Narrativity, Self and the Challenge to Think God: The Reception within Theology of the Recent Work of Paul Ricœur*. Münster: LIT, 2004.
Kant, Immanuel. *Critique of the Power of Judgment*. Edited by Paul Guyer. Translated by Paul Guyer and Eric Matthews. Cambridge: Cambridge University Press, 2000.
Kant, Immanuel. *Einleitung in die Kritik der Urteilskraft*. Leipzig: F. Meiner, 1914.
Kant, Immanuel. *Kritik der Urteilskraft*. Edited by Karl Vorländer. Leipzig: F. Meiner, 1922.
Kaplan, David, ed. *Reading Ricœur*. Albany: SUNY Press, 2008.
Kearney, Richard. *Dialogues with Contemporary Continental Thinkers: The Phenomenological Heritage*. Manchester: Manchester University Press, 1984.
Kearney, Richard. *On Paul Ricœur: The Owl of Minerva*. London: Taylor & Francis, 2017.
Kenny, Peter. 'Conviction, Critique and Christian Theology: Some Reflections on Reading Ricœur'. In *Memory, Narrativity, Self and the Challenge to Think God: The Reception within Theology of the Recent Work of Paul Ricœur*, edited by Maureen Junker-Kenny and Peter Kenny, 92–116. Münster: LIT, 2004.
Kirkbright, Suzanne. *Karl Jaspers: A Biography: Navigations in Truth*. New Haven: Yale University Press, 2004.
Kirkpatrick, Kate. *Sartre on Sin: Between Being and Nothingness*. Oxford: Oxford University Press, 2017.
Klein, Ted. 'Ricœur and Husserl'. *Iliff Review* 35, no. 3 (1978): 27–36.
Klemm, David E., and William Schweiker, eds. *Meanings in Texts and Actions: Questioning Paul Ricœur*. Charlottesville: University Press of Virginia, 1993.
Koci, Martin, and Jason Alvis, eds. *Transforming the Theological Turn: Phenomenology with Emmanuel Falque*. Lanham: Rowman & Littlefield, 2020.
LaCocque, André, and Paul Ricœur. *Thinking Biblically: Exegetical and Hermeneutical Studies*. Translated by David Pellauer. Chicago: University of Chicago Press, 2003.
LaCocque, André, and Paul Ricœur. 'Lettre de Jean-Paul Sartre à Gabriel Marcel'. *Revue de la BNF* 48, no. 3 (2014): 62–63.
Levy, Lior. 'Sartre and Ricœur on Productive Imagination'. *The Southern Journal of Philosophy* 52, no. 1 (2014): 43–60.

Lewis, C. S. *The Collected Letters of C. S. Lewis, volume 3:Narnia, Cambridge, and Joy, 1950–1963*. New York: HarperCollins, 2009.
Magid, Oren. 'Heidegger on Human Finitude: Beginning at the End'. *European Journal of Philosophy* 25, no. 3 (2017): 657–76.
Marcel, Gabriel. 'An Autobiographical Essay'. In *The Philosophy of Gabriel Marcel*, edited by Paul Arthur Schilpp and Lewis Edwin Hahn. Library of Living Philosophers. LaSalle: Open Court, 1984.
Marcel, Gabriel. 'Author's Preface to the English Edition'. In *Metaphysical Journal*. Translated by Bernard Wall, vii–xiii. London: Rockliff, 1952.
Marcel, Gabriel. *Awakenings: A Translation of Marcel's Autobiography*. Translated by Peter Rogers. Milwaukee: Marquette University Press, 2002.
Marcel, Gabriel. *Being and Having*. Translated by Katharine Farrer. 1935. Reprint, London: Dacre Press, 1949.
Marcel, Gabriel. *Coleridge et Schelling*. Paris: Aubier, 1971.
Marcel, Gabriel. *Creative Fidelity*. Translated by Robert Rosthal. 1940. Reprint, New York: Crossroad, 1982.
Marcel, Gabriel. *Du refus à l'invocation*. Paris: Gallimard, 1940.
Marcel, Gabriel. *En chemin, vers quel éveil?* Paris: Gallimard, 1971.
Marcel, Gabriel. *Être et avoir*. Paris: Aubier, 1935.
Marcel, Gabriel. 'Gabriel Marcel to Paul Ricœur', 19 January 1948. 4. Fonds Ricœur.
Marcel, Gabriel. *Homo viator: Introduction to the Metaphysic of Hope*. Translated by Emma Craufurd. New York: Harper Torchbook, 1962.
Marcel, Gabriel. *Homo viator: prolégomènes à une métaphysique de l'espérance*. Paris: Aubier, 1944.
Marcel, Gabriel. *Journal métaphysique*. Paris: Gallimard, 1927.
Marcel, Gabriel. *Le mystère de l'être*. Vol. 1. 2 vols. Paris: Aubier, 1951.
Marcel, Gabriel. *Les hommes contre l'humain*. Belgium: Éditions Universitaires, 1991.
Marcel, Gabriel. *Man against Mass Society*. South Bend: Gateway Editions, 1978.
Marcel, Gabriel. *Metaphysical Journal*. Translated by Bernard Wall. 1927. Reprint, London: Rockliff, 1952.
Marcel, Gabriel. *Pour une sagesse tragique et son au-delà*. Paris: Plon, 1968.
Marcel, Gabriel. 'Some Reflections on Existentialism'. *Philosophy Today* 8, no. 4 (1964): 248–57.
Marcel, Gabriel. *The Mystery of Being*. Translated by G. S. Fraser. Vol. 1. 2 vols. Chicago: Regnery Publishing, 1950.
Marcel, Gabriel. *Tragic Wisdom and Beyond*. Translated by Peter McCormick and Stephen Jolin. 1968. Reprint, Evanston: Northwestern University Press, 1973.
Markus, Arjan. *Beyond Finitude: God's Transcendence and the Meaning of Life*. Frankfurt am Main: P. Lang, 2004.
McFarland, Ian. *From Nothing: A Theology of Creation*. Louisville: Westminster John Knox Press, 2014.
McQuillan, J. Colin. 'Beyond the Analytic of Finitude: Kant, Heidegger, Foucault'. *Foucault Studies*, 2016, 184.
McQuillan, J. Colin. 'Kant, Heidegger, and the In/Finitude of Human Reason'. *CR: The New Centennial Review* 17, no. 3 (2017): 81.

Meillassoux, Quentin. *Après la finitude: essai sur la nécessité de la contingence*. Paris: Éditions du Seuil, 2006.

Meireles, Cristina Amaro Viana. 'Paul Ricœur et l'idée d'une affirmation originaire'. *Revista Contemplação* 10, no. 1 (2015), 105–16.

Meitinger, Serge. 'Entre "intrigue" et "métaphore": la poétique de P. Ricœur devant la spécificité du poème'. In *Paul Ricœur: les métamorphoses de la raison herméneutique*, edited by Jean Greisch and Richard Kearney, 281–301. Paris: Éditions du Cerf, 1991.

Merleau-Ponty, Maurice. *Phenomenology of Perception*. Translated by Donald Landes. 1945. Reprint, London: Routledge, 2013.

Milbank, John. 'Only Theology Overcomes Metaphysics'. *New Blackfriars* 76, no. 895 (1995): 325–43.

Minns, Denis. *Irenaeus: An Introduction*. London: Continuum, 2010.

Mongin, Olivier. *Paul Ricœur*. Paris: Éditions du Seuil, 1994.

Moran, Dermot. 'Husserl and Ricœur: The Influence of Phenomenology on the Formation of Ricœur's Hermeneutics of the "Capable Human"'. *Journal of French and Francophone Philosophy* 25, no. 1 (2017): 132–99.

Moran, Dermot. 'What Does Heidegger Mean by the Transcendence of *Dasein?*' *International Journal of Philosophical Studies* 22, no. 4 (2014): 491–514.

Morgan, Speer. 'Transcendence'. *The Missouri Review* 36, no. 3 (2013): 5–8.

Mounier, Emmanuel. *Existentialist Philosophies: An Introduction*. Translated by Eric Blow. London: Rockliff, 1948.

Mounier, Emmanuel. *Introduction aux existentialismes*. Paris: Éditions Denoël, 1947.

Nabert, Jean. *Le désir de Dieu*. Paris: Éditions du Cerf, 1996.

Nkéramihigo, Théoneste. *L'homme et la transcendance: essai de poétique dans la philosophie de Paul Ricœur*. Rome: Pontificia Universitas Gregoriana, 1984.

Oakes, Kenneth. *Karl Barth on Theology and Philosophy*. Oxford: Oxford University Press, 2012.

Oliva, Mirela. 'Paul Ricœur's Hermeneutics of Creation'. *Revue Roumaine de Philosophie* 54, no. 2 (2010): 197–204.

Oliver, Simon. *Creation: A Guide for the Perplexed*. London: Bloomsbury, 2017.

Olson, Alan. *Transcendence and Hermeneutics: An Interpretation of the Philosophy of Karl Jaspers*. The Hague: Martinus Nijhoff, 1979.

Oord, Thomas Jay. *Theologies of Creation: 'Creatio ex nihilo' and Its New Rivals*. New York: Routledge, 2014.

Pambrun, James R. 'The Relationship between Theology and Philosophy: Augustine, Ricœur and Hermeneutics'. *Theoforum* 36, no. 3 (2005): 293–319.

Pellauer, David. 'Remembering Paul Ricœur'. In *A Passion for the Possible: Thinking with Paul Ricœur* edited by Brian Treanor and Henry Isaac Venema, 41–48. New York: Fordham University Press, 2010.

Pellauer, David. *Ricœur: A Guide for the Perplexed*. London: Continuum, 2007.

'Pierre Thévenaz'. *Esprit*, no. 230/231 (9) (1955): 1640.

Porée, Jérôme. 'Finitude et transcendance: une philosophie à deux foyers'. In *Paul Ricœur: Poetics and Religion*, edited by Jack Verheyden, Theo Hettema, and Pieter Vandecasteele, 189–212. Leuven: Uitgeverij Peeters, 2011.

Possati, Luca M. *Ricœur face à l'analogie: entre théologie et déconstruction*. Paris: Éditions L'Harmattan, 2012.

Priest, Graham. 'The Limits of Thought – and Beyond'. *Mind* 100, no. 3 (1991): 361–70.
Pusar, Güçsal. 'Heidegger on Kant, Finitude, and the Correlativity of Thinking and Being'. *The Journal of Speculative Philosophy* 32, no. 3 (2018): 400.
Raynova, Yvanka, and Paul Ricœur. 'All That Gives Us to Think: Conversations with Paul Ricœur'. In *Between Suspicion and Sympathy: Paul Ricœur's Unstable Equilibrium*, edited by Andrzej Wierciński, 670–96. Toronto: Hermeneutic Press, 2003.
Raynova, Yvanka, and Paul Ricœur. 'Quo vadis? Un entretien avec Paul Ricœur'. *Labyrinth* 2 (2000). http://phaidon.philo.at/~iaf/Labyrinth/2000/ricoeur.html.
Reagan, Charles E. 'Interview avec Paul Ricœur'. *Journal of French and Francophone Philosophy* 3, no. 3 (1991): 155–72.
Reagan, Charles E. *Paul Ricœur: His Life and His Work*. Chicago: University of Chicago Press, 1996.
Reymond, Bernard. *Théologien ou prophète? Les francophones et Karl Barth avant 1945*. Lausanne: L'âge d'homme, 1985.
Ricœur, Paul. *À l'école de la phénoménologie*. Paris: Vrin, 1998.
Ricœur, Paul. *Anthropologie philosophique*. Edited by Johann Michel and Jérôme Porée. Écrits et conférences 3. Paris: Éditions du Seuil, 2013.
Ricœur, Paul. 'Appendix: From Existentialism to the Philosophy of Language'. In *The Rule of Metaphor: Multi-Disciplinary Studies of the Creation of Meaning in Language*. Translated by David Pellauer, 372–81. London: Routledge, 1978.
Ricœur, Paul. *Critique and Conviction: Conversations with François Azouvi and Marc de Launay*. Cambridge: Polity Press, 1998.
Ricœur, Paul. *De l'interprétation: essai sur Freud*. Paris: Éditions du Seuil, 1965.
Ricœur, Paul. 'Doing Philosophy after Kierkegaard'. In *Kierkegaard's Truth: The Disclosure of the Self*, edited by Joseph H. Smith, 325–42. New Haven: Yale University Press, 1981.
Ricœur, Paul. *Du texte à l'action*. Paris: Éditions du Seuil, 1986.
Ricœur, Paul. 'Ethics and Human Capability: A Response'. In *Paul Ricœur and Contemporary Moral Thought*, edited by John Wall, William Schweiker, and David Hall, 279–90. New York: Routledge, 2002.
Ricœur, Paul. 'Evil, A Challenge to Philosophy and Theology'. In *Figuring the Sacred: Religion, Narrative, and Imagination*, edited by Mark I. Wallace, 249–61. Minneapolis: Fortress Press, 1995.
Ricœur, Paul. *Fallible Man*. Translated by Charles A. Kelbley. New York: Fordham University Press, 1986.
Ricœur, Paul. *Figuring the Sacred: Religion, Narrative, and Imagination*. Edited by Mark I. Wallace. Translated by David Pellauer. Minneapolis: Fortress Press, 1995.
Ricœur, Paul. *Finitude et culpabilité*. Philosophie de la volonté 2. Paris: Éditions Points, 2009.
Ricœur, Paul. *Freedom and Nature: The Voluntary and the Involuntary*. Translated by Erazim Kohák. 1950. Reprint, Evanston: Northwestern University Press, 1966.

Ricœur, Paul. *Freud and Philosophy: An Essay on Interpretation*. Translated by Denis Savage. New Haven: Yale University Press, 1970.
Ricœur, Paul. *From Text to Action*. Evanston: Northwestern University Press, 1991.
Ricœur, Paul. 'Gabriel Marcel and Phenomenology'. In *The Philosophy of Gabriel Marcel*, edited by Paul Arthur Schilpp and Lewis Edwin Hahn, 471–94. Illinois: Open Court, 1984.
Ricœur, Paul. *Gabriel Marcel et Karl Jaspers: philosophie du mystère et philosophie du paradoxe*. Paris: Éditions du Temps présent, 1948.
Ricœur, Paul. 'Hegel aujourd'hui'. *Esprit* mars/avril, no. 3 (2006): 174–94.
Ricœur, Paul. *Hermeneutics and the Human Sciences: Essays on Language, Action and Interpretation*. Edited and translated by John Thompson. Cambridge: Cambridge University Press, 1981.
Ricœur, Paul. *Histoire et vérité*. Paris: Éditions du Seuil, 2001.
Ricœur, Paul. *History and Truth*. Translated by Charles Kelbley. Evanston: Northwestern University Press, 1965.
Ricœur, Paul. *Husserl: An Analysis of His Phenomenology*. Translated by Edward Ballard and Lester Embree. Evanston: Northwestern University Press, 1967.
Ricœur, Paul. 'Intellectual Autobiography'. In *The Philosophy of Paul Ricœur*, edited by Lewis Hahn, 3–58. Chicago: Open Court, 1995.
Ricœur, Paul. 'Interpréter la Bible'. *Pardès* 32-33, no. 1 (2002): 31–43.
Ricœur, Paul. *La critique et la conviction: entretien avec François Azouvi et Marc de Launay*. Paris: Calmann-Lévy, 1995.
Ricœur, Paul. *La mémoire, l'histoire, l'oubli*. Paris: Éditions du Seuil, 2014.
Ricœur, Paul. 'La tâche de l'herméneutique'. In *Exegesis: problèmes de méthode et exercices de lecture*, edited by François Bovon and Grégoire Rouiller, 179–200. Neuchâtel: Delachaux & Niestlé, 1975.
Ricœur, Paul. 'L'appel de l'action. Réflexions d'un étudiant protestant'. *Terre nouvelle* 2 (June 1935), 7–9.
Ricœur, Paul. *Le conflit des interprétations. Essais d'herméneutique*. Paris: Éditions du Seuil, 1969.
Ricœur, Paul. 'Le mal: un défi à la philosophie et à la théologie'. In *Lectures 3: aux frontières de la philosophie*, 211–34. Paris: Éditions du Seuil, 1994.
Ricœur, Paul. 'Le renouvellement du problème de la philosophie chrétienne par les philosophies de l'existence'. In *Le problème de la philosophie chrétienne*, edited by Jean Boisset, 43–67. Paris: Presses universitaires de France, 1949.
Ricœur, Paul. 'Le symbole donne à penser'. *Esprit*, no. 275 (7/8) (1959): 60–76.
Ricœur, Paul. *Le volontaire et l'involontaire*. Philosophie de la volonté 1. Paris: Aubier, 1949.
Ricœur, Paul. *Lectures 2: la contrée des philosophes*. Paris: Éditions du Seuil, 1999.
Ricœur, Paul. *Lectures 3: aux frontières de la philosophie*. Paris: Éditions du Seuil, 2006.
Ricœur, Paul. *Living up to Death*. Chicago: University of Chicago Press, 2009.
Ricœur, Paul. *Memory, History, Forgetting*. Translated by David Pellauer and Kathleen Blamey. Chicago: University of Chicago Press, 2004.

Ricœur, Paul. *Méthode réflexive appliquée au problème de Dieu chez Lachelier et Lagneau*. Paris: Éditions du Cerf, 2017.
Ricœur, Paul. 'My Relation to the History of Philosophy'. *Iliff Review* 35, no. 3 (1978): 5–12.
Ricœur, Paul. 'Note sur les rapports de la philosophie et du Christianisme'. *Le Semeur* 38, no. 9 (1936): 541–57.
Ricœur, Paul. 'Note sur l'existentialisme et la foi chrétienne'. *Revue de Théologie et de Philosophie* 56, no. 4 (2006): 307–14.
Ricœur, Paul. *On Translation*. Translated by Eileen Brennan. London: Routledge, 2006.
Ricœur, Paul. *Oneself as Another*. Translated by Kathleen Blamey. Chicago: University of Chicago Press, 1992.
Ricœur, Paul. *Parcours de la reconnaissance*. Paris: Stock, 2004.
Ricœur, Paul. 'Paul Ricœur to Gabriel Marcel', 21 February 1943. Fonds Gabriel Marcel.
Ricœur, Paul. 'Paul Ricœur to Gabriel Marcel', 2 May 1943. Fonds Gabriel Marcel.
Ricœur, Paul. 'Paul Ricœur to Gabriel Marcel', 16 June 1950. Fonds Gabriel Marcel.
Ricœur, Paul. 'Paul Ricœur to Gabriel Marcel', 1 November 1962. Fonds Gabriel Marcel.
Ricœur, Paul. 'Paul Ricœur to Gabriel Marcel, Le Chambon s/Lignon', 25 November 1945. Fonds Gabriel Marcel.
Ricœur, Paul. *Philosophical Anthropology*. Cambridge: Polity Press, 2016.
Ricœur, Paul. 'Philosophie et religion chez Karl Jaspers'. *Revue d'histoire et de philosophie religieuses* 37, no. 3 (1957): 207–35.
Ricœur, Paul. *Réflexion faite*. Paris: Éditions Esprit, 1995.
Ricœur, Paul. 'Réponses aux critiques'. In *'Temps et récit' de Paul Ricœur en débat*, edited by Christian Bouchindhomme and Rainer Rochlitz, 197–205. Paris: Éditions du Cerf, 1990.
Ricœur, Paul. *Soi-même comme un autre*. Paris: Éditions du Seuil, 2015.
Ricœur, Paul. *Sur la traduction*. Paris: Bayard, 2004.
Ricœur, Paul. *The Conflict of Interpretations*. Evanston: Northwestern University Press, 1974.
Ricœur, Paul. 'The Critique of Religion and The Language of Faith'. *Union Seminary Quarterly Review* 28 (1973), 203–24.
Ricœur, Paul. 'The Hermeneutics of Testimony'. Translated by David Stewart and Charles Reagan. *Anglican Theological Review* 61, no. 4 (1979): 435–61.
Ricœur, Paul. 'The Relation of Jaspers' Philosophy to Religion'. In *The Philosophy of Karl Jaspers*, edited by Paul Arthur Schilpp, 2nd ed., 611–42. The Library of Living Philosophers. LaSalle: Open Court, 1981.
Ricœur, Paul. *The Rule of Metaphor: Multi-Disciplinary Studies of the Creation of Meaning in Language*. Translated by Kathleen McLaughlin, John Costello, SJ, and Robert Czerny. London: Routledge, 1978.
Ricœur, Paul. 'The Self in the Mirror of the Scriptures'. In *The Whole and Divided Self*, edited by David Edward Aune and John McCarthy, 201–20. New York: Crossroad Publishing Company, 1997.

Ricœur, Paul. 'The Symbol: Food for Thought'. *Philosophy Today* 4, no. 3 (1960): 196–207.
Ricœur, Paul. *The Symbolism of Evil*. Translated by Emerson Buchanan. Boston: Beacon, 1969.
Ricœur, Paul. 'Translator's Introduction'. In *Freedom and Nature: The Voluntary and the Involuntary*. Translated by Erazim Kohák, xv–xlii Evanston: Northwestern University Press, 1966.
Ricœur, Paul. 'Vérité: Jésus et Ponce Pilate'. *Le Semeur* 44, no. 5 (1946): 381–94.
Ricœur, Paul. *Vivant jusqu'à la mort. Suivi de fragments*. Paris: Éditions du Seuil, 2014.
Ricœur, Paul, and André LaCocque. *Penser la bible*. Paris: Éditions du Seuil, 1998.
Ricœur, Paul, and Gabriel Marcel. *Entretiens*. Paris: Aubier-Montaigne, 1968.
Ricœur, Paul, and Questioners. 'Roundtable Discussion'. In *Memory, Narrativity, Self and the Challenge to Think God: The Reception within Theology of the Recent Work of Paul Ricœur*, edited by Maureen Junker-Kenny and Peter Kenny, 202–16. Münster: LIT, 2004.
Rockmore, Tom. *Heidegger and French Philosophy: Humanism, Antihumanism, and Being*. London: Routledge, 1995.
Rohlf, Michael. 'Immanuel Kant'. In *The Stanford Encyclopedia of Philosophy*, edited by Edward N. Zalta, Summer 2018. Stanford University: Metaphysics Research Lab, 2018. https://plato.stanford.edu/archives/sum2018/entries/kant/.
Sartre, Jean-Paul. *Existentialism and Humanism*. Translated by Philip Mairet. London: Methuen, 1948.
Sartre, Jean-Paul. *Being and Nothingness: An Essay on Phenomenological Ontology*. London: Methuen, 1957.
Sartre, Jean-Paul. *L'être et le néant: essai d'ontologie phénoménologique*. Paris: Gallimard, 1943.
Sartre, Jean-Paul. *L'existentialisme est un humanisme*. Paris: Nagel, 1966.
Sartre, Jean-Paul. 'Translator's Introduction'. In *Existentialism and Humanism*. Translated by Philip Mairet. London: Methuen, 1948.
Schaafsma, Petruschka. 'Philosophical Anthropology against Objectification. Reconsidering Ricœur's Fallible Man'. *International Journal of Philosophy and Theology* 75, no. 2 (2014): 152–68.
Schillebeeckx, Edward. *God among Us: The Gospel Proclaimed*. Translated by John Bowden. London: SCM, 1983.
Schrift, Alan D. *Twentieth-Century French Philosophy: Key Themes and Thinkers*. Malden: Blackwell, 2009.
Scott-Baumann, Alison. *Ricœur and the Hermeneutics of Suspicion*. London: Continuum, 2009.
Scott-Baumann, Alison. *Ricœur and the Negation of Happiness*. London: Bloomsbury, 2013.
Shlomo, Dov Rosen. 'Between the Homunculus Fallacy and Angelic Cognitive Dissonance in Explanation of Evil: Milton's Poetry and Luzzatto's Kabbalah'. In *Evil, Fallenness, and Finitude*, edited by Bruce Ellis Benson and B. Keith Putt, 57–75. Cham: Palgrave Macmillan, 2017.

Sohn, Michael. 'Paul Tillich and Paul Ricœur on the Meaning of "Philosophical Theology"'. *Bulletin of the North American Paul Tillich Society* 39, no. 4 (2013): 23–9.

Soskice, Janet Martin. 'Creation and the Glory of Creatures'. *Modern Theology* 29, no. 2 (2013): 172–85.

Sparby, Terje. *Hegel's Conception of the Determinate Negation*. Leiden: Brill, 2014.

Stambaugh, Joan. *The Finitude of Being*. Albany: SUNY Press, 1992.

Stewart, David. 'In Quest of Hope: Paul Ricœur and Jürgen Moltmann'. *Restoration Quarterly* 13, no. 1 (1970): 31–52.

Stewart, Jon, ed. *Kierkegaard and Existentialism*. Kierkegaard Research: Sources, Reception and Resources 9. Farnham: Ashgate, 2011.

Stiver, Dan R. *Theology after Ricœur: New Directions in Hermeneutical Theology*. Louisville: Westminster John Knox Press, 2001.

Stiver, Dan R. *Ricœur and Theology*. London: T&T Clark, 2012.

Stolorow, Robert D. 'Phenomenological Contextualism and the Finitude of Knowing'. *The Humanistic Psychologist* 46, no. 2 (2018): 204–10.

Sutherland, D. Dixon. 'A Theological Anthropology of Evil: A Comparison in the Thought of Paul Ricœur and Teilhard de Chardin'. *Neue Zeitschrift für Systematische Theologie und Religionsphilosophie* 34, no. 1 (1992): 85–100.

Tanner, John S. '"Say First What Cause": Ricœur and the Etiology of Evil in *Paradise Lost*'. *PMLA* 103, no. 1 (1988): 45–56.

Taylor, Charles. 'History and Truth (Book Review)'. *The Journal of Philosophy* 65, no. 13 (1968): 401–3.

Taylor, George H. 'Ricœur's Philosophy of Imagination'. *Journal of French and Francophone Philosophy* 16, no. 1/2 (2006): 93–104.

Thévenaz, Pierre. 'Dieu des philosophes et dieu des chrétiens'. In *L'homme et sa raison: raison et conscience de soi*, Vol. 1, 309–25. Neuchâtel: Éditions de la Baconnière, 1956.

Thévenaz, Pierre. 'God of the Philosophers and God of the Christians'. Translated by Peter Carpenter. *Studies in Religion/Sciences Religieuses* 5, no. 4 (1976): 338–49.

Thévenaz, Pierre. *La condition de la raison philosophique*. Neuchâtel: Éditions de la Baconnière, 1960.

Thévenaz, Pierre. 'La philosophie sans absolu'. In *L'homme et sa raison: raison et conscience de soi*, 1: 187–206. Neuchâtel: Éditions de la Baconnière, 1956.

Thévenaz, Pierre. *L'homme et sa raison: raison et conscience de soi*. Vol. 1. 2 vols. Neuchâtel: Éditions de la Baconnière, 1956.

Thévenaz, Pierre. *L'homme et sa raison: raison et histoire*. Vol. 2. 2 vols. Neuchâtel: Éditions de la Baconnière, 1956.

Thévenaz, Pierre. 'L'homme normal'. *Revue de Théologie et de Philosophie* 25, no. 3 (1975): 205–11.

Thiselton, Anthony C. *Hermeneutics: An Introduction*. Grand Rapids: Eerdmans, 2009.

Thouard, Denis. 'Kant et l'herméneutique'. *Archives de Philosophie* 61, no. 4 (1998): 629–58.

Tongeren, Paul J. M. van. 'Salvation and Creation: On the Role of Forgiveness in the Completion of Paul Ricœur's Philosophy'. *International Journal of Philosophy and Theology* 75, no. 2 (2014): 169–82.

Vanhoozer, Kevin. *Biblical Narrative in the Philosophy of Paul Ricœur: A Study in Hermeneutics and Theology*. Cambridge: Cambridge University Press, 1990.
Varet, Gilbert. 'Spiritualisme et philosophie réflexive'. *Revue des Sciences Philosophiques et Theologiques* 74, no. 1 (1990): 23–34.
Venema, Henry Isaac. 'The Source of Ricœur's Double Allegiance'. In *A Passion for the Possible: Thinking with Paul Ricœur*, edited by Brian Treanor and Henry Isaac Venema, 62–76. New York: Fordham University Press, 2010.
Verheyden, Jack, Theo Hettema, and Pieter Vandecasteele, eds. *Paul Ricœur: Poetics and Religion*. Leuven: Uitgeverij Peeters, 2011.
Wahl, Jean. *Études Kierkegaardiennes*. Paris: Vrin, 2012.
Wahl, Jean. 'Le problème du choix, l'existence et la transcendance dans la philosophie de Jaspers'. *Revue de Métaphysique et de Morale* 41, no. 3 (1934): 405–44.
Wahl, Jean. *Les philosophies de l'existence*. 2nd ed. Paris: Librarie Armand Colin, 1959.
Wahl, Jean. *Philosophies of Existence: An Introduction to the Basic Thought of Kierkegaard, Heidegger, Jaspers, Marcel, Sartre*. Translated by F. M. Lory. New York: Schocken Books, 1969.
Wahl, Jean. 'The Problem of Choice: Existence and Transcendence in the Philosophy of Jaspers'. *Journal of French and Francophone Philosophy* 24, no. 1 (2016): 224–58.
Wahl, Jean. *Transcendence and the Concrete: Selected Writings*. Edited by Alan Schrift and Ian Alexander Moore. Bronx: Fordham University Press, 2016.
Wahl, Jean. *Vers le concret: études d'histoire de la philosophie contemporaine: William James, Whitehead, Gabriel Marcel*. Paris: Vrin, 2004.
Wall, John, William Schweiker, and David Hall, eds. *Paul Ricœur and Contemporary Moral Thought*. New York: Routledge, 2002.
Wallace, Mark. *The Second Naïveté: Barth, Ricœur, and the New Yale Theology*. Macon: Mercer, 1990.
Watkin, Christopher. 'Ricœur and the Autonomy of Philosophy: A Reappraisal'. *Philosophy Today* 58, no. 3 (2014): 411–25.
Weinandy, O. F. M., Thomas. *Does God Suffer?* Edinburgh: T&T Clark, 2000.
Wells, Harold. 'Theology and Christian Philosophy: Their Relation in the Thought of Paul Ricœur'. *Studies in Religion/Sciences Religieuses* 5, no. 1 (1975): 45–56.
White, Erin. 'Between Suspicion and Hope: Paul Ricœur's Vital Hermeneutic'. *Literature and Theology* 5, no. 3 (1991): 311–21.
Widmer, Gabriel. 'Un essai de philosophie protestante: *L'homme et sa raison*, de Pierre Thévenaz'. *Revue de Théologie et de Philosophie* 12, no. 2 (1962): 93–106.
Williams, Rowan. 'Insubstantial Evil'. In *On Augustine*, 79–105. London: Bloomsbury, 2016.
Wolfe, Judith. *Heidegger and Theology*. London: Bloomsbury, 2014.
Worms, Frédéric. *La philosophie en France au XXe siècle: moments*. Paris: Gallimard, 2009.

Index

Abraham 71, 83, 87
absolute 14, 21, 24–26, 46, 47, 52, 65–71, 73–86, 90, 91, 94, 105, 107–12, 112, 114–17, 125, 135–37, 155, 157, 161, 164, 189, 190, 192, 194, 200, 201, 213, 217, 219–21, 223, 225
abstraction 3, 23, 25, 28, 47–50, 52, 55, 56, 61, 99, 100, 106, 147, 149, 164, 180, 183, 190
absurd 87, 107, 149, 154, 209, 219, 221
Adam 25, 124, 138, 148–53, 155, 156, 160, 164, 169, 179, 216
affirmation, original 15, 78, 86, 111, 112, 114, 116–18, 197, 228
agnosticism 8, 88, 174
Amalric, Jean-Luc 96, 111, 112, 120, 141
ambiguity 41, 55, 66, 69, 75, 83, 84, 95, 119, 142, 192
analogy 77, 78, 165, 168, 169, 172, 173, 182–84, 190, 202, 210, 212, 219, 226
Anderson, Pamela Sue 3, 13, 97, 100, 170, 200, 226
anthropology 2, 3, 6, 10, 13, 70, 73, 80, 88, 89, 92, 94, 96–98, 100, 101, 106, 107, 111–13, 116, 117, 119–21, 124, 125, 129, 137, 141, 142, 146, 148, 149, 161, 163, 164, 166–68, 170, 176, 198–201, 204, 215, 216
anti-systematic 190
apodicticity 21, 40, 70, 88
apologetics 72, 87, 88, 114, 183, 218
apophatic theology 2, 15, 77, 87, 109, 115, 116
Arendt, Hannah 2

Aristotle 1, 12, 13, 150
atheism 6, 83, 84, 88, 90, 91, 124, 174, 204
Augustine of Hippo, St 12, 124, 159–61, 164, 173, 201, 224
authority 4, 56, 130, 166
autonomy 67, 71, 171, 216, 224, 225, 228

Babel, Tower of 72, 104, 105
Bakewell, Sarah 10, 23, 24
Barth, Karl 4, 13, 14, 65, 67, 71, 72, 83, 86, 116, 117, 135, 138, 162, 169, 170, 201, 208, 226, 227
being-in-the-world 75, 99, 103, 106
belief 13, 15, 17, 18, 27, 31, 34, 37–39, 43, 50, 51, 56, 61, 71, 74, 82, 84, 85, 87, 99, 103, 112, 131, 134, 135, 154, 159, 161, 162, 170, 171, 174, 175, 182, 186, 187, 192, 195, 203, 215–19
Benson, Bruce Ellis 92, 119, 161
Bergson, Henri 2, 141
bias 68, 127
Bible, The 6, 11, 16, 87, 88, 104, 114, 115, 124, 134, 135, 146, 152, 155, 160, 162–64, 167–69, 180, 182, 184, 201–3, 208–11, 215, 226, 228
  Scripture 123, 148, 152, 162, 169, 220
Blondel, Maurice 47
Blundell, Boyd 4, 21, 25, 224, 226
Body, The 60, 132, 141, 148, 149, 165, 183, 194, 212, 217, 220
Bonhoeffer 4
Brunschvicg, Léon 11, 20, 67

245

Calvinism 135
Cambridge, University of 1, 2, 4, 6, 13, 19, 23, 99, 106, 169, 172, 175
Camus, Albert 112, 113
Catholicism 6–8, 11, 60, 88, 135, 141
Chesterton, G.K. 178
Chicago, University of 4–6, 9, 15, 33, 51, 52, 74, 88, 167, 169
Christ. *See* Jesus
Christianity 4, 5, 7, 8, 16, 28, 39, 40, 45, 62, 71, 72, 75, 77, 83–85, 87, 88, 90, 91, 114–16, 123–25, 129, 134, 135, 137, 151, 159, 163, 164, 169, 171, 173, 198, 205, 207–11, 215, 216, 219–21, 224–26
christology 169, 179, 206
Church 32, 151
cipher 12, 119, 175–77, 195, 202
Coleridge, Samuel Taylor 8
communication 30, 54, 55, 59–62, 73, 103, 106
consciousness 20, 21, 30, 38, 47, 62, 67, 70, 71, 74, 82, 102, 104, 105, 131, 132, 156, 173, 177, 195, 198, 202, 213–15, 224
consent 17, 139, 193, 194, 206, 211–13, 217–19, 222
contingency 44, 45, 61, 68–71, 78, 86, 90, 92, 95, 118, 122, 133, 139, 144, 145, 149, 166, 202, 213–16, 219
contradiction 26, 42, 57, 79–81, 110, 115, 154, 158, 164, 172, 191, 195, 196, 215, 221, 224, 227
conversion 7, 8, 51, 70, 72, 81, 82, 85, 212, 219
Copernican Revolution 69
correlation 92, 95, 131
creation 3, 4, 11, 13, 16, 17, 28, 39, 41, 60, 65, 83, 100, 107, 118, 124, 125, 127–29, 134, 135, 143, 144, 147, 149, 151–57, 164, 166–71, 178, 180–88, 190, 193–211, 214–23, 225, 227, 228
ex nihilo 187, 200–204

Dalbiez, Roland 21
Dasein 35, 54, 75, 99, 103, 137
Davison, Andrew 16, 88, 223
de Beauvoir, Simone 2
defilement 147, 149, 163, 177
deiformity 135
denegation 112
Depravity, Total 134, 135

désabsolutisation. *See* absolute
Descartes 12, 13, 20, 21, 67, 82, 86, 88, 94–97, 113, 114, 117, 143, 195
despair 14, 39–41, 47, 61, 63, 159, 208, 209, 213–15, 217, 219, 224
determinate 1, 4, 73, 74, 86, 115, 117, 171, 172, 180, 181, 184, 189, 221, 223, 226
determinism 212
Devil, The 163, 164, 166
dieu des philosophes 71, 72, 76
disabsolutization. *See* absolute
disponibilité 29, 30, 139, 165
doctrine 16, 39, 53, 56, 57, 79, 99, 100, 106, 124, 131, 134, 152, 155, 159–64, 166, 169–71, 185–87, 200, 203, 204, 206, 219, 226, 227
dogmatic 29, 45, 53, 56, 73, 160
Dosse 5, 7, 131, 166, 227, 228
dualism 71, 110, 148, 196, 200, 204, 217, 219
Dufrenne, Mikel 10, 33, 45, 55–60, 74, 99, 106, 126, 127, 132, 190, 193, 221
d'absolu 105, 157
d'abstraction. *See* abstraction
d'autrui 131

Ecclesiastes, Book of 86
ecclesiastical. *See* Church
Eden, Garden of 78, 145, 150, 152, 153, 169, 208
eidetics 44, 119, 138, 149, 167, 180, 182, 183, 195
Einheit. *See* unity
Eliade, Mircea 177
Eliot, George 18
Ellul 134, 136, 138, 139, 143, 153, 154, 169, 227
empirical 27, 54, 119, 138, 143, 180, 183, 184, 221
Endlichkeit. *See* finitude
Enlightenment 159
epistemology 13, 18, 28, 39, 42, 44, 45, 55, 65, 122, 127, 135, 142, 191, 224
equivocity 83
eschatology 14, 19, 30, 31, 34, 35, 40, 41, 44, 46, 62, 137, 152, 186, 192, 208, 224, 226
essence 14, 17, 18, 30, 36, 49, 50, 53, 57, 61, 62, 68, 72, 75, 87, 93, 94, 101, 115, 117, 118, 120, 122–24, 129–32, 136, 137, 141, 143, 146, 149, 160, 165, 197, 200, 215, 220, 224, 228

eternity 34, 68, 86, 108, 136, 147, 149, 181, 202
ethics 11, 32, 39, 100, 120, 126, 132–34, 136, 138, 139, 142, 143, 148, 156–59, 161, 162, 168, 170, 181, 206, 212
evil 2–4, 6, 13, 15–17, 31, 32, 36, 62, 92, 96, 111, 118–22, 125–27, 129–34, 138–40, 142–66, 168–70, 173, 175, 177–80, 182, 192, 201–3, 205–11, 215, 216, 218, 219, 221–23, 225, 228
  as privation 91, 146, 161–64, 166, 201, 202
existential 9, 24, 44, 45, 58, 59, 75, 118, 147, 179, 183
existentialism 2, 7–10, 14, 15, 19, 20, 22–26, 30, 31, 33, 43, 47, 48, 54, 56, 58, 59, 63, 75, 91, 118, 123, 125, 126, 129, 133, 145, 147, 182, 197, 198, 215
experience 1, 5, 15, 32, 59, 72, 101, 119–23, 133, 137, 140–42, 145, 147, 152, 157, 158, 160, 165, 174, 176, 178, 181, 188, 192, 202, 220

faith 7, 8, 17, 50–52, 56, 71, 72, 75, 83, 88, 114, 132, 177, 178, 209, 220, 227, 228
fall 3, 16, 25, 49, 53, 74, 92, 107, 115, 122–24, 129–31, 133–35, 137, 139–41, 149–51, 154, 155, 160, 161, 164, 166, 168, 173, 174, 184, 208, 209, 215, 224
  pre-fallen 135, 150
fallibility 119, 127, 146
Falque, Emmanuel 16, 92, 97, 102, 103, 128, 203, 216, 223
Fault, The 119, 121–23, 126, 127, 132, 138, 139, 143, 149, 152, 153, 165, 167, 184, 191, 192, 206, 208, 211, 223
felix culpa 152, 154
fideism 178
finitude 1–4, 6, 13–18, 22, 24, 25, 27, 28, 33, 35, 41, 44, 51–53, 60–62, 65, 68–70, 77–79, 81, 82, 85, 85, 89–97, 100–112, 115–22, 125–35, 138–41, 143–50, 152–58, 160–66, 170, 171, 175, 177–79, 184, 191, 192, 202, 203, 205–7, 211, 213–19, 221–24, 228

for-itself 196, 197, 199, 214
Foucault, Michel 2, 92, 95, 97, 110, 128
fragility 8, 119, 151
freedom 2, 17, 34, 59, 70, 98, 117, 120, 121, 123, 126, 128, 132, 138, 139, 142, 143, 145, 148, 149, 152–58, 160–67, 170, 173, 174, 180–84, 186–88, 194–200, 202–4, 211–20, 222, 224, 228
Freud, Sigmund 21, 129, 147

Gadamer, Hans-Georg 19
Gifford Lectures 131, 220
gift 26, 78, 152, 153, 164, 222
Gnostic 152
God 2–5, 13–17, 21, 24–28, 49–51, 65, 70–72, 75–78, 80–92, 94–96, 98, 99, 107, 113–18, 124–28, 134, 135, 143, 144, 147, 151–56, 163, 164, 167, 182–84, 187, 189, 195–203, 205–11, 214–16, 218–21, 223, 225, 226, 228
Gospel, The 83, 209
Gregor, Brian 2, 11, 20–22, 55, 170
Greisch, Jean 11, 47, 84, 94–97, 102, 128, 137, 181
Gschwandtner, Christina 92, 115, 177
guilt 15, 36, 96, 101–4, 107, 108, 111, 118–27, 129–33, 138–41, 143, 146–53, 155–58, 160–66, 172, 175, 177–79, 184, 191, 202, 203, 205, 211, 216, 221, 223–26

Habermas, Jürgen 19
habit 29, 157, 220
Hackett, Stuart 40, 43–45
Hebrew 148, 152, 155, 162
Hegel, G.W.F. 1, 2, 13, 19, 24, 25, 46, 89, 93, 102, 110, 141, 198
Heidegger, Martin 2, 3, 10, 13, 15, 23, 24, 65, 75, 86, 90–100, 102, 103, 105, 106, 108–10, 115–17, 122, 126, 128, 137, 140–42, 164, 179, 189, 192, 198, 223
  Being and Time 92, 99, 109, 127
  Kant and the Problem of Metaphysics 92, 93, 96
Helenius, Timo 25, 183, 184, 190
hell 181
Hellenism 201
Henry, Michel 2
heresy 12, 206, 207

hermeneutics 2, 4, 5, 10–14, 19–22, 46, 55, 76, 83–85, 89, 106, 111, 114, 115, 119, 141, 147, 167, 169, 170, 172, 174, 175, 181, 182, 185, 201, 224, 226
Hick, John 158, 159
history 2, 5, 6, 9, 12, 14–16, 19, 20, 23, 26, 30–32, 35, 37–43, 45, 52, 53, 55, 59–64, 67, 71, 73, 74, 82, 83, 85, 90, 96, 101, 102, 104–9, 111–13, 118, 122, 125, 129, 130, 132, 133, 136, 144, 145, 147, 149–52, 154, 155, 157, 162, 166, 169, 172, 174, 180, 189, 199, 208–10, 212, 224, 225, 227, 228
holiness 208
hope 11, 14, 17, 19, 25, 28, 35, 39–47, 59–64, 143, 153, 168, 170, 186, 192, 203, 206, 209, 211, 217–21, 224–27
Hughes, John 88
Huguenot 6
Huskey, R.K. 25, 46
Husserl, Edmund 12, 70, 121, 122, 125, 141, 165

iconoclasm 83
idealism 20–22, 38, 41, 48, 49, 58, 67, 69, 74, 77, 110, 189, 190, 192, 194, 213, 215, 217, 219
idolatry 72, 73, 85, 117, 207, 208, 220
Ille, George 13
imagination 3, 6, 11, 79, 94, 120, 130, 135, 137, 140–43, 168, 171, 172, 181, 182
imago dei 78, 117
immanence 3, 26, 55, 67, 68, 75, 82, 183
immediacy 21, 88, 142
imperfection 18, 40, 41, 128, 136
impossibility 34, 46, 49, 85, 90, 108, 113, 174
incarnation 77, 79, 98, 102
infinite 3, 14, 15, 17, 65, 70, 77, 85, 86, 89, 91, 93–97, 100, 102, 103, 105, 107–18, 127–29, 146, 170, 208, 211, 215, 216, 218, 221, 223, 228
innocence 3, 16, 123, 125, 126, 130, 131, 134, 137, 138, 140, 142, 143, 149–55, 167, 169, 184, 202, 208, 209, 227
Insole, Christopher 187
intellectualism 190

interpretation 6, 30, 44, 66, 69, 71, 83, 85, 90, 92, 93, 96, 97, 99, 107, 124, 137, 140, 142, 147, 152, 153, 176, 179, 208
intuitionism 142
Irenaeus of Lyons, St 16, 149, 151, 152, 155, 169

Jackson Ravenscroft, Ruth 92
Janicaud, Dominique 90, 171
Jaspers, Karl 7–13, 23–25, 33–39, 43, 45, 52–61, 65, 73–78, 86, 98, 99, 105, 106, 115–19, 123, 125–27, 131, 132, 149, 156, 173, 176–78, 187, 190–95, 198, 211, 221
  Philosophy 33–35, 38, 52–54, 73–75, 105, 106, 115, 176, 177
  Reason and Existenz 24, 25
Jervolino, Domenico 83, 168, 183, 184
Jesus 40, 41, 71, 77, 134, 143, 144, 151–53, 207–11, 214, 215, 220, 227
Junker-Kenny, Maureen 5, 84, 226
justice 6, 119, 168

Kant, Immanuel 2, 3, 11, 13, 19–21, 39, 46, 61, 67, 69, 70, 88, 92–94, 96, 97, 100, 102, 103, 116, 129, 138, 140, 141, 156, 157, 159, 169–74, 176–78, 180, 181, 184, 186–90, 193, 194, 203, 205, 223, 225, 226
  Critique of the Power of Judgment 11, 140, 170, 172, 173, 181, 188, 189
  post-Kantian 20, 70, 74
  pre-Kantian 76
Kearney, Richard 11, 114, 147, 162, 181, 201, 226
Kierkegaard, Søren 13, 23–25, 36, 120, 126, 184, 187, 190, 191, 194, 198, 206, 208
Kirkpatrick, Kate 124
Koci, Martin 128
Kohák, Erazim 3
Kristeva, Julia 2

Lacan, Jacques 2
Lachelier, Jules 11, 20, 47
LaCocque, André 167, 201, 209
Lagneau, Jules 11, 20, 47
Lessing, Gotthold 149
Lewis, C.S. 106

limit 1–3, 11, 18, 24, 35, 46, 58, 59, 62, 65, 69, 70, 73, 74, 85, 89, 90, 93–96, 102, 109, 110, 112, 122, 123, 126, 127, 132, 134, 146, 148, 158, 159, 164, 166, 169, 171, 177, 181, 186, 189, 194, 202, 203, 209, 211, 212, 216, 217, 221, 225, 228
  as *Grenze* 1, 54, 69, 93, 110
  as limitation 1, 10, 44, 61, 90, 93, 94, 109, 122, 123, 126, 127, 129, 132, 158, 192, 211, 216, 217, 219
  as *Schranke* 1, 2, 69, 93, 102, 110, 117
Liturgy 92
Luther, Martin 160, 173

MacKinnon, Donald 175
Marcel, Gabriel 7–9, 11, 12, 23–30, 33, 35–39, 42, 47–52, 54–56, 60, 61, 65, 67, 73–75, 78–80, 98, 105, 106, 115, 117, 119, 126, 130, 132, 156, 175, 176, 182, 183, 186, 187, 190–94, 198, 206–8, 217, 223
  Being and Having 26, 28, 29, 38, 49–51, 61, 115, 130, 206, 207
  Creative Fidelity 11, 25–30, 78, 79
  Metaphysical Journal 26, 27, 29, 51
  Tragic Wisdom and Beyond 23, 28, 29, 37, 48, 79, 80
Marion, Jean-Luc 97, 117
Martyr, Justin 83
Marx, Karl 48, 129, 198
McFarland, Ian 201
McQuillan, J. Colin 92–94, 97
mediation 5, 14, 19, 33, 43, 45, 46, 54, 60, 65, 106, 129, 142, 177, 188
medieval 115, 195
Meillassoux, Quentin 92
Merleau-Ponty, Maurice 2, 89
metaphor 6, 11, 15, 109, 133, 181, 182
metaphysics 3, 13, 26, 27, 29, 35, 49–51, 61, 70, 73, 75, 91–94, 97, 99, 113, 116, 117, 127, 136, 137, 146, 159–64, 166, 180, 181, 188, 200–202, 211, 218, 222, 223
  anti-metaphysical 201
Milbank, John 117
morality 70, 138, 146, 203
mortality 8
Mounier, Emmanuel 25, 54
mystery 11, 16, 23, 39, 49–51, 60, 69, 116, 146, 155, 159, 160, 162, 178, 186, 187, 190–94, 202, 209, 217, 223

myth, mythology 83, 100, 104, 105, 119, 138, 146–48, 150, 152, 155, 157, 158, 160, 167, 172, 175–77, 179, 184, 202, 203, 224

Nabert, Jean 11, 20, 21, 86, 95, 111, 112, 114, 119, 131, 146
naïveté 13, 59, 150, 177, 226
narrative 6, 10, 11, 124, 145, 146, 150, 166, 177, 180, 201, 202, 215, 228
Nazism 10
negation 5, 15, 33, 41, 76, 90, 93, 94, 107–12, 116, 127, 128, 198, 200, 202, 204, 221, 223, 228
negative 3, 15, 26, 32, 37, 41, 55, 57, 70, 73, 76–80, 87, 95, 99, 106, 108–13, 115–18, 137, 162, 165, 195, 197, 221, 228
Neoplatonic 77
neo-Thomism 88
neutrality 3, 94, 98–100, 108, 174, 183, 195, 201, 203
Nietzsche, Friedrich 24, 25, 190, 198
nihilism 47, 209, 217, 219
Nkéramihigo, Théoneste 183
non-philosophy 159, 173, 174, 187, 222
nothingness 76, 109, 123, 124, 143, 162, 163, 165, 166, 196, 197, 199, 200, 202, 214, 215, 223

Oakes, Kenneth 67
objectivity 17, 24, 27, 34, 44, 45, 49, 51, 55, 76, 106, 112, 120, 142, 187, 194–97, 199, 203, 204, 212
Olson, Alan 10, 12, 76, 106
ontic 122, 137
ontology 15, 18, 33, 39, 41, 42, 45, 46, 49, 50, 57, 58, 60, 65, 68, 91, 95, 96, 99, 100, 102, 120–23, 126, 132, 137, 142, 145–47, 149, 150, 154, 164–66, 171, 180, 184, 186, 191, 192, 194, 196, 197, 210, 224
ontotheological 125, 189
Orphic 148
orthodoxy 206
Other, The 1, 2, 6, 41, 54, 55, 60, 68, 77, 79, 104, 108, 114, 123, 124, 128, 131, 132, 146, 161, 171, 183, 210, 217

paradox 15, 17, 23, 38, 39, 77, 78, 80, 97, 105, 117, 139, 155, 158, 159, 161, 162, 164, 177, 178, 187, 190–95, 221

particularity 14, 43, 48, 58, 62, 90, 95, 105, 106, 146
Pascal, Blaise 71, 87
passions 129, 130, 132, 143, 165
Pelagianism 145, 157, 159, 160
perfection 15, 133, 150–53, 155, 166
phenomenology 2, 4, 11–13, 19, 20, 56, 70, 89, 90, 92, 94, 112, 121–25, 128, 141, 147, 156, 165, 171, 198, 200, 202, 218, 226
philosophia perennis 63
philosophizing 9, 34, 35, 53, 55
Plato 12, 13, 24, 75, 90, 113, 188, 202
Plotinus 76, 125
poetics 11, 16, 100, 163, 164, 167–71, 176, 180–85, 187, 195, 205, 211, 218, 222
Porée; Jérôme 2, 8, 97, 154
Possati, Luca 168, 169, 182–84, 226
post-structuralism 22
prayer 114, 116
predestination 125, 126, 156, 157
pre-philosophical 167
pre-rational 158
presuppositions 37, 38, 49, 54, 60, 61, 79, 102, 104, 113, 132, 136, 140, 148, 156, 174, 175, 178, 182, 183, 204, 225
pretheological 115
pride 26, 28, 41, 215
primordial 3, 104, 120, 123, 129, 130, 133, 135–41, 143, 145, 150, 164, 168
procrustean bed 30, 32
Prometheus 83, 213, 219
Protestantism 5–7, 65–67, 71, 83, 134, 162, 201, 227
psychoanalysis 6, 10, 19, 129, 142, 147, 182
punishment 125, 126, 132, 148
purposiveness 188, 189

rationality 22, 24, 36, 58, 63, 132, 172, 224
Reagan, Charles 5, 85, 179, 227
reality 1, 12, 17, 21, 22, 24–27, 31, 32, 37–41, 43, 45, 47–51, 58, 60, 61, 68, 70, 71, 74–77, 90, 94, 95, 99, 101, 105–7, 109, 111, 113, 118, 119, 122, 128, 129, 131, 136, 137, 141, 142, 146–49, 154, 155, 161, 164, 165, 170, 173, 178–81, 186, 187, 189, 190, 192–94, 196, 197, 199, 200, 203, 204, 211, 214, 216, 218, 228

reciprocity 156, 194, 198, 212, 217
Redemption, doctrine of 16, 137, 150, 206
reflexion 11–14, 19–22, 24, 31, 33, 35, 41, 43, 47, 61–63, 67, 82, 129, 172
Reformation, The 135
refusal 17, 61, 112, 211, 213–17, 219
relativism 45, 61, 68, 80, 81, 178
religion 4, 6, 16, 22, 26, 50, 61, 75, 91, 99, 115, 124, 131, 169, 173, 174, 177, 179, 181, 185, 196, 198, 214, 220, 224, 225
resurrection 154
revelation 4, 26, 62, 65, 72, 81, 83, 85, 87, 89, 114, 115, 166, 176, 178, 179, 181, 207, 220–22, 225
Ricœur, Paul
  Conflict of Interpretations 32, 36, 148, 153, 156–62, 174, 175, 180, 201
  Critique and Conviction 6, 7, 9, 13, 37, 67, 88, 142, 226, 227
  Fallible Man 8, 79, 96, 97, 100–104, 107, 108, 111, 112, 120, 127, 129–31, 140–43, 146, 147, 151, 157, 158, 160, 163, 184, 211
  Figuring the Sacred 19, 31, 39, 47, 62, 116, 168, 225
  Freedom and Nature 3, 16, 17, 87, 89, 99, 100, 110–12, 117, 121, 128, 138, 139, 142, 143, 149, 156, 165, 167, 173, 174, 180, 182–84, 186, 187, 194–98, 200, 202–4, 211–19
  Gabriel Marcel et Karl Jaspers 23, 33, 35, 36, 54, 56, 74, 98, 126, 156, 176, 191, 192
  Hermeneutics and the Human Sciences 19, 174
  History and Truth 19, 30–32, 38–42, 45, 55, 60–64, 102, 104, 106–9, 111–13, 151, 152, 199, 224, 225, 227, 228
  Husserl: An Analysis of His Phenomenology 121, 122, 125, 165
  Rule of Metaphor, The 15, 133, 182
  Symbolism of Evil 121, 125, 126, 133, 138, 139, 147–50, 152, 153, 155, 157–65, 169, 175, 177–79, 182, 201–3, 205, 216
  Thinking Biblically 167, 201, 209

Salvation, doctrine of 144, 145, 168, 221
Sartre, Jean-Paul 2, 9, 17, 23, 24, 47, 75, 90, 91, 98, 123–25, 141, 149, 156, 164, 192, 196–200, 203, 204, 214–17
  Being and Nothingness 123, 124, 163, 196, 197, 199, 214, 215
Satan. *See* Devil, The
Schelling, Friedrich von 8, 141
Schillebeeckx, Edward 118
schizophrenic 227
Schleiermacher, Friedrich 220
Scott-Baumann, Alison 4, 5, 41, 109, 170, 198
sin 15, 105, 116, 118–20, 122–24, 126, 127, 132, 133, 135, 138, 139, 145–47, 149–51, 153–56, 159–63, 165, 166, 169, 173, 177, 180, 184, 201, 205, 206, 208–10, 215, 216, 221, 225, 227
skepticism 61
Soskice, Janet 200
Spinoza, Benedict de 12, 13, 125
spiritualism 20, 22
Stiver, Dan 5, 6, 168, 226
structuralism 10, 22, 129
subjectivity 16, 17, 27, 34, 45, 49, 51, 67, 68, 70, 87, 100, 147, 156, 187, 194–97, 199, 203, 204, 212, 218
suffering 5, 32, 52, 95, 96, 119, 120, 122, 127, 130, 164, 213–15, 217–19, 222
symbol 4, 6, 10, 11, 16, 46, 115, 121, 147, 148, 152, 158–60, 162, 163, 167, 168, 170–80, 184, 185, 187, 191, 202, 203, 205, 211, 222, 223, 226
system 14, 18, 19, 22, 24–43, 49, 55–57, 61, 62, 78, 105, 115, 119, 127, 170, 186–89, 191–94, 200, 203

teleology 95, 150, 187–89, 211
temptation 19, 25–27, 36, 61, 62, 70, 73, 74, 78, 115, 125, 151–54, 158, 161, 211, 215, 216, 218, 219, 222
Tertullian 83

theology 3–6, 11, 13, 15–17, 23, 25, 31, 46, 62, 65–67, 71, 72, 76–78, 80, 82–88, 90–92, 97, 109, 114–17, 120, 121, 129, 134, 135, 151, 159, 165, 168, 169, 171, 173, 179, 181, 184, 185, 189, 200, 201, 203, 206, 216, 221, 223–26
Thévenaz, Pierre 11, 14, 21, 65–74, 76–78, 80–86, 93, 105, 112, 116, 117, 135–37, 139, 142, 225, 226
thing-in-itself 69, 138, 189
Thiselton, Anthony 5
Thomas Aquinas, St. 116, 200, 225
totality (totalising) 14, 18, 22, 24–26, 30–32, 34, 37, 41, 47, 54, 55, 72, 78, 129, 186, 187, 189, 191, 193, 195, 207, 213, 214, 218
transcendence 1, 3, 15–17, 21, 26, 27, 30, 34, 47, 50, 51, 65, 69, 73, 75, 76, 78, 81, 86, 93, 94, 96–100, 102–9, 111, 112, 114, 115, 117, 118, 123, 146, 164, 170, 176, 177, 180, 181, 183, 187, 189, 192, 194, 211, 216–19, 221, 223, 227

unity 14, 16–19, 22, 27, 31, 32, 34, 35, 37–42, 44, 62, 63, 104, 169, 170, 186–90, 192–95, 198, 200, 203–6, 217, 219, 221, 222, 225
universals 4, 14, 21, 22, 24, 43, 44, 47, 49–52, 54, 55, 57–63, 102–4, 106, 119, 178
universal truth 2, 13, 22, 47, 50, 51, 55–57, 61, 63, 104, 131, 177, 191
univocal 174, 175

Vanhoozer, Kevin 169, 226
via negativa / via negationis 75–77, 86, 109, 116–18, 221, 228
voluntarism 62, 156, 212

wager 177–79, 213, 228
worldview 29, 30, 42, 127, 159

For EU product safety concerns, contact us at Calle de José Abascal, 56–1°,
28003 Madrid, Spain or eugpsr@cambridge.org.

www.ingramcontent.com/pod-product-compliance
Ingram Content Group UK Ltd.
Pitfield, Milton Keynes, MK11 3LW, UK
UKHW040328160925
462952UK00012B/359